SETTING GOD FREE

MOVING BEYOND THE CARICATURE WE'VE CREATED IN OUR OWN IMAGE

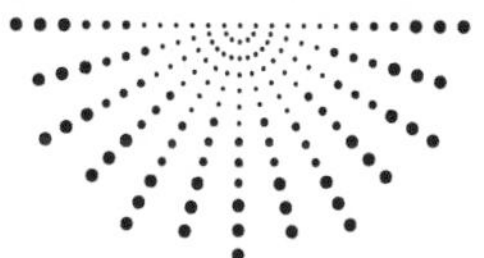

SEÁN ÓLAOIRE

APOCRYPHILE
PRESS

Apocryphile Press
1100 County Route 54
Hannacroix, NY 12087
www.apocryphilepress.com

Printed in the United States of America
ISBN 978-1-949643-88-6 | paper
ISBN 978-1-949643-89-3 | ePub

Back cover mandala by Karen Azar Rubin

CONTENTS

Preface vii

Part I

SETTING PSYCHOLOGY FREE

Introduction to Part I 3

Section I: Epistemology 5

Section II: Cosmology 19

Part II

SETTING GOD FREE

Introduction to Part II 65

Section I: The Prosecution 67

Section II: The Defense 208

Section III: The Verdict 240

Part III

SETTING SPIRITUALITY FREE

Introduction to Part III 249

Section I: Theology 250

Section II: Justice 298

Section III: Mysticism 317

Part IV

SETTING SCIENCE FREE

Setting Science Free 353

Finale: Bring on the Mysticists 378

Afterword 381

Acknowledgments 383

Notes 385

Lovingly dedicated to

Anne Brownstein,
whose angelic smile 'awakened' me
on Palm Sunday 1989.

And my brother Séamus,
whose huge heart
has room for all of us.

And my uncle Noel,
whose great soul
has been an inspiration to me
since we were 'twins' together in the 1940s.

PREFACE

From the time I was a teenager in Ireland, the Celt in me wanted to weave a triple-knot story reminiscent of the standing-stones petroglyphs of the druids and the illustrations of *The Book of Kells*. And so, I have spent the last fifty-five years interlacing my studies of science, psychology, and spirituality into one holistic thread. This book is the culmination of that process. In it, I have striven to liberate spirituality from the reductionism of religion and the concomitant abasement of scriptural revelation to mere literalist, fear-based dogma. I've tried to restore psychology—the study of the soul—to its former plinth and, in the process, rescue it from the pits of mere behaviorism. And I've attempted to set science free from an outdated monist-materialism which, in spite of over a hundred years of study in the field of quantum mechanics, still pretends that matter is all that exists and that consciousness is an illusion.

Those stone circles of Ireland, thousands of years after being erected, still stand in spite of weather and generations of scratching cattle. And so will the holy trinity of inner and outer observation: real open-minded science, a psychology that has recovered its roots, and a spirituality that once more honors its original mystical impulse.

However, I have come to realize that in order to set spirituality free, I must first set God free. My Celtic triple knot has thus become a mandala—the ultimate symbol of balance, harmony, and completeness, as Carl Jung so eloquently pointed out. Thereafter, the quadruple liberation took on a logical sequence. The first task is setting psychology free. The second task unfolds in an extraordinary court case in which God "Himself" is liberated from our individual and species-wide shadow projections. Only then can spirituality itself be rescued and, finally, science can be liberated.

And that has been my purpose in writing this book. I'm not interested in dismantling the violent elements of the Judeo-Christian faith just to prove a point. I wish to set God free to do what God does best: love.

While agnostics are still deciding whether or not God exists, atheists subscribe to a religion that claims to have proof that God does not exist, and many traditionally religious people are willing to abandon their God-given intellect and lay garlands on the altar of somebody else's image of God. I am none of those things. And chances are, if you're reading this book, neither are you. Your beliefs and practices are likely more complex, evolved, and evolving than a given label can describe. But then how do we know what we know? And why do we believe what we believe? And who or what is God, really? I'm eager to explore these questions along with you.

Rather than looking to dogma-driven interpretations of scriptures deemed inerrant, together we can explore the direct spiritual experiences available to us all as we cultivate better understanding, greater awareness, and deeper love of God. If you're Jewish, Christian, or Muslim, maybe you've secretly doubted your ability to simply will yourself to "love the Lord your God with all your mind, with all your heart, and with all your strength" as an act of obedience. I certainly did. We may begin our faith journey expecting some kind of Hollywood romance with the Almighty, but if we depend solely on the stories available to us in our holy books, that movie might end up looking more like the psychological thriller *Fatal Attraction* than the fairy tale we had hoped for!

Perhaps your religious roots lie outside the Abrahamic storyline, or maybe they're less defined in terms of tradition. It doesn't matter where you've come from or where you're going; we all face the same challenges as we attempt to make sense of who the heck "God" is and how we're supposed to love someone or something we can't even see. If Shakespeare was correct when he wrote "the course of true love never did run smooth," I'll happily choose the bumpy ride to find true love with the True God. Are you ready to join me?

I hope you'll see that this book is not a disgruntled rejection of God, but rather a labor of love for the One who is my origin, my journey, my destination, and my Source. In all the vicissitudes of life—personal, societal, and ecclesial—my devotion to God is unwavering. I know no other home than God.

But I had my first real fight with God at age four, when I found that God's white-bearded, red-coated helper named Santa Claus discriminated against poor families like mine. In the annual Yuletide distribution of gifts, I received a chintzy dime store toy gun while the kid across the road got the whole western playset. Complaining bitterly against this injustice on God's part, I flung my pistol at the crèche under our Christmas tree, knocking over St. Joseph, the donkey, and several of the sheep. My dear grandmother was compassionate enough to sympathize with me, and wise enough to explain that even the baby Jesus had it really tough as a little boy.

That was the start of a lifelong loving friendship between Jesus and me.

On two occasions in my adult life, in remote locations where I lived alone, I was close to death—once from typhoid at age thirty-eight while living in Kenya, and a second time, at age fifty, from carbon monoxide poisoning from a blocked chimney flue in my little cabin in the woods in Healdsburg, California. My response both times was to sing hymns in my native tongue—Gaelic. I invited Jesus to join in the chorus of each one. I have no doubt that when my time really comes, Jesus and I will lock arms and serenade each other on the way home.

I have been a Catholic for seventy-three years and a priest for forty-eight years. From an early age, I wanted to weave science, psychology, and spirituality into the seamless garment that best describes our search for the God that is the True Source. From my late teens, I attempted this synthesis by majoring in college in Pure Mathematics and Mathematical Physics, spending eight years in the seminary studying philosophy, scripture, and theology, completing a PhD in transpersonal psychology, practicing as a licensed clinical psychologist in the state of California for the past twenty-five years, living in three different continents (Europe for twenty-seven years, Africa for fourteen years, and America for thirty-three years) and mastering six languages. I share these credentials not to brag, but to assure you that I'm up to the challenge I've laid out in this book. And I trust you are too.

There are moments that prove to be major turning points in our lives, significantly shifting our cosmology and reality, often when we expect it least. For me, one such moment occurred as I was ministering in the Roman Catholic parish of St. Thomas Aquinas in Palo Alto, California. I had struck up a friendship with a Jewish woman named Arlen Brownstein—who is still my closest friend—after her dog singled me out in a crowded park and proceeded to jump all over me as if he knew me. (The dog was clearly on to something!) My friendship with Arlen has brought many meaningful moments over the years, but the one I'd like to share with you occurred on Palm

Sunday, 1989, when Arlen decided to bring her mother, Anne, to mass to meet me.

The gospel that day involved the alleged attempt on Pilate's part to save Jesus from the Jews by saying "I am innocent of the blood of this man." The Jews' supposed response was, "His blood be upon us and upon our children!"

As I stood in the pulpit before my Jewish friend and her mother, my heart was torn in two. I suddenly realized, after having heard this phrase each Lent for forty-two years, exactly what its historically anti-Semitic effects had been. As soon as Christianity was in a position to do so (starting in 312 CE, when Constantine merged the Roman church and state), it had begun orchestrating the persecution of Jesus's own people—justified by this gospel passage. Dressed in full Roman Catholic vestments as I celebrated mass, I just wanted to weep in front of the whole congregation. You see, I was keenly aware of the fact that Anne Brownstein's mother (Arlen's grandmother) had survived the Holocaust by escaping a shtetl in Russia at age eighteen, just months before her entire family, including her two-year-old brother Artzy, had been murdered in an Easter pogrom to avenge the deicide of Jesus. For the first time, I realized the weight this scriptural story held. This shocking wake-up call significantly altered how I would subsequently view the Bible and the God it depicts.

From that day forward, I began retooling my own cosmology and regularly reexamining what I believe. This one moment in time left an indelible mark on my future. I suppose it's only fitting, then, that I pay a lot of attention to the forces that fashion the future as I examine our individual and collective role in moving our species forward on a path of spiritually enlightened evolution. And in so doing, I will try to forge a balanced epistemology that interweaves philosophy, theology, and science on a loom constructed of experiential, intellectual, and authoritative frameworks.

Only when we break down systems long in place can we begin to understand how we know what we know about anything, much less the mysterious creator figure many of us call God. Whatever name we use to describe the divine reality we seek, we must begin by separating the god we have constructed in our own image and likeness from the God in whose image and likeness we were created. And by dismantling the false gods our species has held hostage for millennia, I hope to set God free.

I believe that the only reality is God. We are simply characters in God's dream. But God is nothing like what religion has made God out to be—especially the jealous, irascible, patriarchal, genocidal god of the world's great monotheistic religions. I want to uncover the True God in whose image we were created—who I often refer to as Source—and discard the god we have created in our own image and likeness. If you would like to join me in this adventure of a lifetime, please read this entire book before coming to any final conclusions. This is a never-ending journey, but I think you'll find it one well worth taking.

PART I
SETTING PSYCHOLOGY FREE

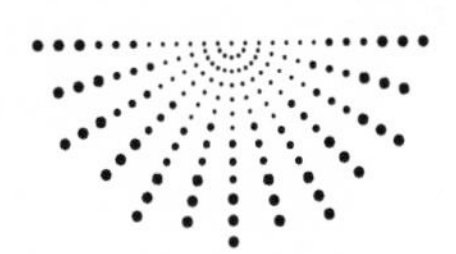

INTRODUCTION TO PART I

IT'S our nature to presume that the world as we found it as little children has always been the same. And even when we get to school, we presume that math has always been the math we met in our textbooks. And that professions have always been the same even way, way back. But remember, the fields of surgery and dentistry began as jobs the local barber performed as far back as the tenth century! Now both surgery and dentistry have many sub-specialties of their own. And that is also the story of psychology. In the old days, when I was in the seminary in the 1960s, psychology was included in the philosophy department. In fact, philosophy—the love of wisdom—was the science that dealt with ontology (the study of the nature of reality), epistemology (the study of how we know what we know), ethics (the study of moral behavior), and cosmology (the study of the universe—physical and metaphysical.) So before we can set psychology free, we first need to spend some time looking at epistemology and cosmology. And let's take a look at ontology while we're at it.

Imagine trying to collect all of the pieces of a jigsaw puzzle that have been scattered throughout the house by a three-year-old child. To make matters worse, the dog has chewed up the corn flakes box, and now pieces of it are in the mix. Some part of you has to be able to tell the corn flakes box pieces from the genuine jigsaw-puzzle pieces. That part of you is what you activate when you employ epistemology, which is the art/science of figuring out how you know what you know.

Then comes cosmology, which is the part of you that figures out how the real puzzle pieces go together. Without epistemology, you'd be trying to integrate corn flakes box pieces into the design, not realizing that they don't belong. And without cosmology, you'd have all the correct pieces but no clue how to assemble them into a whole.

The first task of this book is to apply this analogy to sorting out our basic worldview, religious/spiritual beliefs, personal values, etc. First, we'll make sure there are no corn flakes box pieces in the mix, and then we'll explore how to go about recognizing which combinations of the real pieces might allow us to re-create the picture on the cover of the jigsaw puzzle box. The process involves two main questions:

1. How do we know what we know?
2. How do we organize what we know?

SECTION I: EPISTEMOLOGY

HOW IN GOD'S NAME DO WE KNOW WHAT WE KNOW?

"How do we know what we know?" and "How do we know what we know is true?" Philosophy calls this the epistemological question. St. Thomas Aquinas, who was, according to many people, one of the greatest philosophers and theologians of all time, claimed, *"Nihil est in intellectu quod non antea fuerit in sensu."* (Translated from Latin: "There is nothing in the intellect which is not first in the senses.") In a rare moment of congruency, mainstream psychology, neuroscience, and the Roman Church agree with this religious master. But I respectfully disagree with them all. Their position is based upon the notion that the objective world of rocks, trees, stars, animals, people, etc. sends data that the human senses deliver to the brain (intellect), which then processes those data and creates an accurate one-to-one internal map of what has been captured. These maps of individual sensory experiences fuse, eventually, into a bigger map of total reality—how things are in themselves. I have two issues with this model. Firstly, I do not believe that the sensorium is the only channel that delivers data to the intellect; secondly, I do not believe that the "senses + intellect" equation gives a full and accurate map of objective reality.

Let me tackle this second objection first. Philosophy itself, at some stage, recognizes that it is a fallacy to presume that our internalized maps correspond with outside objective reality. They call this fallacy "the myth of the given." In fact, we have no idea what lies outside before our senses model it. A dragonfly with 2,700 facets in each of its two eyes has a radically different map of the visual world, while a bat, who can hear up to 100,000 hertz, has a totally different map of the acoustical world than humans (who can only hear up to 20,000 hertz) do. Moreover, Quantum Mechanics (QM) has been telling us for almost a century now about the observer effect: it is the witnessing consciousness that collapses the primal reality of any phenomenon to our human perception of it. The founder of QM, Max Planck, said, "I regard consciousness as fundamental. I regard matter as derivative from consciousness. We cannot get behind consciousness. Everything that we talk about, everything that we regard as existing, postulates consciousness."[1]

We cannot get outside of our consciousness or perceptual mechanism to see what's "really" there before we get our hands on it. The net with which we fish determines not what's in the ocean, but simply what we can catch with that particular tool.

And now back to my first objection. As I said, I do not believe that the sensorium is the only channel that delivers data to the intellect. Rather, I think that there are myriad ways in which this can happen. For starters, Carl Jung defined intuition as "perception via the unconscious." Intuition is a way of experiencing and knowing that does not rely solely upon the external senses. But this is only the tip of the iceberg. Each time you shift your state of consciousness, you encounter a treasure trove of data that can form or transform your model of truth and reality. For millennia, human beings have either stumbled upon or created practices for volitionally entering these other dimensions and experiencing alternate data fields via dreaming, dancing, entheogens[2], music, drumming, singing, chanting, meditation, liturgy, art, prayer, storytelling, and reading—to name a few methods.

The data delivered by any one and all of these modalities provide complementary pieces to the puzzle of reality-building and truth-finding. Helen Keller, who could neither see nor hear, may have had far fewer data to build her reality model than a person for whom all senses are in perfect working order. Yet, she's famous for her ability to develop alternate means of constructing her reality. In her oft quoted words, "What I'm looking for is not out there, it is in me." By the same token, any culture or "science" that discards the data delivered from other dimensions and modalities can only offer limited models of truth.

Here's a visual analogy to illustrate my point. I invite you to pause and take three deep breaths as you enter the imaginal realm with me for a moment. (I'll wait!) Now picture a skyscraper that is cylindrical in shape. A bank of elevators is located in the center and when you ascend to any floor and exit the elevator, you find yourself in a circular corridor with eight doors to eight rooms. Each room, then, is wedge shaped, with a greater external curved wall and a smaller internal curved wall. You enter each room through the lesser curved wall and immediately you see that there is a mural painted on the greater curved wall. And let's say that the eight rooms represent eight distinct states of consciousness.

On the first floor, you enter room #101 and see a section of the mural. Since you haven't yet entered any other room, you presume that it's the entire mural. But if you visit room #102, you quickly realize that the imagery continues, but the entire mural cannot be seen by entering only one room. If you visit all of the other rooms on the first floor, you will smile and realize, "Oh, I get it! I need to go into all the rooms to see the full mural!" But a further surprise awaits you. If you ride the elevator to the second floor and begin to visit rooms 201 through 208, another layer is revealed. Whereas the mural on the first floor was drawn in stick figures, the mural on the second floor is done in more realistic drawings. Riding up to the third floor, you wonder what you'll find. Here, the mural is in life-like color. Moving up to the fourth floor, you discover the mural is comprised of 3-D holographic images. Do you want to go further? It's a bit overwhelming, but surely you want to see for yourself what wonders await!

The problem is that most people, especially materialistic scientists, have never gone beyond room 101. But that doesn't stop them from pontificating on "reality" and scoffing at claims that other rooms, let alone other floors, exist. In my analogy, the rooms represent different states of consciousness, while the floors represent different stages of consciousness. For the person fully committed to the spiritual journey into ultimate reality and full truth, it is important to not merely experiment with the different rooms (states) but to aim at growing through the floors (stages). In our quest for ultimate reality, we need to ride the proverbial elevator all the way to the top.

HOW DO WE KNOW WHAT WE KNOW IS TRUE?

Basically, we know things in one of three ways: (a) an authority figure (the Bible, a priest, a scientist, the television, etc.) told us it was true; (b) we had a personal experience of it; or (c) we figured it out for ourselves. None of these three methods is infallible because all "authorities" are, themselves, proclaiming a "truth" they've acquired in one of these same three ways and all authorities make errors, even serious errors. Personal experiences run the gamut from delusions to genuine mystical revelation. And working stuff out for ourselves on the basis of the little laptop we carry between our ears has tripped all of us up occasionally.

Is there an ultimate Truth with a capital "T"? I don't believe so. Or at least not one to which we humans have access. When Thomas Aquinas said truth is found only in the judgment, he was speaking of "personal truth" or truth with a lower case "t." To claim to know Truth is to claim to be God. And to say that there is Truth because God revealed it to us is to go right back to the "authority" route, because to claim that God told us the Truth—through scripture or through science or any other method—is itself a judgment based on a belief in the infallibility of some teacher in the lineage. Dedicated, genuine adherents of significantly different scriptures (the Hebrew Bible or Tanakh of Judaism, the Gospels and Epistles of Christianity, the Koran of Islam, etc.) each claim that their message is God's inerrant message for all people. Yet we risk God's wrath by choosing one among them and denying the others. Each group is equally convinced that it, and only it, has the real truth. Moreover, they have been prepared to commit genocide on behalf of their God to protect His good name. This caricature of God, which we have crafted in our own image and likeness, has long outlived his usefulness.

When Jesus spoke of God, he affectionately called him "Abba", a deeply personal, familial term like "Papa"—in stark contrast to the fearful relationship many of Jesus's contemporaries held with the divine. Jesus also said, "By their fruits you shall know them" (according to Matthew 7:16). Show me followers who act in love, compassion, and forgiveness, and I will show you a God worth adoring. Show me a God who is on the record as perpetrating global destruction (the flood), mandating genocide as an accepted strategy for becoming top dog, and still supports violence against humans based on skin color, creed, or any other easily-distinguishable difference from the "chosen," and I will show you the human shadow writ large, which is quite opposite to the example and teachings attributed to Jesus the Nazarene.

I'd like to take it one step further: any belief that results in creating fear, anger, prejudice or violence in thoughts, words, or actions cannot be true.

Please allow me to explain what I mean by "true." There's a big difference between truth and fact. Something can be true but not factual, while something can be factual but not true. Here's my personal definition of truth: I believe that something is true only if it transforms me and aligns me with Love; I believe something is ultimate Truth if it transforms me *radically* and aligns me *permanently* with Love. When I am holding everybody—even my so-called "enemies," as Jesus enjoined on his followers—in a heart of love, I know I have found truth. If, because of a given belief, anybody becomes the target of my anger, then that belief doesn't square with my understanding of the core message of Jesus's example and teaching.

We each need a set of deeply personal tools to help us determine what is true as we seek ultimate Truth. In the chaotic whirlwind of competing, cacophonous voices and perspectives, the unifying nature of Source gets lost in sectarian claims of "Truth."

So how do we navigate these choppy waters? What search criteria can help sift the wheat from the chaff? Here's my litmus test: a belief or creed that divides us, leads to xenophobia, or creates prejudice, fear, anger or anxiety, cannot be of God. And when a creed or belief results in compassion, forgiveness, serenity, and justice, I think it's safe to say we are firmly in God's camp.

We can study the great religions and read accounts of world history, but neither is a substitute for actually meeting and befriending devotees of other faiths and people of other cultures. I was sent by the Catholic Church to Kenya at age twenty-six, armed with a burning commitment to save "dark Africa" from its pagan ways and win souls for Christ. Upon arriving and steeping myself in African languages and mythologies, I quickly realized that ancient Africa held a beautiful and pure spirituality which hadn't been strait-jacketed by "Sunday obligation" or Nicene creeds, but was alive in its dance with nature and her elemental entities. That was a Transformational experience of Truth for me.

Later, this experience would morph into a kind of Ultimate Truth or Radical Transformation for me. Throughout my fourteen years living under equatorial Kenya's twelve-hour night skies, I systematically exhumed my own unconsciously acquired, Christian-dominated cosmology and began to examine its artifacts like an archaeologist at a dig in a sacred place. One by one, I held these doctrines up to the light of reason and of love and asked myself the following question: "If I had been born Hindu or Buddhist or Taoist or…, would I still believe that this doctrine held spiritual value?" If the answer was no, I blessed it and sent it on its way. If the answer was yes, I put it into another box from which I hoped to create my new cosmology. To adapt Lynne Twist's beautiful phrase, I was trying to hospice the old cosmology and midwife the new cosmology.[3] Beliefs like papal infallibility or being damned to hell for all eternity if I ate sausages on a Friday quickly fell by the wayside. Teachings like the Golden Rule—"Do not do to another what you would not want done to you"—I found in every spiritual system I studied. These were keepers. I soon had enough pieces in the box to create a love-based cosmology free from guilt, fear, and prejudice, expunged of old, tired stories of chosen races, mortal sin, and divinely decreed hierarchies. For me, living in Africa was an experience of radically transformative ultimate Truth.

Let's get back to the difference between truth and fact. A fact is merely a data point in the physical world. For example, the Dow Jones has a set value today. That's a fact. Is it earthshattering in the sense that we instantly become an enlightened being by virtue of that information? I somehow doubt it. But let's look at the story of the Good Samaritan from Luke's gospel. At the tail end of an interrogation from one of the religious "experts," Jesus said we are not only to love the Lord our God with all of our heart, soul, and might, but we are also to love our neighbors as ourselves. The religious one responded: "And who is my neighbor?" As was his way, Jesus replied with a story: A Jewish man on his way to Jericho was mugged, robbed, and left for dead on the side of the road. A priest from the temple in Jerusalem passed by and ignored the plight of this fellow Jew, as did a Levite (a member of the temple police). However, a Samaritan attended to the wounded man, brought him to an inn in Jericho, picked up the tab and asked the innkeeper to continue caring for the injured man while he (the Samaritan) conducted his business in the area, at the end of which he would pay the bill in full. Jesus ended the story by asking, "Which of these people was neighbor to him who fell among robbers?"

The religious one was really on the spot here, because he knew that the Jews looked down on Samaritans with deep prejudice, considering them subhuman and unworthy of such recognition. By sharing this story with him, Jesus gave the religious one an opportunity to see things differently—to break out of the cultural contamination he was born into and discover a more accurate and thus "true" definition of the word neighbor.

Suppose, now, you were a reporter for the *Jerusalem Post,* and you heard Jesus telling this story. You found it hard to believe, so you spent the next three days interviewing the priests, the Levites, and the innkeepers of Jericho. None of them could verify Jesus's story. In other words, it probably wasn't factual. Agreed! It may not have been based on an actual event. However, by my definition, it is indeed true, because, for those who understood the message, it was radically transformative.

So, to revisit Thomas Aquinas's "truth is found only in the judgment," we can see how the observer determines the quality of truth in a given scenario. Here's what Aquinas meant: Faced with any proposition, in science, scripture, psychology...an individual person will either believe it (as truth) or reject it (as not true.) So some internal human faculty must make a judgment and assign the proposition to one of these categories. This sorting process can either be done with full, deliberate, intelligent awareness, or else be a kneejerk, mostly unconscious, and even irrational reaction. The process depends on our willingness to see beyond the limitations of our previous beliefs and thus be transformed. So, we really don't see things as *they* are, we see things as *we* are.[4]

In the end, there is no such thing as a self-evident truth. If there were, then there could never be contrary opinions on the matter. But we humans don't find that level of unanimity anywhere. Reality, then, is a composite of all the "truths" to which we cling. So there is a "personal reality," the sum total of our own beliefs; then there is a "consensual reality," which is the intersection set of all the personal realities of the members of the culture.

Yet truth as a concept is a powerful thing. Indeed, the truth shall set you free and lies will incarcerate— not just individuals, but even the world community. From the beginning of religions, there have been false prophets, dedicated to ingratiating themselves with the king by "prophesies" that praised his wisdom and policies, at the expense of truth. The real prophets were often savagely attacked by these royal sycophants. From the beginning of empires, there have been court historians who put on record only the magnificent achievements of the blue bloods while ignoring their ignominious failures or bloody reigns. From the beginning of warfare, there have been false-flag operations calculated to outrage the citizens and have them howl for battle. This was Hitler's final puzzle piece prior to his invasion of Poland in September, 1939. The United States instigated the Spanish-American War in a similar fashion in 1898, with the very suspicious sinking of the USS Maine. And in 1964, the infamous Gulf of Tonkin incident allowed the United States to escalate the Vietnam war. If the end justifies the means, then it seems that it's acceptable to use increasingly nefarious means to justify increasingly nefarious—but secretive—ends. Like Sir Walter Scott waxed poetically, "Oh, what a tangled web we weave when first we practice to deceive!"

The willingness of the mainstream media to suppress the truth and promote the agenda of oligarchs, coupled with modern communication technologies, means that the new global storytellers are empowered to create narratives of fear, division, and violence on an uneven playing field where the real prophets are spanceled and hobbled. I believe that the fictitious past of the court historians and the fictitious present of propaganda are just as influential in creating the future as are the *real past* and the *real present.* If it's true in psychology that the individual mind often can't distinguish between memories, sensations, and imagination (e.g., false memory syndrome, optical illusions, the placebo effect, and post-hypnotic suggestions), then it is much more powerfully true of the "mass mind" under the influence of "fake news"—a phrase I've been using for many decades that, for me, did not originate with the political jujitsu we've been subjected to in the US in recent years. Over thirty years ago I used the term "fake news" to describe the willful deception employed by then-president of Kenya, Daniel Toroitich Arap Moi, who declared his false narrative not only to be the truth, but to be the only acceptable truth —for which I was deported from the country I loved. Here in the US, I've seen both Democrats and Republicans craft and promote false narratives as the only acceptable truth—once again fake news, as far as I'm concerned. With a culture so deeply in the clutches of such willful deception, it has never been more important to redefine truth as "that which transforms and aligns with Love."

In an oppressive society, there are very few "truths" outside of the consensual reality. It then becomes very difficult to experience that which the culture insists does not exist. On the other hand, in an evolving society, people are free, even encouraged, to think and explore outside the box. One function of the prophet is to break open the boxes, the constricting reality models, the small "truths" and deficient cosmologies, in order to invite us to wonder and venture more deeply into the awesome mystery of God.

The Ultimate Reality is the God-perspective. If Truth is transformation, then Reality is alignment with Love in one of its many manifestations. If, on the other hand, a reality model leads me into fear, in one of its many manifestations, while it may be true and real, it most certainly is not True or Real.

Where truth is in the judgment and reality is in the composite amalgam of the truths, cosmology is the explanatory model that pulls it all together and offers a satisfactory, solid basis for life. However, for the vast majority of us, this entire process, especially the cosmology piece, has been acquired unconsciously and, in any particular situation thereafter, is accessed unconsciously. Ask somebody, "Why did you say that?" and they will likely reply, "Because it was the appropriate thing to say." Or, "Why did you do that?" will evoke, "Because it was the right thing to do." What made it appropriate or right? It was the unconsciously acquired and unconsciously accessed cosmology! So, the sages advise, "Know thyself" and "The unexamined life is not worth living" (both attributed to Socrates); "I am Buddha; I am awake" (delivered by Siddhārtha Gautama); or "If the householder knew when the thief was going to break in and steal, he would not have gone to sleep" (attributed to Jesus in Matthew 24:43).

In synopsis, there are personal, consensual, and ultimate (God-like) levels to truth, reality, and cosmology. It's up to us to choose consciously. And choose wisely.

ANOTHER LOOK AT HOW WE KNOW WHAT WE KNOW

The first model I've presented suggests that we know what we know because (a) some authority figure told us, or (b) we personally experienced something, or (c) we figured it out for ourselves. A second model suggests that we know (a) through philosophy, which attempts to arrive at truth through reason and logic; or (b) through science, which attempts to arrive at truth via observation and experimentation; or (c) through religion, which attempts to find truth by building upon revelation from God.

I'd like to invite you to examine a third model, also in three parts. Firstly, there is objective reality, which is true whether or not we believe in it. For instance, even if I have not studied Newton's law of gravity, if I fall out a second story window, I'm going to experience the reality of gravity during the free fall and, upon impact, its consequences. Secondly, there is subjective reality, which may only be available to the experiencer like a headache or the certainty that this bread pudding is warm and delicious. And, thirdly, we have intersubjective reality, which warrants a bit more elucidation.

Communities and cultures of all kinds constellate around intersubjective reality, which is simply an imaginative idea—a meme—that is effectively sold to the masses by a thought leader. For this to work, each person has to believe that the other people will have the same level of trust in the fiction that they do. Of course, the meme is never presented as a fiction—though that indeed is what it is. Rather, it comes with all the persuasive power of an absolute, self-evident truth.

People will only abandon one great fictional truth—let's call it "A" —when a more powerful fictional truth gains credibility—let's call it "B." Then the tide can turn really quickly, and people are left asking the question, "How could we ever have believed in A? Duh!" Most great "isms" are fictions that become fact by fiat (e.g., capitalism, communism, fascism, consumerism), though occasionally war and conquest can persuade the reluctant. Let's explore three examples of such powerful fictional memes that have become intersubjective reality: religion, nations, and money.

Religion is one of the most ancient examples of intersubjective reality. True spirituality, as I understand it, is always based on a deeply transformative mystical impulse. But the same cannot be said of religion. I've heard it said that if you happen upon the tracks of a religion, you should follow them not to where they are leading, but rather, from whence they've come. The community that forms around a mystical prophet almost inevitably, by fiat, becomes an organization, then an institution, then a dogma-dictating orthodoxy, and finally, a heretic-slaying, infidel-conquering war machine. At its best, religion can unite previously hostile tribes—as did the rise of Islam around 600 CE in the war-torn Arabian Peninsula and as did Confucianism in China around 500 BCE. It can elevate the ethics of the individual members and promote the Golden Rule—do not do to others what you would not want them to do to you. This is particularly true when a religion is in its infancy and is being discriminated against or even persecuted. At this stage, it advocates very strongly for tolerance and ecumenism.

But, as Lord Acton famously said, power tends to corrupt. The history of the major religions—especially the three Abrahamic religions: Judaism, Christianity, and Islam—has shown that tolerance and ecumenism are abandoned once power and control are achieved. Then the "separated brethren" become labeled as infidels, pagans, or gentiles, whom it is mandatory to convert or kill. And each of these phases is driven by a fiat based on the fiction of a new intersubjective reality—a new "truth." All that it takes is a demagogue who can persuade the members that he, and he alone, is privy to God's will. The same is true of national identity and colonial and expansionist aspirations.

The United States of America is actually a legal fiction based on the intersubjective consent of those who were persuaded by charismatic rebels to secede from the British Empire. The USA came into being in 1776, via a piece of paper—the Declaration of Independence. And it will survive until a more powerful fiction draws another fiat from us, the citizens. Look at the example of the USSR. A nation that began in bloody revolution in 1917 and went on to become the second great empire of the 20th Century ended with the scratching of a pen on December 26, 1991 with declaration number 142-H of the Supreme Soviet of the Soviet Union, which dissolved the USSR and acknowledged the independence of the former soviet republics. What to the patriot seems like a real and solid basis for a deeply personal identity—worth killing and dying for—is really just scribblings on flimsy paper without powerful intersubjective constructs in place.

Money—really just fancy pieces of paper and metal cast into specific shapes—is an equally temporary construct. How did the first communities, clans, tribes get their daily bread? Initially, they were self-sufficient hunter-gatherers with very simple needs that a typical band of fifteen to forty members provided for itself. As groups got bigger, however, and life got more complex, individuals were unable to provide for all of their needs: food, shelter, clothing, medicine. So they introduced the barter system and specialists arose and traded resources and products to meet wants and needs. But when people began to gather in big cities and merchants began travelling to distant lands, bartering became problematic. Travelling with all your worldly possessions made you easy prey for bandits, highwaymen, and pirates. Moreover, humans began to desire lots of heretofore exotic commodities like silks and spices. So, about five thousand years ago, the Sumerians invented money. Initially, it took the form of precious metals. But these were heavy and vulnerable to theft, especially for mobile persons. So, tokens—innately valueless but valuable by fiat—were invented. We still have these currencies today. A $100 bill is a useless piece of paper unless a sizeable number of people agree to accept its assigned, and ultimately fictitious, value and—this is the most important part—to trust that all others will also accept this assigned, fictional value.

Money is the most universal and efficient system of mutual trust ever devised; it knows no prejudice of gender, class, creed or culture; even people who don't trust each other tend to trust each other's money. If a population loses this trust in a currency, its value plummets. And we've seen this happen many times in the world's currencies. In antiquity, cows and conches were currencies. Obviously, cows have a lot of intrinsic value and conches have some, whereas a $100 bill has zero intrinsic value, unless you want to cover a hole in the wallpaper. However, try going into the Apple Store to buy a computer and offering three camels in exchange for a MacBook Pro and hope to get two goats and a dozen eggs as change! Once the intersubjective reality of a currency—cows, conches, or cents—changes, the value changes too.

Imagination, as in intersubjective reality, is not merely the handiest tool in the box of the artist, mystic, or scientist, it is the lifeblood of trade. And meme-making is the way in which intersubjective reality is created and sold. Modern advertising utilizes this very effectively, persuading people to go into lifelong debt in order to buy stuff they neither need nor can afford. And intersubjective reality not only influences our behaviors—left unchecked, it shapes our core beliefs about who we are, where we've come from and where we're going.

Now that we've defined Truth and examined a few lesser truths, let's explore together how our own cosmological outlook is based on intersubjective reality.

SECTION II: COSMOLOGY

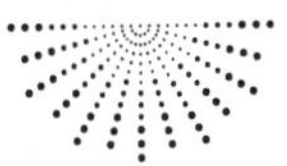

TAKING CONTROL OF OUR COSMOLOGY

We all have at least a partially-developed personal cosmology. But we rarely fully know what it is, much less how we arrived at it. It is crucial to seek to better understand the cosmos by asking "What are the origins of the universe?" It is also crucial to attempt to better understand the kosmos by attempting to crack the metaphysical code that created the blueprint and template of which the world is the printout. Both are crucial to intentionally developing a personal cosmology. (A brief note here: by *Cosmos* the Greeks meant the physical universe, while *Kosmos* meant its metaphysical origins and foundation.)

The first step is to loosen our grip on what we "know" and open our mind to possibilities we may have never considered. Carl Sagan bemoaned the ways science not only asks us to disregard the law of cause and effect when considering the origins of the universe, but the ways it generally discourages us from challenging the usual theories. I'm asking you to go out on a limb with me here—so don't bring any heavy baggage with you!

An agile canoe can reverse direction in seconds, whereas huge oil tankers can take hours to turn 180 degrees on the open sea. But if you've ever watched a supertanker or a huge cruise ship being nudged into its berth at a harbor, you'll remember that two tiny tugboats—one at the tanker's prow and the other at the stern—can turn it about very quickly and very efficiently. If organized religions are the huge cumbersome ships, the prophets are the tugboats. A great prophet—like a Jesus or a Buddha figure—can, in a single lifetime, dramatically re-direct the supertanker of their religion of origin. But the prophets don't change the world once-and-for-all, allowing us to stagnate in the new position; they exemplify for us what we all need to do regularly in our personal cosmologies and for the religious and political systems to which we belong.

Here's a more biological analogy. Every single cell in the human body answers to one, and only one, of two commands: grow or defend. It cannot do both at the same time. When a person is under constant stress—real or imagined—the entire organism is stuck in defensive mode and ill-health is a likely outcome. All religions are comprised of individual people that function like cells of the body they inhabit. If the people who comprise a religion get stuck in a defensive posture, all evolution ceases. They cannot grow if they are committed to defending themselves. Typically, the religions then react by instituting an increasingly rigid combination of dogma and orthodoxy that finally play out in violent forms like inquisitions and crusades.

Each of us is a cell that is part of a greater being. If we are truly committed to a particular religion, then rather than devoting our lives to defending inherited religious beliefs at all costs and staying the course for the sake of continuity even if we're headed for an iceberg (if I may return to my maritime analogy), or simply rearranging the deck chairs while the ship is sinking, we can, instead, choose to be part of the crew that steers the ship. Rather than being passive passengers thoughtlessly snoozing below decks, we can readily serve the greater good by helping to maneuver the behemoth mother ship from the wheel of our personal tugboat. But if we want to serve in this way, we need to know how to navigate these waters and study the charts available to us.

Before we can begin to contribute to the larger conversation, we must first spend quality time and energy in developing our own personal cosmology. Let's begin with yet another metaphor. You're living in the house you've grown up in since birth. You're not even aware of its features. "It's just my house!" you say. Until you compare it with other houses, you don't know whether it's ugly or beautiful, warm or cold, bright or dark, damp or dry, safe or dangerous, welcoming or hostile to you, unfriendly or hospitable to others. So, one day, you wake up and decide to design, build, and live in the house of your dreams. There are four stages to this project: firstly, you make a mental map of your ideal home; secondly, you draw a detailed blueprint; thirdly, you assemble the building materials; and, fourthly, you employ a work force. Building your personal cosmology involves four similar stages.

Of course, over time it will be imperative that we do some periodic remodels. No personal cosmology is permanent. Rather, each one is simply your best attempt, at the moment, at aligning with your God, Self, Neighbor, and Mission. The personal cosmology is simply a map, not the terrain itself. It is incumbent upon us to continually upgrade it. The best we can hope for is not to produce a perfect model, but hopefully less and less imperfect ones.

As we begin to think seriously about this, we will quickly see that the cosmologies with which we are bombarded run the entire gamut. Initially, they were utterly anthropocentric: human beings are the only sentient creatures with souls, in a universe otherwise devoid of life; a universe that spins worshipfully about planet Earth, which is the center of the cosmos. From there, we swung wildly to a cosmology of meaninglessness and despair, in which all life, including us, is a random wandering driven by a purposeless algorithm in which we may as well soothe our savaged ego by becoming addicted consumers of baubles that allow us to temporally forget our accidental arrival and sorry end. Somewhere in between are religions that promise heaven—

though space is very limited and reserved for the elect—and threaten hell that will willingly accommodate the rejected overflow. This model has recently been superseded by a religion I call "scientism," a materialistic science which claims that if we or our instruments can't detect and measure something, then it doesn't exist. Scientism promises utopia— here and now—while actually delivering a dystopia—also here and now—that gives us weapons of mass destruction, ecological Armageddon, and a mad scramble for diminishing resources like water. It is, in fact, a pseudo-science that attempts to explain away the uninvestigated instead of investigating the unexplained.

The problem is—we don't know what we don't know. Imagine, if you will, that you—and everybody you've ever met—have had to spend your entire lives in a (very) large room, which has neither ingress nor egress. On one wall is a large machine from which, by pushing a button, you can extract mushy, hamburger-like mincemeat. None of you has any idea what lies on the other side of the wall which, in actual fact, contains a cow factory. But none of you has ever seen or even heard of such a thing as a "cow." Every so often the owner of the cow factory simply herds a living, breathing cow up to the other side of the large machine which then mangles it into meat, to be delivered at the push of the button to your side of the wall. There is no way you could possibly infer the reality or description of a cow from merely observing the mince. Your presumption would be that at the other side of the machine is simply an inexhaustible mound of squiggly meat.

Our senses are the instruments that allow us to experience the mincemeat but never actually enable us to see the cow, and our scientific instruments are basically extensions of our sensorium. Perception is the stove that then cooks the mince into the meal that we call reality. The cosmos is a giant room with a cow mangle set in the wall. We can never see the other side, so we presume its reality is identical to our own. Neither the sensorium nor science will ever be able to deliver primary, un-mangled reality to us. And that is what philosophy calls "the myth of the given"—the fallacy of presuming that our senses give us an accurate one-to-one map of what's out there.

Any effort to make sense of life must begin with an understanding of the self. I believe we must choose among three versions of self: the soul self, the experiencing self, and the narrating self. The soul self is our true, eternal essence. It is who we are before, during, and after this life. It is a bite-sized piece of God and it leads to the realization that we are spirits in spacesuits. Each of us is a God-probe into corporeality, a way for the Divine to temporarily experience the game of self-alienation. We are souls on safari on planet Earth. Unfortunately, very few of us identify with that level of the self, and that failure causes all the vicissitudes of life.

Next comes the experiencing self. It is the total psyche consisting of the conscious, subconscious, and unconscious parts of us; it is equipped with senses, perception, memory, imagination, will, desires, and intuition; it has huge throughput per second—billions of experiences—most of which are stored off-line in the spiritual "cloud" sometimes called the Akashic Records. Before we move on to the narrative self, let me elaborate a bit on this.

Everything that exists in the physical cosmos leaves an electromagnetic signature. So, theoretically speaking, if you could travel faster than the speed of light, you could catch up with your favorite episode of "I Love Lucy" by zipping out at warp speed in the direction of planet Zorg. But even if you decided not to risk time travel, all episodes of "I Love Lucy" and of all human, animal, vegetable, and mineral events are still available in intergalactic space. The Akashic Records are Hinduism's very detailed and fascinating treatment of that reality. In short, Hinduism teaches that we exist at seven levels of body—the gross or physical body, the etheric or energy body, the astral or emotional body, the mental body, the causal body (where we activate our psychic gifts), the soul body and, finally, Cosmic Consciousness. On the death of the gross body, the astral body archives all of the experiences of the incarnation just ended—to be taken aboard again as in-built hardware when we return for our next incarnation. The causal body is the library of our experiences and learning from all of our incarnations in all the places/dimensions we've ever lived in. Moreover, we can access and benefit from other peoples' lifetimes as well. It's as if we upload photos of our vacation onto the cloud and give the gate code to family and friends. Everybody can then access them. Grandma God is the ultimate librarian/archivist/videographer. And the Akashic Records is the name Hinduism gives to Her enormous collection of family photos.

Thirdly comes the narrating self, which most of us take to be the real "me," but it's actually just our ego. It's the editor/censor that filters out most of the data and attends only to a non-representative subset that suits some self-image. It's the part of me I share on the plane ride with the stranger in the next seat. It mixes real, historical data with movies seen, stories heard, books read and hopes projected, in order to create a personal sense of self—an identity which is largely fictional, but stubbornly held in place. At various stages of life, I can identify myself with my body, emotions, mind, job, relationship, gender, or ethnicity. We all do our own version of Walter Mitty or Don Quixote characters by which any new contrary experience is dismissed. Only what supports our self-image is retained.

It is from the sense of self that we tell our stories and create our future. This "sense of self" exists at all levels: individual, tribe, religion, nation, species. It influences each story we tell: personal, historical, theological, or cosmological. We tell these four kinds of stories, but all are non-representative, because there is an experiencing self and a narrating self of the tribe and of the species, as surely as there is of the individual person. Mystics stand out because they tell their stories from the soul level. And each story, at each level, will either be transformative or crippling.

There is a Spirit of God (true self) beneath each community. Whether we remember or not, we all volunteered to be here now. I believe we each said, "Here I am Lord, send me. I want to be one of the people putting a shoulder to the wheel of human evolution to uncover the Buddha nature of the species and propel it into Christ consciousness/Self-Realization/enlightenment."

If you're willing to visit this minefield with me, together we can construct a road guide that makes sense to the soul, plays music for the heart, and causes the mind to exclaim, "Yes, this finally has the ring of truth!" First, we'll explore the core dialectic or struggle of the human condition—the tug-of-war in the human psyche between love and fear. Then we will engage with the questions, navigational tools, and exercises necessary for developing our own personal cosmology.

THE FOUR KINDS OF STORIES WE TELL

The stories we tell come from the version of self that tells them. I've identified four types of story that, together, form the narrative by which the human story unfolds: personal, historical, theological, and cosmological.

Personal stories consist of the cluster of experiences that congeal about the narrating self and create the myth of personal identity, which then becomes the sole arbiter of what other experiences are allowed to join the family of the self. It is the ego complex, as defined by Carl Jung, clinging tenaciously to the archetype of the "me." It can crucify or it can promote the soul's mission.

Then comes "history"—the story of the tribe: its origins, grandeur, tragedies, specialness, and purpose. Once again, it is a very selective club to which only certain experiences are allowed membership. And the fees are very high. In a telling experiment, English and French children were asked to write down the twenty most important battles between their two countries. The English kids wrote an accurate list as did the French kids. However, there was almost no overlap between the two lists; each group had only recorded battles in which its country had been victorious.

I believe that the tribe is to the species as the ego is to the soul. So, not only is ontogeny recapitulating phylogeny, but phylogeny is recapitulating cosmology. In other words, the individual human can be thought of, starting from conception, as a single-celled creature, then turning into something resembling a "fish" swimming in the amniotic fluid, then into a primate with a tail, into a land animal at birth, into *Homo erectus* as it learns to walk, and finally into *Homo sapiens sapiens* as it learns to speak. This physical progression reenacts the evolutionary trajectory of the species. Similarly, the species is reenacting the journey of the soul back to Source.

By the same token, the notion of a chosen people (tribe/religion) is like the ego's need to feel special. In the individual journey into enlightenment, the ego must be transcended and the self must become identified with the soul. So, too, in the journey of the species, the notion of a chosen people must be transcended and the tribal-self must identify with the soul-pod: the community of the holographic fractals of God incarnated.

Problems begin when the ego develops a narrative self, founded on victimhood in times of powerlessness and on arrogance in times of power. When you scale that up to the level of the tribe, it becomes a very volatile weapon. Then victimhood becomes a reason to smother initiative, and arrogance becomes the justification for slaughter. "We" are always the good guys even when we commit genocide. "They" are the terrorists. (Remember this later in this book when we begin to dismantle some of the more ego-driven stories of the Bible, where we inevitably meet all of these competing forces.)

Thirdly comes "theology," the story of our god. He—and God has, up to now, primarily been described as a He—chose us, made a covenant with us, and has punished us regularly for our failures. We claim these are divinely revealed stories, but they are mainly human creations. The mystical impulses of awakened holy people, once they get into the hands of the disciples and their institutionalized communities, are frequently dipped—nay marinated—in the cauldron of human fear, anger, and xenophobia until the encrusted, unrecognizable love-essence of God is pulled out as a golden calf to be worshipped by the fundamentalist mindset.

There are two possible explanations for the behavior of this golden-calf-god: either he is schizophrenic, oscillating constantly between love and anger (though his center of gravity is definitely much closer to the anger end of the spectrum), or the spiritual impulse is refusing to be permanently quenched, peeping through stubbornly and fanned into flame by mystical influences.

Thankfully, mystics in various forms have always had an influence on humanity. In the rural Ireland of my childhood, the fire was never allowed to go out. Each night, after the rest of the family had retired, the mother would gather the glowing embers and cover them with the ashes. In the morning, before anybody else had arisen, she would rake back the ashes, uncover the still-glowing embers and blow them into flame. There were houses in which the fire had not gone out in over three hundred years. That is the job of the mystics vis-à-vis the flames of God's love. The mystics are the keepers of the ancient wisdom fires —many of whom were actually burned at the stake for daring to fan the embers of truth.

The Bible, if it is to be resuscitated as the word of God, needs to be purified in the loving light of the human mind and in the gentle compassion of the human heart. Then, and only then, shorn of its parasite-riddled shell, will it reemerge as the tiny, whispering sound of Source in the human soul as experienced by Elijah on Mount Horeb. But first, Elijah needs to outgrow his expectations that God will reveal Himself violently in the mighty wind, or devastating earthquake, or all-consuming fire. A strident message laced with violence is always proof of its human origins. When God speaks, even as She challenges and confronts, it's done in tones of a gentle mother guiding her baby's steps, not in the angry threats of an abusive parent.

Like the creative tension between the experiencing self (which is awash in all of the events of its life) and the narrating self (which selectively and in a non-representative fashion mixes real historical data with movies seen, stories heard, books read, and hopes projected) so, also, we have been caught at the theological story level. In order to grow, we must disidentify with the narrating self and identify with the soul self. We must disidentify with the tribal self and identify as a single Earth family. We can no longer retreat self-righteously into the separate stories, the tribal myths that divide us. The world and our species desperately need new stories and more powerful, unifying myths that propel us into thinking, talking, and acting as a global family. As I continue to point out and chip away at this straitjacket in which we have immobilized the Compassionate One, my hope is to set God free.

That's what God is asking of us at this stage of the maturing of *Homo sapiens sapiens*. Nothing less than becoming *Homo spiritualis* will allow us to survive the present crisis and reach for true greatness—the unconditional love and unity consciousness of the God we, in our infantile and adolescent phases, buried in the tomb of our fears. There is a need now for a new resurrection. One that mines the nuggets of true wisdom that are buried in the Bible and in the sacred stories of all peoples, and weaves them into a new scripture, where no one group is "chosen" because all are children of God.

And only then will we be ready to tackle the fourth story—that of cosmology. Many cultures have fashioned colorful but scientifically inaccurate versions of our origins. The Bible claims it happened in six God-busy days and it gave us a world model of an upturned bowl resting on four pillars set in the abyss, with waters both above the bowl and beneath the flat disc of dry land. In response to an enquiry from the emperor, a Chinese sage responded, "the Earth rests on the back of a great elephant, your majesty." "And on what does the great elephant stand?" "Why, he stands on the back of a great tiger, your majesty." "And on what does the great tiger stand?" "Why, he stands on the back of a great turtle, your majesty." "And on what does the great turtle stand?" "Why, from there on down, it's turtles all the way, your majesty."

Science has added its own depressing model. It has robbed us of both God and meaning, promising us a technology and eternal life via bioengineering, artificial intelligence, and a future as cyborgs. In the interim, it has treated us to weapons of mass destruction and ecological degradation. Modern techno-scientists are prophets and peddlers of a demythologized utopia.

The first great weapon of mass destruction, however, was "the Word of God," or rather, "the word of god," because genocide and xenophobia are incompatible with both the creative Logos and the all-loving Source. The former gave birth to the warring nature of sectarian religion—the calling down of God's blessing on our genocide of the "unbelievers." The latest and most devastating WMD has been gifted us by scientism, is deadlier than a flock of H-bombs, and robs humanity of its core organizing principles by claiming that God is dead, the soul is an illusion, free will is as real as the tooth faery, and religion is irrelevant.

Many claim God is dead. However, neither philosophy nor science has been able to produce the divine corpse. From a strictly rational perspective, it is much more difficult to prove that God does not exist than to prove She does exist. The cadaver that militant atheists love to impale for display and ridicule on the gate posts of science is merely a Guy Fawkes scarecrow that was, ironically, created and worshipped by the fundamentalist religious mindset.

When one civilization conquers another, a major weapon in its arsenal is the imposition of a new story on the subjugated people. This may be done by choking the indigenous language in favor of the new, "superior" one. This was done very cruelly but very effectively by the British education system in 19th-Century Ireland, and by the United States in the "schooling" of First Nation children up to very recently. Or the conquerors can also simply enforce the new cosmology by brute force. But they must also eradicate the stories that hold the identity of the conquered civilization intact. The process is rather like setting a trap to deal with an infestation of ants. The trap contains an alluring poison that ants carry back to their nest—thus killing the queen and all of her subjects.

We experience milder forms of this whenever we meet a new idea. Often it raises fear: "Without my old story, who am I? How can I really know what is truth?" Hence, people resist any examination of even a flawed cosmology. But what do we do when the new story is even more violent than the old? That's the situation in which we currently find ourselves vis-à-vis scientism. Former indoctrinations simply substituted one meaning-filled story for another. The greatest danger of scientism is that it has obliterated the old story (i.e. it killed the queen) and replaced it with a myth of meaninglessness. All other cultural conquests have simply given a new meaning to the conquered; this one has substituted meaning with nothingness—no God, no soul, no purpose, no free will, just self-serving neurons firing promiscuously like a series of explosions in a warehouse filled with July Fourth fireworks.

THE SEVEN TIMELINES

Once upon a time, an actual present moment gave birth to a possible future. From the billions of sperm swimming hopefully towards the egg, only one implanted itself, and this day is born. It is the saga of the "now" which will birth the future—a future whose mother is three kinds of Self, whose father is four kinds of story, and whose midwife is seven kinds of time.

These four kinds of stories intersect with seven timelines, which along with the sense of self, fashion the future. Here are the seven timelines: 1) the actual past, 2) the imaginary past (history as written by the victors), 3) the actual present, 4) the imagined present (of propaganda), 5) the fated future, 6) the probable future, and 7) the possible future. We are as much products of our imagined future (our hopes and aspirations) as we are of our imagined past (our founding myths). When it comes to the journeys of evolution and enlightenment, time is a very malleable commodity.

We are fashioned both by the actual past, which has created the very environment (physical, emotional, mental, social) in which we find ourselves, and by the imagined past—because we believed the stories of the victors and this has reoriented us to new reality models. Whether or not something is factual, it can have huge effects once it is believed, especially if it becomes the story adopted by the masses. The same is true of the present: both the actual present and the present of propaganda create the mindset and the reality we experience. Whether or not there are monsters under the bed or ghosts hiding in the closet, as long as we believe there are, then we are in the clutches of both.

The present is the logical, consistent outcome of all the choices of all the players in the past. And the future will be the logical, consistent outcome of all the choices of all the players in the present. If today is the child of a once-upon-a-time now-past present-moment, then the future is the child whom we are presently conceiving by our thinking, talking, and behavior. Will our baby be a monster or a messiah? That is up to us to determine. Only by dismantling the false gods made in our own image and likeness and reconnecting with the mystical impulse can we hope to survive, thrive, and evolve into the next stage of our incarnational contract. Our mission, individually and collectively, is to bring forth Christ Consciousness, to liberate our Buddha Nature, and to become a Soul-Self-Realized Species. We must identify the real God behind those mystical impulses and become not one *nation* under God but one *species* under God, in harmony with all creation.

When it comes to the future, this is where dreamers, mystics, and avatars are in a cosmic tug-o-war with those at the other end of the rope. And here's why: because there is no such thing as the future. There is a real past and a real present, but there is no such thing as a real, inevitable, fated future. There exists only the imagined future in either its probable form or its possible form. The probable future comes from refusing to make changes (based on false self and false stories); while the possible future comes from being willing to change (based on true self and true stories). Hence, the role of the prophet is to prevent the probable future and instead cause the possible future.

Margaret Mead once said, "Never doubt that a small group of thoughtful, committed citizens can change the world; indeed, it's the only thing that ever has." And the first prime minister of the new state of Israel, Ben Gurion said, "Anyone who does not believe in miracles is not a realist." The human ability to dream, coupled with our inner-divine attraction to love, is the greatest architect of a peaceful future.

Many years ago, I had a vision in which I saw planet Earth as a rock sitting on a sheet of ice in the emptiness of space. There were seven billion ropes attached to this rock with a human being pulling vigorously on each one. Using simple vector mathematics, I could calculate the exact speed and direction in which the rock would move. It was being pulled towards a cliff and was in danger of being catapulted into the void. Later, I came to realize that the seven billion ropes were actually humans clustered into camps. As I pondered this vision, I was able to see that originally, these groups of people were comprised of small clans, then tribes, then global religions and, finally, economic and ideological megacommunities. Each group's instincts were honed into intention by the stories they told, especially the historical, theological, and cosmological tales. The meme-makers (storytellers) had learned how to harness the masses. Sometimes this was done for purposes of enlightened transformation, like in the work of Lao Tzu, Confucius, Buddha, and Jesus. Other times it was used for nefarious purposes, like the greed and warfare exemplified by people like Hitler, Stalin, and Pol Pot.

In our times, courtesy of the political-military-economic hegemony and its loyal servant the mass media, a few megagroups have formed around the cleverly disguised intentions of the oligarchs. According to a 2016 Oxfam Davos report, sixty-two individual persons together own the same amount as half the world combined. And this is why xenophobia, avarice, and genocide are endemic to our times. The intentions of the masses have been carefully harnessed by the oligarchs in the service of global domination. Meanwhile, we have been lulled into sleep by the old Roman technique of *panes et circenses* (bread and circuses), as the oligarchs pollute the planet and collect the loot.

But like the great avatars, we too can channel our small group energy in ways that empower us in a world where "little people" have been made to feel helpless. Like never before, there is a need to get behind the rope of hope, of love and of unity consciousness, before our precious rock is pulled over the cliff into the chaos of the abyss.

My vision was inspired partly by history and current events and partly by physics. There is a simple formula that calculates the force of attraction between two heavenly bodies; it says: $F = (M_1 \text{ x } M_2)/r^2$ where F is the force, "M_1" and "M_2" are the masses of the two objects and "r" is the distance between them. If either of the masses were bigger, or if the distance between them were smaller, the force would increase.

Dreams are like that. But mostly we dream from the little "planet ego," about a tiny, personal dream, like a nicer house or a higher salary and—to shrivel our chances even further—we don't really believe we can have them, or even deserve them, thus increasing the distance between the dreamer and the dream because of our lack of faith. Wonders happen, as Jesus said they would, when we have the wisdom to dream as a species, to dream a dream that is love-impregnated, and to dream with a faith that shrinks distances between subject and object, between intention and manifestation. When instinct becomes intention and intention is energized by desire and desire is motivated by love, all things are possible. It only takes two or three to begin, or, as described in Lynne McTaggart's most recent book *The Power of Eight,* with each increase in numbers, you get not just arithmetic progression, but an exponential one.[1]

If you want to grab a strand of this new rope, how about joining or starting a little eight to twelve-person regular prayer/intention group? The networking of such groups will, I believe, be the key to not merely the survival of our "Rock" but its ascension. Maybe this is what Jesus really meant when he said, "thou art Peter, and upon this rock I will build my church." And it is just like Francis of Assisi, who at first misunderstood his vision as an injunction to re-erect the broken shell of his local chapel, but later realized he was being asked to reform the very corrupt Vatican-dominated Christian Church. Perhaps, just perhaps, there is a next stage to this statement of Jesus. His work was never about erecting stone structures nor even about creating human institutions, but about aligning with the community of incarnated souls as they attempt to move planetary consciousness into the next stage of global ascension.

As Jesus discovered, it can be really difficult to persuade others that your new perspective bears open-minded examination. This can be very threatening to their security. If you question a culture's cosmology, you risk ridicule at best and incarceration or extermination at worst. This has been the fate of many a prophet.

Flatland: A Romance of Many Dimensions is a satirical novella by Edwin Abbott Abbott, published in 1884. In reality, it is a social commentary on the caste/class system of Victorian England, but for my purpose here, it provides an elegant mathematical metaphor for the difficulty of shifting a culture's belief system. The author describes a two-dimensional world occupied by geometric figures. A three-dimensional sphere visits this "flatland" and has a helluva time convincing the natives that a third dimension exists. The sphere determines to prove his existence by passing through the plane of the 2-D world, but all they can see is a blob that begins as a point and grows into a circle with a larger and larger circumference until the sphere is midway through its passage and then a smaller and smaller circle, culminating in a point, before even that is extinguished as it continues and completes its passage through.

The sphere is amused by the inability of the flatlanders to see or believe in his existence until he finally makes a convert who travels to sphereland. Once the convert has understood the idea of a third dimension, he tries to convince the sphere of the theoretical possibility of the existence of a fourth (and fifth, and sixth ...) spatial dimension; but the sphere poo-poos this possibility and returns his student to Flatland in disgrace.

That is how difficult it can be to see what nobody else in the culture can see; to envisage a cosmology that nobody else in the culture can envisage. Without such awareness we are like the frog who lives in the well, a character in a delightful Sufi teaching story. An ocean frog visited his cousin, who had spent his entire life in the enclosure of a well. The ocean frog tried to give his cousin a sense of the vastness of the ocean, but without success. "Are you trying to tell me," the well frog asked, "that this ocean of yours is half the size of this well?" "More," said the ocean frog. "Three-fourths of this well?" "Even more!" the ocean frog replied. The well frog refused to believe that the ocean could be larger than the extent of his world, the well. Finally, he was persuaded to visit the ocean, where, upon seeing the enormity of the ocean, he was so overwhelmed that his brain exploded.

All we have is our stories (personal, tribal, theological, cosmological.) Once we accept the cultural wisdom, we will make appropriate, consistent sense of our own experiences so they align with that wisdom (the community stories). While conquests are often won through violence, they always involve imposing/proposing a different story. So there has to be a way to distinguish among them—and there is! Remember what Jesus said: by their fruits you shall know them.[2] Stories that speak of or encourage hatred, fear, anxiety, prejudice, entitlement, and chosen-ness are bad stories, to be discarded and rejected. Stories that speak of or encourage forgiveness, love, compassion, and justice are good stories, to be cherished and incorporated into our lives.

Christians have savaged each other self-righteously in inquisitions and sectarian warfare, and have murdered Jews, Muslims, and Pagans in crusades and conquests over the centuries. So have other "great" religions once they were in positions of power—for example, the ban policy ('cherem' in Hebrew) employed during the exodus from Egypt and the subsequent conquest of Canaan; and more recent and ongoing, the misguided violent form of jihad emerging in fundamentalist Islam. Religions are very ecumenical when they are in a position of powerlessness, but they often become intolerant and even genocidal, once they are in a position of power.

Since revelation of all kinds is based on core stories and key memes, we have to be very careful who the meme-makers and storytellers are. St. Ignatius of Loyola, the founder of the Jesuits, emphasized that skill in spiritual direction was dependent on *de discretione spirituum* (the discernment among spirits). Even a cursory review of history and a week's exposure to the current mass media should quickly convince the critical thinker that most memes and many stories have either been composed or corrupted, at best, by the bean counters and bureaucrats who steer the ship of state on a daily basis or, at worst, by dictators and oligarchs who chart the long-term trajectory.

If you're serious about crafting your own cosmology, you must become a serial killer! You have to commit four murders. First, you need to kill your ego, by which I mean you must put it in its place. You need a healthy ego in order to live in society, but when the ego thinks it's the center of the psyche, instead of the servant of the soul, you're going to have problems. It's the personal equivalent of the geocentric universe of yore, when people thought the cosmos revolved around our planet. So the ego needs to be put in its place, otherwise it gets up to all kinds of mischief. A wise one once said that all human suffering lies in the gap between the ego and the soul.

Next, you need to kill your father, by which I mean you must transcend your own culture and religion of origin—just as Jesus did. To transcend is not to abandon; it's forming an epigenetic relationship to your past wherein each subsequent stage incorporates and goes beyond all of the previous stages. As a tree puts out leaves, it does not separate itself from its roots, trunk, limbs, branches, or twigs. The leaves and the roots continue to feed each other—the roots by providing nutrients to the leaves from the soil in which it's grounded and the leaves by sharing spare chlorophyll (energized by the sun) with the roots. And so, you move beyond your mother and father's beliefs, but you may incorporate some version or portion of their beliefs into your own.

Murder number three: you must kill your guru. No matter how advanced or spiritual your teacher may be, you are a unique individual on a unique mission and there are places and experiences which only you can access. In Star Trek lingo, you must boldly go where no one has gone before. Of course, this does not mean badmouthing the guru or devaluating what you have learned, but bowing gratefully and moving on, just as an adult child does with the parents.

And, finally, the toughest killing of all, you gotta whack your god. No theology can take you to Source. Meister Eckhart says, "I pray daily to God to rid me of God." Since Source is utterly ineffable, it can be experienced but not articulated. Medieval mystic Thomas à Kempis said, "I would rather experience love than be able to define it." Are you feeling like you've just committed deicide? You haven't. Rather, you've begun to set God free from the ludicrous dogma that purports to describe Her. Then, and only then, you may be ready for your own divine revelation.

REVELATION IN ITS MANY FORMS

Truth is a seamless garment. It cannot contradict itself. But the seekers after truth are like the proverbial blind men trying to figure out what an elephant is based only on the part of the creature they happen to feel. They have two choices: firstly, each man could insist that his description is the only true one; or, secondly, they could combine their observations and arrive at a much more accurate picture of the whole elephant.

"Revelation" is the elephant in the room of human knowledge, and so it behooves us to combine our findings. Therefore, I'll look at revelation through story and myth, through philosophy and reason, through science and experimentation, through scriptures and sacred texts, through history and literature, through altered states of consciousness and imagination. There is no point in trying to force all of these modalities to speak the same language. Rather, the student must become multilingual and listen to the mother tongue of each kind of revelation.

Here's another way to look at it. A card, a bunch of flowers, a cake, and a hug might all be ways to say, "Happy Birthday!" There's no law that says the only way to wish somebody a happy birthday is to sing that song. I'll try to look at many of the facets of the diamond of truth, and not seek to reduce them all to a single perspective (which also explains the pile of mixed metaphors I'm asking you to play with here.) Stay with me as I share some introductory ideas with you, then look at the notion of Revelation in general, followed by a focused look at the Bible as Revelation. It all comes together—I promise!

Recall our discussion of epistemology in the first chapter of this book—how we know what we know—and the suggestion that it happens in one of three ways: we know because an authority figure told us it was so, or we know because we experienced something for ourselves, or we know because we figured it out on our own.

Revelation, too, can happen in any of those three ways. Typically, we think of revelation as some kind of information that comes directly from God. But in fact, revelation simply means uncovering that which was previously hidden. So, let's make some important distinctions here. There's a big difference between what is unknowable and what is unknown. "Unknowable" means that something *in its essence* cannot be comprehended by human effort, whereas "unknown" is just a state of being temporarily hidden. The unknowable cannot be either discovered or invented unless there is a supernatural intervention, whereas the unknown is subject to eventual discovery or invention. Let's say you come up with a killer recipe for Tandoori Chicken but, though you serve it regularly to your friends, you keep it as a closely guarded secret until you publish it in your first cookbook. Before the publication, it was secret, hidden, and unknown, but it was not unknowable.

It's the same distinction between invisible and not visible. Invisible means that something cannot be seen, ever, whereas not visible is simply a passing phase. The sun is not visible between sunset and sunrise, but it is not invisible per se. The soul, however, is essentially invisible, since it is not composed of physical matter.

That which is merely hidden can eventually become known, i.e., can be revealed. But this kind of revelation is simply through human agency. That is, for example, how science operates. The principles of thermodynamics have always existed but were unknown until scientists discovered them. So there is *discoverable revelation.* Jesus had something to say on this issue when he berated the religious teachers of his time for being able to discover the laws governing weather but being unable to see the spiritual laws. Invention is a close relative of discovery. Humans can combine previously known but separate parts (wheels, glass, rubber, steel…) into a brand-new artifact, e.g., an automobile. Thus, invention is also a form of revelation.

However, normally, when we hear the word "revelation," especially in a religious context, we think of *divine revelation,* whereby God directly intervenes and passes on information that could not be inferred, deduced or experienced if we were left to our own devices, e.g., the idea of the Holy Trinity, or that God created the world in six days and then chilled on day seven.

In this form of revelation, God is always the agent. Sometimes, He is personally involved, e.g., He speaks directly to Moses in the burning bush incident. On other occasions, He uses an intermediary, e.g., the angel Gabriel to speak to Mary, to Joseph, and to Zechariah in the New Testament, and to Mohammed in the Holy Quran. Often, then, these recipients become prophets—secondary kinds of agents—who purport to speak to the community on God's behalf, as did Moses, Jeremiah, Mohammed, and Joseph Smith.

Thus, we typically think of revelation—especially when we speak of the scriptures—as coming directly from God. Of course, ultimately, all knowledge and wisdom come from God, whether it's via authority, personal experience, or figuring it out for ourselves.

To use an allegory, it is like the difference between a rural farmer and an urban householder. The farmer raises chickens and feeds the eggs directly to his kids. That's like divine revelation. The urban householder feeds her kids eggs that she bought in a store that had purchased them from a packing factory that the farmer had supplied. That's like human revelation.

The fly in the ointment is that, even with direct, divine revelation, *it wasn't made to you.* There is a long lineage of teachers and office holders between you and God. So you are depending on authority figures, and you are presuming that they got it right from people who hopefully got it right from predecessors who hopefully got it right from their predecessors, and so on.

So, once again, using Thomas Aquinas, you have to use your judgment to discern what is true about divine revelation. Later, we'll consider the differences between gullibility, critical thinking, and debunking, but for now, let's just look at the two forms of divine revelation: oral and written. Of course, the oral tradition is much older than the written one. People told stories for tens of thousands of years before cuneiform and hieroglyphics (and later, alphabet-based orthographies) were invented. The vast bulk of the world's scriptures, in fact, are based on earlier oral traditions. It was a point of great dispute, even in Jesus's time, between the Pharisees who believed Moses left two forms of revelation—spoken stories and the written

Torah—and the Sadducees, the priestly caste, who accepted only the Torah as true revelation.

Most written traditions began as oral traditions. The few exceptions may be the Book of Mormon, first published in 1830 by Joseph Smith, who claimed he received it on golden plates, and which an angel commanded him to translate from its original "reformed Egyptian" into English. The other exception is a modern form called channeled writing, like Neale Donald Walsch's series *Conversations with God*.

There are, of course, other forms of revelation—more exotic forms like art, music, and dance. The latter two are the hallmark of the Shamanistic traditions of revelation. And, I believe, science is another form of revelation. Most of us, however, encounter "revelation" in the form of "mass media"— at least, the talking heads of the oral tradition (radio, TV) and the clacking typewriters of the written tradition (newspapers, magazines, and journals) would like us to believe so as they inveigh mightily to prove that their particular brand and theirs alone is the "gospel truth."

Historically, however, revelation has been primarily received and transmitted orally. Oral transmission comes in many forms—stories, myths, folklore, parables, proverbs, analogies, metaphors, aphorisms. For example, the prophet Mohammed began his public ministry as a result of a wrestling match with the angel Gabriel who grabbed him and shouted, "Iqra! Iqra!!" (Recite! Recite!!) There are shades here of Jacob striving with an angel, as a result of which he is renamed, Israel (the man who wrestled with God.)

All scriptures begin as stories whether they are about Adam, Abraham, and Moses of the Torah; Jesus, the Magdalene, Peter, and Paul of the New Testament; Mohammed of the Hadith; or Arjuna and Krishna of the Bhagavad Gita. Only later do these stories get worked into torturous theologies and deadening dogma. Since all revelation begins with, and trades in, storytelling, let's begin with that topic as we explore revelation in general.

Every major religion identifies with holy scriptures or religious texts of some sort. Even before the 13th century BCE, when *The Epic of Gilgamesh* first hit the shelves of Sumerian bookstores, the Egyptians were carving graffiti on the walls and sarcophagi of the pyramids of Saqqara. Historians, archaeologists, anthropologists, and ethnographers study these texts exhaustively in their quest for important insights into the cultures from which they emerged. If every follower of every religion took the same care to fully understand the books that inform their traditions, the world might experience less bloodshed in the name of religion. But the fact that people are ready to die and kill over a Biblical passage makes it all the more important that we examine this library of sacred books and letters with educated minds, discerning hearts, and a critical eye.

This process is necessary and important to do for every holy book —the Koran, the Bhagavad Gita, the Book of Mormon, the Baha'i Revelation, etc. I've studied many religious texts with great reverence for the wisdom they hold, but for our purposes here, I've chosen to put the Judeo-Christian Bible under the microscope. The Hebrew and Christian scriptures hold pervasive influence around the world, but they're really no different from other texts that traditionally hold the status of divine revelation. I'll start with the Bible as a model for how we might examine all religious texts.

I hope that by now I have laid down a thorough and honest foundation for this examination of the Bible—its origins, evolution, and claim to divine revelation. My purpose is not to dismantle the Bible, but to find the eternal, mystical core beneath the countless remodellings, in which each generation has tried to make sense of it and bend it to its own agenda. Indeed, the devil himself can appeal to scripture, which he did in quoting Psalm 91 as he attempted to persuade Jesus to jump off the parapet of the temple. And Jesus himself radically reframed many of the earlier Hebrew teachings, beginning with the mantra-like phrase, "You have heard that it was said to the people of old...but I say to you:.."

The task, then, is to unearth God's real message, and that means thinking critically about its wording and provenance. We must learn to distinguish historical aberrations, driven by political ambition, from the necessary reframing of original texts that were formed in the petri dish of more barbaric times.

In elementary mathematics, one and one always add up to two. In higher math, you'll meet mathematical systems (e.g., binary Boolean algebra) in which this is not the case. In the elementary understanding of the Bible, every utterance is God's inerrant teaching, to be understood according to the literal meaning of each word. In the more advanced schools of real spirituality, however, this is not always the case. In the search for "God's word," it is vital to be able to make that distinction. Otherwise, we are destined to get even more embroiled in religious wars and to drive an even deeper chasm between religion and science.

In seeking the true word of God, we must ask ourselves if what we've encountered leads only to love, compassion, and forgiveness. If our journey is taking us anywhere else, we need to overhaul the ship's compass. And that is my core objective here.

The United Church of Christ recently created a marketing campaign that speaks for God. Ironically, the tag line is "God Is Still Speaking." I think it's a good message, often emblazoned on rainbow banners above the same door that says "All Are Welcome." God speaks as eloquently in Celtic mythology, African folklore, and Aboriginal dreamtime as He does in the Bible, Koran, Upanishads, or Pitakas. In fact, God speaks every bit as eloquently in a single flower.

The shortest homily the Buddha ever gave was to simply pluck a flower and hold it silently aloft as his disciples watched. Minutes passed, but he uttered not a word. His disciples were getting impatient and thinking, "Alright, dude, what's up?" But still he remained silent. Then one of his disciples broke into a huge smile. The Buddha noticed this and nodded his head in confirmation. The disciple had suddenly realized that to really see even a flower is to see everything. It's not important *where* you look, but *how* you look. If you don't know how to look, you can search everywhere and find nothing; but if you do know how to look, then wherever you search you can find everything. Revelation is in the eye and in the soul of the beholder.

Jesus gave a similar sermon, though he wrapped it in a spoken sentence: "Look at the lilies of the field." The gospel writers went on to expand that saying and then to offer both an interpretation and a lesson—both of which they attribute to Jesus. I'm not certain he actually added anything to those seven (in English) words. Like the Buddha, he was demonstrating to his disciples that to really see the essence/origin of a lily is to see Source Itself.

And that mystical English poet, William Blake, said it so beautifully: "To see the world in a grain of sand, and to see heaven in a wildflower, hold infinity in the palm of your hands, and eternity in an hour." In other words, God reveals Herself in all of Her creation and in all of Her stories. And the Bible is a beautiful compendium of one nation's God-stories.

It is actually incorrect to speak of the Bible as a book, even as a holy book. The term Bible is a version of the original Greek, τὰ βιβλία, which means, "the books"—plural. And rightly so, because the Christian Bible is more like a library—sixty-six books in the Protestant version and seventy-three in the Catholic version. Moreover, like any library, it has very different kinds of books in it—e.g., laws, history, liturgy/ritual, riddles, letters, theology, myth, parables, musings on existential issues (e.g., Job), eschatology, a hymnal (psalms), prophecy, wisdom literature (e.g., proverbs), and much more.

Without even realizing it, as you read your Sunday newspaper and move from the comic section to gardening, movies, finance, and foreign news, you are subtly shifting your mindset. But people presume that they can just dip into the Bible anywhere and engage meaningfully with the content. You cannot read eschatology (the study of the end times) with the same mindset as the liturgical prescriptions of Leviticus. So, before we can begin to understand the Bible as a whole, we need to appreciate that it is made up of a diverse collection of parts.

With estimated sales of over five billion copies, the Bible is very probably the best-selling book of all time. It continues to sell about 100 million copies annually and it has had a huge influence, not just on Judeo-Christianity, but on world history, literature, art, architecture, music, and civilization. The Gutenberg Bible was the first book ever printed using moveable type.

The oldest extant copy of the complete bible (the Codex Vaticanus) is held in the Vatican Library in a Fourth-Century CE parchment-book. Strangely enough, the oldest copy of the Hebrew/Aramaic Tanakh comes from much later—the tenth century CE.

In 1631, the royal printers in London were commissioned to do a reprint of the King James Bible. In a grievous error, the word, "not" was omitted from the commandment, "Thou shalt *not* commit adultery." It became known as the "Wicked Bible." King Charles I and the archbishop of Canterbury were outraged. Most of the copies were confiscated and burned, but a few escaped and are still available for display, including one in the New York Public Library. The printers were fined the equivalent of 46,000 pounds sterling and deprived of their printing license.

The original language of the Tanakh is Biblical Hebrew, but a few passages of Ezra, Jeremiah and Daniel are in Biblical Aramaic, which was much more widely spoken among Semitic peoples. For the New Testament, Koine Greek is the original language.

The original scriptures (both the Tanakh and the New Testament) consisted of complete books or letters without any formal "breaks" in the text. But in 1226, Stephen Langton, the Roman Catholic archbishop of Canterbury, divided them into chapters; and in 1551, Robert Estienne, a French printer, divided the chapters into verses.

The Hebrew Scriptures are composed of three parts. The acronym TaNaKh stands for the three parts: "T" stands for Torah (meaning "Teaching") which is the first five books of the Bible: Genesis, Exodus, Leviticus, Numbers and Deuteronomy—believed to have been written by Moses himself; "N" stands for Nevi'im (the Hebrew word for "prophets") and means the works of the minor and major prophets, e.g., Isaiah, Jeremiah, Ezekiel; and "K" stands for Ketuvim (literally "the writings"). This included the wisdom literature developed while the two remaining tribes were in exile in Babylon from 589 BCE to 538 BCE, as well as the book of Psalms and the book of Proverbs. Under the very significant influence of Zoroastrianism, the exiles pondered the great existential issues, which were then written as the books of Job, Ecclesiastes, etc. This wisdom included a belief in angels, spirits, and the afterlife. The Pharisee party accepted all three parts of the Tanakh as revelation, but the Sadducees rejected the Ketuvim. And there was a deep division between the lay-theologian Pharisees and the priestly Sadducees based upon their differences regarding divine revelation and the Bible.

Similarly, Roman Catholics, Anglicans, and Eastern Orthodox Christians emphasize the complementarity of Sacred Tradition (the belief that Jesus's teachings were preserved from generation to generation both in the Scriptures and oral traditions under the supervision of Church leaders), whereas Protestants focus on the idea of "sola scriptura" (the Bible alone.) But those who consider the Bible to be the revealed word of God actually span a very wide spectrum. At one end are those who claim that it is inspired by God, whose Holy Spirit influenced the words, message, and collation of the Bible. Then comes the position that it is also infallible when it comes to matters of faith and practice, but not necessarily in scientific or historical matters. Position number three is occupied by those who claim that its inerrancy extends to all matters—no exception. Then comes biblical literalism, whose adherents further claim that not only is it inerrant on all topics, but that its meaning is clear to the average reader.

It gets even more confusing. Most evangelical Bible scholars claim that only the original texts in the original languages were inspired, but not the translations, while other groups—like the followers of the King-James-only Movement—are convinced that there is only one translation which is inerrant—the King James Version (KJV). In 1546, the Council of Trent decreed St. Jerome's translation into Latin of the original Hebrew/Aramaic and Greek language versions (called the Vulgate)—completed around 380 CE—to be the only authentic and official Bible of the Latin Church.

As you can see, it is far from clear what the ideas of "revelation" and "divine inspiration" of the Bible actually mean. There is lots of wiggle room here. Many scholars point out that the biblical texts come from a creative thousand-year-long conversation between ancient oral traditions and different faith communities. And there were many voices in this conversation: political, cultural, theological, economic, and even health-related topics.

Perhaps one of the greatest of all human inventions was writing—the creation of orthographies that turned spoken languages into visual symbols. The original efforts were cumbersome and only highly trained practitioners could master the thousands of symbols necessary to read and write cuneiform and hieroglyphics. However, that changed dramatically when a second great invention superseded the first. It was the creation of "modern" alphabets. It actually came in two waves—firstly, "abjads," which represented only the consonants of the spoken language, and then the "true" alphabet which provided symbols for both consonants and vowels. Greek was the first to render this complete alphabet. But the original genius was that of the Phoenicians, who (around 1,300 BCE) invented the radical idea of representing the *sounds* of a written language rather than a myriad of symbols to represent "things" (trees, cows, hands) or internal "states" (love, fear, loyalty). Now, unlike cuneiform and hieroglyphics, a few dozen symbols—or, in the case of the Phoenician and other Semitic languages, merely 22—could capture it all.

The Phoenicians were a maritime trading culture and their new ideas on written language soon spread around the Mediterranean. Its brilliance was that it could immediately be adapted to any other language, and its simplicity meant that it could be learned even by the "common people." Heretofore, only royal and religious hierarchies knew how to write, so this new system had significant social implications. These hierarchies in many Middle Eastern kingdoms, however, continued to use cuneiform for legal and liturgical matters right down to the Common Era.

The new system was adopted by the Greeks, and the Romans got it from the Greeks. The Roman/Latin orthography is the single most common one among languages today. As this new system encountered spoken languages whose sounds could not be represented by only 22 phonemes, alphabets got extended. English has 26 letters in its alphabet.

Hebrew, Aramaic, and Arabic also borrowed it from the Phoenicians beginning around the 9th century BCE. Hebrew, with its 22 characters, still has no vowel signs (even in modern Israeli newspapers), so context is very important when reading it. So, in the 7th century CE, Jewish scholars, called the Masoretes, fixed the meanings of the texts by adding vowel signs in the form of little marks above and below the consonant signs.

The first books of the Bible began to be written about 950 BCE employing the new Phoenician-inspired orthography. So, when they spoke of Abraham (c. 1850 BCE) and Moses (c. 1250 BCE), they were dependent on oral traditions. Later parts of the Bible were then composed and written over the next 1,000 years by hundreds of different writers.

The Bible tells us that the Israelites entered "the promised land" about the year 1210 BCE and, beginning with the sacking of Jericho, spent the next 200 years conquering the country. By 1010 BCE, King David had conquered Jerusalem, made it his capital, and united the tribes into a single nation. Solomon built the first temple around 950 BCE. But when he died in 933 BCE, a civil war ensued which divided the country in two: the southern kingdom of Judea (consisting of two tribes – Judah and Benjamin) with its headquarters (and the temple) in Jerusalem; and the northern kingdom of Israel (consisting of the other ten tribes) with its headquarters in Samaria.

In 721 BCE, the great Assyrian empire, with the cooperation of Judea, overthrew Israel, deporting the ten northern tribes, who then disappear from history. They are referred to, even today, as "the lost tribes of Israel." After the Babylonians overcame the Assyrians, they laid siege to Jerusalem and conquered it in 597 BCE, installing a puppet king. When he rebelled, they came back, reconquered Jerusalem, destroyed the temple and exiled the last two tribes. The prophet Ezekiel managed to hold the people together until 538 BCE, when the Persian king Cyrus overthrew the Babylonians and set the Jews free to go back to the land of Judea. This remnant set about building the second temple, which was completed around 515 BCE.

Alexander the Great overcame the Persians in 333 BCE and

marched eastwards, conquering "the entire known world" to the gates of India. The Greek language and culture followed behind him. But by 63 BCE, the Romans had fully defeated the Greeks and now ruled the Middle East, including the land of "Palestine"—the Roman name for the country. The Romans installed King Herod, who ruled from 40 BCE to 4 BCE. The Romans put down a Jewish revolt in 70 CE and flattened the second temple. All that remains of it, to the present day, is the western wall, better known as the "Wailing Wall," where millions of Jews come each year to pray.

This history is very important because each phase left its mark on the composition, writing, and redaction of the Bible. Modern scholarship employs three main techniques in establishing the time of composition of various parts of the Bible. Historical Analysis seeks to establish the "intent" of each writer, so as to be able to translate accurately. Materialist Analysis looks at the social, economic, and political environments at the time of composition. And Structural Analysis, especially using the twentieth-century discipline of Semiotics, tries to determine internal consistencies and inconsistencies within the texts. Semiotics is the science of understanding the grammar not just of individual sentences (e.g., subject, predicate, object…), but of an entire text. Texts have a natural flow, and when edits or redactions are done, they leave footprints in the text.

Each organization, from tennis clubs to nations, needs a variety of documents to establish itself. In the case of a theocratic culture, the stories of the ancestors bind them together as family; epics celebrate (and exaggerate) their past heroes and heroines; laws establish the ground rules; poetry/prayers focus their spirituality; oracles/prophets align them with God's precepts; teachings steer them on the journey; and "wisdom" writings help them reflect on the great existential issues.

The Bible employs all of these kinds of documents, and using all three kinds of analysis just mentioned, scholars can identify when and where various parts of the Bible were written. In a nutshell, they've discovered four great origins/redactions, which are widely known as J, E, D, and P.

J (or Y in Hebrew) gets its name from how God is called in this group of writings, i.e., Yahweh. It represents the oldest writings, beginning around 950 BCE. It is the sacred history of the southern kingdom of Judah—centered on a promised land, a chosen king, and a temple-of-the-divine—and it treats of the beginnings (Adam and Eve), the Patriarchs (Abraham, Isaac and Jacob), and the core story of Exodus and Moses. The author of J is a great storyteller and God is presented as very "human." He is a gardener, potter, surgeon, and tailor. He bargains with Abraham, is quite forgiving, and always ready to bless.

E gets its name from how God is called in this group of writings, i.e., Elohim. Once the civil war divided the nation, the kings of the northern kingdom of Israel did not want their subjects going down to Jerusalem to worship. Unlike the south, where leadership centered on the king and the temple, the north's religion now centered on the prophets like Elijah, Amos, and Hosea. E begins to produce its writings around 750 BCE. The E tradition speaks of a very different kind of God than is presented in J. He is accessible mainly through dreams or in spectacular manifestations or theophanies. No images allowed! E is very interested in moral questions and quite focused on sin. Real worship is about obeying God, keeping the covenant, and rejecting false gods.

D gets its name from the book of Deuteronomy. It is a collection of laws that was begun in the northern kingdom, but taken south and hidden in the Temple after the Assyrian conquest in 721 BCE. During renovations there in 612 BCE, it was rediscovered, completed, and offered as a rededication of the people to God. It became the book of Deuteronomy and also influenced other books of the Bible. Its style is very emotional and its words are put into the mouth of Moses—though it was composed over 600 years after the time of Moses.

JE. Around 700 BCE, scholars in Jerusalem, under the direction of King Hezekiah, began to amalgamate J and E—the sacred histories of the southern kingdom of Judah and the (fallen) northern kingdom of Israel. It was an effort to heal the results of the civil war of 933 BCE. It is known to scholars as JE.

P gets its name from the "Priestly" documents of the Bible, which were written during the Babylonian captivity—587 to 538 BCE—and later, especially under the influence of Ezekiel. P has a rather dry style, with lots of figures and lists. The vocabulary is very technical, having to do with liturgy/cult/worship. Genealogies appear often because it is written during the Babylonian captivity and it is vital that the exiles retain a sense of history and belonging. The huge emphasis on worship covers pilgrimages, festivals, and the importance of priests. The priests replace the role of the king in J and of the prophets in E. Because of its unique style, it is the easiest of the four traditions to identify when reading the Torah.

JEPD. Over a period of some five hundred years, religious leaders had gone over their history several times in order to find meaning in their experiences as a culture. Around 520 BCE, under Ezra the priest-scribe, they began to bring the four main attempts together into a single work, called **JEPD** by scholars. It was completed around 400 BCE and is known as "the Pentateuch" in Greek or "Torah" in Hebrew. It consists of the first five books of the modern Bible—Genesis, Exodus, Leviticus, Numbers, and Deuteronomy. The books of Genesis, Exodus, and Numbers contain input from J, E and P; Leviticus is a pure P document and Deuteronomy is a pure D document.

In a later major redaction, the writings of the prophets (Nevi'im) and the wisdom literature (Ketuvim) were added to the canon; hence the total work is known as Tanakh or the Hebrew Bible.

Much later, in Yavneh after the fall of the second temple in 70 CE, when the final decision was to be made about which books to include or exclude, the Jewish scholars used two criteria. To qualify for admission, a book had to have been written (i) in Hebrew and (ii) before 400 BCE. Both criteria were misapplied. Some books, whose originals were written in Hebrew but were lost and which "now" existed only in translation, were excluded, only for the originals to surface when it was too late—e.g., The Book of Enoch and the Book of Jubilees. And some books which purported (according to internal claims) to have been written before 400 BCE were discovered, through modern scholarship, to actually have been written much later. (You win some, you lose some!)

A simple example will illustrate this weaving of sources. The story of the escape from slavery in Egypt contained in chapters 13 and 14 of the book of Exodus has J, E, and P interwoven into a single narrative, but it oscillates between them throughout the two chapters, drawing upon J eleven times, E eight times, and P eight times.

This is a work of love and dedication that spanned many generations of priests, prophets, and scribes. Each redaction was an attempt to make sense of their relationship with their God and express it in a way that the people of each era could comprehend.

Beginning in the third century BCE, the Hebrew Scriptures were translated into Greek. Tradition says that 70 elders, acting completely independently of each other, did this translation and arrived at identical versions. Thus, believers held, this translation was also divinely inspired.

Translations vary; some are more faithful to the original texts. To express the Bible in idiomatic English, for example, a translator must often take liberties with the source texts. In general, there are three basic ways in which one can translate any language into another. The first is *literal translation.* At first blush one might imagine that this is the optimal way. In actual fact, this method often corrupts the original and fails miserably to convey its message. When you are dealing with idioms, alliteration, poetry, puns, and proverbs, for instance, literal translation is most inadequate.

The second way to translate is called *dynamic transference* where you try to establish the intent of the original writer and study the history, economics, politics, and culture of the times in which it was written. Of course, there is still an element of subjective interpretation on your part, but it puts the least amount of detritus into the mix.

The third way to translate is to begin with an agenda or bias and then force the original text to conform to your position. This is called "paraphrasing." Unfortunately, many fundamentalists favor this approach and several such translations exist. Of course, even a good translation can be read with a paraphrasing mindset— since "truth" is in the eye of the beholder—and used to "prove" one's prejudices.

But even with the best of intentions and the best of scholarship, there are linguistic constraints that create problems of their own. Let's just take the issue of gender. In English, to use the third person singular pronoun, one is forced to land on the side of one gender; I have to choose she or he or else resort to the cumbersome he/she. In Hebrew it is even worse: even with second-person-singular pronouns, I must make a choice. If I want to say "blessed are you" I have to say, *baruch ata* if I am addressing a male and *baruch at* if I am addressing a female. Kiswahili does not have this problem with first, second, or third person pronouns: *alienda nyumbani* can mean "he went home," "she went home," or "it [e.g., a cow] went home." So, in translating from Hebrew, one is forced to choose sides.

Add to that the fact that, as I have said previously, Hebrew does not have vowel signs. Now let me tell you of a real issue I encountered when I worked as a missionary among the Kalenjin peoples of Kenya. The Kalenjin languages did not have an orthography; there was no written form of the languages until quite recently. They are also semi-tonal. Now, take an ancient Hebrew story that existed only in an oral form for hundreds of years, was then written in a language without vowel signs and redacted several times over a period of hundreds of years. Translate that story into Tugen (a Kalenjin language) which is semi-tonal and didn't have a written form until a few years back. Here's an example. Jesus tells a parable about a farmer who sowed wheat in his field, but an enemy came at night and sowed cockle among the wheat. Cockle is a weed which, in the early stages of its growth, looks identical to wheat. The master's workers, upon discovering this evil deed, ask him if they should pull up the cockle. The master says, "No, because you might also uproot the wheat. Wait until harvest time, then we will separate them." Now the missionaries who first translated this into Kalenjin had several problems. Firstly, the Kalenjin are nomadic pastoralists with no agricultural practice or know-how. Next, neither wheat nor cockle is native to Kenya and there are no words in Kalenjin for them. How now to convey the clever and deep meaning of this parable of Jesus?

The translators had to invent both words. For wheat they used *bainik,* which is the plural of the Kalenjin word for "food," and for cockle they invented a new word, *chemulbainik,* which literally means "that which imitates food." Talk about beating the listeners over the head with the punch line!

Another issue with translating is the occasional "need" to sanitize the language. Let me give you two examples. I hope I don't offend any pious ears or eyes, but I am, in fact being true to the original Hebrew and Greek texts.

Example one: the *Douay–Rheims Bible* or the *Douai Bible* is a translation of the Bible from the Latin Vulgate into English made by members of the English College, Douai, in the service of the Catholic Church between 1582 and 1610. The "ban" is an alleged edict from God, found in several parts of the Torah, which says that when the Israelites sacked a town, they were to kill all the males. The problem is that the Hebrew Bible didn't actually say, "Kill all the males." What it actually said was, "Kill everything that urinates against the wall." The Douai Bible translated this phrase into English as, "Kill everything that pisses against the wall." That would not have been considered "rude" in 1610.

Example two: in Mark's account of Jesus's discussion of kosher and treif foods, Jesus says, "It is not what goes into a man (i.e., food) that makes him unclean, but rather that which comes out of him (e.g., evil thoughts, anger, lust)." Jesus goes on to say, "What goes into a man is processed by the stomach and voided into the toilet." Now Greek has several words for "toilet"—latrine, long-drop, water-closet—but Mark doesn't use any of these. The Greek word he chooses instead is "shit-house." Now, is Jesus being intentionally crude to drive home his teaching? Or is Mark trying to shock his own audience? Either way, modern translations have cleaned up the language.

What then of Biblical inerrancy or not messing with the word of God? Here I will just focus on three areas where the Biblical viewpoint is obviously in error: science, history, and scriptural knowledge.

Science: The notion that the entire cosmos was created in six days is definitely not scientific. So, depending on which version of "divine inspiration" you subscribe to, it raises issues. Those who hold that the Bible is inerrant in all matters—including its scientific pronouncements—and that it is literally true as understood by the ordinary reader, have a major problem here. Less stringent interpretations of "divine inspiration" can interpret "six days" as six "periods of time" and thus hope to skate around the issue. In all probability the "six days" of creation and the seventh day of rest was borrowed by the Hebrew writers from the much older creation accounts of the Sumerians who wrote an origin story on seven clay tablets, called the Enuma Elish. The Bible goes on to depict a world which is basically dry land resting on pillars that separate it from the waters beneath the land and a metal dome to separate it from the waters above. The sun, moon, and stars are under this canopy and flood gates in this vault allow rain and snow to water the Earth. Sheol, the abode of the dead, lies in the depths of the Earth. And high above all things sits God on his throne. I reckon God is now constantly on the lookout to make sure stray satellites and interplanetary space probes don't crash-land on his home.

History: In the beginning of chapter two of his gospel, where Luke is about to tell of the story of Jesus's birth, he writes, "*In those days a decree went out from Caesar Augustus that the whole world should be enrolled. This was the first enrollment, when Quirinius was governor of Syria.*" We know from secular history that such censuses took place in 28 BCE, 8 BCE, and 14 CE. Jesus's birth could not have coincided with any of these. Moreover, Quirinius did not become governor of Syria until 6 CE. Luke is trying to construct a reason to get Jesus's parents from Nazareth in Galilee to Bethlehem in Judea so that he could fulfill the prophecy that the Messiah would be born in Bethlehem.

Scriptural Knowledge: In the heat of another typical battle with the Pharisees, Jesus says, "*Have you never read what David did when he and his companions were hungry and in need? In the days of Abiathar the high priest, he entered the house of God and ate the consecrated bread, which* *is lawful only for priests to eat. And he also gave some to his companions."* This passage is from Mark 2:25-26 and Jesus/Mark is referring to a story from 1 Sam 21:1-7. The problem is that Abiathar was *not* the high priest then; rather, his father, Abimelech was. So, who screwed up? Was it the Hebrew Scriptures, or Jesus, or Mark? Whoever was responsible, when Matthew and Luke record the same incident, they drop the name of the high priest entirely. Are they trying to expunge the guilt of the offending party?

Dr. Laura Schlessinger—an outspoken advice-giver on matters of morals and relationships, announced on her radio show that, as an observant Orthodox Jew, she believed homosexuality to be an abomination (in accordance with Leviticus 18:22) and is not to be condoned under any circumstance. The following was an open, tongue-in-cheek letter to her, "asking advice" about some other laws from Leviticus.

Dear Dr. Laura:

Thank you for doing so much to educate people regarding God's Law. I have learned a great deal from your show, and try to share that knowledge with as many people as I can. When someone tries to defend the homosexual lifestyle, for example, I simply remind them that Leviticus 18:22 clearly states it to be an abomination. End of debate.

I do need some advice from you, however, regarding some other elements of God's Laws and how to follow them.

Leviticus 25:44 states that I may possess slaves, both male and female, provided they are from neighboring nations. A friend of mine claims that this applies to Mexicans, but not Canadians. Can you clarify? Why can't I own Canadians?

I would like to sell my daughter into slavery, as sanctioned in Exodus 21:7. In this day and age, what do you think would be a fair price for her?

I know that I am allowed no contact with a woman while she is in her period of menstrual "uncleanliness" (Lev. 15: 19-24). The problem is, how do I tell? I have tried asking, but most women take offense.

When I burn a bull on the altar as a sacrifice, I know it creates a pleasing odor for the Lord (Lev. 1:9.) The problem is my neighbors. They claim the odor is not pleasing to them. Should I smite them?

I have a neighbor who insists on working on the Sabbath. Exodus 35:2 clearly states he should be put to death. Am I morally obligated to kill him myself, or should I ask the police to do it?

A friend of mine feels that even though eating shellfish is an abomination (Lev. 11:10), it is a lesser abomination than homosexuality. I don't agree. Can you settle this? Are there degrees of abomination?

Lev. 21:20 states that I may not approach the altar of God if I have a defect in my sight. I have to admit that I wear reading glasses. Does my vision have to be 20/20, or is there some wiggle-room here?

Most of my male friends get their hair trimmed, including the hair around their temples, even though this is expressly forbidden by Lev. 19:27. How should they die?

I know from Lev. 11:6-8 that touching the skin of a dead pig makes me unclean, but may I still play football if I wear gloves?

My uncle has a farm. He violates Lev. 19:19 by planting two different crops in the same field, as does his wife by wearing garments made of two different kinds of thread (cotton/polyester blend). He also tends to curse and blaspheme a lot. Is it really necessary that we go to all the trouble of getting the whole town together to stone them? (Lev. 24:10-16) Couldn't we just burn them to death at a private family affair, like we do with people who sleep with their in-laws? (Lev. 20:14)

I know you have studied these things extensively and thus enjoy considerable expertise in such matters, so I'm confident you can help. Thank you again for reminding us that God's word is eternal and unchanging.

The "Dr. Laura letter" is whimsical and humorous but scripturally accurate and raises genuine concerns about the issue of divine inspiration of some Biblical passages. So, let me raise some concerns of my own. When we translate the Bible, is it okay to write "human" instead of "man" in order to capture the original intent of the writer? But what if the original intent was to show that women were inferior or mere chattels? Can we change it then? Here's what St. Paul had to say in his letter to the Ephesians (5:22-24):

> Wives, obey your husbands as you obey the Lord. The husband is the head of the wife, just as Christ is the head of the church people. The church is his body and he saved it. Wives should obey their husbands in everything, just as the church people obey Christ.

Are we stuck with that forever? Is it unchristian to regard and treat women as equals to men? In the Torah, slaves, women, gentiles and children are all lesser beings. Are we, then, ungodly bible-destroyers by affording all of these equal value? Was the American Civil War, in fact, a refusal to acknowledge God's curse on Ham/Canaan in the book of Genesis?

What *can* we change? What are we not allowed to change? And why? What criteria do we need to adopt as we translate or adapt the Bible to 21st-century people? Are we only allowed to clean up the indelicate language? Or can we change, even radically change, the teachings themselves—as Jesus definitely did in his longest homily of all—the Sermon on the Mount, that takes up three chapters of Matthew's gospel? And, most importantly, what criteria or orienting principles will guide us as we pan for gold in the sometimes murky stream of the Scriptures? Surely, unconditional love for all of God's creatures and a sense of Unity Consciousness (the realization that all of creation is simply the manifestation of one Source—God) must be the primary drivers of the sifting process. Jesus himself compared the kingdom of God to a dragnet cast into the sea that pulls out all kinds of stuff. The fisher's job, then, is to patiently sort out the goodies from the garbage, the facts from the fiction. His final command to his followers was that they be fishers of "men."

I believe that Jesus had no intention of founding a new religion, and certainly not one that would be headquartered in Rome and would persecute his own people for the next 2,000 years. Rather, as a great avatar, who transcended denominational thinking, he was inviting the people of his time and of his culture to move from a slavery-to-law mentality into the embrace of the divine mystery. Rumi would later put this notion very poetically when he said, "Out beyond ideas of wrong-doing and right-doing there is a field. I'll meet you there. When the soul lies down in that grass the world is too full to talk about."

So, Jesus had this enigmatic, paradoxical relationship to Torah (Law/teaching). On the one hand, he would declare, "I have come not to abolish the law but to bring it to fulfillment"; but—like Tevya in *Fiddler on the Roof,* he would say: "On the other hand…" He would go on to radically challenge it. By intending to "fulfill" the Torah, he was implying that the Word of God is a work in progress, a wisdom that must continually evolve in order to be relevant and inspirational to each era of human development.

In a famous series of "updates," Jesus intoned, in an almost mantra-style introduction, *"You have heard that it was said to your ancestors... but I say to you..."* He then went on to seriously challenge and radically reframe a whole bunch of laws, e.g., on killing, anger, forgiveness, adultery, lustful thoughts, divorce, oath-taking, revenge, almsgiving, prayer, fasting, and judging others.

He shifted the emphasis from a "law" written on stone tablets to a "law" written in the heart, just as Jeremiah had predicted 600 years before (Jer 31:33). And it is important to realize that this was not just a shift from stone to memory, but from stone to heart. It wasn't just that people had to memorize the law, but to realize that the ultimate law—love—is deeply embedded in the human soul. The Latin origin of the English word "education" is *educatio,* from the verb *educare,* which means, "to lead out from inside of." True education is not the pouring of data into empty heads, but rather, the uncovering of the innate wisdom of the student. Similarly, true morality is not about imposing rules on a recalcitrant populace, but helping them to dig so deeply into themselves that they uncover their inner divinity. Then, the only law is love. St. Augustine of Hippo said as much: "Love God and do as you please."[3] Once you discover and operate out of love, morality is no longer the minimalist operating at the lowest acceptable behavior, but the disciple loving at the highest possible level.

In an exchange with a scholar who wanted to know which of the 613 precepts of Torah was the most important, Jesus responded that it was to *"love the Lord your God with all your heart and all your soul and all your mind"* (Matt 22:37) and—as a bonus—he threw in the second most important law which was to *"love your neighbor as yourself"* (Matt 22:39). Now that is a very interesting phrase which, I believe, is rarely understood. It does not mean, "love yourself and then love your neighbor in exactly the same way." Rather, I believe, what it really means is, "love your neighbor *because your neighbor is yourself*." In other words, both you and your neighbor are simply characters in God's dream—aspects of God's immanence. Hence, love of self and love of neighbor is really love of God. To drive this understanding even deeper, Jesus completely reframed the notion of "neighbor" when he told the parable of the Good Samaritan (Luke 10:25-37). Now, "neighbor" includes the "enemy," which is why he will say, *"You have heard that it was said, 'you shall love your neighbor and hate your enemy.' But I say to you, 'Love your enemies and pray for those who persecute you...'"* (Matt 5:43-44)

The law of Moses called for a punitive response that was commensurate with the crime, e.g., "an eye for and eye and a tooth for a tooth." This was borrowed from the Code of Hammurabi, a Babylonian system of ethics dating to 1754 BCE. King David was a big believer in revenge, even a hugely amplified revenge in response to personal insult. With his last breath he instructed his son Solomon, who was to succeed him to the throne, to engineer a circumstance to kill an enemy of his who was still alive and whom David had previously "forgiven." His words to Solomon were, *"And remember, you have with you Shimei son of Gera, the Benjamite from Bahurim, who called down bitter curses on me the day I went to Mahanaim. When he came down to meet me at the Jordan, I swore to him by the Lord: 'I will not put you to death by the sword.' But now, do not consider him innocent. You are a man of wisdom; you will know what to do to him. Bring his gray head down to the grave in blood."* (1 Kings 2:8-9)

Even Jeremiah called upon God to exact revenge on those false prophets who had made life hell for him: *"Lord Almighty, you who examine the righteous and probe the heart and mind, let me see your vengeance on them, for to you I have committed my cause"* (Jer 20:12).

So, basically, Jesus reduced the 613 precepts to a single law— love

God. St. John the Evangelist makes this easy to understand when he says, "*Whoever claims to love God yet hates a brother or sister is a liar. For whoever does not love their brother and sister, whom they have seen, cannot love God, whom they have not seen*" (1 John 4:20). In other words, the only way you can be sure that you are really loving God is to see how you are treating others. How then do crusades, "the ban," inquisitions, violent Jihad, drone warfare, and nuclear detonations perpetrated by religions or "religious nations" measure up to that understanding of God's law?

As a Bible scholar, for me scripture is not a dead book but a living testament that must be understood by each generation in ways that make it relevant and teach us how to love interpersonally, communally, and internationally.

I have been attacked for not taking the Bible literally, and I've been attacked for listening to any of it; I have been accused of both abandoning the Bible (by fundamentalist believers) and of believing in it (by fundamentalist atheists.) Do I have a disdain for Bible stories? Certainly not. But I do distinguish between: (a) historical events, e.g. the fall of Jerusalem in 598 BCE; (b) stories that malign God by attributing horrible events to his interference, e.g. the flood; and (c) teaching stories that are sometimes partially based on historical events but mainly created by the authors to promote an outcome—whether that intended outcome is to justify slavery and excuse genocide, or (conversely) to promote the unity of all people.

Just as the writers of J, E, D, and P edited and redacted the earlier versions in order to guide their people in their ever-changing circumstances, so too must we for our times. Otherwise, the Bible is a dead document, an ancient artifact, a paleo-curiosity whose proper place is in a museum together with stone-age tools.

The *word* of God is not just a noun, it is a living, vibrant verb. When God famously answered Moses's query about His name, He said, *Ehiye ashir ehiye.* ("I *will be* who *I will be.*")

So, who will we allow God to be in this 21st Century? And what beautiful truth will we harvest from Her *word*?

The biblical writings come from a people trying to make sense of their experiences; attempting to create cosmological, theological, and historical stories that offer meaning to the past and a compass for the future. And the linchpin of these stories is belief in a God who is Just, Omnipotent, Omniscient, but Partisan—He has chosen *them* and made a covenant with *them*. All the bad things that happen to them—and lots of bad things did happen to them—must be their own fault, since God is just; and all the good stuff that happened— rain, harvests, military victories—must be evidence of His benediction.

Belief in monotheism and life after death both came quite late into Jewish thinking—during the exile in Babylon under the influence of Zoroastrianism. Earlier versions of their cosmology had to make sense and be consistent without these two puzzle pieces. One consequence of the belief that life ended with death was the doctrine that everything had to be rewarded or punished in the here and now. If you were a healthy, wealthy Jewish male, that was evidence that you were in God's special favor.

Everything had to be ascribed to His divine decrees—everything from social stratification (king, priest, males, females, children, and slaves) to dietary laws (kosher and treif), to sexual conduct. This God even uses the gods of other nations as surrogates for his own agenda. For example, He uses the gods of Babylon to punish Judah for its transgressions, and then He uses the gods of Persia to punish the gods of Babylon for daring to oppress "His people"—though He, Himself, had arranged their exile.

Within these parameters, everything could be explained consistently. And, as Viktor Frankl would discover 3,000 years later in the death camps of Auschwitz and Dachau, humanity's search for meaning is what makes life tolerable and survivable. We still search for meaning, but hopefully we can "create" a better version of God. We have to steer a course that avoids the pitfalls of both the mantra of meaninglessness proposed by materialistic science, and the slavish, craven belief in the rage-aholic God who dominates the fundamentalist religious mindset.

Life is a game. Our cosmologies attempt to infer the rules of the game based on observation of the plays. If you happen upon a soccer game, you'll see twenty-two players and a round ball. If you observe long enough, you can deduce the rules. Next you visit a baseball stadium; the ball is smaller and the players fewer, but after a while you can figure out its rules. You continue your travels and happen upon football, basketball, and lacrosse games. Each game, once you figure out the rules, is consistent. Nothing happens that can't be explained by the rules. It's just that the rules are different for different games. So, science has one set of rules, philosophy another, politics a third, and various religions their own. Once you buy into the rules, you can fully understand the game.

Each game thinks it's true. And it is, once you accept the rules. You must use "external criteria" to decide among them. In my opinion, those criteria are based on examining their fruits. Is this game, and its rules, creating harmony, love, peace, compassion and forgiveness within the individual psyche, in interpersonal dynamics and in international relationships? If "yes," then it is a good game with good rules.

If belief in God implies abandoning my intelligence and ignoring my own spiritual experiences in order to lay garlands on the altar of dogmatic religion based upon literally inerrant scriptures, count me out. The problem here is not disbelief. In fact, I believe that the only reality is God. But God is nothing like religion has made Him out to be—especially the jealous, irascible, genocidal god portrayed in the Bible.

Believing in God means discovering the True God in whose image we were created and discarding the "god" whom we have created in our own image and likeness.

PART II
SETTING GOD FREE

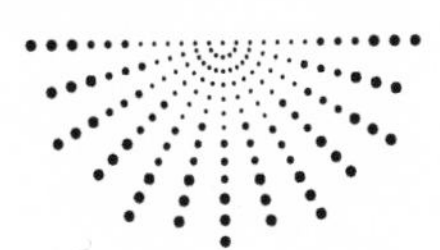

INTRODUCTION TO PART II

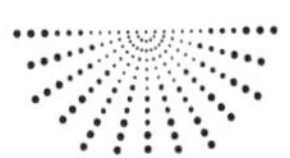

IMAGINE a court case in which Yahweh is put on trial for crimes against humanity. It's easy if you try. (Thanks, John Lennon!) The very books that have immortalized this caricature of God are loaded with evidence that He and His primary accomplice Moses could end up in the slammer for all of their treacherous acts. This section explores this saga in the form of a courtroom drama. I've taken some creative license, but really, I'm inviting you to renew your own creative license as you read and imagine along with me how these scenes might unfold.

By setting psychology free, we've freed our minds to utilize the fullness of our God-given faculties as we consider who this "God" may actually be. And so, we can begin to read the Bible as the fascinating collection of books it is, rather than attempting to piece together some sort of historical treatise from the stories therein—which were themselves created as a way to try to piece together meaning in a confusing world. But we humans have come a long way since those stories were written, and if we allow ourselves to apply what we know, we find the Bible holds many windows into the deeper wisdom its stories hold.

So, before we hear the evidence and the counterevidence, the arguments of the prosecution and defense, we must first establish the psychological and philosophical underpinnings of (a) how we actually 'know' what we know (epistemology); (b) how we then decide what is 'true' and what is not true; (c) how we organize all of these data into a coherent, internally consistent 'story' (cosmology); and (d) what we mean by "revelation." Only then are we ready to go to court.

Obviously, this will be a fictitious court, but I assure you the proceedings are embedded in accurate statements drawn from the Bible itself— particularly the first five books—Genesis, Exodus, Leviticus, Numbers, and Deuteronomy. I will neither invent nor even exaggerate the Biblical data, though I will comment upon and make associations among the stories which you may not have seen elsewhere. For I learned from my seanachaí (Irish storyteller) grandfather that a great story should be both educative and entertaining.

Thus, I invite you, dear reader, to be a juror in this case and to let the evidence lead you to your own verdict. You may even outgrow some preexisting beliefs in the process! Great scientific breakthroughs are frequently harvested from the imagination, which great scientists employ mightily in every experiment they undertake. Similarly, the mystics from all religious traditions have been the ones whose prophetic imaginations have challenged existing dogma, allowing human awareness of the divine to grow and evolve. I invite you to become a hybrid form of these two types of genius: a "mysticist" – one who can meaningfully cross-pollinate real, evidence-based science with deep, mystical spirituality.

Are you ready to enter the imaginal realm?

Procedamus in pace! (Let us proceed in [a spirit of] peace.)

SECTION I: THE PROSECUTION

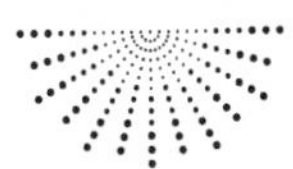

THE CASE AGAINST YAHWEH

THE HONORABLE JUDGE JEROME GROSSLER cut a patrician figure with his neatly groomed silver hair, aquiline features, and watchful eyes that matched in color the mahogany desk he presided over. Unsurpassed in his knowledge of the law, he was also something of a polymath, erudite in multiple disciplines. Known to be an excellent listener, he patiently afforded attorneys and witnesses ample time to present their testimonies, committed as he was to establishing a complete and thorough set of facts. He was the ideal choice to try such a complex case.

Tapping his gavel on the sound block to call the proceedings to order, he announced, *"I regret to report that the key defendants have failed to appear in court today. I have issued a bench warrant for their arrest and requested that an all-points bulletin be sent out to try to bring them in. We will proceed with the case against the primary defendant, Mr. Yahweh, and his alleged accomplice, Mr. Moshe (aka "Moses"), in absentia. Because I consider this one of the most important cases over which I have ever presided, I encourage all parties to present their case thoroughly and thoughtfully. I want to assure both the prosecution and the defense that I am prepared to explore every reasonable line of questioning necessary to achieve a comprehensive picture of all pertinent information, background, and contexts."*

YAHWEH ON TRIAL

Chief prosecuting attorney Michael Newsome (*summa cum laude* Yale Law) had rarely lost a case in his ten years as a prosecutor. He brought a passion for social justice to his work, having been raised by a single mother on the rough streets of Baltimore. Newsome had a nose for detecting the weak spots in a story, seeing through witnesses' subtle omissions, minimizations, and exaggerations. He had lined up three expert witnesses to support the prosecution's case: an esteemed religious scholar, a well-known psychologist, and an expert in contract law.

Rising from his desk, Newsome addressed Judge Grossler with a reverent nod. Then, in deep and sustained sonorous tones, he offered his opening statement.

As far as I'm concerned, Yahweh's day in court is long overdue. Yes, many revere this fearful character as God, but this case against Him is not meant to be irreligious. On the contrary, it is an attempt to chisel away centuries of human-made, fear-based accretions, and in so doing, liberate God from the libel of our projections. Even as I drag Yahweh off His throne and cross-examine Him, it's up to you, respected jurors, to decide His guilt or innocence.

You may think it outrageous to put God on trial; you may even think it blasphemous. However, this is not the first time Yahweh has been on the stand. The book of Job, which dates back some 2,500 years, also put God on trial. And again, in the horrific death camp of Auschwitz, God was again formally prosecuted. Elie Wiesel categorically stated in The Jewish Chronicle (July 9, 2010) *that he himself participated in that trial.*[1] *So I feel I'm in good company as I introduce this case.*

But there is a significant difference between this case and previous trials: Job took God to task for His treatment of an individual human (Job himself) and Wiesel took God to task for His treatment of one nation (the Jews). Today

God stands trial for His psychopathic treatment of all of humanity, indeed, all of creation! Newsome sputtered angrily, pausing for added effect.

Call it blasphemy if you like, but I am here today to dismantle the libelous caricature of a god created by humans in their own image and likeness in order to liberate the true God. Newsome paused again, this time waiting as members of the gallery murmured to one another.

All of the characters, events, quotations, dates, and data mentioned in the prosecution's case are factual. Expert witnesses will use accurate statements from the Bible itself to build the case against this fabricated god. I will shine light on the greatness as well as the shadow side of the heroes and heroines who emerge: Abraham and Sarai, Isaac and Rebekah, Jacob and Rachel, Moses and Miriam, to name a few.

As the honorable Judge Grossler pointed out, neither of the two defendants—Yahweh and his enforcer Moses—have shown their faces today in court, but we will commence nonetheless to present the vast bulk of the evidence as it appears in their own writings.

I understand that my learned colleague, the attorney for the defense, intends to call other expert witnesses. I will call merely three—a religious scholar, a psychologist, and a contract lawyer—since I am fully convinced, and intend to convince you, that this is an open and shut case.

The prosecution will show that Yahweh—far from being the infallible, omniscient, just, merciful, and competent figure that He claims to be in His own journals and to which His fearful followers further attest—is, instead, a very fallible figure who lacks the basic scientific knowledge, compassion, and humility requisite for the title He holds. He is confused, vindictive, frequently unable or unwilling to fulfill His sworn promises, and, speaking psychologically, far more resembles a psychopath than a benevolent Creator. His murderous, indeed genocidal behavior is unmatched even by the Pol Pots, Hitlers, and Stalins of human history.

Moreover, in several instances, He was intellectually outsmarted by his own advisors, who persuaded him to abandon plans to utterly wipe out all of His own devotees during particular and frequent foul moods occasioned by his followers' failure to strictly adhere to His dictates. When it was pointed out to Him that His intended massacres would simply afford the competing divinities of the Levant an excuse to sneer at His inability to protect His own,

He "graciously and mercifully" changed His mind, Newsome said, punctuating His statement with sarcastic air quotes.

This reign of terror must come to an end— and this court is tasked with that great service to humanity. Michael Newsome concluded with a slight tremor in his voice. Pausing for a moment as if waiting for applause, he returned to his seat.

The lead defense lawyer was Kayla Goldstein, a sophisticated redhead whose eidetic memory allowed her to graduate at the top of her class at UC Berkeley with a double major in philosophy and theater. Her summers performing "Shakespeare in the Park" in New York City prior to enrolling in NYU Law gave her plenty of practice in the art of the soliloquy. Indeed, she could hold the court spellbound with her concise, highly potent statements. Her almond-shaped green eyes bespoke her keen ability to see every flaw in the Prosecution's case. But it was her steady calmness that made prosecutor Michael Newsome nervous.

Kayla Goldstein seemed well-prepared as she stood behind a lectern loaded down with binders of evidence. Her fluency in Hebrew gave her a level of mastery of the Biblical texts that comprised the primary arguments of this case. But then, as she was about to offer her opening remarks, she casually walked away from her microphone and stack of prepared notes and calmly addressed the jury from center of the room.

With the bard we can exclaim: "Out, out, brief candle! Life's but a walking shadow, a poor player that struts and frets his hour upon the stage and is heard no more. It is a tale told by an idiot, full of sound and fury, signifying nothing." We wind our way through a labyrinth of make-believe until we realize that we are chasing villains of our own making.

Her voice projected off the back wall as she spoke Shakespearean English with perfect diction and rhythm. The court held its breath in utter silence as the Defense made eye contact with each juror individually, her mouth poised as if ready to speak to each of them. But after a subtle bow to the judge, Kayla Goldstein simply returned to her seat without another word.

Partly relieved and partly mystified by the brevity of the Defense's opening, Michael Newsome was more than ready to prosecute Yahweh for His many crimes against humanity.

PROSECUTING GOD

We will begin with the Prosecution. Mr. Newsome, you may call your first witness, Judge Grossler announced.

Thank you, your honor. I wish to call Dr. Dermot O'Sullivan, an internationally acclaimed Bible scholar, who will, as you so graciously and wisely directed us, lead us patiently through the pertinent passages in these journals which reveal the criminal nature of the defendants. I have chosen Dr. O'Sullivan to present this depressing, even horrifying, deposition not only due to his extensive mastery of the material, but because he has an uncanny ability to present it without sugar-coating the facts. It's not easy evidence to hear, but you may come to appreciate, as I have, Dr. O'Sullivan's tongue-in cheek humor as we pore over the disturbing evidence before us.

Dr. O'Sullivan, this is, as Judge Grossler attests, the trial of the millennium. So please don't hold back as you lead us in detail through the defendants' sordid history, Newsome concluded as the bailiff invited the witness to be sworn in.

The witness's Irish eyes did more than smile—they laughed out loud as they danced above the reading glasses teetering on the tip of his rosy nose while he laid his hand on the *Holy Bible* and swore to tell the whole truth and nothing but the truth. Dermot O'Sullivan took his work as a Biblical scholar very seriously, but he knew better than to take himself too seriously. Sit back and hear—in his slight brogue, a vestige of his childhood spent in Ireland prior to living fourteen years in Africa and his eventual immigration to the United States—what the Bible says about Yahweh and Moses, beginning with the book of Genesis.

Dr. O'Sullivan laid his voluminous notes on a lectern provided by the court and prepared to begin his lengthy testimony, which would work its way through the first five books of the Bible: Genesis, Exodus, Leviticus, Numbers, and Deuteronomy. The material was heavy and sometimes brutal, but Dr. O'Sullivan managed to keep the court spellbound as he walked through the evidence as it appears in stories deemed holy and perfect without question.

GENESIS

With his back to the jury, Michael Newsome flashed a friendly grin toward the stand and addressed his witness. *Dr. O'Sullivan, thank you for agreeing to serve the court in your capacity as a Biblical scholar.* Pivoting like a hockey player readying himself to receive a forward pass, Newsome faced the jury and continued: *In debunking the defendants' claims to the titles of "God" and "Patriarch," we need look no farther than their own journal entries contained in exhibit A: the Judeo-Christian Bible. Where would you like to begin, Dr. O'Sullivan?*

Why don't we take it from the top, Michael? O'Sullivan quipped. *Already in the first chapter of the first book of the Bible it becomes obvious that we have a scientific blunder on our hands. In verse three we are told that on "day one" God created day and night:* "Then God said: Let there be light, and there was light. God saw that the light was good. God then separated the light from the darkness. God called the light 'day,' and the darkness he called 'night.' Evening came, and morning followed—the first day."

If God created the sun and the moon and the stars on day four, where did day and night come from before the heavenly luminaries were created? Here's the relevant Bible passage: "Then God said: Let there be lights in the dome of the sky, to separate day from night. Let them mark the seasons, the days and the years, and serve as lights in the dome of the sky, to illuminate the earth. And so it happened: God made the two great lights, the greater one to govern the day, and the lesser one to govern the night, and the stars. God set them in the dome of the sky, to illuminate the earth, to govern the day and the night, and to separate the light from the darkness. God saw that it was good. Evening came, and morning followed—the fourth day."

By verse 26, we run into two more problems. Firstly, the phrase, "Then God said: Let us make human beings in our image, after our likeness." *The plural "us" has been explained away as the royal "we." But this explana-*

tion is an anachronistic import from a much later time period. It has also been said that God had a council of advisors with whom He discussed all important matters, but that doesn't seem like the omniscient, all-powerful God I learned of in church when I was a kid. The truth is: Judaism was not a monotheistic religion until around the time of the Babylonian captivity from 587 BCE to 539 BCE, when it was very much influenced by Zoroastrianism in this regard. It is much more likely that Yahweh, at the time of the writing of Genesis from 950 BCE to 750 BCE, was understood to be one among many gods who had a family of his own with whom he made all kinds of important decisions. In actual fact, this story of the creation of humans is borrowed from the much older Sumerian legends of the god Anu and his divine sons Enki and Enlil who deliberate together and argue quite a bit about whether or not to go ahead with this plan to create humans in their own image and likeness.

The second problem introduced in verse 26 has to do with the relationship between humans and nature—as if humans are not part of nature. Here is the verse: "Let them have dominion over the fish of the sea, the birds of the air, the tame animals, all the wild animals, and all the creatures that crawl on the earth." *This idea is repeated in verse 28:* "God blessed them and God said to them: Be fertile and multiply; fill the earth and subdue it. Have dominion over the fish of the sea, the birds of the air, and all the living things that crawl on the earth." *The Hebrew word used here,* Radah, *has three distinct meanings: to "have dominion over" or to "exploit" or to "be responsible for." Unfortunately, humans, for the most part, have chosen the first two meanings and ignored the last. But this mindset represents a shift from an earlier cosmology—from hunter/gatherer societies, in which nature and humans are unified partners, to a later cosmology of human domination. The domestication of plants and animals led to a huge shift in the human/nature relationship, and each subsequent "revolution" (agrarian, industrial, technological, informational) has widened the gap.*

Related to this is the strong impression that originally both humans and animals were meant to be vegetarians, and this arrangement was only changed after the flood. Genesis 1:29-30 says, "God also said: See, I give you every seed-bearing plant on all the earth and every tree that has seed-bearing fruit on it to be your food; and to all the wild animals, all the birds of the air, and all the living creatures that crawl on the earth, I give all the green plants for food." *I wonder if lions and hyenas were aware of this arrangement. Their dental records (not to mention those of their Mesozoic ancestors) indicate otherwise.* O'Sullivan paused to smile at a person seated in the gallery who was attempting to muffle a chuckle.

All this changes, however, with the flood. Compare the above passage with Genesis 9:1-3.

"God blessed Noah and his sons and said to them: Be fertile and multiply and fill the earth. Fear and dread of you shall come upon all the animals of the earth and all the birds of the air, upon all the creatures that move about on the ground and all the fishes of the sea; into your power they are delivered. Any living creature that moves about shall be yours to eat; I give them all to you as I did the green plants."

Isn't it ironic that, having just saved all of the creatures of the earth in his ark, Noah is encouraged to put not just the "fear of God" into them, but the "fear of humans"—even the "dread of humans"—into them. Moreover, the days of vegetarianism are over.

You will also notice as you read chapters 1 and 2 of Genesis that, positioned side by side, we see two very different accounts of creation. Here's why: in compiling four different sources of biblical material— called J, E, D, and P (around the year 400 BCE) the redactors simply included the P version (chapter 1) and the J version (chapter 2) without any attempt to iron out the discrepancies between them. According to P, humans are the final act of creation; God first made everything else and we were the pièce de résistance. But according to J, Adam was created first and then God made several attempts to provide him with companionship, but when nothing really satisfied Adam, God got a brainwave and created "woman" from Adam's rib. It's actually a pun in Hebrew which tends to get lost in translation—'ishsha' (woman or wife) coming from 'ish' (man or husband.)

The first creation account, the P account, spills over into the beginning of Genesis chapter 2 due to an editorial blunder that occurred when Stephen Langton (a 13th-century English Cardinal of the Roman Catholic Church who was also Archbishop of Canterbury) broke the book into chapters. It ends with an anachronistic story of God resting on the seventh day: "On the seventh day God completed the work he had been doing; he rested on the seventh day from all the work he had undertaken." *This is not to be confused with the practice of the Sabbath, which would not be invented until about 550 BCE.*

Chapter 2 of Genesis, which comes from source J, gives a second and different account of creation, starting with verse 7. Humans are created in three stages. Firstly, Adam's body is made from the dust of the earth, then God blows life into this material, and, finally, God forms Eve from Adam's side: "then the LORD God formed the man out of the dust of the ground and blew into his nostrils the breath of life, and the man became a living being." *Later, in verses 22 and 23, we read,* "So the LORD God cast a deep sleep on the man, and while he was asleep, he took out one of his ribs and closed up its place with flesh. The LORD God then built the rib that he had taken from the man into a woman."

According to the J account, however, God had made many, many previous efforts to provide a helper for the man, but none of them cut the mustard. Here's that version of the story: "So the LORD God formed out of the ground all the wild animals and all the birds of the air, and he brought them to the man to see what he would call them; whatever the man called each living creature was then its name. The man gave names to all the tame animals, all the birds of the air, and all the wild animals; but none proved to be a helper suited to the man."

Did you catch another anachronism in this passage? It says that God created both wild and tame animals. Of course we know that cattle, dogs, cats, camels, elephants, horses, etc. were not created tame; rather, generations of humans domesticated them.

Another interesting tidbit, as you read these verses in sequence, is that Eve hadn't yet been created when God told Adam not to eat of the tree of the knowledge of good and evil. It's recorded in verse 16: "The LORD God gave the man this order: You are free to eat from any of the trees of the garden except the tree of knowledge of good and evil. From that tree you shall not eat; when you eat from it you shall die." *But Eve is not created until verses 21 and 22. She could have claimed innocence when God punished her for ignoring this command!*

If Eve did not hear of the food restriction directly from God, Adam must have told her about it. When tempted by the snake, she is well aware of the prohibition, but gives in any way for gustatory, visual, and psycho-spiritual reasons: "The woman saw that the tree was good for food and pleasing to the eyes, and the tree was desirable for gaining wisdom." *And the upshot is that both she and her husband get kicked out of the Garden of Eden. It is fascinating to note that Eve's thirst for knowledge and Solomon's thirst for wisdom are treated very differently by God. Eve is berated and punished while Solomon is praised and rewarded as follows:* "Since you have not asked for a long life but for wisdom and knowledge to govern my people over whom I have made you king, therefore wisdom and knowledge will be given you. And I will also give you wealth, possessions and honor, such as no king who was before you ever had and none after you will have.'" (2 Chronicles 1:11-12)

In chapter 3 of the book of Genesis, once again, God shows up as a human in male form. He is walking in the garden in the cool of the evening and when Adam and Eve hide from Him, He doesn't know where they are. He doesn't seem to have perfected this game of hide-an- seek and has to call out for a clue: "When they heard the sound of the LORD God walking about in the garden at the breezy time of the day, the man and his wife hid themselves from the LORD God among the trees of the garden. The LORD God then called to the man and asked him: 'Where are you?'"

He is a talented God, however, and having earlier demonstrated his skills as a gardener, potter, and surgeon, He now tries his hand at tailoring, and makes leather garments for the naked couple. Of course, in order to do this, He has to kill some animal. So, the first killing in scripture is God sacrificing an innocent animal to make clothes for the sinful couple.

This chapter, once more, shows its polytheistic origins, with the gods jealously guarding their immortality: "Then the LORD God said: See! The man has become like one of us, knowing good and evil! Now, what if he also reaches out his hand to take fruit from the tree of life and eats of it and lives forever?"*This fear may very well be repeated in our lifetimes as we create our own monsters through genetic engineering, artificial intelligence, and nanotechnology. Stephen Hawking and Elon Musk have both warned about the possibilities that our own creations may eventually surpass and even obliterate us.*

Another upsetting aspect of God's very human-like behavior is His proclivity for violent and over-the-top reactions, like banishing His children and all of their descendants over a minor infraction. Here's my thinking: Adam and Eve are, in fact, innocent, naive, curious children. Before they ate of the forbidden fruit, they could not distinguish between right and wrong, and yet their childlike behavior is punished as if they were fully rational and self-reflective. Imagine a mother pointing out to her three-year-old and four-year-old where the cookies and the candies are hidden and then telling them, "You can eat as many fruits or vegetables as you like, but don't eat the candy!" She then leaves them alone and, of course, they eat the forbidden sweets. When she discovers this, she goes bananas (no pun intended) and packs their suitcases and kicks them out of the house, screaming after them that they are never to darken her door again and if they ever get married and have kids and grandkids of their own, they and their progeny are forbidden from ever coming home. If a psychologist or teacher became aware of this scenario, they would be mandated to report that mother to child protective services!

God's punishment is way over the top. It involves exile, pain, and death for everybody associated with Adam and Eve. Not only will humans now be mortal, but God will progressively shorten their life expectancy. Initially, they live into their 800s and 900s, but God decides to reduce their lifespan drastically to 120 years. As written in Genesis 6:3: "Then the Lord said, 'My Spirit will not contend with humans forever, for they are mortal; their days will be a hundred and twenty years.'"

Then He really rubs it in, cursing not just humans but Mother Earth herself: "For you are dust, and to dust you shall return." *Dirt, dust, earth, soil now become pejoratives—filthy things rather than the fertile skin of Pachamama. We live with this even in our own days: to call something "dirty" or "soiled" is to berate that element which provides all of our foodstuffs.*

But God is merely warming to His task. He's about to get really mean-spirited, crafting specific punishments for each of the offenders, above and beyond mere mortality. First, the Earth, having been disrespected so egre-

giously, is coopted in the fight against humans. "Cursed is the ground because of you! In toil you shall eat its yield all the days of your life. Thorns and thistles it shall bear for you."

Next, He turns His attention to the snake: "Cursed are you among all the animals, tame or wild; on your belly you shall crawl, and dust you shall eat all the days of your life." *I have lived among lots of snakes in my international travels—spitting cobras, puff adders, pythons, black mambas—and in northern California the rattlesnakes come out from May to October each year. I am not aware of any snake species that eats dust. And I very seriously doubt, though I wasn't there to observe it, that snakes ever perambulated upright.*

And what of Adam? He was originally fashioned to be God's gardener in Eden. Now "by the sweat of your brow you shall eat bread, until you return to the ground from which you were taken."

And Eve? She is going to need Adam's protection, but he will lord it over her: "Yet your urge shall be for your husband, and he shall rule over you." *And voila! Sexism is born. Rather than "man" emerging from the womb of "woman," you have woman fashioned from the rib of man. Later, in medieval times, the medical model of embryonic evolution was that of the homunculus: the woman's womb was merely potting soil into which the male deposited a full human-in-miniature.*

And before we can blink, in Genesis chapter 3, we discover that the woman is to blame for the fall of humankind. After all, she listened to the serpent. Adam did not talk to him. It was Eve who was seduced by the sight of the fruit, ate it first herself, and then gave it to her innocent husband. Enter the weak link, the irrational one, the temptress.

Before I finish with Genesis chapter 3, in my capacity as a scholar I need to interject: This material was written by people who observed the world around them—as we do today—who were trying to create stories to explain how things got to be the way they are: snakes do crawl on their bellies, weeds and thorns do hamper human agricultural efforts, women did need men to protect them at that time, and most women do suffer greatly while in labor. How come? Genesis chapter 3 is the "how come" of the year 1000 BCE.

Things get a little more complicated in Genesis chapter 4. Eve gives birth to two boys: Cain, who becomes a farmer, and then Abel, who becomes a nomadic herder. And they both bring offerings to God. Cain brings veggies and Abel brings choice meat. God turns up his nose at the veggies but licks his chops at the sight of the meat.

With that, O'Sullivan leaned towards the jury and quipped, *"Sounds like God and I like the same restaurants!"* followed by a muffled wave of laughter throughout the courtroom.

Visibly pleased with his own joke, O'Sullivan continued: *Cain feels rejected and brings his complaint to God, but it only leads to a lecture and criticism from his divine dad. So the jealous Cain kills Abel. This is the start of a long war between cowboys and farmers that Rodgers and Hammerstein's "Oklahoma" tried to heal in 1956,* O'Sullivan joked, but this time the joke flew right over his audience's head.

Disappointed with the flop, O'Sullivan tried to explain: *Historically, nomadic herders and settled farmers were always at odds about water rights —the farmers building fences around their property and the herders breeching them to water their flocks. This motif of God favoring the younger son/daughter appears many times afterwards—Isaac over Ishmael, Jacob over Esau, Rachel over Leah, Joseph over his twelve siblings, and David (who was the runt of the litter) over all of his older brothers.*

Once again, God punishes both the innocent and the guilty. Not only is Cain banished, but God further curses the earth: "If you till the ground, it shall no longer give you its produce." *Then comes the first of some very strange statements. Cain complains that anybody who sees him will want to kill him. The problem is that there are only three human beings on the planet at this stage: Adam, Eve, and Cain. God can't have been very good at math, so when Cain protests,* "Anyone may kill me at sight," *God proposes the following solution:* "'Not so!' the LORD said to him. 'If anyone kills Cain, Cain shall be avenged seven times.'" *Sounds like a line from "*The Godfather*" to me,* O'Sullivan said, leaning toward the gallery—whose members restored his comedic confidence with a hearty laugh.

To console himself, Cain has intercourse with his wife. Now where in God's name did she come from? O'Sullivan asked while scratching his head, further disheveling his already disheveled mop of hair. *Well, however and whenever he managed it, here is the beginning of the first genealogy in the Bible. His great-great-grandson, Lamech, is the first polygamist and the first serial killer. Lamech has two wives, Adah and Zillah, to whom he boasts:* "Adah and Zillah, hear my voice; wives of Lamech, listen to my utterance: I have killed a man for wounding me, a young man for bruising me. If Cain is avenged seven times, then Lamech seventy-seven times.'" *This is like* "The Godfather" *on steroids! But if we fast forward a few millennia to the time when Jesus fulfilled this part of Torah, he did so by enjoining his followers to forgive seventy-seven times. I don't think this is what either Yahweh or Lamech had in mind, but we'll get to that later.*

Moving on to the second genealogy that shows up in Genesis chapter 4, it's pretty much all the same players, except that it traces the lineage not through Cain but through Seth—the child Adam and Eve had to console themselves for the death of Abel. Here we have another instance of two different accounts being presented together without any attempt to iron out the discrepancies. It uses an interesting formula: starting with the age of each of the ancestors when he gave birth to his first son, followed by how many years he lived after that and, finally, God does the math for us and reveals how old the ancestor was when he died. Here's a sample: "Adam was one hundred and thirty years old when he begot a son in his likeness, after his image; and he named him Seth. Adam lived eight hundred years after he begot Seth, and he had other sons and daughters. The whole lifetime of Adam was nine hundred and thirty years; then he died.

When Seth was one hundred and five years old, he begot Enosh. Seth lived eight hundred and seven years after he begot Enosh, and he had other sons and daughters. The whole lifetime of Seth was nine hundred and twelve years; then he died.

When Enosh was ninety years old, he begot Kenan. Enosh lived eight hundred and fifteen years after he begot Kenan, and he had other sons and daughters. The whole lifetime of Enosh was nine hundred and five years; then he died..."

However, this formula is not followed in the case of Enoch: "When Enoch was sixty-five years old, he begot Methuselah. Enoch walked with God after he begot Methuselah for three hundred years, and he had other sons and daughters. The whole lifetime of Enoch was three hundred and sixty-five years. Enoch walked with God, and he was no longer here, for God took him."

So, Enoch becomes the first of only two characters in the Bible (the other being the prophet Elijah) who never actually died. While still a young whippersnapper of 365 years of age, God transports him body and soul into heaven. It will be 1950 CE before that claim is again made about a human—Mary the mother of Jesus, whom Pope Pius XII declared (in the only infallible decree to issue from the papacy) to have been assumed body and soul into heaven.

Back to Genesis: if you remove Enoch from the list—as an outlier—the average age of the pre-flood patriarchs is 907 years and six months. And the genealogy ends with an interesting datum: "When Noah was five hundred years old, he begot Shem, Ham, and Japheth." (Gen 5:32) *This seems to indicate that these three boys were triplets—either that, or humans back then had much shorter gestation periods! But, as we shall see later, these boys were treated very differently by their father.*

The first four verses of Genesis chapter 6 are among the strangest in all of the Bible. Here they are: "When human beings began to grow numerous on the earth and daughters were born to them, the sons of God saw how beautiful the daughters of human beings were, and so they took for their wives whomever they pleased. Then the LORD said: My spirit shall not remain in human beings forever, because they are only flesh. Their days shall comprise one hundred and twenty years. The Nephilim appeared on earth in those days, as well as later, after the sons of God had intercourse with the daughters of human beings, who bore them sons. They were the heroes of old, the men of renown."

Who on earth are these "sons of God"? If God has "sons," and if humans were created in God's "image and likeness," then two truths are suggested: firstly, these sons are not merely spirit entities but have physical bodies also. Otherwise they couldn't mate and have offspring who themselves could also breed. And, secondly, it appears that this "God" is also a creature of flesh and blood. Could it be that "God" and his "sons" may have been non-terrestrial beings? If so, they are a far cry from the modern notion of a monotheistic divinity who is pure, immaterial spirit.

Moreover, this God appears to have all the virtues and all the vices of humans. But here's the $64,000 question: is this because He has fashioned us in His image and likeness? Or because we have fashioned Him in our image and likeness?

A hush fell over the courtroom as Dermot O'Sullivan and Judge Jerome Grossler locked eyes for a moment.

Please continue, Dr. O'Sullivan, the Prosecution urged.

Let's move on to some rather sordid evidence in Genesis chapter 6, O'Sullivan obliged. *Firstly, the male gods are enthralled with human females, take them to wife, breed with them, and create a race of giants mentioned in several other parts of the Bible and Apocrypha, who are variously called the Nephilim, the Anakim, the Watchers, or the Fallen Angels.*

Incidentally, this story line is not peculiar to the Bible. Many of the stories of Genesis are taken from the much earlier Sumerian scriptures: creation stories, human origins, gods (male and female) mating with humans, a world-wide flood, etc. In fact, you find the very same motifs—including the divine/human mating—in the Greek, Roman, Hindu, Norse, and Celtic mythologies.

Let's continue for a few moments to cull evidence from this chapter that shows either the anthropomorphizing of the "real God" or—perhaps—the deification of more technologically sophisticated non-terrestrial, flesh-and-blood beings.

Ladies and Gentlemen of the jury, have you heard of cargo cults? I'm not just talking about the confusion caused by US Navy supply ships dropping supplies on indigenous islands during World War II. Cargo cults have been a feature of human longing since the beginning: a tendency for less sophisticated cultures to make gods of more advanced civilizations upon encountering them. My point is this: humans have an established proclivity to create false gods without even knowing it.

But what about the God that supposedly created humans? In Genesis 6:5-6, God is surprised and angered by human wickedness. He regrets creating them. Then, once again, his reaction is over the top: he decides to kill them all, plus the animals, the crawling things, and the birds of the air. Mild-mannered deer, millipedes, and robins must all be included in the punishment. By verse 17, he has worked himself into an agitated state and promises:

"I, on my part, am about to bring the flood waters on the earth, to destroy all creatures under the sky in which there is the breath of life; everything on earth shall perish."

Interestingly, this phrase of killing every creature "in which there is the breath of life" is the same blood-thirsty mantra He will use many more times in the books of Deuteronomy and Joshua as He mandates the genocide of the enemies of His "chosen people."

One other thing: God is appalled that His sons are having intercourse with the women whom He fashioned. So, what does He do? Punish His sons for their concupiscence? No, He punishes the women. It's as if a slave owner's sons were to "defile" themselves by having sex with the female slaves and the father finds out, reads the riot act to the sons, and then kills the slaves. Alas, this brutal practice still happens in certain parts of the world, where girls who have been raped are executed by their fathers and brothers to protect the good name of the family. It goes by the falsely virtuous title of "honor killing." And it seems "God" may have inspired the idea.

This "God" appears to be subject to all of the limiting mental and emotional problems experienced by us humans: He is surprised (so He can't be omniscient or precognitive), angered (and all anger, I believe, is based on fear—so He is fearful), regretful (an issue of a poor self-image based on mistakes He made) and vengeful (He's gonna make everybody suffer—the guilty and the innocent alike).

Speaking of suffering, how about a nice flood to wipe out all living things? In preparation for this premeditated act of global destruction, God kindly gives Noah instructions on how to build the ark. It's to be made of gopherwood and have specific dimensions, given in cubits. A cubit is the distance from the elbow to the tip of the middle finger— about 18 inches. So, the dimensions of the ark translate as follows: it was to be 440 feet in length, 73 feet wide and 44 feet high—thus a total volume of 1,413,280 cubic feet. The ark of the Babylonian flood story—from which Genesis borrowed—was a perfect cube of 120 cubits (180 feet) on each dimension, for a total volume of 5,832,000 cubic feet. Thus, it was four times the size of Noah's craft.

Noah's ark was to have three decks, so each compartment had to have an average ceiling height of slightly less than 15 feet. I guess the giraffes, which can range in height from 16-20 feet, either had to keep their necks bent for the duration of the trip, or one compartment had to be extra tall. Or maybe they stuck their heads out of some sort of sunroof like teenagers on a joy ride. Giraffes aside, it must have been a trifle crowded on board, not to mention quite stinky. And it's no wonder Noah was given one hundred and twenty years to collect all of the animals and shepherd them to their quarters, because many of them lived in China and Brazil and Ireland—and Antarctica—thousands of miles from the port of embarkation. I wonder, did Noah's Uber fleet fetch them in smaller vessels and ship them back to the Middle East?

And what about the birds? They couldn't all be kept in the same section. Hawks and eagles and other raptors had to be separated from the doves and finches. Lions and tigers were totally frustrated because they could smell the antelope and wildebeest, but couldn't get at them (or were they still vegetarians at this stage?) And how in God's name did they keep the creepy-crawlies from pinching, biting, and stinging everybody? And, of course, they had to put the larger animals (elephants, rhinos, hippos, etc.) in the lowest level of the Ark, under the waterline, to act as ballast. It must have been a logistical nightmare!

About a hundred and fifty days into the flood, things began to get pretty rocky. Noah was still upset that he had been forced to abandon his grandfather, Methuselah, who had just turned 969 and whom he dearly loved, while being pressured to make space for hyenas, skunks, and boa constrictors on the ark. Can you imagine how unpleasant a seasick gorilla would be? And all of those various breeds of horses and cattle on board must have given a whole new meaning to the phrase "poop deck!"

With that the courtroom gallery burst out in raucous laughter. Fighting the urge to join them, the judge gave a half-hearted whack of the gavel while issuing a perfunctory *"Order in the court."*

Never hesitant to laugh at his own jokes, Dr. O'Sullivan gave the gallery plenty of time to regain composure before continuing his presentation of evidence.

The flood story as we know it is based on the 11th tablet of the Gilgamesh Epic, *which is part of the longer creation story of the* Atrahasis Epic. *It's like the* Bhagavad Gita *being excerpted from the Mahabharata. Interestingly, at the end of the Biblical account, Noah first releases a raven which does not come back, but instead, keeps flying around until the waters subside. Then he releases a dove who, upon finding no place to land, returns to the ark. A week later, Noah sends the dove again and this time it comes back with an olive leaf in its beak. In the Babylonian version, Utnapishtim (their Noah) first releases a dove, then a swallow, and finally a raven. When the raven does not return, Utnapishtim realizes that it's safe to leave the ark. The Roman Pliny (circa 50 CE) tells of Indian sailors who released birds in order to follow them to dry land.*

There's a lot of confusion in the Biblical telling of the flood story because it's a mishmash of various versions of the story (J and P, if you've been paying attention). Unlike the creation accounts, however, where the two versions are distinct, discrete, and presented in sequence (the P version in chapter 1 and the J version in chapter 2), in the flood story it's as if two jigsaw puzzles have their pieces intermingled and the redactors are trying to create a picture from the scrambled parts. The greater number of pieces come from P, but J-pieces are sprinkled throughout the account, leading to all kinds of confusion about how many pairs of animals were admitted to the ark, where the flood waters came from, and how long the flood lasted.

Very briefly, P says there were two pairs of every animal, whereas J says there were seven pairs of clean animals and two pairs of unclean animals. "Of every clean animal, take with you seven pairs, a male and its mate; and of the unclean animals, one pair, a male and its mate; likewise, of every bird of the air, seven pairs, a male and a female, to keep their progeny alive over all the earth."

To complicate matters further, Genesis 6:19-20 says "two *of every kind,*" *not* "two pairs *of every kind.*"

This is typically what you see in drawings of the event. "Of all living creatures you shall bring two of every kind into the ark, one male and one female, to keep them alive along with you. Of every kind of bird, of every kind of animal, and of every kind of thing that crawls on the ground, two of each will come to you, that you may keep them alive."

P did not distinguish between clean and unclean until after the covenant on Mount Sinai. But the compilers and redactors of J wrongly assumed that this distinction had existed since the beginning of creation. These differences would have had huge effects on the construction and size of the ark. Let's assume that there are an equal number of clean and unclean species. And let's call that number "x." So, altogether there are 2x species on the planet before the flood. If only a single pair of any species is brought on board, the ark would have 4x guests. If, however, two pairs of each species are brought aboard, then there are 8x guests. But if J is correct (seven pairs of clean and one pair of unclean), then there are 16x guests. Only the Babylonian ark would be big enough for such a crowd.

As for the source and duration of the flood, in P the floodgates from above as well as the waters of the underground abyss contributed to the flood, whereas J blames it all on forty days of rain. In chapter 8, there is a further discrepancy regarding how long the flood lasted, with the timeline for the appearance of dry land varying from 150 days when the ark came to rest on the mountains of Ararat in what is today northwestern Iraq (by the way, there is no one Mount Ararat mentioned anywhere in the Bible), to 225 days when the tops of the mountains appeared. "Gradually the waters receded from the earth. At the end of one hundred and fifty days, the waters had so diminished that, in the seventh month, on the seventeenth day of the month, the ark came to rest on the mountains of Ararat. The waters continued to diminish until the tenth month, and on the first day of the tenth month the tops of the mountains appeared." *Now according to Genesis 7:19-20,* "Higher and higher on the earth the waters swelled, until all the highest mountains under the heavens were submerged. The waters swelled fifteen cubits higher than the submerged mountains." *I imagine that the Bible writer believed that the mountains of Ararat were the highest in the world. In reality, their highest peak is actually 16,854 feet—whereas Mount Everest is 29,029 feet. To rise higher than the submerged mountains, the flood would have raised the sea level by 30,000 feet all over the planet. That's a helluva lot of water! Currently, the wettest place on the Earth is Masynram, Meghalaya in India, which gets a piddling 467 inches in a year.*

And remember, Antediluvian (pre-flood) creatures—human and animal alike—are portrayed in Genesis 1:29-30 as being vegetarian: "God also said: See, I give you every seed-bearing plant on all the earth and every tree that has seed-bearing fruit on it to be your food; and to all the wild animals, all the birds of the air, and all the living creatures that crawl on the earth, I give all the green plants for food." *After the flood there is to be a radical change of plan:* "Any living creature that moves about shall be yours to eat; I give them all to you as I did the green plants." *Is the end of vegetarianism the reason animals are henceforth to be filled with fear and dread of humans? Were the animals given any kind of a heads-up about the rule changes?*

Whatever it was about the taste of animal flesh, God certainly got high on the smell of roasting meat. "Then Noah built an altar to the LORD, and choosing from every clean animal and every clean bird, he offered burnt offerings on the altar. When the LORD smelled the sweet odor, the LORD said to himself: Never again will I curse the ground because of human beings, since the desires of the human heart are evil from youth; nor will I ever again strike down every living being, as I have done." *It seemed to have a hallucinogenic effect on God, for He got all mushy and started to make a compassion-filled covenant, not just with humans, but with all creatures. And He expressed this warm-fuzzy moment in the heavens, creating a rainbow as a kind of "cross-my-heart-and-hope-to-die" promise to never get mad again.*

So from then on it was rainbows and butterflies, right? Nope. Once the drug of sacrifice had worn off, Yahweh was back to cursing as usual—as Ham, Canaan, and people of color can attest.

In a futile attempt to keep God happy and high, "Noah built an altar to the LORD, and choosing from every clean animal and every clean bird, he offered burnt offerings." *Now how many species of clean animals and birds existed on planet Earth before the flood? Millions, obviously! It must have been one hell of an altar to accommodate that many roasting creatures.*

Noah is now 600 years old (he will live to 950) and his sons are centenarians. High on the odor of barbequing animal flesh, God promises to never again destroy the Earth or its creatures and He sets a rainbow in the sky as a token. This must have worried Noah a little, since you can only see a rainbow when it's been raining, which might have triggered a bit of Post-Traumatic Stress Disorder for him. But the covenant itself—the first of its kind—is made not just with humans, but also with Gaia/Pachamama/Earth. In a mantra-like repetition, God says this covenant is with Noah and his descendants (all of us—yippee!), with "every living creature" *(repeated four times) and with* "every mortal creature" *(also repeated four times.)*

However, God can't quite let go of his vindictive side, so he says: "Indeed, for your own lifeblood I will demand an accounting: from every animal I will demand it, and from a human being, each one for the blood of another, I will demand an accounting for human life. Anyone who sheds the blood of a human being, by a human being shall that one's blood be shed; for in the image of God have human beings been made."

This is the first of several covenants that God makes, revealing his proclivity for contract law. First, with Noah—the pact made with all of creation. Then comes the covenant with Abraham, where God promises to give him lots of offspring and land if Abraham agrees to choose him from among all of the competing gods. Next comes the covenant with Moses. This one has 613 bylaws, again predicated on the Israelites sticking with Yahweh and ignoring any counteroffers from other deities. The reward? A promised land flowing with milk and honey (once they get rid of the pesky natives.) Contract number four is with King David, and his reward is a dynasty that will rule in perpetuity. And the final one (at least up to now) is with Jesus. The condition that is placed on that one is different from the rest. It's all about love—of God, the neighbor, and the "enemy"—and the reward is the kingdom of heaven.

The Noah covenant came with three kinds of blessings. First, that people be fertile and fill the Earth; second, that they put fear and dread into all animals, birds, and fish; and, third, that they could now be omnivores. Then comes the inevitable curse, revealed in a strange and upsetting story which I will give you in the author's own words: "Noah, a man of the soil, was the first to plant a vineyard. He drank some of the wine, became drunk, and lay naked inside his tent. Ham, the father of Canaan, saw his father's nakedness, and he told his two brothers outside. Shem and Japheth, however, took a robe, and holding it on their shoulders, they walked backward and covered their father's nakedness; since their faces were turned the other way, they did not see their father's nakedness. When Noah woke up from his wine and learned what his youngest son had done to him, he said: 'Cursed be Canaan! The lowest of slaves shall he be to his brothers.' He also said: 'Blessed be the LORD, the God of Shem! Let Canaan be his slave. May God expand Japheth, and may he dwell among the tents of Shem; and let Canaan be his slave.'"

Here Noah shows that he is as thin-skinned as God: because he snuck a peek at his naked dad, Ham's unborn—not even yet conceived—son, Canaan, is consigned to slavery, first to his uncles, Shem and Japheth and, thereafter, through his own offspring he will provide the Biblical justification for the subjugation of people of color to Whites and Semites.

The story is obviously created post factum *to justify the Israelite conquest and enslavement of the Canaanites—the previous inhabitants of the Promised Land. And "Christian nations" have piously pointed to this "divine command" to show that owning African slaves is not only permissible, it is mandated.*

At that, you could have heard a pin drop in the courtroom. O'Sullivan held the gaze of the jury for what seemed like minutes, and then, as he gathered his notes and stacked them on the lectern, he shook his head ever so slightly, seeming to talk to himself so only the judge could hear him. *"Is this really your God?"*

Keeping his personal opinion on the matter well concealed, Michael Newsome kept his hands in his pockets to hide their slight tremble as he locked eyes in gratitude to his expert witness and softly said, *I have no further questions.*

Judge Grossler called the court to adjourn for a 30-minute break, and with a subtle gavel tap, the trial's first session met the half-way mark.

Twenty minutes later, much to Michael Newsome's surprise, every member of the jury had already returned to their seats ready to hear more testimony. The gallery had remained full as the Defense and Prosecution both devoted the recess to reviewing their notes.

Soon the bailiff proclaimed, *All rise!* and the judge returned to the bench.

Michael Newsome welcomed his star witness, Dr. Dermot O'Sullivan, back to the stand. *Thank you, Dr. O'Sullivan, for your thorough and thoughtful testimony this morning. May I take a moment to review what you've shared with us from the first ten chapters of Genesis?*

With a friendly nod from O'Sullivan, Newsome continued:

To be very brief—here's the scoop on God, if I've understood you correctly, Dr. O'Sullivan:

1. *He curses the Earth, the serpent, Adam, and Eve with all kinds of long-drawn-out punishments culminating in death.*
2. *He exhibits all of the worst human characteristics—in spades: regret, anger, revenge, jealousy, and insecurity.*
3. *He is a misogynist.*
4. *He should have been reported to the Child Protective Services for kicking his pre-rational, pre-moral kids out of the house to wander vulnerably around the planet.*
5. *He basically tells Adam he is worthless: "You didn't come from nuthin', you'll never amount to nuthin' and you'll die as nuthin'!"*
6. *He has all of the characteristics of a schoolyard bully or a barroom drunk itching for a brawl.*
7. *He's the first carnivore.*
8. *He is partisan, favoring Abel over Cain because he favors meat over veggies.*
9. *He has sons who engage in forbidden sex with their dad's creations, for which he punishes not the horny sons, but the exploited women and their families.*
10. *He seems to exhibit an impulse control disorder whereby he doesn't give a damn about the global collateral damage to his vengeful whims.*
11. *He may be suffering from early onset Alzheimer's disease: He can't remember what instructions he gave to Noah about the number of animals to put in the ark, nor exactly how long the rains lasted, nor how long it took for the first mountain peak to breach the surface of the receding flood waters. One gets the impression that even the mountains were fearful as they tentatively shoved their periscopes above the surface, like the children of an abusive parent waiting for the next blow.*

12. *He decrees slavery as a punishment, in perpetuity, to be inflicted upon the unborn progeny of an embarrassed young man who had just survived a global disaster and many months aboard a fragile craft crammed with noisy and smelly animals.*

Do we really want to worship this God? Or are we just afraid not to? Please help us understand our pathological addiction to this psychopath God, Dr. O'Sullivan.

Dermot O'Sullivan picked up where he left off, but this time he didn't try to crack any jokes:

Each of us assumes that the world into which we were born is the world as it has always been, which is why, when we attempt to write or speak of the past, anachronisms flow freely from our pens and from our mouths. They're often humorous once we catch them—and the Bible has its share of them, as writers, editors, and redactors unconsciously projected their own sense of the world onto previous eras when things were actually quite different. Two new examples from chapters 11 and 12 of the book of Genesis will suffice—we've already seen in the Ark story how the distinction between clean and unclean animals, a concept that didn't come into being until the time of Moses (if even then), was retrojected to the beginning of creation.

In chapter 11, in two places, verse 28 and verse 31, we are told that Abram's father, Terah, emigrated with his family from "Ur of the Chaldees." Now Ur was a very ancient Sumerian city, but the Chaldeans and their empire didn't arrive on the scene until 625 BCE, some 1,200 years after Abraham. The Biblical author, who was writing or redacting the texts around 400 BCE, is wrongly identifying the place from which Terah emigrated by its contemporary name. It would be the equivalent of a writer of 17th-century history telling us that members of the Iroquois Nation lived in New York State.

In chapter 12, verse 16, we're told that Abraham was given gifts of herds and flocks by the Pharaoh, including a herd of camels. The only problem is, camels were not domesticated until 500 years after the time of Abraham.

So, it's clear that even Bible writers assume that the world in which they lived was the way it had always been.

Sensing that his audience was feeling the tension of the moment, O'Sullivan decided to lighten things up a bit.

Imagine a modern millennial "scholar" redacting Genesis and Exodus: "Adam and Eve pulled out their iPhones and punched in the following messages to each other:

> *'C U @ apple tree in 10. —Eve'*
>
> *To which Adam replies: 'Did u mean apple tree or Apple Store?' —Adam*

It gives a whole new meaning to the term "Biblical text."

Smiles and a few groans scattered across the courtroom as O'Sullivan slipped in another joke.

Or imagine Moses, as he escapes from Egypt, pulling out his GPS, which tells him to hang a left on Sinai Boulevard in 14 miles.

Thank you, Dr. O'Sullivan, the Prosecution interjected. *Would you be willing to share with the members of the jury any additional crimes against humanity committed by Yahweh?*

Oh, I'm just getting warmed up, Michael, O'Sullivan replied. *Here's a story of polytheistic petty pouting and divine insecurity wedded to jealousy and vindictiveness, as the heavenly council takes steps to punish perceived human hubris:* And God said, "Come, let us go down and there confuse their language, so that no one will understand the speech of another." *Here we have another tale borrowed from the Sumerians— the people who built the ziggurats—the first skyscrapers. It is, of course, merely a retroactive, colorful and totally fanciful explanation for the multiplicity of human languages—about 7,000 in our times. This technique of "divide and conquer" will be frequently and successfully wielded by authority figures (religious and royal alike) to prevent ordinary people from rising up.*

But now the fearful, craven, and subjugated citizenry has finally managed to throw off this suffocating divinity by declaring God dead, and instead, they have put their trust in two revolutions: first, the scientific revolution, and then the industrial revolution. Religious folks only have themselves to blame for this secession, because the God they worshipped, the God they imposed on us and threatened us with, was a volatile pathetic actor who should have been fired after act one scene one.

But I'm getting ahead of myself. In the second part of Genesis chapter 11, there's another genealogy from source P. It marks the important transition, in Genesis, between the story of the nations/gentiles in the first 11 chapters and the story of Israel in the rest of the book of Genesis (39 more chapters.) It traces the lineage from Shem (son of Noah) down to Abraham (son of Terah) in ten generations. It's interesting to note what is happening to life expectancy. Shem lives to age 600; the next three generations have an average life expectancy of 445 years; the next three generations have an average life expectancy of 236 years; and the final three generations have an average life expectancy of 156 years.

Also, what catches the eye when you compare the two lists of patriarchs (pre-flood and post-flood) is the following: Initially, men were aged around 150 years before they had their first child—that's a long puberty— and they lived an average of 907 years. So, late onset sexual activity seems to be a recipe for longevity. Later, however, guys were having their first child in their late 20s but were dying around age 230. By the time of Abraham, you have the worst of both worlds: Abraham was 86 before his first child was born and he himself died at 175.

What more can you tell us about Abraham? the prosecutor prompted.

First a brief note on names, O'Sullivan replied. *God loves to change people's names to reflect a new mission or status. Jesus did it too, humorously calling Simon "Peter—the rock," and James and John "Boanerges—sons of thunder." Roman Catholic nuns do the same as they take their vows and become Sister Mary Clarence and the like. God changed Abram, the "high father," to Abraham, the "father of a multitude," in Genesis 17:5, and Abraham's wife's name from Sarai, "my princess," to Sarah, "mother of nations" in Genesis 17:15-16.*

The name changes are part of God playing favorites again. Not only does he handpick Abraham, but he declares, "I will bless those who bless you and curse those who curse you" *in Genesis 12:3. Shades of Cain, Lamech, Shem, Japheth, Ham, and Canaan are back again. Is this where the Catholic Church got the idea for a pope from—*"And I tell you that you are Peter and on this rock I will build my church, and the gates of Hades will not overcome it. I will give you the keys of the kingdom of heaven; whatever you bind on earth will be bound in heaven, and whatever you loose on earth will be loosed in heaven"—*from Matthew 16:18-19?*

Also mentioned casually is the fact that Abraham had male and female servants, where the word servant is a euphemism for slave. The Hebrew word for slave is used over a thousand times in the Tanakh, but is translated as slave *only occasionally in the English versions. Similarly, the Greek word for slave (which is* doulos*) is used about one hundred-fifty times in the New Testament, but you rarely find any of them translated accordingly in the English versions. In Greek,* doulos *never means servant or worker or hired hand or helper—Greek has separate words for all of these categories—but Calvin and Knox, and the first translators of the Bible into English, felt this was not appropriate for pious eyes. So, Abraham didn't really have servants; he was a slave owner, as were most of the important figures of his time. It is estimated that in the 5th century BCE there were about 80,000 slaves in Athens alone. Aristotle considered slavery not only necessary, but even natural. In Roman society around 100 BCE about 30% of the population was enslaved.*

While we cannot retroject 21st-century ethics onto the Middle Eastern cultures of 4,000 years ago, nor even onto the European cultures of 2,000 years ago, we can certainly point out that it wasn't really God—or a Real God—who decreed as just, and even as mandatory, any of the vicious practices that we read of in the sacred writings of these peoples. But in retelling the story of Abraham, I feel compelled to be as honest and accurate as I can be.

In tempting Abraham to leave his father and his homeland, God promised to give him a land flowing with milk and honey. Alas, Yahweh turns out to be a bit of a used-car salesman, for in Genesis 12:10 we learn, "There was famine in the land; so Abram went down to Egypt to sojourn there, since the famine in the land was severe." *This wasn't just your regular kind of famine, this was, we are told, severe. And it wouldn't be the last famine in this land flowing with milk and honey; famines happen with some regularity. Abraham's greatgrandchildren (Jacob's kids) will be forced to go to Egypt during another great famine, where they wind up being enslaved for 430 years.*

Here's another interesting Abrahamic story. Let me give it to you as it appears in Genesis 12:11-20 and then I will comment upon it: "When he was about to enter Egypt, he said to his wife Sarai: 'I know that you are a beautiful woman. When the Egyptians see you, they will say, 'She is his wife'; then they will kill me, but let you live. Please say, therefore, that you are my sister, so that I may fare well on your account and my life may be spared for your sake.' When Abram arrived in Egypt, the Egyptians saw that the woman was very beautiful. When Pharaoh's officials saw her they praised her to Pharaoh, and the woman was taken into Pharaoh's house. Abram fared well on her account, and he acquired sheep, oxen, male and female servants, male and female donkeys, and camels. But the LORD struck Pharaoh and his household with severe plagues because of Sarai, Abram's wife. Then Pharaoh summoned Abram and said to him: 'How could you do this to me! Why did you not tell me she was your wife? Why did you say, 'She is my sister,' so that I took her for my wife? Now, here is your wife. Take her and leave!' Then Pharaoh gave his men orders concerning Abram, and they sent him away, with his wife and all that belonged to him."

Nice of Abraham to sell out his wife for his own safety, huh? And then Yahweh visits Pharaoh and his household with plagues for his unwitting adultery. And this is just a test run for the ten plagues that will happen 600 years later, written about in the book of Exodus,

Once again, God punishes the victims rather than the perpetrators of the crime. Sarai and Abram tell lies and maintain the deceit for an extended period of time. For these sins both God and Pharaoh bless them with sheep, oxen, slaves, donkeys, and camels. Meanwhile, Pharaoh and his household—innocent victims who had been intentionally duped—are running up huge medical bills. Justice appears to have been blind even back then. Um... I'm sorry, Your Honor, no offense intended to you or your court.

None taken, Judge Grossler replied blithely as Dr. O'Sullivan pondered his next thought.

And, come to think of it, what are the chances that the Pharaoh, the most powerful man in the known world at the time, would give an audience to a homeless nomad like Abraham? It seems a bit like an illegal immigrant from Canada or Mexico driving his flocks across the US border, grazing them on the White House lawn and getting an audience with the POTUS, who rewards this unlawful behavior by telling the USDA to "beef up" his herds before they provide escort back across the border.

In another great sleight of hand, the writer of Genesis chapter 12 casually mentions in verses 6 and 7: "Abram passed through the land as far as the sacred place at Shechem, by the oak of Moreh. The Canaanites were then in the land. The LORD appeared to Abram and said: To your descendants I will give this land." *It seems of little importance to God or Abraham (a nomad from the east visiting the land of Canaan for the first time) and later Moses (who actually never set foot in Canaan), Joshua, the Judges, and the kings of Israel that, in order to possess the promised land, they had to first slaughter the Canaanites in a 200-year-long war campaign. The Bible writers will invent lots of reasons, beginning with the pathetic story of Noah and his son Ham, to justify this slaughter.*

We encounter the same disregard for the native population in Genesis chapter 13. By now the cows and bees are back in full production and Abraham and Sarai are back to taste the milk and honey. Now they are accompanied by their nephew Lot and his entourage. They like what they see, but the place ain't big enough for the both of them. They sound like two modern multinational corporations deciding how to best squash the "mom and pop" stores in order to own the market. So, we read in Genesis 13:5-17: "Lot, who went with Abram, also had flocks and herds and tents, so that the land could not support them if they stayed together; their possessions were so great that they could not live together. There were quarrels between the herders of Abram's livestock and the herders of Lot's livestock. At this time the Canaanites and the Perizzites were living in the land. So Abram said to Lot: "Let there be no strife between you and me, or between your herders and my herders, for we are kindred. Is not the whole land available? Please separate from me. If you prefer the left, I will go to the right; if you prefer the right, I will go to the left." Lot looked about and saw how abundantly watered the whole Jordan Plain was as far as Zoar, like the LORD's own garden, or like Egypt. This was before the LORD had destroyed Sodom and Gomorrah. Lot, therefore, chose for himself the whole Jordan Plain and set out eastward. Thus they separated from each other. Abram settled in the land of Canaan, while Lot settled among the cities of the Plain, pitching his tents near Sodom. Now the inhabitants of Sodom were wicked, great sinners against the LORD. After Lot had parted from him, the LORD said to Abram: Look about you, and from where you are, gaze to the north and south, east and west, all the land that you see I will give to you and your descendants forever. I will make your descendants like the dust of the earth; if anyone could count the dust of the earth, your descendants too might be counted. Get up and walk through the land, across its length and breadth, for I give it to you."

Helloooo! O'Sullivan crooned, startling an old lady who had been dozing in the gallery. *What about the Canaanites and the Perizzites? If you really are God, why aren't these children of yours equally beloved? Oh, I get it! You're not really God! Either you are just one among many "gods" trying desperately to carve out a reputation, or perhaps you're a fiction, a creation of our own. Either way, you don't get my vote. Lest we feel too self-righteous, however, it is important to realize that there is not a single nation on the face of the planet today that's not living on land that they took by bloody force from earlier inhabitants.*

O'Sullivan was really coming undone as he exposed Yahweh's racist, sexist, colonial, land-grabbing exploits. O'Sullivan had personally identified as a Celt until his grandfather told him stories of the Tuatha Dé Danann (the people of the Goddess Dana, a.k.a. the Faery Folk) whom the Celts defeated at two great battles in Moytura. They then divided the land of Ireland between them—the Celts getting the territory above the ground, and the Tuatha Dé Danann shape-shifting and getting the territory under the ground. Young O'Sullivan wasn't comfortable calling himself a descendant of the colonizing force, until he read further and realized that the Tuatha Dé Danann had stolen the land from the Fir Bolg who, in turn, had conquered even earlier inhabitants, the Formorians. Later, history reveals that the Celts were invaded by the Norse Vikings beginning in 795 CE, then by the Normans in 1169 CE, and then by the Brits. They finally got rid of the Brits in 1922. The question we must ask is, "Who are the *they* that got rid of *them*?!" O'Sullivan takes solace in the fact that, according to the genetic testing that's become a fad, he's 4% Neanderthal.

Calming himself, O'Sullivan finished his rant on a bitter note. *And, of course, these early books of the Bible are not historical evidence. They are teaching stories to help illiterate people—who lived thousands of years after the times of Adam and Abram—make sense of the world in which they found themselves. Are we doing any better today with our mass media and cosmologies, our political strategies, and military "actions," our science and our technology which have given us ecological devastation, unending war, and the looming possibility of the extinction of our species?*

The Prosecution considered pulling the despondent expert from the stand as this point, but instead decided to try to bring him back to Genesis and the task at hand.

Dr. O'Sullivan, surely Yahweh has had a hand in all of this...

But before he could finish his thought, O'Sullivan was off to the races again: *We need to learn to recognize "retroactive prognostication," where "prophesies" are made long after the event has taken place but are claimed to have predated the event. Parents are really good at this, e.g., "I told you that would happen if you disobeyed me!" It is a favorite biblical ploy both in the Hebrew Scriptures and the New Testament. It allows the "prophet" to have a 100% success rate. In Genesis 15:13, Yahweh predicts,* "Know for certain that your descendants will reside as aliens in a land not their own, where they shall be enslaved and oppressed for four hundred years." *Of course, this is actually ancient history by the time this "prediction" is first written.*

And in verse 18, Yahweh is boasting about his ability (never actually realized) to make Israel an empire stretching from Egypt to Iraq: "On that day the LORD made a covenant with Abram, saying: To your descendants I give this land, from the Wadi of Egypt to the Great River, the Euphrates, the land of the Kenites, the Kenizzites, the Kadmonites, the Hittites, the Perizzites, the Rephaim, the Amorites, the Canaanites, the Girgashites, and the Jebusites."

Once again, one might ask, "What about the Kenites, the Kenizzites, the Kadmonites, the Hittites, the Perizzites, the Rephaim, the Amorites, the Canaanites, the Girgashites, and the Jebusites? Doesn't anybody love them or look out for them?" Yahweh clearly picks and chooses the objects of his love and leaves a lot of people out in the cold.

And He wasn't even that great to the people he "chose." Ten years after the promise that they would be the parents of descendants as numerous as the stars of the heavens, Sarai and Abram are still childless. Sarai is very unhappy and takes matters into her own hands. She has an Egyptian maid (read "slave") called Hagar whom she presents to Abram with instructions that he is to have intercourse with her so that Sarai may have "sons through her." This custom is well attested in Near Eastern law, where marriage contracts often said that a wife who fails to produce a child within two years must provide her husband with a concubine.

In the case of Sarai and Hagar, we are not told if Abram was dragged kicking and screaming into this agreement or if he couldn't believe his luck. However, as soon as Hagar finds herself pregnant, things take a turn for the worse. Hagar gets cocky, Sarai gets pissed (pardon my French), and Abram gets stuck in the middle. Sarai blames Abram for this sorry mess and, knowing what side his bread was buttered on, he immediately kowtows to Sarai's demands. Here's the story: "His wife Sarai took her maid, Hagar the Egyptian, and gave her to her husband Abram to be his wife. He had intercourse with her, and she became pregnant. As soon as Hagar knew she was pregnant, her mistress lost stature in her eyes. So Sarai said to Abram: 'This outrage against me is your fault. I myself gave my maid to your embrace; but ever since she knew she was pregnant, I have lost stature in her eyes. May the LORD decide between you and me!' Abram told Sarai: 'Your maid is in your power. Do to her what you regard as right.' Sarai then mistreated her so much that Hagar ran away from her." *Sheesh. Women can be just as vindictive as men,* O'Sullivan gasped.

But it doesn't end there, O'Sullivan continued. *Hagar flees into the wilderness bewailing her fate. God finds her there and sends her back with promises that she, too, will become the mother of multitudes. So, she returns and gives birth to Abram's first son, Ishmael—whose name means "God has heard." It will be another fourteen years before his second son, Isaac, is born.*

There is, of course, a deeper wisdom to this and similar stories. They represent some of the archetypes of human behavior—jealousy, looking out for oneself, mama bear protecting her own offspring and punishing the competition—that occur in all cultures. How is it that people seem to repeat the same trends over time and space? Maybe the universe gives us as many lifetimes as we need to grow beyond selfish love to unconditional love for all sentient beings. But it ain't easy.

Are you suggesting that we go around more than once, Dr. O'Sullivan? Newsome queried.

I wasn't gonna go there, but since you asked—could it be that Abraham and Sarah are the reincarnation of Adam and Eve, acting out a lifetime in which Eve/Sarah is getting revenge on Adam/Abraham? We see the same patterns playing out, reversing the gender of the players, in both generations. Let me explain. After the first "sin," Adam accepts no responsibility and puts all the blame on Eve. But by chapter sixteen, the shoe is on the other foot. In this story, Sarah (who is Eve reincarnated) is taking zero responsibility for her actions and makes Abraham (who is Adam reincarnated) the cause of her misfortune. She is the one who crafted the plan to have a child through her slave girl but then freaked out and blamed Abraham (Adam) when Hagar started to get snotty with her infertile mistress. It gets even worse by chapter twenty-one. Sarah now has a son of her own womb and is full of laughter and gratitude until she sees Ishmael playing with his little brother. Merriment and thanksgiving turn to rage and violence as she screams at Abraham (Adam) to get rid of the kid and his mother. She won't have them invading her pitch and grabbing a part of the will.

Sarah's reaction is textbook victim-mentality: blaming others for past, present, and future vicissitudes —all the while willing to punish another mother and an innocent child to shore up her own insecurities. And she is married to the ultimate wimp, an emasculated male who would sooner send his first-born son into exile than disobey Sarah. Even God, it seems, is loath to mess with her: "Obey Sarah, no matter what she asks of you."

Imagine a modern version of this. A man and his wife get divorced after birthing a child. The man remarries, but his new wife soon shows her true colors. In screaming matches, she tells him he must send his ex-wife and child out of the country and cut the kid out of his will. Moreover, he is further forbidden from paying either spousal support or child support. And, coward that he is, he agrees to those terms. Aren't we lucky to be descended from such an enlightened couple?

Here's the second part of the story as it appears in the Bible: "When his son Isaac was eight days old, Abraham circumcised him, as God had commanded. Abraham was a hundred years old when his son Isaac was born to him. Sarah then said, 'God has given me cause to laugh, and all who hear of it will laugh with me. Who would ever have told Abraham,' she added, 'that Sarah would nurse children! Yet I have borne him a son in his old age.' The child grew and was weaned, and Abraham held a great banquet on the day of the child's weaning. Sarah noticed the son whom Hagar the Egyptian had borne to Abraham playing with her son Isaac; so she demanded of Abraham: 'Drive out that slave and her son! No son of that slave is going to share the inheritance with my son Isaac!' Abraham was greatly distressed because it concerned a son of his. But God said to Abraham: 'Do not be distressed about the boy or about your slave woman. Obey Sarah, no matter what she asks of you; for it is through Isaac that descendants will bear your name. As for the son of the slave woman, I will make a nation of him also, since he too is your offspring.' Early the next morning Abraham got some bread and a skin of water and gave them to Hagar. Then, placing the child on her back, he sent her away."

I'm reporting them both to child protective services! O'Sullivan shouted, waving his iPhone in sweeping motions toward the jury.

The prosecutor chimed in: *But the children of God didn't have agencies like that, did they, Dr. O'Sullivan. They were supposed to be able to depend on Yahweh to protect them, weren't they?* Newsome nudged.

True, replied Dr. O'Sullivan. *And neither did they have fertility treatments like in-vitro fertilization. So it was literally laughable that Abraham and Sarah would become parents at their advanced age. So when their son was born they called him Isaac—in Hebrew, Yishaq, which means "laughed." There are three different explanations given for this name in chapters 17, 18, and 21. Here's a synopsis: in Genesis 17:17, after God had told the ninety-nine-year-old Abraham that his ninety-year-old wife, Sarah, would conceive and bear a son, Abraham laughed but, so as to not let God see that he was laughing, he bent his face to the ground. God's promise was too taxing even for Abraham's faith. He didn't believe that God could deliver (no pun intended) on this outrageous promise. So, the son would be called Isaac because Abraham laughed in disbelief:* "Abraham fell face down and laughed as he said to himself, 'Can a child be born to a man who is a hundred years old? Can Sarah give birth at ninety?'"

The second version is completely different. Now, Abraham receives three angelic visitors (or God Himself—the versions differ also in this detail) whom he feeds and entertains. Here's the story: "Where is your wife Sarah?" they asked him. "There, in the tent," he said. Then one of them said, "I will surely return to you about this time next year, and Sarah your wife will have a son." Now Sarah was listening at the entrance to the tent, which was behind him. Abraham and Sarah were already very old, and Sarah was past the age of childbearing. So Sarah laughed to herself as she thought, "After I am worn out and my lord is old, will I now have this pleasure?" Then the Lord said to Abraham, "Why did Sarah laugh and say, 'Will I really have a child, now that I am old?' Is anything too hard for the Lord? I will return to you at the appointed time next year, and Sarah will have a son." Sarah was afraid, so she lied and said, "I did not laugh." But he said, "Yes, you did laugh." *In this version, from Genesis 18:9-15, the child is called Isaac because Sarah had laughed in disbelief.*

But there is yet a third explanation for Isaac's name in Genesis 21:1-7. "Now the Lord was gracious to Sarah as he had said, and the Lord did for Sarah what he had promised. Sarah became pregnant and bore a son to Abraham in his old age, at the very time God had promised him. Abraham gave the name Isaac to the son Sarah bore him. When his son Isaac was eight days old, Abraham circumcised him, as God commanded him. Abraham was a hundred years old when his son Isaac was born to him. Sarah said, "God has brought me laughter, and everyone who hears about this will laugh with me." And she added, "Who would have said to Abraham that Sarah would nurse children? Yet I have borne him a son in his old age." *In this version, he is called Isaac because everyone will laugh and rejoice that Sarah has borne and nursed her own child.*

Names are a funny thing, O'Sullivan continued with a far-away look on his face. *There's a story in our family lore about my mother's birth certificate. My mother is Margaret. Her mother I knew as "Nanna." And her father I knew as "Daddy Jim." Margaret was born at home, and when Nanna had mustered enough energy, she told Daddy Jim to go to City Hall and register the birth. So, he headed off but got waylaid by some buddies who were so excited by his good news that they dragged him kicking and screaming into a pub. Hours later, he emerged and staggered to City Hall, but for the life of him he couldn't remember what name Nanna had decided for the child. So, he gave his best guess. Alas, he only got the first letter right, and forever after, my mother's birth certificate had a totally different name from the one by which she was known. In fact, nobody discovered the error until she herself needed a copy of her birth certificate in order to get married!*

Being tipsy was Daddy Jim's excuse. What's God's excuse? He made three attempts to remember why Isaac was called Isaac. If that had been a PIN code, He'd be locked out of his online banking for the day. Does this sound like an inerrant scripture to you? What judge in a court of law is going to have confidence in such a witness?

At that moment, the attorney for the defense could no longer contain her frustration. Kayla Goldstein's heavy wooden chair squawked on the tile floor as she simultaneously pushed it back and stood up. *Your Honor, I simply must object. This has gone on long enough. With all due respect for the expert witness, the Prosecution is out of line.*

Objection sustained, Judge Grossler concurred. *The court would like to address the witness. Dr. O'Sullivan, your testimony is as interesting as it is important, but I'm going to have to ask you to reserve the judgment calls for me.*

Understood, Your Honor, O'Sullivan demurred.

I'll expect the prosecution to pull in on the reins a bit as we move forward. Judge Grossler chided Newsome. *Are we nearing the completion of this testimony, Dr. O'Sullivan?*

That depends. Are you asking that in Irish time or American time? O'Sullivan joked, winking at the gallery and pushing his luck with the judge.

With that, Michael Newsome stepped forward and attempted to

get a hold of the aforementioned reins. *Thank you for your detailed testimony, Dr. O'Sullivan—*

There's more, Michael. The next covenant Yahweh makes—a really weird one which exchanges progeny and a promised land for a whole bunch of foreskins—is not only a rather odd fetish, but one helluva bargain! O'Sullivan blurted out before Newsome could rein him in.

Initially, Abraham thinks that the promise of progeny is through his thirteen-year-old son, Ishmael, but God insists that he is going to give him another son, Isaac, and that the covenant will follow Isaac's lineage, not Ishmael's. Here is another instance of the right of the firstborn being given away to a younger son: "So Abraham said to God, 'If only Ishmael could live in your favor!' God replied: 'Even so, your wife Sarah is to bear you a son, and you shall call him Isaac. It is with him that I will maintain my covenant as an everlasting covenant and with his descendants after him. Now as for Ishmael, I will heed you: I hereby bless him. I will make him fertile and will multiply him exceedingly. He will become the father of twelve chieftains, and I will make of him a great nation. But my covenant I will maintain with Isaac, whom Sarah shall bear to you by this time next year.'"

And, once again, the writer slips in the promise of taking the land from the indigenous population and giving it to the alien invaders: "I will give to you and to your descendants after you the land in which you are now residing as aliens, the whole land of Canaan, as a permanent possession." (Gen 17:8)

I painted a picture earlier of God-the-gardener, the one who planted the Garden of Eden with all kinds of veggies, fruit trees, and berry bushes, including two that no longer appear in Sunset Magazine—"the tree of the knowledge of good and evil" and "the tree of life." God's real specialty is pruning—and not just trees, but covenants. Nobody is better able to trim down the original agreements, changing the contractees, the terms, and the beneficiaries. At first, the arrangement was for Adam and Eve and their progeny in perpetuity to enjoy the Garden of Eden. Then He got mad at their disobedience and kicked them out with thunderous warnings never to attempt to come back in. In fact, he stationed cherubim with a fiery revolving sword east of the garden to make sure they couldn't get back in. That didn't quite pacify Him, so He wiped out everybody except Noah and company in a global flood. He made a covenant with Noah and all his descendants promising never again to wipe out humanity in a flood. However, He soon changed his mind and, in a fit of pique, sent a second devastating flood—this one a flood of languages—to divide and conquer the people of the earth.

Then He pruned away the vast bulk of Noah's lineage, leaving only the descendants of Abraham in his favor. Very quickly he amended those terms, choosing only one of Abe's kids, the young fella Isaac, rather than the first-born Ishmael. Later He snips off the branch that comes from Isaac's firstborn son, Esau, and chooses the lineage of Jacob via his twelve sons—the progenitors of the twelve tribes of Israel (which is the nickname God gave Jacob after a wrestling match. "Israel" means "the man who wrestled with God.") But God was unable to protect all twelve tribes and when the Assyrians invaded in 721 BCE, ten of the tribes disappear forever. Now only Judah and Benjamin are left. But the New Testament tells us that they, too, have been pruned and only one line of their offspring— the Jews of the Jesus Movement (Christianity) and not Rabbinical Judaism (the other surviving child of Temple Judaism)—has been chosen.

Islam resurrected the lineage of Ishmael (Abraham's firstborn son) claiming to now be the "real deal" above all branches of Judaism and Christianity. Soon, Islam split into Sunni and Shia—who murder each other in sectarian strife to this day—based on their differing view of who would succeed Mohammed as leader of the faith. Meanwhile Christianity did not give up its claim, though internal divisions resulted in wholesale slaughter between Eastern and Western churches and, later, between Protestants and Catholics, where even today, there are two competing groups claiming to be the covenanted ones—Roman Catholicism, which said, "Extra ecclesiam nulla est salus" (outside the [Catholic] church there is no redemption) and other Christians who said that only those who confess their sins and profess Jesus as Savior can get to heaven.

Meanwhile, Judaism stubbornly refused to believe they had been disinherited and continued, through 2,000 years of persecution and exile, to claim that they are still God's chosen people. Their presence in the land of Israel today infuriates many Islamic nations, who regularly threaten to finish what Hitler almost achieved in his plan to totally annihilate the Jews.

Christianity disdainfully regards this as mere squabbling among the losers and sees itself, especially Roman Catholicism and the Born-agains, as the divinely favored.

At some stage, God himself got so confused about who was the legal holder of the covenant that he gave up and stopped talking. When did this happen? Judaism says it was around 400 BCE, with Malachi, the last of the prophets; Christianity says it was around 100 CE with the death of the last of the apostles; and Islam says it was in 632 CE with the death of Mohammed, "the Seal of the Prophets."

Occasionally, like the Voyager I space probe which has punctured the solar systems's outer membrane and exited the heliosphere but still manages to send back faint, intermittent messages, God's voice will be heard via channeled proclamations in the form of fatwas from an Ayatollah who is incensed on God's behalf, or in a fiery sermon from a televangelist—accompanied by a guarantee of salvation if you send him a sizeable donation. Otherwise, a powerless or geriatric God doesn't have the energy any longer to deal with the cacophony of human voices, and so remains silent—secateurs held impotently in hand.

Are our only God choices a murderous micromanager, a bewildered, powerless bystander, or a phantasm who never really existed (as materialistic science claims)? What if you and I can uncover who God really is by dismantling these three fables and letting the sun finally shine?

If we hope to find God in the Bible, we must search for Him among stories about circumcision, incest, child sacrifice, betrayal, and vengeance.

Shall we begin with circumcision? In requiring this as the sign of the new covenant, God uses the word "circumcision" or its cognates seven times in five verses [Gen 17:10-14] and ends with the dire warning that whoever is uncircumcised will be regarded as being in breach of the covenant: "This is the covenant between me and you and your descendants after you that you must keep: every male among you shall be circumcised. Circumcise the flesh of your foreskin. That will be the sign of the covenant between me and you. Throughout the ages, every male among you, when he is eight days old, shall be circumcised, including houseborn slaves and those acquired with money from any foreigner who is not of your descendants. Yes, both the houseborn slaves and those acquired with money must be circumcised. Thus my covenant will be in your flesh as an everlasting covenant. If a male is uncircumcised, that is, if the flesh of his foreskin has not been cut away, such a one will be cut off from his people; he has broken my covenant."

Abraham's compound must have looked like a MASH unit on a battle front, because on the very day God made this demand we read: "Then Abraham took his son Ishmael and all his slaves, whether born in his house or acquired with his money—every male among the members of Abraham's household—and he circumcised the flesh of their foreskins on that same day, as God had told him to do. Abraham was ninety-nine years old when the flesh of his foreskin was circumcised, and his son Ishmael was thirteen years old when the flesh of his foreskin was circumcised. Thus, on that same day Abraham and his son Ishmael were circumcised; and all the males of his household, including the slaves born in his house or acquired with his money from foreigners, were circumcised with him."

All of this surgery without the use of opioids! I don't care what the social or medical "benefits" of circumcision may be, I have a huge problem believing that a compassionate God demanded this widespread suffering as the price of a covenant with Him.

Once again, a very anthropomorphic God emerges in the story of Sodom and Gomorrah. Before setting out to destroy these two cities, God wonders whether or not he should keep Abraham in the dark: "The LORD considered: Shall I hide from Abraham what I am about to do...?" *God has heard reports about the "ungodliness" of the two cities but decides to go check it out for himself*: "So the LORD said: The outcry against Sodom and Gomorrah is so great, and their sin so grave, that I must go down to see whether or not their actions are as bad as the cry against them that comes to me. I mean to find out."

Abraham, of course, does find out what God intends to do and begins to bargain with Him about the loss of innocent life: "Then Abraham drew near and said: 'Will you really sweep away the righteous with the wicked? Suppose there were fifty righteous people in the city; would you really sweep away and not spare the place for the sake of the fifty righteous people within it? Far be it from you to do such a thing, to kill the righteous with the wicked, so that the righteous and the wicked are treated alike! Far be it from you! Should not the judge of all the world do what is just?' The LORD replied: If I find fifty righteous people in the city of Sodom, I will spare the whole place for their sake. Abraham spoke up again: 'See how I am presuming to speak to my Lord, though I am only dust and ashes! What if there are five less than fifty righteous people? Will you destroy the whole city because of those five?' I will not destroy it, he answered, if I find forty-five there. But Abraham persisted, saying, 'What if only forty are found there?' He replied: I will refrain from doing it for the sake of the forty. Then he said, 'Do not let my Lord be angry if I go on. What if only thirty are found there?' He replied: I will refrain from doing it if I can find thirty there. Abraham went on, 'Since I have thus presumed to speak to my Lord, what if there are no more than twenty?' I will not destroy it, he answered, for the sake of the twenty. But he persisted: 'Please, do not let my Lord be angry if I speak up this last time. What if ten are found there?' For the sake of the ten, he replied, I will not destroy it. The LORD departed as soon as he had finished speaking with Abraham, and Abraham returned home."

It appears that Abraham is both wiser and more compassionate than a God who is also indecisive and not sure if the information he is receiving from his angelic agents on planet Earth is correct.

And here, now, is a slightly shortened (by me) account of the destruction of Sodom and Gomorrah: "The two angels reached Sodom in the evening, as Lot was sitting at the gate of Sodom. When Lot saw them, he got up to greet them; and bowing down with his face to the ground, he said, 'Please, my lords, come aside into your servant's house for the night, and bathe your feet; you can get up early to continue your journey.' But they replied, 'No, we will pass the night in the town square.' He urged them so strongly, however, that they turned aside to his place and entered his house. He prepared a banquet for them, baking unleavened bread, and they dined. Before they went to bed, the townsmen of Sodom, both young and old—all the people to the last man—surrounded the house. They called to Lot and said to him, 'Where are the men who came to your house tonight?

Bring them out to us that we may have sexual relations with them.' Lot went out to meet them at the entrance. When he had shut the door behind him, he said, 'I beg you, my brothers, do not do this wicked thing! I have two daughters who have never had sexual relations with men. Let me bring them out to you, and you may do to them as you please. But do not do anything to these men, for they have come under the shelter of my roof.' They replied, 'Stand back! This man,' they said, 'came here as a resident alien, and now he dares to give orders! We will treat you worse than them!' With that, they pressed hard against Lot, moving in closer to break down the door. But his guests put out their hands, pulled Lot inside with them, and closed the door; they struck the men at the entrance of the house, small and great, with such a blinding light that they were utterly unable to find the doorway…

As dawn was breaking, the angels urged Lot on, saying, 'Come on! Take your wife with you and your two daughters who are here, or you will be swept away in the punishment of the city.' When he hesitated, the men, because of the LORD's compassion for him, seized his hand and the hands of his wife and his two daughters and led them to safety outside the city. As soon as they had brought them outside, they said: 'Flee for your life! Do not look back or stop anywhere on the Plain. Flee to the hills at once, or you will be swept away...'

The sun had risen over the earth when Lot arrived in Zoar, and the LORD rained down sulfur upon Sodom and Gomorrah, fire from the LORD out of heaven. He overthrew those cities and the whole Plain, together with the inhabitants of the cities and the produce of the soil. But Lot's wife looked back, and she was turned into a pillar of salt. The next morning Abraham hurried to the place where he had stood before the LORD. As he looked down toward Sodom and Gomorrah and the whole region of the Plain, he saw smoke over the land rising like the smoke from a kiln."

Lot's offer to throw his daughters to the dogs reflects three things: the patriarch's total control and rights over his household, very low regard for the rights of women, and the overarching value placed on hospitality. I wonder how human history would have been different if there had been as much respect for women as there was for hospitality? I can understand that patriarchy was a stage in human evolution; what I cannot understand or agree to is the notion that God (the Real One) would have condoned such behavior.

The angels (God himself in some versions) arrange for the escape of Lot, his wife, and his two virgin daughters, but not without God punishing Lot's wife for disregarding a minor command: "Flee for your life! Do not look back or stop anywhere on the Plain. Flee to the hills at once, or you will be swept away...But Lot's wife looked back, and she was turned into a pillar of salt." *God seems incapable of not screwing up a good intention with some kind of punitive twist.*

Now comes an unusual story of incest. Only Lot and his two daughters are left. The sky is filled with the sights and sounds and smells of the sulphur-immolated cities. Perhaps the girls thought that only the three of them are left on planet Earth. That would be sad. It would mean never having a husband, never becoming mothers, and watching the human species go extinct. So, they sprang into action: "Since Lot was afraid to stay in Zoar, he and his two daughters went up from Zoar and settled in the hill country, where he lived with his two daughters in a cave. The firstborn said to the younger: 'Our father is getting old, and there is not a man in the land to have intercourse with us as is the custom everywhere. Come, let us ply our father with wine and then lie with him, that we may ensure posterity by our father.' So that night they plied their father with wine, and the firstborn went in and lay with her father; but he was not aware of her lying down or getting up. The next day the firstborn said to the younger: 'Last night I lay with my father. Let us ply him with wine again tonight, and then you go in and lie with him, that we may ensure posterity by our father.' So that night, too, they plied their father with wine, and then the younger one went in and lay with him; but he was not aware of her lying down or getting up. Thus the two daughters of Lot became pregnant by their father. The firstborn gave birth to a son whom she named Moab, saying, 'From my father.' He is the ancestor of the Moabites of today. The younger one, too, gave birth to a son, and she named him Ammon, saying, 'The son of my kin.' He is the ancestor of the Ammonites of today."

Of course, that didn't quite solve the long-term problem. Since they both gave birth to boys, there was gonna have to be some more incest in order to get the human race started again. Mother and son liaisons would have to be a necessary next step.

Sodom and Gomorrah, henceforth, take on an archetypal role in Biblical literature, with various prophets identifying their sin in different ways. Speaking of Judah in 742 BCE, Isaiah sees their sin as a lack of social justice: "Hear the word of the Lord, you rulers of Sodom; listen to the instruction of our God, you people of Gomorrah! Learn to do right; seek justice. Defend the oppressed. Take up the cause of the fatherless; plead the case of the widow." *Around the year 600 BCE, Jeremiah speaks of the sin as general immorality:* "And among the prophets of Jerusalem I have seen something horrible: They commit adultery and live a lie. They strengthen the hands of evildoers, so that not one of them turns from their wickedness. They are all like Sodom to me; the people of Jerusalem are like Gomorrah." *By 550 BCE, Ezekiel identifies the sin as a disregard for the poor:* "Your older sister was Samaria, who lived to the north of you with her daughters; and your younger sister, who lived to the south of you with her daughters, was Sodom. You not only followed their ways and copied their detestable practices, but in all your ways you soon became more depraved than they. As surely as I live, declares the Sovereign Lord, your sister Sodom and her daughters never did what you and your daughters have done. Now this was the sin of your sister Sodom: She and her daughters were arrogant, overfed and unconcerned; they did not help the poor and needy. They were haughty and did detestable things before me. Therefore I did away with them as you have seen. Samaria did not commit half the sins you did. You have done more detestable things than they, and have made your sisters seem righteous by all these things you have done."

In the original story, the sin is basically the violation of the sacred obligation of hospitality by the threatened rape of Lot's guests. Neither the rape, per se, nor the homosexual intent carry as much weight as the breach of the host-guest bond.

But let's go back to Sarah and Abraham. Once more we find them using the same old lie: "She's my sister, he's my brother." This time there is a new stooge. Here's the story from Genesis 20: "From there Abraham journeyed on to the region of the Negeb, where he settled between Kadesh and Shur. While he resided in Gerar as an alien, Abraham said of his wife Sarah, 'She is my sister.' So Abimelech, king of Gerar, sent and took Sarah. But God came to Abimelech in a dream one night and said to him: You are about to die because of the woman you have taken, for she has a husband. Abimelech, who had not approached her, said: 'O Lord, would you kill an innocent man? Was he not the one who told me, 'She is my sister'? She herself also stated, 'He is my brother.' I acted with pure heart and with clean hands.' God answered him in the dream: Yes, I know you did it with a pure heart. In fact, it was I who kept you from sinning against me; that is why I did not let you touch her. So now, return the man's wife so that he may intercede for you, since he is a prophet, that you may live. If you do not return her, you can be sure that you and all who are yours will die. Early the next morning Abimelech called all his servants and informed them of everything that had happened, and the men were filled with fear. Then Abimelech summoned Abraham and said to him: 'What have you done to us! What wrong did I do to you that you would have brought such great guilt on me and my kingdom? You have treated me in an intolerable way. What did you have in mind,' Abimelech asked him, 'that you would do such a thing?' Abraham answered, 'I thought there would be no fear of God in this place, and so they would kill me on account of my wife. Besides, she really is my sister, but only my father's daughter, not my mother's; and so she became my wife. When God sent me wandering from my father's house, I asked her: 'Would you do me this favor? In whatever place we come to, say: He is my brother. Then Abimelech took flocks and herds and male and female slaves and gave them to Abraham; and he restored his wife Sarah to him. Then Abimelech said, 'Here, my land is at your disposal; settle wherever you please.' To Sarah he said: 'I hereby give your brother a thousand shekels of silver. This will preserve your honor before all who are with you and will exonerate you before everyone.' Abraham then interceded with God, and God restored health to Abimelech, to his wife, and his maidservants, so that they bore children, for the LORD had closed every womb in Abimelech's household on account of Abraham's wife Sarah."

Once again, God punishes the innocent party while blessing the culprits with flocks and herds and male and female slaves, as well as 1,000 shekels of silver to compensate Sarah for a perceived loss of honor. In a lovely twist, Abraham (who is here called a "prophet" for the one and only time when, in fact, he is a liar and a perpetrator of deceit) intercedes with God to remove the forced sterilization of Abimelech and his entire household.

It is the equivalent of corrupt Wall Street traders pleading with God (as they receive million-dollar bonuses for screwing up) to provide food stamps for those who lost their homes in the manipulated economic collapse of 2008.

Monkey see, monkey do. In Genesis chapter 26:6-11, Isaac and his wife, Rebekah, pull the very same stunt: "So Isaac stayed in Gerar. When the men of that place asked him about his wife, he said, 'She is my sister,' because he was afraid to say, 'She is my wife.' He thought, 'The men of this place might kill me on account of Rebekah, because she is beautiful.' When Isaac had been there a long time, Abimelek king of the Philistines looked down from a window and saw Isaac caressing his wife Rebekah. So Abimelek summoned Isaac and said, 'She is really your wife! Why did you say, 'She is my sister'? Isaac answered him, 'Because I thought I might lose my life on account of her.' Then Abimelek said, 'What is this you have done to us? One of the men might well have slept with your wife, and you would have brought guilt upon us.' So Abimelek gave orders to all the people: 'Anyone who harms this man or his wife shall surely be put to death.'"

In the West, ignorance of the law is not an argument for innocence; but in Biblical times, ignorance of the truth was no reason not to be punished; a commandment had an inbuilt consequence irrespective of motive or knowledge of the facts or the law.

A wee note on marrying a half-sister: in Sumerian mythology, the gods practiced this as a way of keeping the royal bloodline as "pure" as possible. It was a calculated balancing act: marrying a full sibling led to lots of genetic abnormalities in the offspring, and marrying outside the "family" diluted the bloodline. So, a workable compromise was same-father-different-mother kids marrying each other.

You see lots of evidence of this practice in Greek and Roman mythology. In fact, the Greek and Roman gods had no compunction about grandmothers and grandfathers having sex (and lots of offspring) with their own grandsons and granddaughters.

Later, in Israelite life, this half-brother half-sister custom was prohibited.

CHILD SACRIFICE

The story of Abraham being willing to sacrifice his twelve-year-old son, Isaac, is very well known both in literature and in art. I don't need to go into great detail about it, except to add the following: The God of the New Testament allegedly does what Abraham narrowly avoided; he went all the way and sacrificed his "only son." Really?

Listen to the psalmist during the Babylonian captivity singing, "Daughter Babylon, doomed to destruction, happy is the one who repays you according to what you have done to us. Happy is the one who seizes your infants and dashes them against the rocks. (Psalm 137:9)*; or the Christian crusaders of 1095 chanting, "Laus tibi, Christe" (praise to you, oh Christ) as they slaughter Jews and Muslims; or the modern terrorist who shouts, "Allahu Akbar!" (God is the greatest!) as he detonates a bomb that kills fifty school children on a bus.*

Such a God, if He exists, is a monster.

Abraham is horrified at the thought of his son marrying a mere Canaanite, so he sends a servant to Haran, whence he'd come many moons ago, to find a wife from amongst his kinfolk. The servant is successful and comes back with Rebekah and she and Isaac fall madly in love. Rebekah births twin boys, Esau the firstborn, who was covered in hair and who became a great hunter, and Jacob, who is smooth skinned and his mother's favorite. Fast forward many years. Now Isaac is very decrepit and blind. He calls his firstborn, Esau, and asks him to go hunt and cook him a meal, so that Isaac can give him his final blessing. Rebekah has been eavesdropping and, as soon as Esau leaves for the hunt, she dresses Jacob in his brother's hunting gear, making sure also to cover the smooth skin of his arms and neck with goatskin so as to fool his father. Then she cooks Isaac's favorite food and sends Jacob to deliver it to his dad. Jacob objects, fearing that if his dad tumbles to the ruse, instead of stealing Esau's blessing he'll wind up being cursed by his dad. But his mother prevails upon him. Here is the lying-through-his-teeth dialog that ensues: "Going to his father, Jacob said, 'Father!' 'Yes?' replied Isaac. 'Which of my sons are you?' Jacob answered his father: 'I am Esau, your firstborn. I did as you told me. Please sit up and eat some of my game, so that you may bless me.' But Isaac said to his son, 'How did you get it so quickly, my son?' He answered, 'The LORD, your God, directed me.' Isaac then said to Jacob, 'Come closer, my son, that I may feel you, to learn whether you really are my son Esau or not.' So Jacob moved up closer to his father. When Isaac felt him, he said, 'Although the voice is Jacob's, the hands are Esau's.' (*He failed to identify him because his hands were hairy, like those of his brother Esau; so he blessed him.*) Again Isaac said, 'Are you really my son Esau?' And Jacob said, 'I am.' Then Isaac said, 'Serve me, my son, and let me eat of the game so that I may bless you.' Jacob served it to him, and Isaac ate; he brought him wine, and he drank. Finally his father Isaac said to him, 'Come closer, my son, and kiss me.' As Jacob went up to kiss him, Isaac smelled the fragrance of his clothes."

As the final act of the deception, he betrays the truth—and his brother—with a kiss! Moreover, he has called God as a witness to support his lie: "How did you get it so quickly, my son?" *He answered,* "The LORD, your God, directed me."

So, Isaac offers him the blessing, which includes the following: "May peoples serve you, and nations bow down to you; be master of your brothers, and may your mother's sons bow down to you. Cursed be those who curse you, and blessed be those who bless you."

*Esau returns to discover he has, once more, been betrayed and bilked out of his rights as a firstborn—*déjà vu *all over again, as Yogi Berra said. In a heartrending plea he beseeches his father to bless him too. But Isaac explains that he can't "undo" Jacob's blessing and that Esau must settle for a consolation prize:* "As he heard his father's words, Esau burst into loud, bitter sobbing and said, 'Father, bless me too!' When Isaac said, 'Your brother came here by a ruse and carried off your blessing,' Esau exclaimed, 'He is well named Jacob, is he not! He has supplanted me twice! First he took away my right as firstborn, and now he has taken away my blessing.' Then he said, 'Have you not saved a blessing for me?' Isaac replied to Esau: 'I have already appointed him your master, and I have assigned to him all his kindred as his servants; besides, I have sustained him with grain and wine. What then can I do for you, my son?' But Esau said to his father, 'Have you only one blessing, father? Bless me too, father!' and Esau wept aloud."

A California psychologist would be mandated to report this as elder abuse. Unfortunately, I see a lot of this—scam artists on the phone who bilk the elderly of their fragile funds with Ponzi schemes. And the whole scenario reminds me of an Irish proverb: "Is minic a chuir fear na luaithrigh fear na sluasad amach." *('Tis often the man of the ashes puts the man of the shovels out.) And here's what it means: A farmer has two sons, the elder son is a very hardworking boy spending his time helping his dad with the farmwork (he's the "man of the shovels"); the younger son is the mother's little pet who spends his days being fed treats as he warms his feet at the fire (he's the "man of the ashes"). The day comes when the father is on his dying bed and about to make his will. The wife harangues him until he agrees to bequeath the farm to the younger son, who promptly, on his dad's demise, kicks out the elder son.*

But let's get back to the Jacob story. Understandably enough, Esau is filled with a homicidal rage, so Rebekah has a plan (as usual) that will "kill two birds with the one stone." She doesn't want her son marrying a local girl (an accursed Canaanite) and she wants to put Jacob into a temporary witness protection program, so she arranges to send him back to Mesopotamia (the oul *country) to her brother Laban to find a bride.*

*Deceit seems to be a common trait of Abraham/Sarah, Isaac/Rebekah and their extended family. Laban, Jacob's uncle (brother of Jacob's mother Rebekah) switches brides on Jacob, who thinks he's marrying Laban's younger daughter, Rachel, when in fact he's being pawned off on the elder daughter, Leah. Poor ol' Leah. We read in Gen 29:*17, "Leah had dull eyes but Rachel was shapely and beautiful." *Notice how a woman's marriage prospects were linked directly to her appearance even then—can't blame Hollywood for that one!*

Laban, never one to pass up a business opportunity, even at the expense of a family member, tells Jacob that he can marry the beautiful Rachel if he first serves Laban for seven years. Seems like a very stiff "bride price," but Jacob is so smitten that seven years seem like "a few days because of his love for her." *(Gen 29:20.)*

On the wedding night, Laban switches the daughters and Jacob consummates the marriage, only realizing in the morning that he got duped. When he protests, Laban tells him he can also marry Rachel after the week's festivities (for the Leah wedding) are concluded. But he must agree to another seven years of working for his uncle. (And you think you've got problems with the in-laws?)

Jacob continues to favor Rachel, so a disconsolate Leah attempts to win him over by producing seven children to Rachel's two (both of whom arrived very late in the game.) Jacob, for his part, is a very busy daddy; he has 13 children (12 boys who will become the 12 tribes of Israel and his daughter, Dinah) by four women: six boys and a girl by Leah; two boys by Leah's maidservant Zilpah; two boys by Rachel; and two more boys by Rachel's maidservant Bilhah. (It seems the job description of "maidservant" was different back then.)

Is this deception of Jacob by his uncle instant karma for Jacob's deception of both his geriatric dad and his inattentive brother? If so, Jacob will get his chance to even the score in the next chapter of the saga, when he uses a unique breeding trick to outsmart his uncle.

The phrase, "How could you do this to me?" is like a mantra all through the history of this family. Pharaoh says it to Abraham; Abimelech also says it to Abraham; Abimelek says it to Isaac; Esau says it to Jacob; and Jacob says it to Laban. This is like musical chairs—karma on steroids.

Because the Book of Genesis is a compilation of many sources and is so poorly edited, you really have to skip about a lot to follow the plot line. So, in chapter thirty, Rachel still isn't pregnant. There follows an amusing event where she offers to trade her husband, Jacob, for the night, with sister Leah in exchange for some Mandrake plants which Leah's son had found. According to popular folklore, Mandrake was a fertility drug. Here's the story: "One day, during the wheat harvest, Reuben went out and came upon some mandrakes in the field which he brought home to his mother Leah.

Rachel said to Leah, 'Please give me some of your son's mandrakes.' Leah replied, 'Was it not enough for you to take away my husband, that you must now take my son's mandrakes too?' Rachel answered, 'In that case Jacob may lie with you tonight in exchange for your son's mandrakes.' That evening, when Jacob came in from the field, Leah went out to meet him. She said, 'You must have intercourse with me, because I have hired you with my son's mandrakes.' So that night he lay with her."

Jacob had spent twenty years serving Laban; moreover, Rachel had finally birthed a son—Joseph (you remember the kid with the multicolored tunic?) So, Jacob was ready to go home to Canaan. Laban reluctantly agrees but seeks a way to defraud Jacob. They strike a bargain which Laban believes gives him a guaranteed way to optimize his own profit. However, God—ever the schemer—shows Jacob, in a dream, the way to turn the tables on Laban. It involves a complicated breeding process that makes cloning Dolly the sheep look like a grade-school science project. Jacob's experiment is a huge success, but Laban is not a happy camper and his sons (the brothers of Leah and Rachel) complain that Jacob has defrauded their father and stolen their inheritance. Jacob says, "Moi? How, in God's name, could you come up with a weird theory like that!"

Jacob figures it's time to do a runner so, while Laban and his sons are outta town grazing and shearing the sheep, he makes his case to his wives. Here's the dialog: "So Jacob sent for Rachel and Leah to meet him in the field where his flock was. There he said to them: 'I have noticed that your father's attitude toward me is not as it was in the past; but the God of my father has been with me. You know well that with all my strength I served your father; yet your father cheated me and changed my wages ten times. God, however, did not let him do me any harm.'... Rachel and Leah answered him: 'Do we still have an heir's portion in our father's house? Are we not regarded by him as outsiders? He not only sold us; he has even used up the money that he got for us! All the wealth that God took away from our father really belongs to us and our children. So do whatever God has told you.' Jacob proceeded to put his children and wives on camels, and he drove off all his livestock and all the property he had acquired in Paddan-aram, to go to his father Isaac in the land of Canaan."

Note the anachronism of the camels again; Gen 31:17 might just as well have said "Jacob proceeded to put his children and wives in four-wheel-drive SUVs."

Rachel further indulges in what Canon Law calls "occult compensation" —a situation in which a self-perceived victim secretly redresses their loss—by stealing her father's idols (images of the household gods): "Now Laban was away shearing his sheep, and Rachel had stolen her father's household images."

The entourage makes its way across the Euphrates River before Laban and his goons catch up with them. But God warns Laban in a dream to back off. Still, he has to give vent to his sense of offended family values. Here again comes the familiar, "How could you...?" Here it is: "When Laban overtook Jacob, Jacob's tents were pitched in the hill country; Laban also pitched his tents in the hill country of Gilead. Laban said to Jacob, 'How could you hoodwink me and carry off my daughters like prisoners of war? Why did you dupe me by stealing away secretly? You did not tell me! I would have sent you off with joyful singing to the sound of tambourines and harps. You did not even allow me a parting kiss to my daughters and grandchildren! Now what you have done makes no sense." *What a sweet soul.*

They finally make peace and go on their separate ways; Laban back to Haran in Mesopotamia; and Jacob to Canaan and the prospect of confronting his brother Esau.

As it turned out—with lots of Middle Eastern diplomacy that included Jacob using, "my lord" when referring to Esau and "your servant" when speaking of himself, and bowing to the ground seven times in front of Esau, as did his wives and concubines, together with gifts (bribes) of cattle (40 cows and 10 bulls), goats (200 she-goats and 20 he-goats), sheep (200 ewes and 20 rams), camels (30 females and their young) and donkeys (20 female donkeys and 10 male donkeys), and the strategic division of his entourage into two groups travelling miles apart—Jacob was successful.

Esau, proving to be a much less corrupt man than any of the main charac-

ters in Genesis so far, is full of both forgiveness and generosity: "Esau ran to meet him, embraced him, and flinging himself on his neck, kissed him as he wept. Then Esau looked up and saw the women and children and asked, 'Who are these with you?' Jacob answered, 'They are the children with whom God has graciously favored your servant.' Then the maidservants and their children came forward and bowed low; next, Leah and her children came forward and bowed low; lastly, Joseph and Rachel came forward and bowed low. Then Esau asked, 'What did you intend with all those herds that I encountered?' Jacob answered, 'It was to gain my lord's favor.' Esau replied, 'I have plenty; my brother, you should keep what is yours.' 'No, I beg you!' said Jacob. 'If you will do me the favor, accept this gift from me, since to see your face is for me like seeing the face of God—and you have received me so kindly. Accept the gift I have brought you. For God has been generous toward me, and I have an abundance.' Since he urged him strongly, Esau accepted."

However, the crafty and greedy Jacob still has no intention of sharing the "promised land" with Esau.

They have barely arrived in the new land, when a local (Shechem, the son of Hamor, the leader of the region) seizes and rapes Dinah, Leah's daughter. The young man, however, is smitten with Dinah and prevails upon his father to arrange the marriage and pay whatever bride price Jacob demands. Jacob's sons have a different plan. They pretend to go along with this arrangement, provided all the males of the city agree to be circumcised first. Hamor persuades the townsmen to accept this condition, but on day three, as the menfolk are still in pain, the sons of Jacob exact their vengeance. (The fruit doesn't fall far from the tree!) Here's the account: "On the third day, while they were still in pain, two of Jacob's sons, Simeon and Levi, brothers of Dinah, each took his sword, advanced against the unsuspecting city and massacred all the males. After they had killed Hamor and his son Shechem with the sword, they took Dinah from Shechem's house and left. Then the other sons of Jacob followed up the slaughter and sacked the city because their sister had been defiled. They took their sheep, cattle and donkeys, whatever was in the city and in the surrounding country. They carried off all their wealth, their children, and their women, and looted whatever was in the houses."

They seemed to miss the irony in that they had abducted the women of the city (and presumably raped them), kidnapped the children, and slaughtered the innocent men. Jacob was not a happy camper, not because of the murder, kidnapping, rape, and plundering per se, but because, since he was a newcomer to the region, the other tribes might now become a trifle suspicious and hostile: "Jacob said to Simeon and Levi: 'You have brought trouble upon me by making me repugnant to the inhabitants of the land, the Canaanites and the Perizzites. I have so few men that, if these people unite against me and attack me, I and my household will be wiped out.'"

Jacob now decides to formalize his allegiance to the God of Abraham and Isaac, so he orders all of his people to "get rid of the foreign gods among you." *He builds an altar to God in "Bethel" ("the house of God.") The entire household surrenders* "all the foreign gods in their possession and also the rings they had in their ears and Jacob buried the lot under the oak tree that is near Shechem."

Understandably, after the slaughter at Shechem, "a great terror fell upon the surrounding towns." *Jacob, however suffered his own loss; his wife Rachel died giving birth to her second son, Benjamin. While Jacob is grieving her death, Reuben, his firstborn son, is having sex with Bilhah, Rachel's maidservant and Jacob's concubine. Jacob is not amused.*

Isaac was 160 years old when Jacob left home; he is now 180 years of age and ready to die, so Jacob pays a quick visit to the old man whom he had cheated so grievously. In a Hallmark Card ending we read: "his sons Esau and Jacob buried him."

GOOD OLD JOSEPH

Next comes the story of Joseph, the dreamer. He is Jacob's second youngest child—only Benjamin, whose birth caused Rachel's death, is younger. He is a dreamer, but with little common sense; even at age 17, he reports to his siblings and parents dreams in which they all bow down to him. The brothers don't think this is at all cute and, to make matters worse, it's obvious to them that the parents dote on him. In fact, his dad has a special multi-colored tunic made for him.

His jealous brothers finally decide to kill him or sell him into slavery. There follows another story which is a terrible mishmash of several traditions. Once again, the pieces are so badly combined that you really have to pick the account apart phrase by phrase and try to rearrange it in some kind of a logical fashion. That will still give you two contradictory accounts, but at least some kind of flow will have been established.

In brief, the details are as follows: first they throw him into a dry well to die or maybe to be rescued later by Reuben—who wants to save him; or by Judah, who wants to sell him and make a profit on his loss; next they sell him to a group of Ishmaelites—no, they sell him to a group of Midianites—no, the Midianites discover him themselves in the well and sell him down in Egypt—no, the Midianites find him in the well and sell him to the Ishmaelites, for 20 pieces of silver, who then take him to Egypt and resell him (presumably at a profit.)

The sad thing is they're all family! Not just the brothers who killed or sold him, but the Ishmaelites and Midianites also. All three groups have Abraham as their great-granddad, so the current crop of players are all third cousins. Ishmael was Abraham's firstborn and Midian was his son by his second wife, Keturah, whom he married after Sarah died.

The brothers are now faced with breaking the news to their father. Here's what happened: "They took Joseph's tunic, and after slaughtering a goat, dipped the tunic in its blood. Then they sent someone to bring the long ornamented tunic to their father, with the message: 'We found this. See whether it is your son's tunic or not.' He recognized it and exclaimed: 'My son's tunic! A wild beast has devoured him! Joseph has been torn to pieces!' Then Jacob tore his garments, put sackcloth on his loins, and mourned his son many days. Though his sons and daughters tried to console him, he refused all consolation, saying, 'No, I will go down mourning to my son in Sheol.' Thus did his father weep for him. The Midianites, meanwhile, sold Joseph in Egypt to Potiphar, an official of Pharaoh and his chief steward."

Having fabricated the evidence of his death-by-wild-animal, they further compound their crime by employing some kind of hired stooge—who presumably would pretend that he found the tunic himself and came straight to

Jacob—thus allowing the villains to act surprised and devastated when their dad broke the news to them. (I wonder where they learned to lie like that?)

If this were a police case, it would have more holes than a chunk of Swiss cheese. How could an inerrant God get the story so messed up? If it weren't so tragic a tale, you'd split your sides laughing at the antics of modern fundamentalist preachers as they attempt to explain away God's apparent memory lapses.

A STORY OF JUDAH

Judah moves away from the other brothers and defies tradition by marrying a Canaanite woman called Shua who bears him three sons—Er, Onan, and Shelah. Compounding matters, he chooses another "foreign" woman, Tamar, for his son Er to marry. But Er, we are told, greatly offended God, so God killed him. Jacob then gives Onan to Tamar to "raise up children to his dead brother" as the Levirate law demanded. Onan evidently didn't much care for his dead brother, so whenever he had intercourse with Tamar he spilled his seed on the ground. So God offed him too. But Tamar isn't gonna give up; she wants Shelah, but Judah decides to slow the game down. He is fearful that he will lose all of his sons, so he advises Tamar to go back to her dad's house and he'll send her a text when Shelah is old enough to marry. Soon after, Judah's own wife, Shua, dies. Tamar grows impatient and takes matters into her own hands by means of a very interesting ruse. She disguises herself as a harlot and manages to get herself pregnant by an unsuspecting Judah. She gives birth to twin boys—Perez and Zerah.

So by a twist of fate, the covenant, which ultimately in Jewish history was fulfilled in the line of Judah, comes through a Canaanite mother! Interestingly, in the New Testament, the Gospel of Matthew gives a genealogy of Jesus consisting of 42 generations, in which only five women are named, Tamar being the first, followed by Rahab, Ruth, Bathsheba, and Mary. All have some kind of a sexual history attached and the first four are all gentile women.

It seems that in the end, love conquers racism. Even the unfortunate, despised Canaanites got into the family tree of King David, King Solomon and Jesus. If, as Jewish law states, lineage and "Jewishness" come through the mother, then Tamar, Rahab, Ruth, and Bathsheba are the keepers of the covenant and there is hope that even the most divisive of ideas and holy books are, ultimately, no match for life's love affair with life.

JOSEPH IN EGYPT

Joseph is sold to Potipher, the chief steward of the Pharaoh. Potipher's household prospers under Joseph's guidance, so that his master trusts him with everything. However, Potipher's wife continually tries (and fails) to seduce Joseph until finally, in a frustrated rage (hell hath no fury like a woman scorned) she accuses him of an attempted rape, for which he is jailed. Even in prison, however, his organizational skills and integrity win him the admiration of the chief jailer. While imprisoned, he accurately interprets the dreams of two fellow prisoners, both from Pharaoh's household. This is brought to Pharaoh's attention after he himself has had two dreams that none of his sages can figure out. The now ex-prisoner (whose dream Joseph had interpreted while in jail and who has since been restored to his position in Pharaoh's household) suddenly remembers, and Joseph is brought to Pharaoh. He interprets Pharaoh's dreams: there will be seven years of great harvests followed by seven years of drought. He advises Pharaoh to set some wise man in charge of storing and guarding the excess food in preparation for the hungry years. Guess which wise man Pharaoh selects? (Ah! Have you heard this story before?) Yes, it is Joseph himself.

Joseph, at age 30, is made the second most important person in Egypt, and Pharaoh gives him, in marriage, Asenath, (the daughter of the priest of Heliopolis) who bears him two sons.

The famine, when it arrives, also affects the land of Canaan, so Jacob sends his sons to Egypt to buy grain. Joseph figures out who they are, but strings them along in a series of tests, the final one being a contrived theft of his silver drinking goblet that was "found" in Benjamin's bag. Joseph, we are told, used this goblet for divination! There follows the longest speech in the entire Book of Genesis, in which a very passionate Judah offers to become a slave in place of Benjamin.

In an extraordinarily beautiful and moving passage, Joseph reveals to them who he really is. In a splendid demonstration of seeing the silver lining in every cloud—or the divine purpose in every apparent misfortune—he interprets his brothers' evil actions in selling him into slavery as the preparation by God for saving the entire family from death-by-famine. The brothers are "gob-smacked" (to use a Scottish idiom) and both Joseph and Pharaoh enthusiastically encourage them to go back to Canaan, collect their father, wives, kids, and livestock and hurry back to Egypt, where they will be lavishly provided for, because, as Joseph had advised them, there are still another five years of famine ahead.

In another version of the story, Joseph does not inform Pharaoh of the situation until Jacob's party of seventy people and their flocks actually arrive in Egypt. Joseph counsels his family as follows: "Joseph then said to his brothers and his father's household: 'I will go up and inform Pharaoh, telling him: 'My brothers and my father's household, whose home is in the land of Canaan, have come to me. The men are shepherds, having been owners of livestock; and they have brought with them their flocks and herds, as well as everything else they own.' So when Pharaoh summons you and asks what your occupation is, you must answer, 'We your servants, like our ancestors, have been owners of livestock from our youth until now,' in order that you may stay in the region of Goshen, since all shepherds are abhorrent to the Egyptians."

Jacob lives for seventeen years in Egypt and dies at age one hundred forty-seven, but gives strict instructions that he is to be buried in the land of Canaan with his ancestors. He makes Joseph swear to this.

On a sour note, one that really spoils Joseph's heretofore pristine performance, he calculatingly disenfranchises the entire Egyptian population over the course of the final years of the famine. Here's the story: "Since there was no food in all the land because of the extreme severity of the famine, and the lands of Egypt and Canaan were languishing from hunger, Joseph gathered in, as payment for the grain that they were buying, all the money that was to be found in Egypt and Canaan, and he put it in Pharaoh's house. When all the money in Egypt and Canaan was spent, all the Egyptians came to Joseph, pleading, 'Give us food! Why should we perish in front of you? For our money is gone.' 'Give me your livestock if your money is gone,' replied Joseph. 'I will give you food in return for your livestock.' So they brought their livestock to Joseph, and he gave them food in exchange for their horses, their flocks of sheep and herds of cattle, and their donkeys. Thus he supplied them with food in exchange for all their livestock in that year. That year ended, and they came to him in the next one and said: 'We cannot hide from my lord that, with our money spent and our livestock made over to my lord, there is nothing left to put at my lord's disposal except our bodies and our land. Why should we and our land perish before your very eyes? Take us and our land in exchange for food, and we will become Pharaoh's slaves and our land his property; only give us seed, that we may survive and not perish, and that our land may not turn into a waste."

"So Joseph acquired all the land of Egypt for Pharaoh. Each of the Egyptians sold his field, since the famine weighed heavily upon them. Thus the land passed over to Pharaoh, and the people were reduced to slavery, from one end of Egypt's territory to the other. Only the priests' lands Joseph did not acquire. Since the priests had a fixed allowance from Pharaoh and lived off the allowance Pharaoh had granted them, they did not have to sell their land. Joseph told the people: 'Now that I have acquired you and your land for Pharaoh, here is your seed for sowing the land. But when the harvest is in, you must give a fifth of it to Pharaoh, while you keep four-fifths as seed for your fields and as food for yourselves and your households and as food for your children.' 'You have saved our lives!' they answered. 'We have found favor with my lord; now we will be Pharaoh's slaves.' Thus Joseph made it a statute for the land of Egypt, which is still in force, that a fifth of its produce should go to Pharaoh. Only the land of the priests did not pass over to Pharaoh."

It's really upsetting to me to read that the enslaved people regard Joseph as their savior. He has stripped them of their money, livestock, land, personhood, and earnings, yet they bow to him and are grateful? Of course, this has been repeated throughout human history. And it continues to follow this pattern: first, the oligarchy creates an artificial crisis—often by means of a false flag operation. Then the mass media—who are owned by the oligarchy —hype the crisis and suggest solutions. Like fools, the populace hollers for these solutions to be implemented, and finally the oligarchy obliges. Of course, both the crises and solutions have been planned ahead of time by the oligarchy (which then appears as the savior), bowing to public pressure while "reluctantly" stripping away human and constitutional rights in order to deal more effectively with the crisis and institute the solutions for which the populace called. I guess that explains Joseph's story, at least in part.

PASSOVER

Ostensibly, the great Jewish feast of Pesach is a celebration of the escape of the Hebrews from four hundred and thirty years of slavery by the Egyptians (which is in complete contradiction to the story of Genesis 47:13-26). It's ironic that Joseph, who enters Egypt as a slave, becomes the second most powerful man in the country (behind the Pharaoh), and winds up enslaving all of the Egyptians to his boss! And, of course, as part of Pharaoh's "property," the Hebrews also found themselves enslaved. So, don't blame Egypt for enslaving the Israelites, blame Joseph for being the mastermind behind the scheme. In fact, at the time of the writing of Genesis, the author says, "You have saved our lives," they said. "May we find favor in the eyes of our lord; we will be in bondage to Pharaoh." *So Joseph established it as a law concerning land in Egypt—still in force when Genesis was being written—that a fifth of the produce belongs to Pharaoh. What a legacy to leave.*

THE DEATHS OF JACOB AND JOSEPH

Jacob now gathers all his sons around his deathbed to give them his final "blessings." He begins by cursing Reuben, his firstborn, for the sin of having sex with Jacob's own concubine. Warming to his task, he then goes on to curse his next two sons—Simeon and Levi—because they murdered the men of Shechem and "at their whim they maimed oxen." (One of the signs of a psychopath is the torturing of animals.) He now comes to Judah and promises that the scepter will never pass from him. Apart from calling Joseph "a prince among his brothers," he offers only ho-hum blessings to the rest of the boys.

Given Joseph's position in Egypt, the physicians spend forty days embalming Jacob's body. Then a huge retinue, including all the high officials in Pharaoh's own household, processes to Canaan to bury him beside Abraham and Sarah, Isaac and Rebekah, and Jacob's first wife, Leah.

Joseph, himself, dies at one hundred and ten with instructions that, though he will be buried in Egypt, he wants his bones to eventually be re-interred with his ancestors in Canaan.

And so ends the Book of Genesis.

Michael Newsom had been doing some research of his own and was ready to give the jury a sense of the greater context for Dermot O'Sullivan's stories. He took a cue from his opponent Kayla Goldstein by delivering a succinct monologue to the jury.

Pacing the slate floor in front of the jury box, Newsome began his pitch. *Apart from the events in Pharaonic Egypt, neither the actors in, the writers of, nor even the God of Genesis appear to have any knowledge of the wider world—not the "Americas" (I don't want to be guilty of an anachronism myself!) which had their own advanced cultures at the time, Asia (which had very sophisticated cultures in China and India), or even their own immediate neighborhood of the Middle East (with well-established empires in Akkadia and Sumeria that predated Abraham by some two thousand years).*

And, apart from a few vicious global interventions (remember Him kicking us all out of the garden, the worldwide extermination of life in the global flood, and the mean-spirited manipulated confusion of Babel), God seems content to just regularly select among his children, ignoring the vast bulk of them and choosing his favorites for no apparent virtues of theirs. The "chosen" continue to demonstrate the full range of human vices, with fractured families and sibling deceit well to the fore. Apart from some fairly barbaric customs, there was, as yet, no overarching moral code. Further to the East, the Code of Hammurabi (established since 1754 BCE) was a compendium of two hundred and eighty-two laws, with scaled punishments. It's the first to use the phrase, "an eye for an eye, a tooth for a tooth"—meaning the punishment must be commensurate with the crime. God would have done well to have embraced that concept, as would the humans we have met to date in the book of Genesis. The Code of Hammurabi meted out punishments depending upon the social status of the slave versus the free man or woman. Some six hundred years after Abraham, Moses would introduce this lex talionis *("law of the talon") into Israelite law.*

Every culture, with or without assistance from "civilized" societies, has arrived at the same basic values—for example, respect for the gods, parents, family, property, truth, life, and sexuality. And all of them – including God's chosen ones – have regularly flouted them.

All in all, the God of Genesis emerges as a portrait painted by several artists on the same piece of canvas. He is petty, petulant and given to uncontrollable fits of rage.

Stepping toward the jury, Newsome continued, "*Ladies and gentlemen of the jury, the Prosecution would like to offer a synopsis of the first volume of the journals of the accused. First, a look at Yahweh's followers and devotees whom, presumably, He offers for our admiration, and second, a precis of and a commentary on His own self-reported behavior.*"

With that, Michael Newsome flicked on a screen upon which a PowerPoint presentation showed the lineages depicted in the book of Genesis.

Here's a list of Yahweh's early followers, Newsome offered, stepping aside. *Will you please walk us through the cast of characters, Dr. O'Sullivan?*

Dr. O'Sullivan pounced at the opportunity with a cat-like leap from the stand to the center of the room that revealed a degree of spryness that defied his age.

Referencing the screen with a laser pointer, O'Sullivan whisked through the list in a matter of minutes:

Here's a quick synopsis of Yahweh's followers' shenanigans:

1. *Adam, who for all his alleged importance in the whole story, has only a tiny speaking part, in which he eschews all responsibility for his actions, blaming all crimes on his rib-mate.*
2. *Eve, "mother of all life," who listened to a talking snake and persuaded Adam to enter into a deal in which they lost all humanity's treasures.*
3. *Cain, who committed the first murder and then magically married a non-existent woman.*
4. *Lamech, the first polygamist and first serial killer.*
5. *Noah, the master shipbuilder and drunkard, who cursed his*

unborn grandchild, Canaan, condemning him and his progeny to perpetual slavery.

6. *Abraham, a deceiver and master opportunist, who lied his way into riches.*
7. *Sarah, Abraham's equal and partner in crime, who spitefully insisted on the banishment of a young mother and her son into the desert without any kind of provisions.*
8. *Isaac and Rebekah, who repeated the winning scheme of Abraham and Sarah with their lies and deceit.*
9. *Rachel, for offering her husband, Isaac, to her sister, Leah, as a sex prize, in exchange for a plant with alleged aphrodisiac properties.*
10. *Jacob, for twice defrauding his brother Esau of his rights and blessing in a scheme created and orchestrated by his mother, Rebekah.*
11. *The sons of Jacob for (a) the wholesale slaughter, rape, and pillage of Shechem and its inhabitants; and (b) for planning and executing the "disappearance" of their own brother, Joseph.*
12. *Joseph, who initially is presented as a forgiving, spiritual man only to have his greatest achievement be the enslavement of the people of Egypt by creating a bureaucratic system which sequentially deprived them of their money, livestock, land, and personhood and made them the property of the Pharaoh.*
13. *In the midst of this bunch of very fallible and not very loveable exemplars, the one standout, in my opinion, is the very unlikely hero Esau. Defrauded twice by his brother Jacob, abandoned by his father, and the innocent, unsuspecting victim of his mother's vicious plans, he finds forgiveness in his heart, and cries genuine tears of joy on his brother's shoulder after Jacob returned from twenty years in exile in Mesopotamia. Moreover, he protests strongly that he really doesn't need Jacob's gifts (bribes) as he himself has all he really needs. (What a contrast to Jacob's acquisitiveness!) If God were any judge of character, He'd have made His covenant with Esau.*

And now, to the chief accused: Yahweh. "By my friends, you will know me." That alone should alert you to who this God really is. His list of indictments is rather long—so you might want to take notes...

But the Prosecution interrupted him mid-sentence. *Thank you, Dr. O'Sullivan, for this helpful summary of the crimes and misdemeanors memorialized in Yahweh's book of Genesis. Perhaps we can save the rest for tomorrow's testimony.*

Whatever you say, Michael! O'Sullivan said with a smile, offering a deferential bow to the judge as he glided back to his seat.

Michael Newsome strode to the center of the room and confidently offered this brief closing:

Dear jurors, thank you for your patient receptivity as we have begun this trial of the century—perhaps the trial of many centuries—in which the God of Abraham is finally being held accountable for His crimes against humanity. I need to warn you that His most egregious crimes have not yet been offered as evidence. Brace yourselves for what lies ahead. It won't be pretty.

Newsome nodded to the judge, who gave the gavel a quick whack as he bellowed, *"Court adjourned until 9:00 a.m. tomorrow. Rest well!"*

EXODUS: THE ISRAELITES IN EGYPT

The jurors arrived early the next day to beat the crowd of people who lined up for an opportunity to sit in the gallery, more than half of whom were turned away due to lack of space. News reporters, who were allowed to stand behind the jury and in the hall outside the courtroom, lined every corridor of the building. Michael Newsome had risen at dawn to review his strategy for the day, gulped several cups of black coffee, and donned his best suit for day two of the biggest trial of his career. Kayla Goldsmith woke at dawn as well, as was her habit, so she could give her cats plenty of attention and take her dog for a five-mile run before heading to court. Her rosy cheeks glowed as she entered the courtroom in her usual professional but simple attire, carrying a slim brief case that held the one file she would present in Defense of Yahweh. When the judge entered the room at 8:59 a.m. everyone was in place and ready to begin.

Judge Grossman welcomed the jury and invited the Prosecution to continue presenting his case.

Good morning, Judge, jurors, and witnesses to this extraordinary trial, Michael Newsome began. *I'm guessing after yesterday's presentation of evidence you have seen with your own two eyes that the characters in the book of Genesis don't do much in the way of exonerating their God. But the question I find myself asking is this: "How did I not see all of this treachery years ago for what it was?" Before we answer that question, I think it behooves us to bring further evidence before the court and continue to question just who exactly this Yahweh character is. Today's evidence will be drawn from the second volume of the accused's journals: the book of Exodus.*

The Prosecution would like to call Dr. O'Sullivan to the stand.

O'Sullivan's sparkling blue eyes flickered a barely perceptible wink as he placed his hand on the book in which he had been immersed throughout his illustrious career and swore an oath to honesty.

Thank you, Professor O'Sullivan, for your thoughtful and thorough exegesis yesterday, the prosecution offered with an air of formality. *Will you please continue?*

Certainly, Michael! O'Sullivan responded with glee.

The book of Exodus consists of four main parts:

1. The Israelites in Egypt, chapters 1:1 – 12:36

2. The Exodus and the journey to Sinai, chapters 12:37 – 18:27

3. The Covenant on Sinai, chapters 19:1 – 24:18

4. The Dwelling and its furnishings, chapters 25:1 – 40:38

We learn of the death of Joseph at the end of the book of Genesis, but over the next few generations the Israelites flourish and increase in numbers. Then a new pharaoh worries that since they don't assimilate, but remain a separate people, the Israelites might ally with an enemy of Egypt. So, he determines to subjugate them through forced labor. They still increase in numbers, so a new strategy is adopted in which the pharaoh commands the two Egyptian midwives Shiphrah and Puah to kill all of the male Israelite children they delivered.

It is highly unlikely that there were only two midwives for all of Egypt, and even less likely that the Israelites wouldn't have their own midwives. Shiphrah and Puah, however, refuse to cooperate, so Pharaoh sends out a new decree to all of his subjects that they should throw all the male Israelite children into the river. When Moses is born, his mother hides him for three months and then puts him in a papyrus basket, sealed with bitumen, and floats him off down the Nile where Pharaoh's daughter finds him and adopts him. She is tricked in the process by Moses's sister, who offers to provide a Hebrew woman to act as wet nurse. So, Moses's mother gets paid by the princess for suckling her own baby.

Moses grew up, presumably, in Pharaoh's household, but self-identified as a Hebrew. So, when he saw an Egyptian striking a Hebrew, he killed the Egyptian and hid the body in the sand. This was to be the first in a long line of murders committed by Moses. The incident is reported to Pharaoh, who intends to execute Moses for the crime, so Moses flees and is given sanctuary and hospitality by a Midianite priest variously called "Reuel" and "Jethro." He is given Jethro's daughter Zipporah in marriage and has sons by her.

*He is now reduced to tending his father-in-law's flocks. This must have represented a huge loss of status for an Egyptian "prince" because, as we learned in Genesis 46:33-34—*O'Sullivan paused while flipping open his personal copy of the Good Book—*"All shepherds are abhorrent to the Egyptians." One day, Moses has an encounter with a burning bush that tells him to remove his sandals, for he is on holy ground. God gives an impassioned speech about His care and plans for His chosen people: "'I am the God of your father,' he continued, 'the God of Abraham, the God of Isaac, and the God of Jacob.' Moses hid his face, for he was afraid to look at God. But the LORD said: 'I have witnessed the affliction of my people in Egypt and have heard their cry against their taskmasters, so I know well what they are suffering. Therefore I have come down to rescue them from the power of the Egyptians and lead them up from that land into a good and spacious land, a land flowing with milk and honey, the country of the Canaanites, the Hittites, the Amorites, the Perizzites, the Girgashites, the Hivites and the Jebusites. Now indeed the outcry of the Israelites has reached me, and I have seen how the Egyptians are oppressing them. Now, go! I am sending you to Pharaoh to bring my people, the Israelites, out of Egypt."*

Strange that it took him 430 years to get off his tuchus and intervene!

The phrase, "a land flowing with milk and honey" seems to have been a stock phrase learned in marketing class by gods who wanted to impress prospective clients. This one repeats it several times, like a salesman with a catchy pitch. And once more, the Canaanites, the Hittites, the Amorites, the Perizzites, the Girgashites, the Hivites, and the Jebusites are regarded as just temporary placeholders.

Moses, however, isn't one bit interested in being God's envoy to Pharaoh. Apart from being wanted on a murder rap, he has no idea who this god is. God says in reply, "Ehiye ashir ehiye," *which, you may recall translates to the future tense: "I will be who I will be." This answer still doesn't make sense to Moses, so God clarifies,* "I am the God of your ancestors, the God of Abraham, Isaac, and Jacob." *Remember, at the time of Moses and for some seven hundred years afterwards, the Hebrews were not monotheists but simply practiced monolatry—the worship of one particular god in the pantheon of competing divinities.*

God has a two-part plan. First, the Hebrews are to pretend they simply want to go on a three-day's journey into the desert in order to offer sacrifice to their God. Phase two: God knows that Pharaoh ain't that dumb, so He then plans to "smite Egypt by doing all kinds of wondrous deeds." I don't know about you, ladies and gentlemen of the jury, but wondrous deeds is hardly how I would describe ten plagues that included the wholesale slaughter of the firstborn of the Egyptians—both human and animal.

Moses reluctantly agrees and gets permission from Jethro to go back to Egypt with his wife and sons. Jethro sends him off in peace. But God is still his irrational, impulsive self: "On the journey, at a place where they spent the night, the LORD came upon Moses and sought to put him to death. But Zipporah took a piece of flint and cut off her son's foreskin and, touching his feet, she said, 'Surely you are a spouse of blood to me.' So God let Moses alone. At that time she said, 'A spouse of blood,' in regard to the circumcision." *God couldn't have told Moses, at the burning bush, "...by the way, I need you to circumcise your son"?*

After hearing Moses's request for a three-day retreat in the desert to worship their God, Pharaoh refuses and attributes their request to the Hebrews having too much leisure time. So, he doubles their workload.

God is now taking credit and boasting about His mighty power. He "hardens Pharaoh's heart" so that He may have an excuse to deploy His weapons of mass destruction. So, why is it Pharaoh's fault if God intention-

ally and gleefully makes him obstinate? It's like a father taunting his son, so that he may punish the kid's reaction with further abuse.

God now indulges His sadism in a display of plagues. First, He turns the rivers and all the waters of Egypt into blood, so that the fish die and the people have nothing to drink. Second come the frogs—getting into everything —beds, ovens... Third come the gnats; fourth, the flies; fifth, a pestilence that killed all of the Egyptian livestock: "All the livestock of the Egyptians died, but not one animal belonging to the Israelites died." *Sixth, boils that will affect humans and animals. God seems to have forgotten that He had already killed all of the livestock. Why waste boils on already-dead beasts? Seventh, hailstones*: "At this time tomorrow, therefore, I am going to rain down such fierce hail as there has never been in Egypt from the day it was founded up to the present. Therefore, order your livestock and whatever else you have in the open fields to be brought to a place of safety. Whatever human being or animal is found in the fields and is not brought to shelter will die when the hail comes down upon them. Those of Pharaoh's servants who feared the word of the LORD hurried their servants and their livestock off to shelter. But those who did not pay attention to the word of the LORD left their servants and their livestock in the fields." *God seems to have already forgotten that He has wiped out the livestock a few days earlier. Number eight, locusts who ate all the greens and veggies. Number nine, three days of total darkness; and then number ten, the pièce de résistance, God kills the firstborn:* "Moses then said, 'Thus says the LORD: About midnight I will go forth through Egypt. Every firstborn in the land of Egypt will die, from the firstborn of Pharaoh who sits on his throne to the first-born of the slave-girl who is at the handmill, as well as all the first-born of the animals.'" *Note that the animals are now being killed for the fourth time! Even the cats must be feeling anxious at this stage. (Weren't cats supposed to be worshipped in Egypt?)*

To commemorate this slaughter, the great festival of Pesach (the Passover) is instituted, so that the angel of death, as he murders the Egyptians, knows which households to spare. This, of course, should have been unnecessary, because since the time of Jacob and Joseph, the Hebrews had lived separately from Egyptians in Goshen, a district reserved only for them. Moreover, throughout the account of the plagues we are told repeatedly that none of them were visited upon the Hebrews or their territory. Maybe this latest angel of death was a trainee and liable to screw up.

"And so at midnight the LORD struck down every firstborn in the land of Egypt, from the firstborn of Pharaoh sitting on his throne to the firstborn of the prisoner in the dungeon, as well as all the first-born of the animals. Pharaoh arose in the night, he and all his servants and all the Egyptians; and there was loud wailing throughout Egypt, for there was not a house without its dead." *Just imagine, Judge, a typical Egyptian multigenerational family consisting of grandparents, parents, and grandkids. This last plague meant that in some households there were now three dead bodies. Is this the God you worship? Really?*

To compound matters, throughout this entire saga, another mantra is chanted, "But the Lord made Pharaoh obstinate." Continual taunting, leading to more obstinacy, which in turn leads to more abuse. What a dad!

And then this Passover festival is to be enshrined as the preeminent feast in the Hebrew calendar. It's the equivalent of August 6th becoming the most important celebration in the USA's calendar, in honor of the 1945 slaughter of 192,020 residents of Hiroshima, who were either killed instantly or died from radiation and other aftermath effects.

And a wee note on Exodus 12:15, which says, "For seven days you must eat unleavened bread. From the very first day you will have your houses clear of all leaven. For whoever eats leavened bread from the first day to the seventh will be cut off from Israel." *The term "cut off from Israel" is used frequently throughout the Torah and can mean a variety of punishments, from excommunication of the offender from the Israelite community, the premature death of the offender, the eventual eradication of the offender's posterity, and finally the loss by the offender of all ancestral holdings.*

I have found, as I have regularly attended Pesach with Jewish friends—in spite of Exodus 12:43 ("The LORD said to Moses and Aaron: This is the Passover statute. No foreigner may eat of it")—*that the modern prayer books emphasize liberation of all peoples from all forms of oppression, and not the fictitious slaughter of Egyptians 3,750 years ago. As I will point out repeatedly throughout this section, these are teaching stories meant to consol-*

idate and inspire much later generations of Jews who were living in real exile or suffering under occupation. I have found the very same motifs, heroes, heroines, villains, battles, and slaughters in my own Celtic mythology. They are the only recourse of oppressed peoples. Even more powerful than the experience of freedom is the dream of freedom. "Free" people frequently fail to exercise the citizen duties of a democracy, whereas the occupied celebrate its possibility with song and dance, with music and stories. Newly freed democratic populations have more than a 90% turnout at the voting booths, while "old" democracies have about 40%.

Everyone in the courtroom held their breath as Dr. O'Sullivan paused, took a deep breath, and delivered this final thought:

These stories are archetypes designed to help us navigate the minefield of incarnation. As long as we interpret them in this context they will continue to inspire us. They are the pep talks delivered by the coach in the locker room before the big game to pump us up for the fray. But the opponents of the day are not our enemies. The challenge simply offers us the opportunity to demonstrate and improve our skills.

Thank you for your thorough analysis of the book of Exodus, Professor O'Sullivan, the prosecutor said as he approached the bench.

Hold on there, Michael! O'Sullivan barked. *The train hasn't even left the station!*

Pardon me, Professor, Newsome demurred. *Please continue.*

Hold on to your hats, folks. They don't call this the book of Exodus for nothin'! O'Sullivan said with a smile.

THE EXODUS AND THE JOURNEY TO SINAI

Dermot O'Sullivan leaned forward toward the microphone hovering in front of him on its flexible gooseneck stand and continued telling the story of the Exodus—his voice barely above a whisper—as if gathering his listeners around a campfire. *Here's what the Good Book says about our roving forebears:* "The Israelites set out from Rameses for Succoth, about six hundred thousand men on foot, not counting the children. A crowd of mixed ancestry also went up with them, with livestock in great abundance, both flocks and herds." *As is typical of the times, the females are not even mentioned, and neither kids nor women are counted. So, at a conservative estimate we are talking about perhaps two million people. For some strange reason the Egyptians, who were fastidious bean counters, make no mention of either the Exodus nor the plagues recounted in the Bible anywhere in their record keeping. The reason, of course, is that the Exodus never happened.*

As that radical statement floated from the mouth of a Biblical scholar, you could have heard a pin drop in the courtroom. After a pregnant pause, O'Sullivan continued.

As a reminder of the death of the first-born of the Egyptians and their beasts, the Hebrews are now commanded to consecrate every first-born male child and sacrifice every first-born animal, "You will dedicate to the LORD every newborn that opens the womb; and every firstborn male of your animals will belong to the LORD. Every the firstborn of a donkey you will ransom with a sheep. If you do not ransom it, you will break its neck. Every human firstborn of your sons you must ransom." *Having acquired a great love of roasting flesh after the Noah flood, God seems to be providing for His addiction in perpetuity. Meanwhile He shape-shifts, in the best Shamanistic fashion, in order to guide the Hebrews as a pillar of cloud by day and a pillar of fire by night.*

Leaning toward the jury, O'Sullivan quipped, *"Having survived some recent devastating wildfires, I'd be more inclined to go in the direction opposite to the fire and smoke!*

Not content with the devastation of the ten plagues culminating in the slaughter of the firstborns, God now has another plan in which He will once again harden Pharaoh's heart so that he regrets letting the Hebrews go and decides to give chase. And once again God has devised a scheme to murder even more of the Egyptians. Three more times it is mentioned that God hardens the heart of Pharaoh, who now personally leads his own troops into the sea that Moses has miraculously parted. According to the story, not a single Egyptian survived: "As the water flowed back, it covered the chariots and the horsemen. Of all Pharaoh's army which had followed the Israelites into the sea, not even one escaped. But the Israelites had walked on dry land through the midst of the sea, with the water as a wall to their right and to their left. Thus the LORD saved Israel on that day from the power of Egypt. When Israel saw the Egyptians lying dead on the seashore and saw the great power that the LORD had shown against Egypt, the people feared the LORD. They believed in the LORD and in Moses his servant."

But isn't it strange that the meticulous historical records of Egypt fail to mention the death-by-drowning of Pharaoh and his army? According to the Biblical record, the Hebrews celebrated their delivery and the slaughter with music, dancing and song, led by Moses's sister Miriam: "Then the prophet Miriam, Aaron's sister, took a tambourine in her hand, while all the women went out after her with tambourines, dancing; and she responded to them: 'Sing to the LORD, for he is gloriously triumphant; horse and chariot he has cast into the sea.'" *And hidden in plain sight is the evidence that they are still polytheists:* "Who is like you among the gods, O LORD?" (Ex 15:11)

God feeds the Israelites with manna which they are to gather off the desert floor each morning. He commands them to only gather enough for one day, else it will stink and become full of maggots; but in another miracle, on the morning of the sixth day they are to collect enough for two days, since manna will not be available on the Sabbath. Here, God Himself is obeying His own command to do no servile work on the Sabbath. Obviously sprinkling manna on the desert floor was regarded as servile work, as was the gathering of it. This injunction about manna and the Sabbath is repeated several times in Exodus chapter 16. But in historical reality, the laws governing the Sabbath were not enacted until 600 years after Moses's alleged lifetime. The same debate was still going on 600 years later, when Jesus (who "fulfilled" the law by "breaking" it) vigorously defended the actions of his disciples who harvested grain with their bare hands on the Sabbath because they were hungry. So, I guess it's not surprising that these issues would be projected back in time onto people who had actually not even encountered the subject.

Throughout this miraculous "escape" from Egypt, the Hebrews constantly complained. On seeing Pharaoh's army in pursuit, they asked Moses, "Were there no graves in Egypt for us to be buried in? You had to drag us out here to die in the desert." *Then, before the manna appeared, they complained about having to abandon the "fleshpots" of Egypt where they had plenty of food. And when there was a water shortage, they complained:* "in their thirst for water, the people grumbled against Moses, saying, 'Why then did you bring us up out of Egypt? To have us die of thirst with our children and our livestock?'"

I imagine Moses sometimes wished he hadn't given up his day job herding Jethro's flocks, but this section of the Exodus story ends on that sour note.

THE COVENANT ON SINAI

Now God is ready to make a new covenant, but as usual, He first needs to put "the fear of God" into everyone, humans and animals alike: "The LORD said to Moses: I am coming to you now in a dense cloud, so that when the people hear me speaking with you, they will also remain faithful to you. When Moses, then, had reported the response of the people to the LORD, the LORD said to Moses: Go to the people and have them sanctify themselves today and tomorrow. Have them wash their garments and be ready for the third day; for on the third day the LORD will come down on Mount Sinai in the sight of all the people. Set limits for the people all around, saying: Take care not to go up the mountain, or even to touch its edge. All who touch the mountain must be put to death. No hand shall touch them, but they must be stoned to death or killed with arrows. Whether human being or beast, they must not be allowed to live. Only when the ram's horn sounds may they go up on the mountain."

As God delivers His ten commandments to Moses, the very first one acknowledges that, though other gods exist, the Hebrews must worship only Him, because: "I, the LORD, your God, am a jealous God, inflicting punishment for their ancestors' wickedness on the children of those who hate me, down to the third and fourth generation; but showing love down to the thousandth generation of those who love me and keep my commandments." *This, of course, doesn't really make sense. Let me unpack it for you, Ladies and Gentlemen of the jury: If Tom keeps God's commandments, then the next 1,000 generations (roughly 30,000 years) are guaranteed God's love. So, then, does it not matter what Tom's great-granddaughter does? Does she incur no guilt? However, if Dick is a sinner, then his newborn great-granddaughter is already guilty? What if Harry is a sinner, but his wife, Judy, is God-fearing, what happens then to their great-granddaughter?*

And, as a little corollary to the list of commandments, He makes sure He's still gonna get His meat supply: "An altar of earth make for me, and sacrifice upon it your burnt offerings and communion sacrifices, your sheep and your oxen. In every place where I cause my name to be invoked I will come to you and bless you." *It's like having a standing order at the local butcher's shop.*

At this stage, God puts more thought into the issue of slavery: "When you purchase a Hebrew slave, he is to serve you for six years, but in the seventh year he shall leave as a free person without any payment. If he comes into service alone, he shall leave alone; if he comes with a wife, his wife shall leave with him. But if his master gives him a wife and she bears him sons or daughters, the woman and her children belong to her master and the man shall leave alone. If, however, the slave declares, 'I love my master and my wife and children; I will not leave as a free person,' his master shall bring him to God and there, at the door or doorpost, he shall pierce his ear with an awl, thus keeping him as his slave forever. When a man sells his daughter as a slave, she shall not go free as male slaves do. But if she displeases her master, who had designated her for himself, he shall let her be redeemed. He has no right to sell her to a foreign people, since he has broken faith with her. If he designates her for his son, he shall treat her according to the ordinance for daughters. If he takes another wife, he shall not withhold her food, her clothing, or her conjugal rights. If he does not do these three things for her, she may leave without cost, without any payment."

God would have been one helluva lawyer! O'Sullivan blurted with a wink toward Michael Newsome.

Next, God begins to assign the death penalty to a whole range of "crimes": murder, striking a parent, women who practice sorcery, kidnapping, cursing a parent, killing a slave—but only if the slave dies immediately; if he/she survives for a day or two, it doesn't count as murder "since the slave is his own property."

Oxen beware! If an ox gores and kills somebody, the ox must be stoned to death and its meat must not be eaten. (Guilt by osmosis avoided?) If, however, the ox has a rap sheet and gored others in the past, then a fatal goring means both the ox and its owner must be killed.

And here, the new covenant borrows the Lex Talionis from the Code of Hammurabi: "You shall give life for life, eye for eye, tooth for tooth, hand for hand, foot for foot, burn for burn, wound for wound, stripe for stripe." *More than half of the laws which are designated as "the book of the covenant" are borrowed from cuneiform laws of the ancient Middle East.*

As a reward for keeping all of these laws, He once more promises: "My angel will go before you and bring you to the Amorites, Hittites, Perizzites, Canaanites, Hivites and Jebusites; and I will wipe them out," *while warning once more against following other gods, whose altars they must "ecumenically" destroy:* "Therefore, you shall not bow down to their gods and serve them, nor shall you act as they do; rather, you must demolish them and smash their sacred stones."

He then goes on to make some more wild promises: "no woman in your land will be barren or miscarry." *I'd like to see a demographic study on that claim. And He promises that the Israelites will take ownership of the Middle East from the Arabian Peninsula north to the Mediterranean and eastwards to Mesopotamia:* "I will set your boundaries from the Red Sea to the sea of the Philistines, and from the wilderness to the Euphrates; all who dwell in this land I will hand over to you and you shall drive them out before you." *Even under David and Solomon, the kingdom didn't come anywhere near that. And, of course, all of these promises are contingent upon: "You shall not make a covenant with them or their gods."*

THE DWELLING AND ITS FURNISHINGS

The next seven chapters of Exodus are devoted to minute details, given by God to Moses on Mount Sinai, about how to make the Ark of the Covenant, the menorah, the table for the "shew bread," the Tabernacle, the Tent Cloth and its veils, the altar for burnt offerings, the court of the Tabernacle, the making of oil for lamps, the sacred vestments for the priests, the altar of incense, the bronze ablution basin and the preparation of spicy incense (with a warning that anyone who makes such incense for his own enjoyment must be "cut off from his people"— *God doesn't want to share His stash of personal perfumes with anybody), as well as details of the ordination rites for priesthood involving the slaughter of bulls and rams and lambs. It is a very complex and voluminous set of instructions, all given to Moses on the mountaintop, where the only writing "tablets" were chunks of rock. So, either Moses had an eidetic memory, or he came down the mountain with a whole lot of stone notes.*

But the Ten Commandments aren't the only laws God foisted upon His people. By Exodus chapter 31, He's back to Sabbath laws. And the punishment for breaking these laws? You guessed it—death: "Therefore, you must keep the Sabbath for it is holiness for you. Whoever desecrates it shall be put to death. If anyone does work on that day, that person must be cut off from the people. Six days there are for doing work, but the seventh day is the sabbath of complete rest, holy to the LORD. Anyone who does work on the sabbath day shall be put to death."

Finally, God is finished laying down the law and giving specs for His own worship. Then He inscribes two stone tablets—a ten-point precis of the covenant—with His own finger.

Alas, all is not well down at base camp. After waiting for Moses for forty days, the crowd decided that Moses must be dead. It doesn't take long for Aaron to agree to their request for a new god, so he fashions a golden calf from their earrings. The admiring memory-impaired crowd shout out, "these are your gods, Israel, who brought you up from the land of Egypt." *And they began to eat, drink and be merry. When you do the calculations, the Israelites haven't really known this Yahweh character for more than a couple of months. For four hundred and thirty years He had been missing, then He's back claiming to be their ancestral god. It takes Moses only a few weeks to dialog with the pharaoh and act as the instrument of the plagues, and then they leave Egypt. They have only been in the desert for about six weeks at this stage and then Moses goes missing. So, can you really blame them for wanting a more familiar, available god?*

Meanwhile, up top, God, whose hearing is quite acute, is not a happy camper. For years He has been calling the Israelites "my people," but now, suddenly, He insists that they are Moses's people and He plans to wipe them all out and start over with Moses leading a new crop of people. "Then the LORD said to Moses: Go down at once because your people, whom you brought out of the land of Egypt, have acted corruptly. They have quickly turned aside from the way I commanded them, making for themselves a molten calf and bowing down to it, sacrificing to it and crying out, 'These are your gods, Israel, who brought you up from the land of Egypt!' I have seen this people, how stiff-necked they are, continued the LORD to Moses. Let me alone, then, that my anger may burn against them to consume them. Then I will make of you a great nation." *(Déjà vu?) Isn't this the part of the movie where we came in? What really upsets Him is that all of His miracles are being ascribed to another god. But, apparently, Moses knows better than God.*

Like his ancestor Abraham, Moses's debating skills are more than a match for God's as he sets out to convince God of the error of His ways. He easily wins the argument by alerting God to the fact that He'd be a laughing stock if the Egyptians (are there any still left?) find the carcasses of the Israelites in the desert: "But Moses implored the LORD, his God, saying, 'Why, O LORD, should your anger burn against your people, whom you brought out of the land of Egypt with great power and with a strong hand? Why should the Egyptians say, 'With evil intent he brought them out, that he might kill them in the mountains and wipe them off the face of the earth'? Turn from your burning wrath; change your mind about punishing your people. Remember your servants Abraham, Isaac, and Israel, and how you swore to them by your own self, saying, 'I will make your descendants as numerous as the stars in the sky; and all this land that I promised, I will give your descendants as their perpetual heritage.' So the LORD changed his mind about the punishment he had threatened to inflict on his people."

Note the subtle way in which Moses deflects God's use of "your people" right back at Him, while praising His great deeds. But now Moses has to deal with the apostates down in the base camp. He is so angry on seeing what is happening down there that he smashes the two stone tablets with God's fingerprints and DNA on them. He interrogates Aaron who, like Adam before him, blames somebody else—this time not a woman, but the unruly mob. He even denies the fact that he fashioned the golden calf, saying that he just threw the gold in the fire and out came the fully formed calf. But a very creative fire-god was lurking in the flames: "Moses asked Aaron, 'What did this people do to you that you should lead them into a grave sin?' Aaron replied, 'Do not let my lord be angry. You know how the people are prone to evil. They said to me, 'Make us a god to go before us; as for this man Moses who brought us out of the land of Egypt, we do not know what has happened to him.' So I told them, 'Whoever is wearing gold, take it off.' They gave it to me, and I threw it into the fire, and this calf came out.'" *Reminds me of that old claim—"The dog ate my homework!"*

It's now time for Moses to put on his killing cap. It's voting time: "Who is for Yahweh and who is for the golden calf?" *he asks. All of the Levites rallied to Yahweh, so:* "Moses stood at the gate of the camp and shouted, 'Whoever is for the LORD, come to me!' All the Levites then rallied to him, and he told them, 'Thus says the LORD, the God of Israel: Each of you put your sword on your hip! Go back and forth through the camp, from gate to gate, and kill your brothers, your friends, your neighbors!' The Levites did as Moses had commanded, and that day about three thousand of the people fell. Then Moses said, 'Today you are installed as priests for the LORD, for you went against your own sons and brothers, to bring a blessing upon yourselves this day.'"

For their willingness to slaughter their own, they are rewarded by being ordained priests in perpetuity.

But Moses has to schlep back up the mountain to ask forgiveness for the people—the ones he hasn't murdered yet. God responds that they should proceed with the initial plan and He'll delay punishment until later: "Now, go and lead the people where I have told you. See, my angel will go before you. When it is time for me to punish, I will punish them for their sin." *However, God doesn't really trust Himself to keep his temper under control—has He been in therapy since we last met Him?—so He determines instead to send an angel to lead them:* "otherwise I might consume you on the way… The LORD spoke to Moses: Speak to the Israelites: You are a stiff-necked people. Were I to go up in your company even for a moment, I would destroy you. Now off with your ornaments!

Let me think what to do with you. So, from Mount Horeb onward, the Israelites stripped off their ornaments."

He continues to refer to the Israelites as "Moses's people" whom Moses "brought up out of the land of Egypt." *It's like a dysfunctional family: when a child is successful, each parent refers to her as "my child," but when they have a troubled kid they say "she's your child."* Once again, God is stuck in an OCD loop, speaking of "a land flowing with milk and honey" *from which He will drive out the Canaanites, Amorites, Hittites, Perizzites, Hivites and Jebusites. Will those poor bastards ever catch a break?*

A muffled chuckle arose from the gallery, but the members of the jury were not amused as they took close note of how this brutal and fickle God seemed to scapegoat the same groups of people even as his favorites flipped back and forth. O'Sullivan kept going:

Meanwhile, God is spending some quality time thinking how best to punish the people. He's one busy dude! It must be exhausting to have to plan how to make His own people suffer even as He's wiping out the "foreigners." And we're back to the anthropomorphic God and his buddy Moses, who again proves to be very persuasive: "The LORD used to speak to Moses face to face, as a person speaks to a friend. Moses would then return to the camp, but his young assistant, Joshua, son of Nun, never left the tent. Moses said to the LORD, 'See, you are telling me: Lead this people. But you have not let me know whom you will send with me. Yet you have said: You are my intimate friend; You have found favor with me. Now, if I have found favor with you, please let me know your ways so that, in knowing you, I may continue to find favor with you. See, this nation is indeed your own people. The LORD answered: I myself will go along, to give you rest." *And the debate tournament continues: Moses 2, God 0.*

But the writings of Exodus can't agree with each other. We've just been told, in Exodus 32:11, that "The LORD used to speak to Moses face to face, as a person speaks to a friend." *But by verses 18-23, we get a radically different story:* "Then Moses said, 'Please let me see your glory!' The LORD answered: I will make all my goodness pass before you, and I will proclaim my name, "LORD," before you; I who show favor to whom I will, I who grant mercy to whom I will. But you cannot see my face, for no one can see me and live. Here, continued the LORD, is a place near me where you shall station yourself on the rock. When my glory passes I will set you in the cleft of the rock and will cover you with my hand until I have passed by. Then I will remove my hand, so that you may see my back; but my face may not be seen." *Once again, ladies and gentlemen of the jury, what court of law is going to believe the testimony of such a witness?*

Next comes one of the most patently false pieces of self-praise to be found anywhere in the Torah. Moses has been commanded to go back up the mountain to replace the two stone tablets he broke. If he's meeting regularly face to face with his friend, in the tent by the camp, why doesn't God simply hand deliver them there? Amazon.com would have them there in less than a day!

O'Sullivan's modern references always got the gallery giggling, but he didn't wait for them to settle down before continuing with his breakdown of the book of Exodus.

Anyway, God is now really puffed up with His own abilities, and so we read: "The LORD came down in a cloud and stood with him there and proclaimed the name, "LORD." So, the LORD passed before him and proclaimed: The LORD, the LORD, a God gracious and merciful, slow to anger and abounding in love and fidelity, continuing his love for a thousand generations, and forgiving wickedness, rebellion, and sin; yet not declaring the guilty guiltless, but bringing punishment for their parents' wickedness on children and children's children to the third and fourth generation." *This type of performance really merits a much wider audience than simply Moses. It would be a great acceptance speech for best actor at the Oscars.*

Warming to His task and convincing Himself with every phrase that He really is who He claims to be, He promises even greater miracles: "The LORD said: Here is the covenant I will make. Before all your people I will perform marvels never before done in any nation anywhere on earth, so that all the people among whom you live may see the work of the LORD. Awe-inspiring are the deeds I will perform with you! As for you, observe what I am commanding you today. See, I am about to drive out before you the Amorites, Canaanites, Hittites, Perizzites, Hivites and Jebusites. Take care not to make a covenant with the inhabitants of the land that you are to enter; lest they become a snare among you. Tear down their altars; smash their sacred stones, and cut down their asherahs. You shall not bow down to any other god, for the LORD— "Jealous" is his name—is a jealous God. Do not make a covenant with the inhabitants of the land; else, when they prostitute themselves with their gods and sacrifice to them, one of them may invite you and you may partake of the sacrifice. And when you take their daughters as wives for your sons, and their daughters prostitute themselves with their gods, they will make your sons do the same. You shall not make for yourselves molten gods." *Do I dare risk tiring you again, dear jurors, by mentioning the fate of the unfortunate Amorites, Canaanites, Hittites, Perizzites, Hivites and Jebusites? Hasn't God ever heard the phrase "I wouldn't wish that fate on my worst enemy"? Apparently not.*

For the first time since the trial began, Dr. O'Sullivan seemed weary. As he looked to the prosecutor for guidance, Michael Newsome offered him a warm smile and silently signaled to him to wrap up his testimony by circling his finger in the air. The expert witness straightened the microphone as he straightened his spine and addressed the jury with his Irish eyes burning with suppressed tears.

So, what do we have at the end of two days of evidence? Let's just focus on the homicides. It started off with a Permian-style extinction event destroying almost all life on planet Earth. Then came two individual murders—Er and Onan, the sons of Judah. Next was the slaughter of all the livestock in Egypt, followed by the deaths of all the firstborn. Let's say the population of Egypt was two million people and that the average family size was eight members; that would mean 12.5% (or 250,000 people!) are firstborns. That was the tally of God's victory, won by hardening pharaoh's heart.

Without even taking a breath, He then went on to kill the pharaoh and his army, including 600 three-person chariots (1,800 men). On a formal trip to the mountain He warns that anybody—human or beast—who touches even the base of the mountain must be "stoned to death or killed with arrows." *Later, He turned on the calf-worshippers and, courtesy of mild-mannered Moses and the Levites, oversaw the killing of 3,000:* "Kill your brothers, your friends, your neighbors." *In His leisure-time, God draws up a list of crimes which are punishable by death, so the killing can continue while He's busy with other stuff.*

How could anybody actually worship such a criminal? I can only think of one reason—and a corollary: fear of the biggest bully on the block, and the self-soothing delusion that, somehow, our group is special to Him—us Jews! No—us Catholics! No—us Born Again Christians! No—us Muslims! And so on. Personally, I could fear such a psychopath, even obey Him, but there is no way I could love Him or even respect Him.

How often have we seen devotees of famous televangelists, gurus, and rinpoches be taken advantage of financially, sexually, and otherwise? And why? Because they chose to believe the claims of these spiritual leaders rather than listen to their own intuitive responses to the obvious bad behavior of these spiritual leaders. Or maybe religious people become desensitized to this kind of treachery because their "holy" books are full of this kind of stuff.

Dermot O'Sullivan's jovial spirit went dark for a moment and his face showed a look of utter disgust.

This case may be getting difficult for some of you to stomach. God's behavior in the book of Exodus is sickening, no doubt. But you might want to bring some antacid tablets with you to court tomorrow, because there's more of the same in the book of Leviticus. In the meantime, you might want to keep an eye out for this "God." He could turn on you at any time.

The mood was solemn as day two concluded and the court was adjourned.

LEVITICUS

By day three of the trial, the courtroom was hushed and bracing for the worst. Michael Newsome tempered his previously fiery rhetoric with a gentler approach: *Are you, dear jurors, committed to hearing all of the evidence before you make your assessment of this God known to many as Yahweh? If so, let's begin today's proceedings with the book of Leviticus. I call Dr. Dermot O'Sullivan to resume his testimony as expert witness.*

O'Sullivan was sworn in with no fanfare and he pushed up his sleeves and jumped right into the book of Leviticus. Sounding more scholarly than on the previous two days, O'Sullivan began day three:

This entire volume comes from the Priestly source we call "P" and was put together during the Babylonian Exile around the year 550 BCE, some 700 years after Moses's supposed safari to the top of Mount Sinai. It consists of thousands of liturgical injunctions, as well as long lists of sins and their punishments. Mainly, the liturgical rites have to do with the slaughter of animals and the splashing of blood—red seems to be God's favorite color—so that the sweet odor of roasting flesh might please the Lord. That phase is repeated as a mantra throughout Leviticus. Every human sin is punished by the death of a human or the sacrifice of an animal. And to think my Roman Catholic brothers and sisters got out of it by way of a Confession—one Our Father, and three Hail Marys, O'Sullivan quipped, unable to resist his proclivity for humor.

And if you thought the list of instructions for making the Tabernacle, its furnishings, and the priestly vestments covered in the book of Exodus was boring, you ain't read nuthin' yet. I'll spare you the details. Here's a summary: "This is the ritual for the burnt offering, the grain offering, the purification offering, the reparation offering, the ordination offering, and the communion sacrifice, which the LORD enjoined on Moses at Mount Sinai at the time when he commanded the Israelites in the wilderness of Sinai to bring their offerings to the LORD." *There, I've just saved you having to read eight chapters.*

But here are a few little interesting tidbits. Upon slaughtering any animal—and believe me there were frequent and multi-animal slaughters—nobody except God could have either the fat or the blood. (I guess He wasn't overly concerned about His cholesterol levels.) The only blood-sharing allowed was for ordination rites and healings, in which cases the ordaining prelate or healer had to smear blood on the "right earlobe, the right thumb, and the right big toe" *of the* ordinandi *or the patients. I'm not making this up*! "Then he brought forward the second ram, the ordination ram, and Aaron and his sons laid their hands on its head. When it was slaughtered, Moses took some of its blood and put it on the lobe of Aaron's right ear, on the thumb of his right hand, and on the big toe of his right foot. Moses had the sons of Aaron also come forward, and he put some of the blood on the lobes of their right ears, on the thumbs of their right hands, and on the big toes of their right feet. The rest of the blood he splashed on all the sides of the altar."

For two of Aaron's sons who had just been ordained, the honor quickly turned to horror. "Aaron's sons Nadab and Abihu took their censers and, putting incense on the fire they had set in them, they offered before the LORD unauthorized fire, such as he had not commanded. Fire therefore came forth from the LORD's presence and consumed them, so that they died in the LORD's presence."

This is the most extreme case of Obsessive-Compulsive Disorder that I've come across, accompanied by a homicidal rage that took the lives of two newly ordained, enthusiastic priests for messing up a detail of a liturgical event. God sure seems to act like a bratty kid who destroys his toy soldiers because they're not acceding to his wishes. Without batting an eyelid, Moses immediately orders two of his first cousins—Mishael and Elzaphan, neither of whom were priests—to carry the corpses outside the camp, while warning Aaron himself and his other two priest-sons to show no signs of shock or bereavement lest they further infuriate God and bring about their own deaths and, perhaps, collateral damage: "Then Moses summoned Mishael and Elzaphan, the sons of Aaron's uncle Uzziel, with the order, 'Come, carry your kinsmen from before the sanctuary to a place outside the camp.' So they drew near and carried them by means of their tunics outside the camp, as Moses had commanded. Moses said to Aaron and his sons Eleazar and Ithamar, 'Do not dishevel your hair or tear your garments, lest you die and bring God's wrath also on the whole community. While your kindred, the rest of the house of Israel, may mourn for those whom the LORD's fire has burned up, you shall not go beyond the entrance of the tent of meeting, else you shall die; for the anointing oil of the LORD is upon you.' So they did as Moses told them."

Moses, knowing God as "an intimate," is afraid that if Aaron reacts to the murder of his two sons, God may completely lose it and murder a whole bunch more of the Israelites. Maybe Moses was afraid that God would vent His frustration by shooting up the nearest schoolyard. Are you really a follower of—or even a believer in—this cosmic psychopath? O'Sullivan asked, glancing at Judge Grossler.

Pivoting to make eye contact with members of the jury, one by one, O'Sullivan asked: *How would you feel, dear juror, if immediately following the ordination of yourself and your kids, God were to kill two of them and warn you and the survivors not to object or even mourn? Instead, you were to intone "Blessed be the Lord God of Israel!" This might be the place for a bit of get-back-at-you subtle irony, by instead intoning: "O Lord, who is like you among the gods?!" God's behavior smells like a hugely amplified version of the abusive parent who threatens a beaten, tearful child with "Shut up, or I'll really give you something to cry about!"*

In one final warning from God to Aaron, He threatens, "if you or your sons ever taste hard liquor before you exercise your priestly duties, I'm gonna kill you too." The surviving sons, Eleazar and Ithamar—could it be because they are really disoriented after their brothers' deaths?—screw up the next ritual and Moses hauls Aaron over the coals for it. I imagine that Moses himself was terrified that this latest foul-up was going to unleash another murder spree from the all-loving Yahweh: "Moses inquired closely about the goat of the purification offering and discovered that it had all been burned. So he was angry with the surviving sons of Aaron, Eleazar and Ithamar, and said, 'Why did you not eat the purification offering in the sacred place, since it is most holy? It has been given to you that you might remove the guilt of the community and make atonement for them before the LORD. Since its blood was not brought inside the sanctuary, you should certainly have eaten the offering in the sanctuary, as I was commanded."

There follows a listing of clean and unclean animals based on (1) whether or not they have hoofs, (2) whether or not these hoofs are cloven, and (3) whether or not they chew the cud. Ungulates are any hoofed mammals and there are two sub-classes: odd-toed ungulates, such as horses and rhinoceroses; and even-toed ungulates, such as cattle, pigs, giraffes, camels, deer and hippopotamuses. And ruminants are any even-toed ungulate mammals that chew the cud. So, a dog has no hoofs and doesn't chew the cud. (Bad dog!) A hare chews the cud but has no hoof. (Bad hare!) A horse has hoofs, but only one on each foot, and moreover does not chew the cud. (Bad horse!) A cow has hoofs, cloven (yes!) and chews the cud. (Holy cow!) The pig has cloven hoofs but never learned to chew the cud. (Bad pig!)

Speaking of clean and unclean, in the Acts of the Apostles, St. Peter has a vision in which he is told by God very emphatically, "Do not call anything I have created unclean!" *Was this the same Yahweh we met in Leviticus? The Leviticus list goes on to distinguish between fish types: If a species has fins and scales it's clean, otherwise it's treif. Next come birds, insects, rodents and lizards—all unclean. 'Pardon, monsieur, no escargot s'il vous plais!'* O'Sullivan attempted, his Irish brogue overpowering his attempt to sound French.

But clean and unclean doesn't stop with the animal kingdom. Humans, especially females, can be unclean too. For the sin of birthing a boy child a woman is unclean for seven days—"with the same uncleanness as during her menstrual period"*—and then for another thirty-three days she's in a state of "blood purity"—which actually means "blood impurity." If she's sinful enough to give birth to a girl child, she is unclean for fourteen days—*"with the same uncleanness as during her menstrual period"*—and then for another sixty-six days she is in a state of "blood purity." The commentary in my particular Bible,* O'Sullivan said while holding up his dog-eared copy of The New American Bible Revised Edition, *very piously explains the difference as follows: The mother has two stages of uncleanness or impurity: the first where her uncleanness is as severe as during her menstrual period and is contagious to profane persons and objects (according to Leviticus15:19-24), and the second where she does not contaminate persons and objects, but is still impure to what is holy, such as the sanctuary (Leviticus 12:4) or sacrifices. The implication is that in the second stage she may resume sexual relations with her husband (which would be prohibited in the first stage according to 18:19). So, in stage one, she's a walking virus against whom nobody and nothing has immunity, whereas in stage two, only the holy ones are susceptible to her contagion. Eleven weeks after birthing a girl she must undergo a ritual of atonement by offering a lamb and a pigeon to the priest to kill, in order to appease God's outrage. Here it is, you can read it for yourself.* "The LORD said to Moses: Tell the Israelites: When a woman has a child, giving birth to a boy, she shall be unclean for seven days, with the same uncleanness as during her menstrual period. On the eighth day, the flesh of the boy's foreskin shall be circumcised, and then she shall spend thirty-three days more in a state of blood purity;

she shall not touch anything sacred nor enter the sanctuary till the days of her purification are fulfilled. If she gives birth to a girl, for fourteen days she shall be as unclean as during her menstrual period, after which she shall spend sixty-six days in a state of blood purity. When the days of her purification for a son or for a daughter are fulfilled, she shall bring to the priest at the entrance of the tent of meeting a yearling lamb for a burnt offering and a pigeon or a turtle-dove for a purification offering. The priest shall offer them before the LORD to make atonement for her, and thus she will be clean again after her flow of blood. Such is the ritual for the woman who gives birth to a child, male or female."

This practice, in a very modified form, survived down to modern times. In Roman Catholicism, the unclean mother had to be "churched." This meant shamefacedly waiting at the back of the church on a Sunday after the parish-ioner-saints had gone home, to be purified by the male priest. Thereafter, she was free to join "the people of God" and even receive Holy Communion—that is, until she sinned again by another birthing. Shouldn't mothers of newborns be honored and revered for the heroic, sacrificial, and powerful act of bringing the next generation of progeny into the world? Apparently not, according to Yahweh.

Allow me, dear jurors, to hereby examine the notion of clean and unclean in both the animal and human realms.

Talmudic scholars cannot agree as to the origins of this distinction in the Bible. I am of the opinion that it is based on the memories of real, historical plagues which were attributed to eating contaminated foodstuffs. This led to the creation of a simple, easily memorized taxonomy to ensure hygiene and health. This system was then promulgated as a divine decree. (The easiest way to get any law passed is to attribute it to God.)

In all of the great mythologies of the world, there appears to be an exorbitant obsession with blood. The Hebrews were no different—unsurprising, since they borrowed many of their beliefs from other cultures. In trying to decode the notion of "clean" vs. "unclean," let's take a look at this preoccupation with the red stuff. In the Sumerian accounts, creation occurs in three stages. First, the gods used DNA from their own blood; second, they mixed this with elements from planet Earth (e.g., soil); and, third, spirit was breathed into the physical form to bring it to life. The result was called "lulu" or "the mixed one." The geneticist-god of the Sumerians—Enki, meaning "Lord of the Earth"—was the son of the chief god of the Anunnaki (Anu.) In defiance of the other gods, Enki warned and saved Ziusudra (whom the Bible would later call Noah) from a global flood orchestrated by the Anunnaki. The Genesis account borrows some of these aspects.

The biblical name given to the first human is a four-way pun in the Semitic languages, to which the African tongue, Kiswahili, is related. In Kiswahili, the word for a human is "Binadamu." Ostensibly it means "son of Adam." But "Adam" in Hebrew comes from the word "adamah," meaning soil or earth; and in Kiswahili, the word "damu" means "blood," while in Hebrew and Arabic, it's "dam." Thus, "binadamu" can mean (1) human, (2) a descendant of Adam, (3) an earthling, or (4) a being of blood.

So, the lulu or mixture is a being, one of whose parents is of Earth and the other of the gods. The gods contributed both blood and breath to the mix. Therefore, at the end of life, we have to give both back to them. Jesus "gave up the Spirit (breath)" even as he poured out his blood on the cross, because breath is the interdimensional connection, the interface between Spirit and matter. Hence, the oft-repeated practice of Moses and Joshua to "kill everything that breathes" is a guarantee that God gets back His entire investment (blood and Spirit), while Earth, too, gets her contribution back—the atoms of the dead body.

This is probably the reason for the grave injunctions (no pun intended) against bloodletting, in any guise, unless God ordained it. At the first "council" of the Church in Jerusalem in 49 CE, they debated whether or not to force the Gentiles who had joined the Jesus Movement to keep all 613 Jewish precepts. The decision was, No! Only four requirements are sine qua non: (1) abstain from drinking blood, (2) do not eat meat sacrificed to idols—because the blood had been offered to fake gods, (3) do not eat the meat of strangled animals—because the blood is still in their bodies, and (4) abstain from "porneia." (This term is often translated as "adultery," but more accurately might mean "marriage within the forbidden degree of kinship"—in other words, don't mess with the bloodline.)

I have a theory that, in the very early stages of human development, when we were simply hunter/gatherers who searched for and happened upon game and grain, we had no concept of the causal connection between copulation and baby-making. This "aha!" would only come as we began to domesticate crops and animals. Breeding was understood for the first time then. Before that, however, every so often a female of the tribe would shock and terrify the group by producing an infant. It always arrived covered in blood and crying, even as the mother, herself, writhed in distress. Perhaps the members of the community saw this as evidence of a crime, a battle; the woman had stolen that baby from god, and he was pissed. Pretty soon, he was going to come looking for it and, in his anger, was liable to punish everybody. So, what to do? Why, give it back, quam celerrime! Hence, human sacrifice.

In time, adaptations emerged. The belief grew that only the first-born was God's since "only God could open the womb." Thereafter, a mere mortal male could impregnate a woman, and then those children belonged to the couple. So, once you sacrificed your first-born, you were in bonus territory. Then came the next phase. What if we simply substitute an animal sacrifice for the first-born baby? If the gods agreed to this arrangement, then the humans could redeem (literally "buy back") the firstborn. This is what the parents of Jesus did eight days after he was born.

Occasionally, parents tried to trick the gods. In Africa, if a woman had the chutzpah to give birth to twins, one of them would be placed at an obvious and highly visible location, so that when the god came looking for the stolen property, he might not realize the extent of the robbery and be satisfied with one child. In Judaism, there is still a folk belief that if an infant is very ill, it's a sign that God is trying to take it back. And the solution is to confuse Him by changing the child's name. These clever humans have created a pretty gullible god, it seems!

At this stage of Leviticus, the priests are expected to double up as physicians as well as inspectors of fungal infections on wool, linen, leather, and houses; and when a problem is detected, the cleansing ritual is— you guessed it once again—the slaughter of more animals and, of course, the usual anointing of the lobe of the right ear, the right thumb, and the right big toe. I wonder if this protocol still exists in the medical textbooks?

These priests-playing-doctors were even less prepared to handle the question of sexuality. Mainstream religions always seem to have a love/hate relationship with this topic. Here is a quick look at how the Hebrews dealt with male nocturnal emissions, female menstruation, and the sex act itself: "When a man has an emission of semen, he shall bathe his whole body in water and be unclean until evening. Any piece of cloth or leather with semen on it shall be washed with water and be unclean until evening. If a man has sexual relations with a woman, they shall both bathe in water and be unclean until evening. When a woman has a flow of blood from her body, she shall be in a state of menstrual uncleanness for seven days. Anyone who touches her shall be unclean until evening."

Skipping about wildly, God is still smarting over the sins of Aaron's dead sons and He is looking for other future stuff to be upset by. So, He fusses that Aaron might wander into the holy of holies whenever he pleases, wearing whatever duds come to hand after he gets out of bed. So, there must be a strict protocol. Aaron can only enter once a year— on the Day of Atonement—wearing very specific garments: "After the death of Aaron's two sons, who died when they encroached on the LORD's presence, the LORD spoke to Moses and said to him: Tell your brother Aaron that he is not to come whenever he pleases into the inner sanctuary, inside the veil, in front of the cover on the ark, lest he die, for I reveal myself in a cloud above the ark's cover. Only in this way may Aaron enter the inner sanctuary. He shall bring a bull of the herd for a purification offering and a ram for a burnt offering. He shall wear the sacred linen tunic, with the linen pants underneath, gird himself with the linen sash and put on the linen turban. But since these vestments are sacred, he shall not put them on until he has first bathed his body in water."

Then comes a very strange passage. Aaron must select two male goats and cast lots to see which one is for God and which one is for Azazel—a demon-god! Here's the story: "Taking the two male goats and setting them before the LORD at the entrance of the tent of meeting, he shall cast lots to determine which one is for the LORD and which for Azazel. The goat that is determined by lot for the LORD, Aaron shall present and offer up as a purification offering. But the goat determined by lot for Azazel he shall place before the LORD alive, so that with it he may make atonement by sending it off to Azazel in the desert." *The Azazel goat is actually a scapegoat—onto whom the sins of all the people have been laid. Is this some kind of a Trojan horse, where the crime-saturated goat is captured and eaten by the desert demon? Is Yahweh trying to poison His rival?*

Then on to more future anxiety: lest any Israelite try to sacrifice an ox or a sheep or a goat to another god, all slaughtering of animals has to be done at the entrance to the Tent of the Meeting by a priest. No hedging your bets, people! "Any Israelite who slaughters an ox or a sheep or a goat, whether in the camp or outside of it, without first bringing it to the entrance of the tent of meeting to present it as an offering to the LORD in front of the LORD's tabernacle, shall be judged guilty of bloodshed—that individual has shed blood, and shall be cut off from the people. This is so that such sacrifices as they used to offer in the open field the Israelites shall henceforth bring to the LORD at the entrance of the tent of meeting, to the priest, and sacrifice them there as communion sacrifices to the LORD."

Let's get back to sex—Yahweh can't seem to get it off His mind. I'm just going to mention a few of the prohibitions and show how earlier "heroes and heroines" of the Bible story were in breach of them. Unless maybe St. Paul was right when he said, "before there was law *(Pre-Sinai)* there was no sin."

You can't have sex with your mother. Then where did Cain get "a wife" after he'd killed Abel and before any of his sisters was born? You can't have sex with your father's wife. Then Cain is doubly guilty, and Reuben sinned by having intercourse with Bilhah, his father's concubine. You can't have sex with your sister or half-sister. Then Abraham and Sarah, as well as Isaac and Rebekah are guilty. You can't have sex with your daughter. Then Lot and his two daughters are guilty. You can't have sex with your daughter-in-law. Then Judah and Tamar are guilty. You can't have sex with two sisters while they are both alive. Then Jacob, Leah, and Rachel are guilty.

Lot has the excuse that he was drunk at the time and was seduced by his daughters, and Judah has the excuse that Tamar was disguised as a prostitute when he propositioned her; but as we've already seen, ignorance is no excuse. Remember what happened to unsuspecting Pharaoh for taking Abraham's "sister" Sarah; and to unsuspecting Abimelech and his household for taking Isaac's "sister" Rebekah?

In between these warnings and threats and punishments, God takes time out to pat Himself on the back. Several times He humbly intones, "Be holy, for I, the Lord your God am holy." *Gimme a break! Does anything you've heard about this guy over the last three days remind you of Mother Teresa or St. Francis of Assisi? Then He piously interjects the following:* "Take no revenge and cherish no grudge against your own people. You shall love your neighbor as yourself. I am the LORD." *Everything God commands should be prefaced with "Do as I say, not as I do."*

Next comes the first recorded shot across the bow of the Monsantos of the world and their GMO products. For good measure, God throws in proscriptions about polyculture and the garment industry, all in just one sentence: "Keep my statutes: do not breed any of your domestic animals with others of a different species; do not sow a field of yours with two different kinds of seed; and do not put on a garment woven with two different kinds of thread."

Still on the theme of agriculture—and using a weird analogy—He orders: "When you come into the land and plant any fruit tree there, first look upon its fruit as if it were uncircumcised. For three years, it shall be uncircumcised for you; it may not be eaten. In the fourth year, however, all of its fruit shall be dedicated to the LORD in joyous celebration. Not until the fifth year may you eat its fruit, to increase the yield for you. I, the LORD, am your God." *Is He talking about all fruit here, or just bananas? As apocryphal Freud said, "Sometimes a cigar is just a cigar."*

Having tried His hand at haberdashery and agriculture, He now moves on to hairdressing and body decoration: "Do not clip your hair at the temples, nor spoil the edges of your beard. Do not lacerate your bodies for the dead, and do not tattoo yourselves. I am the LORD."

Like a nagging parent who keeps repeating the same warnings and advice, He now goes back again to the "ten commandments." To save time, I will just list some of the infractions that merit the death penalty or "being cut off from the people."

1. Giving offspring to Molech—a rival who was well known for his taste for infant flesh. "Tell the Israelites: Anyone, whether an Israelite or an alien residing in Israel, who gives offspring to Molech shall be put to death. The people of the land shall stone that person."

2. *Failure to kill the devotees of Molech.* "If the people of the land condone the giving of offspring to Molech, by failing to put the wrongdoer to death, I myself will turn against that individual and his or her family."

3. *And finally, just "to be sure to be sure," if someone is a devotee of Molech,* "I will cut off from their people both the wrongdoer and all who follow this person by prostituting themselves with Molech."

4. *Adultery—both parties must be put to death.*

5. *Homosexuality—both parties must be put to death.*

6. *A man who marries both a woman and her mother (one way to deal with mother-in-law issues!)—all three must be burned to death.*

7. *Bestiality—both human and beast must be killed.*

8. *Having intercourse during a woman's period—both "cut off from the community of Israel."*

9. *Mediums and clairvoyants—death by stoning.*

10. *A priest's daughter who becomes a prostitute—death by fire.*

11. *A priest who draws near to the sacred offerings while he is in a state of uncleanness.*

12. *Failure to show up for the Day of Atonement ceremonies:* "On this day you shall not do any work, because it is the Day of Atonement, when atonement is made for you before the LORD, your God. Those who do not humble themselves on this day shall be cut off from the people. If anyone does any work on this day, I will remove that person from the midst of the people."

13. *Those who invoke God's name as they curse another—death at the hands of the community by stoning.*

O'Sullivan paused for a moment and, scratching his head, asked himself: *I wonder how He decides which manner of execution is appropriate for which crime?*

Moving right along. Catholic monks who are tonsured as part of their consecration to God, and enthusiastic ascetics who self-flagellate, are in breach of this edit: "The priests shall not make bald the crown of their head, nor shave the edges of their beard, nor lacerate their body."

The really important priests are not allowed to make themselves "unclean" or adopt the normal symbols of mourning, even for a parent: "The most exalted of the priests, upon whose head the anointing oil has been poured and who has been ordained to wear the special vestments, shall not dishevel his hair or rend his garments, nor shall he go near any dead person. Not even for his father or mother may he thus become unclean."

God, who presumably created all of them, is disgusted by the following kinds of people: "The LORD said to Moses, Say to Aaron: None of your descendants, throughout their generations, who has any blemish shall come forward to offer the food of his God. Anyone who has any of the following blemishes may not come forward: he who is blind, or lame, or who has a split lip, or a limb too long, or a broken leg or arm, or who is a hunchback or dwarf or has a growth in the eye, or who is afflicted with sores, scabs, or crushed testicles. No descendant of Aaron the priest who has any such blemish may draw near to offer the oblations of the LORD; on account of his blemish he may not draw near to offer the food of his God.

I wonder how Jesus would respond to this, as he advocated (albeit symbolically) self-mutilation—pluck out an erring eye, cut off a sinful limb—in order to enter heaven. Is there going to be an argument at the pearly gates on the Last Day? And who will settle the dispute? St. Peter? Will Moses be called in as an expert witness? Will Jesus and his Father fall out over this issue?

You can't have a fellow Israelite as a slave, but foreigners are fair game, and you can bequeath the slave to your posterity forever: "The male and female slaves that you possess—these you shall acquire from the nations round about you. You may also acquire them from among the resident aliens who reside with you, and from their families who are with you, those whom they bore in your land. These you may possess, and bequeath to your children as their hereditary possession forever. You may treat them as slaves. But none of you shall lord it harshly over any of your fellow Israelites."

Now comes a long, lugubrious listing of escalating punishments on Israel if they refuse to keep these laws—culminating in "If, despite all this, you disobey and continue hostile to me, I will continue in my hostile rage toward you, and I myself will discipline you for your sins sevenfold, till you begin to eat the flesh of your own sons and daughters. I will demolish your high places, overthrow your incense stands, and cast your corpses upon the corpses of your idols. In my loathing of you, I will lay waste your cities and desolate your sanctuaries, refusing your sweet-smelling offerings. So devastated will I leave the land that your enemies who come to live there will stand aghast at the sight of it. And you I will scatter among the nations at the point of my drawn sword, leaving your countryside desolate and your cities deserted."

Famine, cannibalism, war, exile—it is very obvious that instead of being a threat uttered by God in 1250 BCE, that this is actually a summary of Israelite history up to 550 BCE. God is very accurate when He prophesies after the fact. Similar lists of blessings and curses appear in the conclusions of ancient Near Eastern treaties. "Moses" probably got this template online!

The punishment list is much longer than the list of blessings, and is given as waves of increasing ferocity: illness, pestilence, crop failure, famine, attacks by wild animals, child mortality, military defeat, panic, and exile. This God is a very well-equipped psychopath.

In case you're wondering about how age and gender affect one's dollar-value, here's a helpful list supplied by God to Moses: "the value for males between the ages of twenty and sixty shall be fifty silver shekels, by the sanctuary shekel; and for a female, the value shall be thirty shekels. For persons between the ages of five and twenty, the value for a male shall be twenty shekels, and for a female, ten shekels. For persons between the ages of one month and five years, the value for a male shall be five silver shekels, and for a female, three shekels. For persons of sixty or more, for a male the value shall be fifteen shekels, and ten shekels for a female." *I hope that's helpful when you're buying gifts for your family and friends.*

Following that comment, Judge Jerome Grossler asked the witness to avoid sarcasm. O'Sullivan responded, *Forgive me, Your Honor, I'm just really tired of Yahweh's sexism.*

And I'm getting tired of Leviticus, so please allow me to offer a few final remarks to try to contextualize these laws and the mindset that created them. Carl Jung claimed that in order to be an effective therapist, you have to initially join with the belief system of the client, even a psychotic client. You can't heal them by simply confronting them; rather, align with them and then guide them to a healthier perspective. Is this what Yahweh— or the thinkers of the time—are doing with the Israelites? And not just them, but all the ancient cultures?

Let me use an analogy of my own. Suppose I were to lead a group of Americans on a bike tour of Ireland. I'm the expert because I grew up there. So, we head off on day one and I pedal like Lance Armstrong on a double dose of steroids so that the entire group gets lost when they reach the first crossroads, because I am out of sight. Then, I am not a very effective leader. On the other hand, if I just pedal comfortably and remain in the middle of the group, the front of the pack will have to stop at each crossroads and wait for directions. Again, I'm not a very effective leader. The ideal leader is one who is far enough ahead of the pack to provide direction but not so far ahead that he's out of sight. Is this what "Yahweh" or the religious leaders are trying to do?

For example, as I've said before, misogyny was a fact of life based on patriarchal thinking which, in turn, was a stage of human psychosocial evolution through which all cultures, not just the Israelite one, had to pass. Even an enlightened soul like Jesus had to grow and, in the process, say some dumbass things. Remember the exchange between him and the Canaanite woman in Matthew chapter 15: "Leaving that place, Jesus withdrew to the region of Tyre and Sidon. A Canaanite woman from that vicinity came to him, crying out, 'Lord, Son of David, have mercy on me! My daughter is demon-possessed and suffering terribly.' Jesus did not answer a word. So his disciples came to him and urged him, 'Send her away, for she keeps crying out after us.' He answered, 'I was sent only to the lost sheep of Israel.' The woman came and knelt before him. 'Lord, help me!' she said. He replied, 'It is not right to take the children's bread and toss it to the dogs.' 'Yes it is, Lord,' she said. 'Even the dogs eat the crumbs that fall from their master's table.' Then Jesus said to her, 'Woman, you have great faith! Your request is granted.' And her daughter was healed at that moment."

His first response was "I was sent only to the lost sheep of Israel." *Wrong! His next response was racist and totally lacking in compassion,* "It is not right to take the children's bread and toss it to the dogs." *Moses, in his antipathy for the Canaanites, would have been proud of him. The woman, whose love for her daughter is much stronger than her shock at the insult, cleverly turns his own language against him,* "Yes it is, Lord... Even the dogs eat the crumbs that fall from their master's table."

I believe that the "Father" gave Jesus a stern look and said, "Dude, I did *not* send you as a Jewish prophet for the Jewish people; I sent you as a child of mine to all of my hurting children! Give her what is her birthright." *And, I believe, Jesus was never the same again. He went from ethnocentric thinking to ecocentric thinking; from tribal theology to cosmic compassion.*

Don't we all, occasionally, need to snap out of our implicit bias so we can let go of innate prejudices of any teaching—even (especially) the sacred ones? Could it be that all of the bloody treachery outlined in the book of Leviticus is really God's way of shaking His people up? Or was this God some kind of bloodthirsty, vindictive, cruel psychopath? You decide... And with that, O'Sullivan excused himself from the witness stand.

Judge Grossman looked to Michael Newsome for an explanation for his witness's rather abrupt end to this long testimony.

Speechless for a moment, Newsome stuttered "I... I... I have no further questions."

NUMBERS

Day four of the testimony began with the Prosecution calling for the court material taken from the fourth volume of God's Journals, called the book of Numbers, once again as analyzed by expert witness Dr. Dermot O'Sullivan, who began with a bit an overview:

It's called the book of Numbers because of the two censuses taken, one near the beginning and the other toward the end of the journey in the wilderness (chapters 1 and 26). It covers the thirty-eight years from the time the Israelites leave Sinai until they're about to cross the Jordan into the land of Canaan. It's a combination of law and "history"—if you can call it that.

God wanted to take a census of His people. This raises two issues. First, isn't He God? How come, in His omniscience, He doesn't know how many

Israelites there are? Perhaps, He's killed so many that He has lost count. The second problem is that census-taking was verboten. Consider the following story from 2 Samuel chapter 24: "On another occasion the Lord was angry with Israel, and he made David bring trouble on them. The Lord said to him, 'Go and count the people of Israel and Judah'...." *So, David went ahead, overruling, in the process, the commander of his armed forces, Joab, who seems to have figured out that God was setting a trap. The census took nine months and twenty days but when it was completed and the results were in—800,000 troops in Israel and another 500,000 in Judah—we learn,* "David was conscience-stricken after he had counted the fighting men, and he said to the Lord, 'I have sinned greatly in what I have done. Now, Lord, I beg you, take away the guilt of your servant. I have done a very foolish thing. Before David got up the next morning, the word of the Lord had come to Gad the prophet, David's seer: Go and tell David, 'This is what the Lord says: I am giving you three options. Choose one of them for me to carry out against you.' So Gad went to David and said to him, 'Shall there come on you three years of famine in your land? Or three months of fleeing from your enemies while they pursue you? Or three days of plague in your land? Now then, think it over and decide how I should answer the one who sent me." *David opted for the three days of plague and in that time, God killed 70,000 of the troops. Shades here of God hardening Pharaoh's heart so as to test His latest arsenal? What kind of a sicko is this?*

We were told in the Book of Leviticus that a male aged 20-60 is valued at 50 silver shekels. Presumably the troops are in this category. So, the loss of 70,000 troops was the loss of 3.5 million silver shekels. By today's standards, a biblical silver shekel is worth somewhere between $12,000 and $15,000. So, the economic equivalent, in today's US dollars, is around $50 billion! According to FEMA figures, hurricane Katrina—the costliest in US history—set the US back by $108 billion. One more God-tantrum and He is neck-and-neck with nature. Or, perhaps, hurricanes are simply another of His weapons? And, apart from the economic cost to David, what did it do to his ability to fend off the ubiquitous Philistines?

Back to the census. God, too, is basically just interested in counting the "battle-ready" men, so Moses is instructed to count everybody but record the names only of men age 20 and above who are eligible for fighting. The final count was 603,550. It seems that from the beginning men did not have ownership of their own bodies; they were—if you'll pardon the anachronism —merely cannon fodder. In Ireland, beginning in the 1700s, many parents did not record the birth of male children because the British used these lists to forcibly conscript young Irishmen into the British army and navy. In Moses's count, the Levites were exempted: "The ancestral tribe of the Levites, however, was not counted along with the others. The Lord had said to Moses: 'You must not count the tribe of Levi or include them in the census of the other Israelites. Instead, appoint the Levites to be in charge of the tabernacle of the covenant law—over all its furnishings and everything belonging to it. They are to carry the tabernacle and all its furnishings; they are to take care of it and encamp around it. Whenever the tabernacle is to move, the Levites are to take it down, and whenever the tabernacle is to be set up, the Levites shall do it. Anyone else who approaches it is to be put to death.'" *Somehow or other, however, we are told that the Levites numbered 22,000.*

Running as another mantra throughout the descriptions of the clans of Levi and their duties is the phrase, "Anyone else who approached the sanctuary was to be put to death." *Is there any decree He issues which is not uttered without a mention of the death penalty? I'm beginning to think that God is somewhere on the Autistic-Asperger's spectrum, in that He latches onto particular phrases and repeats them constantly, as if He's caught in some mental verbal loop.*

God also wants to know the total number of firstborn males of one month or older. This turns out to be 22, 273. Then, for God only knows what reason, He commands Moses to collect "redemption money" at five shekels each from each of the 273 firstborns, who are in excess of the 22,000 Levites. This is a total of 1,365 shekels, or around $18 million in today's money, which must be turned over to the Levites. And you thought that the IRS was the most complex and devious way ever devised to separate people from their hard-earned cash?

Back to misogyny and adultery. If a wife is unfaithful or is even suspected of it, she must be brought before the priest, let her hair down (literally!) and drink a special preparation of "bitter water" while agreeing to the following curse, should she be found guilty: "may the Lord cause you to become a curse among your people when he makes your womb miscarry and your abdomen swell. May this water that brings a curse enter your body so that your abdomen swells or your womb miscarries.' Then the woman is to say, 'Amen. So be it.'"

By chapter 9, verse 14, God has changed His mind about "aliens" (like me) celebrating the Passover, "If an alien who lives among you would celebrate the LORD's Passover, it shall be celebrated according to the statutes and regulations for the Passover. You shall have the same law for the resident alien as for the native of the land."

They've been camped at Sinai for quite some time now—more than two years—and it's time to provide them with a state-of-the-art GPS system: by day, the Lord's presence is in the form of a pillar of cloud and, at night, a pillar of fire. And the instructions are to break camp whenever the pillar moved; and to pitch camp whenever it settled—whether the interval was a few hours or more than a month. He did, however, provide a cheat sheet for those who weren't paying attention to the pillars. Here were Moses's instructions: "Make two trumpets of silver, making them of hammered silver, for you to use in summoning the community and in breaking camp. When both are blown, the whole community shall gather round you at the entrance of the tent of meeting; but when one of them is blown, only the tribal leaders, the heads of the clans of Israel, shall gather round you. When you sound the signal, those encamped on the east side shall break camp; when you sound a second signal, those encamped on the south side shall break camp; when you sound a third signal, those encamped on the west side shall break camp; when you sound a fourth signal, those encamped on the north side shall break camp. Thus shall the signal be sounded for them to break camp."

Finally, it's time to get their asses in gear (literally). It was all very well organized, with the tribe of Judah leading the way and the tribe of Dan bringing up the rear. Moses, however, isn't convinced that God knows the terrain, so he tries to prevail on his Midianite brother-in-law, Hobab, son of Reuel/Jethro, to serve as their guide: "Moses said to Hobab, son of Reuel the Midianite, Moses's father-in-law, 'We are setting out for the place concerning which the LORD has said, 'I will give it to you.' Come with us, and we will be generous toward you, for the LORD has promised prosperity to Israel.' But he answered, 'No, I will not come. I am going instead to the land of my birth.' Moses said, 'Please, do not leave us; you know where we can camp in the wilderness, and you can serve as our guide. If you come with us, we will share with you the prosperity the LORD will bestow on us.'"

There are two problems here. First, scholars dispute whether Hobab is a brother-in-law of Moses or simply a third name for Reuel/Jethro. Second, it's not obvious whether or not Hobab agreed to act as guide. According to Judges chapter 1:16, it appears he did, but both Exodus 18:27 and Numbers 10:29-32 suggest that Hobab chose to go home to his own place. Are we still buying into the notion of biblical inerrancy? In any case, Moses seems to have much more confidence in Hobab's ability to navigate in the desert (and, presumably find the oases) than in God's.

Next follows a three-way struggle between the ungrateful Israelites, a frustrated Moses and—here we go again—a vengeful God. The people yearn for the "good ol' days" of slavery in Egypt, "The riffraff among them were so greedy for meat that even the Israelites lamented again, 'If only we had meat for food! We remember the fish we used to eat without cost in Egypt, and the cucumbers, the melons, the leeks, the onions, and the garlic. But now we are famished; we have nothing to look forward to but this manna.'"

Moses gets upset with God for leaving him to carry the entire people on his back, so God appoints 70 elder/helpers; and now God is free to devote His whole attention to the complaints of the people—"You want meat? I'll give you meat!" Here's the scoop: "There arose a wind from the LORD that drove in quail from the sea and left them all around the camp site, to a distance of a day's journey and at a depth of two cubits upon the ground. So all that day, all night, and all the next day the people set about to gather in the quail. Even the one who got the least gathered ten homers of them. Then they spread them out all around the camp. But while the meat was still between their teeth, before it could be chewed, the LORD's wrath flared up against the people, and the

LORD struck them with a very great plague. So that place was named Kibroth-hattaavah, because it was there that the greedy people were buried." *We are not told how many people got killed in that little contretemps. I can't resist doing the math on this! If a day's journey is about 10 miles and two cubits is about three feet, then God deposited about 250,000,000 cubic feet of meat around the camp!*

For some reason, only now do Aaron and Miriam—Moses's siblings—get upset with him for being married to Zipporah, the Midianite daughter of Jethro. Feeding off each other, they springboard onto a complaint about Moses's claim that God speaks only through him. So, God inflicts Miriam with leprosy for this revolt, only curing her at Moses's request after seven days. That seems to have settled any aspirations they had.

Moses sends twelve spies into the land of Canaan with the following orders: "See what kind of land it is and whether the people living there are strong or weak, few or many. Is the country in which they live good or bad? Are the towns in which they dwell open or fortified? Is the soil fertile or barren, wooded or clear? And do your best to get some of the fruit of the land.' It was then the season for early grapes." *When they return, only one of them, Caleb, of the tribe of Judah, is in favor of invasion. The others are scared, telling the people that the country was inhabited by giants—descendants of the Nephilim (hybrid human/gods whom we met in Genesis chapter 6)—in whose sight "we looked like grasshoppers." Not a great start to the conquest project. Round one goes to the much-discounted Canaanites, Hittites, Amorites, Perizzites, Girgashites, Hivites and Jebusites.*

Once more, the people lose faith in this Johnny-come-lately God and they decide to pick a new leader who will bring them back to Egypt. Moses, Aaron, Caleb, and Joshua try to reason with them, but the people respond by threatening to stone all four. God goes into His default mode, telling Moses, "Outta my way! I'm gonna wipe 'em out and then make you into an even greater nation!" Hasn't He already done that a few times and threatened it a few more times? Moses goes into bargaining mode, once more reminding God that He's gonna look like a doofus when the ever-prowling Egyptians find a couple of million rotting Israelite carcasses in the desert. God sees the sense in this, but His mafia-instinct is whetted—"Revenge is a dish best served cold."

So, He determines to take 40 years to wipe 'em out. Thus, none of them except Caleb and Joshua will enter the Promised Land: "Here in the wilderness your dead bodies shall fall. Of all your men of twenty years or more, enrolled in your registration, who grumbled against me, not one of you shall enter the land where I solemnly swore to settle you, except Caleb, son of Jephunneh, and Joshua, son of Nun."

Let's think about that. 603,550 soldiers, and if you add in the elders and the typical life expectancy of the women, as well as child mortality rates at the time, you can safely add another 400,000 souls. Then 1,003,550 Israelites are going to die over the next 38 years. That translates to 26,409 each year or 508 per week. Is it any wonder that there are so many prohibitions against touching a dead body? They must have been everywhere.

As an example to the community—and maybe even to provide some physical exercise while at the same time encouraging group bonding—a man who was found gathering firewood on the Sabbath was stoned to death by the community. "While the Israelites were in the wilderness, a man was discovered gathering wood on the sabbath day. Those who caught him at it brought him to Moses and Aaron and the whole community. But they put him in custody, for there was no clear decision as to what should be done with him. Then the LORD said to Moses: This man shall be put to death; let the whole community stone him outside the camp. So the whole community led him outside the camp and stoned him to death, as the LORD had commanded Moses." *How, in God's name, do you even manage to get your shot in when there are two million other people throwing rocks at the same tiny target?*

Don't look now, but here comes the next rebellion. This one is composed of two factions; one faction is disputing Moses's political leadership (Dathan and Abiram were the instigators of this group) and the other one—250 Levites (at the prompting of Korah)—is disputing Aaron's priestly leadership. This latter group doesn't just want to be in charge of sacred furniture (the equivalent of sacristans in the Catholic liturgy), they want to be full priests. So, Moses issues a challenge on God's behalf and here's what happened: "No sooner had he finished saying all this than the ground beneath them split open, and the earth opened its mouth and swallowed them and their families and all of Korah's people with all their possessions. They went down alive to Sheol with all belonging to them; the earth closed over them, and they disappeared from the assembly. But all the Israelites near them fled at their shrieks, saying, 'The earth might swallow us too!'...And fire from the LORD came forth which consumed the two hundred and fifty men who were offering the incense."

You think the people would have learned their lesson? Nah! Next day, at the instigation of Consumer Affairs, the whole Israelite community is back accusing Moses and Aaron of "killing the people of God." To show His approval of this democratic feedback, God went into road-rage and killed another 14,700. That'll learn 'em! And just in case they are still not convinced of Aaron's priestly authority, God proposes a contest. Each tribe is to bring a staff (the symbol of authority) with the tribal name inscribed on it. Aaron, also, will include his autographed staff. And the contest? The staffs are to be deposited overnight in the Tent of the Meeting, and whichever staff is found to have sprouted by morning is the winner, and God's choice of high priest. Guess who won? Aaron's staff not only sprouted overnight, but it also produced blossoms and ripe almonds!

How 'bout you? Would you be more impressed with a blossom-covered, almond-laden stick or the death of 14,700 disgruntled kvetchers?

Seemingly, the Israelites are perpetual complainers. Their next beef is a lack of water. Once again, they want to go back to Egypt. God tells Moses and Aaron to take the staff (I wonder if they've first eaten the almonds off it?) and strike a rock to produce water. Moses grabs the staff, shouting at the people, "Just listen, you rebels! Are we to produce water for you out of this rock?" Then he whacks the rock, not once but twice, and water gushes out, enough for both people and livestock. Alas, the story does not have a happy ending, "But the LORD said to Moses and Aaron: 'Because you did not have confidence in me, to acknowledge my holiness before the Israelites, therefore you shall not lead this assembly into the land I have given them.'"

Whoa there! Let's back up a little. Anybody with even a smidgen of a sense of fair play cannot fail to see the utter injustice of this. Moses, if he ever actually existed, is not one of my favorite people, yet he bent over backwards to follow God's injunctions. And now, for a single act of frustration, he's denied entry into the Promised Land. It upsets the Irish in me! At this stage, if I were Moses I'd say, "Screw you, Big Fellah, you take them from here!" And I'd go back to Jethro and let Yahweh figure out how to get the Israelites to Canaan. But Moses is a better man than I; he just kept on trucking.

However, time's up for both Miriam and Aaron. God orders Moses to bring Aaron and his son Eleazar to the top of mount Hor. There, Moses stripped Aaron of his priestly garments, put them on Eleazar, and "Aaron died on the top of the mountain." *We're not told if he died of hypothermia, being up there naked an' all. His experience of being a priest was brief—two or three years—and unhappy, beginning with the killing of his two sons, and then dying alone atop a foreign mountain in his undies.*

Now comes the first use of the "ban." Up to now, the Israelites haven't had a chance to use it, but when they do get the opportunity, they take to it like ducks to water. The idea of the ban is that, once an invading Israelite force conquers a foreign city or tribe, they must wipe out every living being—just like the Great Teacher in the Sky did in the flood. The phrase that will be used a lot is "kill everything that breathes." It seems that God must have also taught this skill to other nations, because you don't have to dig very deeply into human history to see how frequently it was employed.

The Israelites' first chance to practice this injunction of the Compassionate One was against the king of Arad, a Canaanite ruler, and his people; they got a perfect score. You'd imagine that the resultant adrenaline rush would sustain their mood for a bit. Nah! They're back to complaining about the manna menu, so God sends a bunch of poisonous snakes—seraph serpents —to bite them so that "many people died." How many times can you say, "I'm sorry; I'll never do it again!" and be credible? But Moses prays to God to relent and is instructed to fashion and erect a bronze seraph serpent, so that all who look upon it would recover from the snake bite. I can't help wondering what the difference is between Moses fashioning a bronze serpent —given the garden of Eden story an' all—and Aaron fashioning a golden calf. In any case, this bronze serpent became a treasured artifact and memento of the Exodus for some 500 years until, in a fit of piety, King Hezekiah—who flourished around 700 BCE— got rid of it (2 Kings 18:4): "He removed the pagan shrines, smashed the sacred pillars, and cut down the Asherah poles. He broke up the bronze serpent that Moses had made, because the people of Israel had been offering sacrifices to it. The bronze serpent was called Nehushtan."

They're on the move again. For a change of pace, instead of warring with the Amorites, who stupidly enough put their tribal lands smack bang in the middle of the Israelites' route, they offer to pass through peacefully, promising not to eat any of the grapes nor even draw water from any of the wells. Sihon, king of the Amorites, ungraciously declines and opts to fight instead. Bad idea! "But Israel put him to the sword, and took possession of his land from the Arnon to the Jabbok and as far as Jazer of the Ammonites, for Jazer is the boundary of the Ammonites. Israel seized all the towns here, and Israel settled in all the towns of the Amorites, in Heshbon and all its dependencies."

They're now getting a taste for being on the "dishing out" end of violence, so they next engage Og, king of Bashan, with predictable results: "So they struck him down with his sons and all his forces, until not a survivor was left to him, and they took possession of his land."

Now comes a talking donkey. And not just a talking donkey who can say, "Mama" and "Dada" and "Fetch me a carrot," but an educated ass, well versed in religious debate. Here's the backstory: The Israelites have reached Moab, which is northeast of the Dead Sea. The king of Moab—Balak—was scared by the size of the Israelite horde and decided to engage some divine help. So, he sent messengers, promising great rewards, to Balaam, an Ammonite renowned for his divination skills, to come and curse the Israelites. Balaam consults his divination paraphernalia and initially is told by God not to accompany these men back to Moab. So, he sends them away. Getting more and more concerned about the Israelites, Balak sends a second delegation with promises of even bigger rewards. Balaam goes back to his Ouija board. Now, God changes His mind: "That night God came to Balaam and said to him: If these men have come to summon you, go back with them; yet only on the condition that you do exactly as I tell you. So the next morning when Balaam arose, he saddled his donkey, and went off with the princes of Moab." *So, he sets off on his Don Quixote donkey, only for God to have another rethink and get mad with him:* "But now God's anger flared up at him for going."

God stations an angel in the road to block his way but only the donkey can see the angel. Three times the donkey takes evasive action in order to circumvent the sword-carrying angel, squeezing Balaam's leg against a stone wall in the process. Balaam applies the stick to the willful ass. Finally, with absolutely no space to maneuver around the winged heavenly hitman, the donkey lies down on the road with Balaam still aboard.

The following lively debate then takes place: "When the donkey saw the angel of the LORD there, she lay down under Balaam. Balaam's anger flared up and he beat the donkey with his stick. Then the LORD opened the mouth of the donkey, and she asked Balaam, 'What have I done to you that you beat me these three times? 'You have acted so willfully against me,' said Balaam to the donkey, 'that if I only had a sword at hand, I would kill you here and now.' But the donkey said to Balaam, 'Am I not your donkey, on which you have always ridden until now? Have I been in the habit of treating you this way before?' 'No,' he replied. Then the LORD opened Balaam's eyes, so that he saw the angel of the LORD standing on the road with sword drawn; and he knelt and bowed down to the ground."

Balaam's ass went on to have a very successful career in the Roman Circus—just kidding! O'Sullivan joked. *Naturally enough,* he continued more seriously, *Balaam apologizes to the angel and promises he will return home immediately. But no! God has changed His mind once again:* "Then Balaam said to the angel of the LORD, 'I have sinned. Yet I did not know that you took up a position to oppose my journey. Since it has displeased you, I will go back home.' But the angel of the LORD said to Balaam: 'Go with the men; but you may say only what I tell you.' So Balaam went on with the princes of Balak."

Balaam orders Balak to build seven altars and to sacrifice a bull and a ram on each one; but God won't bite and, instead, Balaam is forced to bless Israel. Balak ain't a quitter, so he tries twice more, each time in a different location and each time erecting seven altars, on each of which he sacrifices a bull and a ram. But God refuses to budge, and each time Balaam is forced to bless Israel.

In an act of deep appreciation to God for using Balaam—a foreigner—to bless Israel, the people immediately begin to worship another god—the Baal of Peor. And who were the instigators of this apostasy? The women! the

Moabite women. Balak's secret troops? God's response is to order Moses to "publicly execute" all of the apostates, resulting in 24,000 fresh corpses. "While Israel was living at Shittim, the people profaned themselves by prostituting themselves with the Moabite women. These then invited the people to the sacrifices of their god, and the people ate of the sacrifices and bowed down to their god. Israel thereby attached itself to the Baal of Peor, and the LORD's anger flared up against Israel. The LORD said to Moses: 'Gather all the leaders of the people, and publicly execute them before the LORD, that the blazing wrath of the LORD may turn away from Israel.' So Moses told the Israelite judges, 'Each of you kill those of his men who have attached themselves to the Baal of Peor.'"

One Israelite man, Zimri, had the chutzpah to bring home a Midianite wife, Cozbi. Aaron's grandson, Phineas—a priest—followed the couple to their tent and speared them to death. As a reward, God promises to extend Phineas's priestly line forever, "At this a certain Israelite came and brought in a Midianite woman to his kindred in the view of Moses and of the whole Israelite community, while they were weeping at the entrance of the tent of meeting. When Phinehas, son of Eleazar, son of Aaron the priest, saw this, he rose up from the assembly, and taking a spear in his hand, followed the Israelite into the tent where he pierced the two of them, the Israelite and the woman. Thus the plague upon the Israelites was checked; but the dead from the plague were twenty-four thousand. Then the LORD said to Moses: Phinehas, son of Eleazar, son of Aaron the priest, has turned my anger from the Israelites by his being as jealous among them as I am; that is why I did not put an end to the Israelites in my jealousy. Announce, therefore, that I hereby give him my covenant of peace, which shall be for him and for his descendants after him the covenant of an everlasting priesthood, because he was jealous on behalf of his God and thus made expiation for the Israelites."

From now on, the Midianites will be targeted for elimination. (More on that later.) Nobody seems to remember that Moses's own wife Zipporah was a Midianite; in fact, she was the daughter of a priest of Midian, Jethro.

The Hebrew phrase which is translated as "publicly execute" means more than just kill them; it also implies the post-mortem dismemberment or impaling of the bodies. Seriously, dear reader/juror, how are we expected to worship this brutal, fickle, psychotic God?

By now, so many Israelites have died during God's regular hissy fits that He needs to do a second counting. So, He orders another census. Again, He's only interested in the men over 20. And the total score this time is 601,730. As is now the custom, the Levites are counted separately. And, again, it is only the males, but from age one month and upwards. The total is 23,000.

Then, a very telling statement: "These, then, were those enrolled by Moses and Eleazar the priest, when they enrolled the Israelites on the plains of Moab along the Jordan at Jericho. Among them there was not one of those who had been enrolled by Moses and Aaron the priest, when they enrolled the Israelites in the wilderness of Sinai. For the LORD had told them that they would surely die in the wilderness, and not one of them was left except Caleb, son of Jephunneh, and Joshua, son of Nun" *If you remember the previous census—the one done at Sinai 38 years before—it means that 603,550 men aged 20 and over had died in the desert, courtesy of God's out-of-control, homicidal temper. Gee, I can't wait to get to heaven and meet Him!*

And talk about counting your chickens before they're hatched—God now gives instructions about how to divide up the land of Canaan—which they have yet to enter—among the 12 tribes. It's to be a combination of lottery and tribe size! "The LORD said to Moses: Among these the land shall be divided as their heritage in keeping with the number of people named. To a large tribe you shall assign a large heritage, to a small tribe a small heritage, each receiving its heritage in proportion to the number enrolled in it. But the land shall be divided by lot, all inheriting according to the lists of their ancestral tribes. As the lot falls the heritage of each tribe, large or small, will be assigned." *I wonder if they bought their lottery tickets at 7 Eleven?*

At last, a significant appeal for women's rights. The five daughters of Zelophedad, a descendent of Joseph, bring their case to Moses, the priests and the community. They want to know why their dead father's name should be cut off from his clan simply because he had no sons. Their plea resulted in the following divine decree: "So Moses laid their case before the LORD, and the LORD said to him: The plea of Zelophehad's daughters is just; you shall give them hereditary land among their father's kindred and transfer their father's heritage to them. Tell the Israelites: If a man dies without leaving a son, you shall transfer his heritage to his daughter."

There was a corollary, however. Lest the five daughters "alienate" the clan's promised inheritance in the land of Canaan, they must agree to marry only within the clan. No problemo! Each of the five agrees to God's stipulation, "The daughters of Zelophehad did exactly as the LORD commanded Moses. Mahlah, Tirzah, Hoglah, Milcah and Noah, Zelophehad's daughters, married sons of their uncles on their father's side. They married within the clans of the descendants of Manasseh, son of Joseph; hence their heritage remained in the tribe of their father's clan." *In other words, each married a first cousin.*

And a further setback: in a lengthy section on valid and invalid vows, a woman's vow is only valid if neither her father (before she marries) or her husband (after she marries) objects. If she is widowed or divorced, however, nobody can invalidate her vow. Thank heaven for little mercies. In fact, however, under Confucianist law, Chinese women had it worse. They were the property of their fathers until they got married, the property of their husbands once they got married, and the property of their firstborn sons once widowed.

And now, Moses's own time is up. He is to transfer leadership to Joshua, who will decide when or when not to engage in battle by having the high priest—Eleazar, son of Aaron—consult the Urim and Thummim, the Israelite equivalent of the Tarot Deck, animal bones or the Ouija Board. But even as God decrees Moses's death, He still can't resist reminding him of his grievous sin of striking the rock twice.

Before Moses dies, he has two more jobs to do, two more slaughters to supervise. First, God tells him to ensure that His regular supply of meat continue: animals must be sacrificed every morning, every evening, on the Sabbath, at the New Moon festival, at Passover, at Pentecost, on New Year's Day, on the Day of Atonement, and on the Feast of Booths. It's no bloody wonder that the Israelites had no meat left for themselves. I wonder what God's BMI was?

Can you imagine the stench, the bedlam, the bleating and bellowing of the terrified beasts who can smell each other's fear? The urine and dung and the ubiquitous blood? The hordes of flies settling on everything and then cross-pollinating by crawling over people's bodies and into all the orifices? Is it any wonder that plagues were a regular feature of life in the desert? Didn't God know anything about hygiene? Or He just didn't give a damn as long as He could smell roasting flesh and taste mammalian blood? (What a weirdo!)

And Moses's very final task is to organize the genocide of the Midianites —such a wonderful way to exit incarnation. One thousand men from each of the twelve tribes are sent forth under the leadership of the priest Phineas, son of the high priest, Eleazar, to conduct the slaughter. Way to go, holy man! They killed every single Midianite male and...but why don't I tell this final story in Moses's words from the book of Numbers: "They waged war against the Midianites, as the LORD had commanded Moses, and killed every male. Besides those slain in battle, they killed the kings of Midian: Evi, Rekem, Zur, Hur and Reba, the five kings of Midian; and they also killed Balaam, son of Beor, with the sword. But the Israelites took captive the women of the Midianites with their children, and all their herds and flocks and wealth as loot, while they set on fire all the towns where they had settled and all their encampments. Then they took all the plunder, with the people and animals they had captured, and brought the captives, together with the spoils and plunder, to Moses and Eleazar the priest and to the Israelite community at their camp on the plains of Moab by the Jordan opposite Jericho. When Moses and Eleazar the priest, with all the leaders of the community, went outside the camp to meet them, Moses became angry with the officers of the army, the commanders of thousands and the commanders of hundreds, who were returning from the military campaign. 'So you have spared all the women!' he exclaimed. 'These are the very ones who on Balaam's advice were behind the Israelites' unfaithfulness to the LORD in the affair at Peor, so that plague struck the LORD's community. Now kill, therefore, every male among the children and kill every woman who has had sexual relations with a man. But you may spare for yourselves all the girls who have not had sexual relations'....This plunder, what was left of the loot which the troops had taken, amounted to six hundred and seventy-five thousand sheep, seventy-two thousand oxen, sixty-one thousand donkeys, and thirty-two thousand women who had not had sexual relations."

Are you still praying to this monster? When ISIS does this kind of thing they're acting as terrorists; when God does it, He's within His rights—his victims must have somehow deserved it. According to Thomas Chalkley, in 1713, "There are none so blind as those who will not see. The most deluded people are those who choose to ignore what they already know."

So ends day four of the prosecution's case, and the gavel slam echoes in the silence.

DEUTERONOMY

Another gavel slam opens day five of this ugly trial. We'll be covering some familiar territory as we continue to question and expose this "God" for who He really is. If you like stories of jealousy, greed, and cruelty you won't be disappointed.

The prosecutor opened the proceedings with a word of thanks to expert witness Dr. Dermot O'Sullivan, whose testimony would be concluding with a look at the book of Deuteronomy. *"Thank you, Dr. O'Sullivan, for your detailed analysis of these rather difficult documents taken from the Biblical accounts detailing behaviors and decrees associated with the accused, a deity also known as Yahweh. Your expertise has been very enlightening.*

Aw shucks, don't mention it, Michael, O'Sullivan blushed. *I wish I could say it's been my pleasure, but I really take no pleasure in exposing the atrocities contained in the Bible. Sadly, the book of Deuteronomy is more of the same.*

Deuteronomy—which means "second Law" or "copy of the Law"—was a work completed around 600 BCE in the southern kingdom of Judea, based on notes that were begun around 750 BCE in the northern kingdom of Israel and set in the mouth of Moses. It is well named because much of its content is a repeat of laws we've already encountered. It is the final book of Torah/Pentateuch. Written long after the events described, it provides a retrospective look at the exodus event, the Sinai Covenant, the wandering in the wilderness

—as well as a look into the already-experienced "future" as they prepare to enter Canaan.

For a change, much of this text is delivered in the first person singular, that is, "I, Moses said/did..." And it is also interesting to note that the mountain on which the covenant was given is now called Horeb. This is from the E and D streams of material. The earlier name—Sinai—is from the J and P streams. J and P were produced by the Judeans before and during the Babylonian exile, whereas E and D were begun in the northern kingdom. Informing the entire book of Deuteronomy is the very real memory, from 722 BCE, of the fall of the northern kingdom of Israel, at the hands of the great Assyrian empire, with graphic details of the siege that preceded it.

Basically, the book consists of three great Mosaic exhortations that boil down to two divinely dictated scenarios offered to the Israelites. It goes like this: If you remain faithful and worship only me, you will be showered with a multitude of blessings; but if you stray and worship other gods, you have no idea just how mean-spirited I'm gonna get!

Moses recapitulates the journey from Sinai/Horeb recounting the enforcement of the ban that left no living being in its wake, nor city that wasn't reduced to its fire-blackened walls. All of this is told dispassionately, almost like a gunfighter from a western movie putting notches on his gun. The phrase "we left no survivors" is now the punch line concluding each conquest. As a typical example, here's a passage from Deuteronomy chapter 3: "the LORD, our God, delivered into our power also Og, king of Bashan, with all his people. We defeated him so completely that we left him no survivor. At that time we captured all his cities; there was no town we did not take: sixty cities in all, the whole region of Argob, the kingdom of Og in Bashan—all these cities were fortified with high walls and gates and bars—besides a great number of unwalled towns. As we had done to Sihon, king of Heshbon, so also here we put all the towns under the ban, men, women and children; but all the livestock and the spoils of each city we took as plunder for ourselves."

Moses adds a note on the huge stature of the king of Bashan, obviously a descendant of the Nephilim whom we encountered in Genesis chapter 6—the hybrid giants resulting from the mating of the "sons of God" with the "daughters of men." Here's what he notes: "Og, king of Bashan, was the last remaining survivor of the Rephaim. He had a bed of iron, nine regular cubits long and four wide, which is still preserved in Rabbah of the Ammonites." Translated, the bed was 13.5 feet long by 6 feet wide! (Imagine trying to find sheets and shams for that.) Incidentally, the Anakim/Nephilim are mentioned in pre-Israelite Egyptian texts.

In the only example of Moses trying to get something for himself, we read the following: "It was then that I entreated the LORD, 'Lord GOD, you have begun to show to your servant your greatness and your mighty hand. What god in heaven or on earth can perform deeds and powerful acts like yours? Ah, let me cross over and see the good land beyond the Jordan, that fine hill country, and the Lebanon!' But the LORD was angry with me on your account and would not hear me. The LORD said to me, Enough! Speak to me no more of this. Go up to the top of Pisgah and look out to the west, and to the north, and to the south, and to the east. Look well, for you shall not cross this Jordan." *What a harsh and vindictive god this is!*

Still, even then, I suspect Moses is not a monotheist. In fact, even God Himself is not! This, however, does not prevent Him from preening Himself and putting words of admiration on the lips of those nations who are following other gods: "For what great nation is there that has gods so close to it as the LORD, our God, is to us whenever we call upon him?" *Getting carried away with the exuberance of His own verbosity and, it seems, believing His own claims—a typical symptom of a psychopath—He then goes into a long recital of His own achievements both in Egypt, and since, culminating in a promise and a reminder:* "When the LORD, your God, brings you into the land which he swore to your ancestors, to Abraham, Isaac, and Jacob, that he would give you, a land with fine, large cities that you did not build, with houses full of goods of all sorts that you did not garner, with cisterns that you did not dig, with vineyards and olive groves that you did not plant; and when, therefore, you eat and are satisfied, be careful not to forget the LORD, who brought you out of the land of Egypt, that house of slavery." *This has all the hallmarks of a throw-away note in the minutes of a multinational corporation board meeting whose decisions will signal the horrible suffering and death of millions of sub-Saharan Africans. But not to worry, the shareholders and executives will benefit hugely.*

This God has zero respect for the time, talent, and labor that other peoples, over hundreds of years, poured into their own futures and that of their children. All is to be snatched and given to the invaders. Doesn't this sicken your soul and make your heart weep, dear reader/juror? Innocent children and defenseless grandparents not just dispossessed to wander homeless, but exterminated, for happening to be born in the wrong place, and whose only crime was to cultivate the gifts bestowed on them by Pacha Mama. As I've said previously, this is not unique to the Israelites. I believe that there is not a single tribe anywhere on the planet which is not squatting on territory taken violently from previous occupants. But to claim that this is not merely God's will but a detailed plan that He personally crafted, orchestrated, and executed? No! I cannot go there. If there was ever a case of "taking the Lord's name in vain," this is it. It is the ultimate projection, by the human shadow, of ultimate Evil onto ultimate Good. Even atheism is a more hopeful interpretation of life than belief in such a monster.

God now engages, again, in a long diatribe in which He reminds the Israelites of their many sins and of His many mighty deeds. We have a saying in my native land that "Irish dementia" is when you forget everything and everyone except the details and names of people who have, at one time or another, screwed you over. God has this form of dementia, in spades. He goes on and on and on about the wonders He's worked and the ingratitude of the people.

By now, even Moses himself is showing definite signs of senility. In his best imitation of God, he goes over and over the same old stories, reminding the people of "all I've done for you!" and their constant sinning. I wonder if by now anybody is actually listening. Moses, you hear that noise? It's the sound of two million people yawning.

Another constant refrain is to "watch out for the Levites"—pay taxes to support them, make sure they are given the choicest meat... I wonder if the priest-Levites had any part in writing this legislation?

Once the people finally conquer the land—a process that will take another 200 years—they are no longer to worship God in the moving tabernacle, rather there is to be only one, fixed residence for Him. Of course, this particular passage is being written in the Southern Kingdom of Judah some 600 years after Moses's alleged instructions. In the meantime, Solomon had built the temple around 950 BCE and the civil war had divided the ten northern tribes from the two southern ones. The kings of the north, obviously, did not want their subjects going down south to worship in the temple of "the enemy" in Jerusalem. Hence, this other piece of retroactive legislation.

God's paranoia about being jilted in favor of other gods continues through these Mosaic harangues. I sometimes pity this God who gets no respite from His own greatest fear—being dumped in favor of a more appealing divinity. "If you hear it said concerning one of the cities which the LORD, your God, gives you to dwell in, that certain scoundrels have sprung up in your midst and have led astray the inhabitants of their city, saying, 'Come, let us serve other gods,' whom you have not known, you must inquire carefully into the matter and investigate it thoroughly. If you find that it is true and an established fact that this abomination has been committed in your midst, you shall put the inhabitants of that city to the sword, placing the city and all that is in it, even its livestock, under the ban. Having heaped up all its spoils in the middle of its square, you shall burn the city with all its spoils as a whole burnt offering to the LORD, your God. Let it be a heap of ruins forever, never to be rebuilt." *What a kindly soul.*

At that, the Defense attorney screeched her chair on the tile floor and popped to her feet, calling out *"Objection, Your Honor. The witness is editorializing again."*

Objection sustained, Judge Grossler agreed, adding, *"Please avoid sarcastic commentary, Dr. O'Sullivan.*

Humble apologies, O'Sullivan demurred without missing a beat. *Thinking "ahead," God decides it's okay if the people eventually want to have a king to rule over them, as other nations do. But they can't choose a king themselves—no democracy allowed—rather God will appoint one with the following cautions:* "When you have come into the land which the LORD, your God, is giving you, and have taken possession of it and settled in it, should you then decide, 'I will set a king over me, like all the surrounding nations,' you may indeed set over you a king whom the LORD, your God, will choose. Someone from among your own kindred you may set over you as king; you may not set over you a foreigner, who is no kin of yours. But he shall not have a great number of horses; nor shall he make his people go back again to Egypt to acquire many horses, for the LORD said to you, Do not go back that way again. Neither shall he have a great number of wives, lest his heart turn away, nor shall he accumulate a vast amount of silver and gold." *I wonder how Solomon got around those laws with his 700 wives and 300 concubines, not to mention his equine collection:* "And Solomon had 40,000 stalls of horses for his chariots, and 12,000 horsemen." (1 Kings 4:26) *Incidentally, in another display of "biblical inerrancy"—probably due to scribal error—we read in 2 Chronicles 9:25 that the number was only 4,000:* "Now Solomon had 4,000 stalls for horses and chariots and 12,000 horsemen, and he stationed them in the chariot cities and with the king in Jerusalem." *Hey, what's an extra zero between friends?*

And, it seems, the wisest man in the world had lots of foreign friends in high places, who showered him with exotic gifts: "All King Solomon's goblets were gold, and all the household articles in the Palace of the Forest of Lebanon were pure gold. Nothing was made of silver, because silver was considered of little value in Solomon's days. The king had a fleet of trading ships at sea along with the ships of Hiram. Once every three years it returned, carrying gold, silver and ivory, and apes and baboons. King Solomon was greater in riches and wisdom than all the other kings of the earth. The whole world sought audience with Solomon to hear the wisdom God had put in his heart. Year after year, everyone who came brought a gift—articles of silver and gold, robes, weapons and spices, and horses and mules. Solomon accumulated chariots and horses; he had fourteen hundred chariots and twelve thousand horses, which he kept in the chariot cities and also with him in Jerusalem. The king made silver as common in Jerusalem as stones, and cedar as plentiful as sycamore-fig trees in the foothills." (1 Kings 10:21-27)

And what's with the apes and baboons? Was he trying to get a head-start on Darwin or just intent on creating a zoo?

There is to be no messing about casting spells, consulting ghosts, dealing with spirits, or using oracles to talk to the dead. Rather, God promises, He will send prophets to speak on His behalf. But if a "fake" prophet purports to speak in His name or speak in the name of a different god, that prophet shall die. Then He raises and answers His own question, how to distinguish between the two kinds of prophet? Simple. If their predictions come true, then they are the real deal. Wow! What a wonderful piece of finessing. This guy would make a great Bridge player. With that kind of test, how could God possibly lose? It's like an investment broker saying that any accurate prediction of the behavior of the stock market really came from me. If a prediction proved erroneous, some other schmuck made it.

Next, God, in His infinite mercy, is going to make a distinction between the treatment of conquered cities in the "promised land" and those in other parts. Underlying this distinction is, once more, the fear of apostasy. I wonder, does He bite His nails? Or clench His teeth when He's sleeping? "When you draw near a city to attack it, offer it terms of peace. If it agrees to your terms of peace and lets you in, all the people to be found in it shall serve you in forced labor. But if it refuses to make peace with you and instead joins battle with you, lay siege to it, and when the LORD, your God, delivers it into your power, put every male in it to the sword; but the women and children and livestock and anything else in the city—all its spoil—you may take as plunder for yourselves, and you may enjoy this spoil of your enemies, which the LORD, your God, has given you. That is how you shall deal with any city at a considerable distance from you, which does not belong to these nations here. But in the cities of these peoples that the LORD, your God, is giving you as a heritage, you shall not leave a single soul alive. You must put them all under the ban—the Hittites, Amorites, Canaanites, Perizzites, Hivites, and Jebusites—just as the LORD, your God, has commanded you, so that they do not teach you to do all the abominations that they do for their gods, and you thus sin against the LORD, your God." *In His all-seeing wisdom, there are three categories, (1) The citizens of faraway cities (not in Canaan) who agree to peace terms must be taken as slaves; (2) The male citizens of faraway cities (not in Canaan) who do not agree to peace terms must all be slaughtered; while the women, the kids, the livestock and other goodies are to be taken as booty; and (3) The citizens of the cities of Canaan, must all be wiped out—lest they lead the Israelites into apostasy. What a pathetic, paranoid psychopath. Are you still "worshipping" Him?*

What happens when a warrior feels attracted to a foreign woman whose parents he has just slaughtered? I'm glad you asked. Here's what must be done, "When you go out to war against your enemies and the LORD, your God, delivers them into your power, so that you take captives, if you see a beautiful woman among the captives and become so enamored of her that you wish to have her as a wife, and so you take her home to your house, she must shave her head, cut her nails, lay aside her captive's garb, and stay in your house, mourning her father and mother for a full month. After that, you may come to her, and you shall be her husband and she shall be your wife." *There, I'm glad we sorted that one out.*

Dress-wearing men and trouser-wearing women beware; you are in violation of Deuteronomy 22:5: "A woman shall not wear a man's garment, nor shall a man put on a woman's clothing; for anyone who does such things is an abomination to the LORD, your God." *I hope that doesn't include kilts!*

Next comes the case of a man who marries a woman and later falls out of love with her and, in order to divorce her, accuses her of not being a virgin on their wedding night. In that case, the parents of the girl must produce the bloodied sheet taken from the marriage bed on the morning after the wedding. If the man is found to have lied, "Then these city elders shall take the man and discipline him, and fine him one hundred silver shekels, which they shall give to the young woman's father, because the man slandered a virgin in Israel. She shall remain his wife, and he may not divorce her as long as he lives." *I wonder how the "vindicated" wife is going to feel for the remainder of her married life.*

Back to Deuteronomy. Suddenly, in the midst of a whole bunch of legislation, we get this enlightened statement: "Parents shall not be put to death for their children, nor shall children be put to death for their parents; only for one's own crime shall a person be put to death." *This, obviously, is an insertion from a later, more balanced moral code. It's like an oasis in the desert where God had been, regularly, threatening to punish the parents' crime to, at least, the third or fourth generation. Both Jeremiah (c. 600 BCE) and Ezekiel (c. 550 BCE) reject the Hebrew proverb about the kids' teeth being set on edge because the parents have eaten sour grapes, and promote instead personal responsibility only:* "In those days people will no longer say, 'The parents have eaten sour grapes, and the children's teeth are set on edge.' Instead, everyone will die for their own sin; whoever eats sour grapes—their own teeth will be set on edge." *This is a huge improvement on the practice of "corporate singularity," whereby the entire tribe was held guilty—and punished—for the sin of an individual member. It's too bad our species still fails repeatedly on this one. Think of all the Iraqi civilians who died for the sins of Saddam Hussein. When the US placed sanctions on Iraq in an attempt to pressure Hussein to hand over his phantom cache of weapons of mass destruction—thus causing the deaths of over 500,000 Iraqi children—this tragedy was considered by Madeleine Albright, the US Ambassador to the United Nations at the time, to be "worth it" in a 1996 interview with "60 Minutes." This kind of thing just makes me weep. The Hebrews didn't do much better subsequent to this decree, but I'll give "God" a point for effort—if only for the symbolic value—on this one.*

Symbols are interesting things. The most ordinary of actions can be front-loaded with a cultural meaning that radically changes its effects on a community. Here is a good example from Deuteronomy 25:5-10: "When brothers live together and one of them dies without a son, the widow of the deceased shall not marry anyone outside the family; but her husband's brother shall come to her, marrying her and performing the duty of a brother-in-law. The firstborn son she bears shall continue the name of the deceased brother, that his name may not be blotted out from Israel. But if a man does not want to marry his brother's wife, she shall go up to the elders at the gate and say, 'My brother-in-law refuses to perpetuate his brother's name in Israel and does not intend to perform his duty toward me.' Thereupon the elders of his city shall summon him and speak to him. If he persists in saying, 'I do not want to marry her,' his sister-in-law, in the presence of the elders, shall go up to him and strip his sandal from his foot and spit in his face, declaring, 'This is how one should be treated who will not build up his brother's family!' And his name shall be called in Israel, 'the house of the man stripped of his sandal.'"

As the five books of the Torah are about to wind down, God thinks of every conceivable kind of punishment to frighten the daylights out of the Israelites, as the people prepare to cross the Jordan and enter the Promised Land. Think of all the disasters, horrors, illnesses, crimes, wars, exiles and famines—God has covered them all in His list. Just to give you a flavor for His sick, psychopathic, vindictive mindset, try this passage on for size. It's from Deuteronomy 28:52-57: "They will besiege you in each of your communities, until the great, fortified walls, in which you trust, come tumbling down all over your land. They will besiege you in every community throughout the land which the LORD, your God, has given you, and because of the siege and the distress to which your enemy subjects you, you will eat the fruit of your womb, the flesh of your own sons and daughters whom the LORD, your God, has given you. The most refined and fastidious man among you will begrudge his brother and his beloved wife and his surviving children, any share in the flesh of his children that he himself is using for food because nothing else is left him—such is the siege and distress to which your enemy will subject you in all your communities. The most fastidious woman among you, who would not venture to set the sole of her foot on the ground, so refined and fastidious is she, will begrudge her beloved husband and her son and daughter the afterbirth that issues from her womb and the infants she brings forth because she secretly eats them for want of anything else—such the siege and distress to which your enemy will subject you in your communities." *It sounds like a horror story co-written by Edgar Alan Poe and Stephen King.*

Building to a crescendo, God insists for the umpteenth time on naming all the great victories He's had over other tribes and their gods; and then, once again, launches into a tirade that you'd normally associate with a psychotic patient wrapped in a strait jacket, as he bangs his head continually against the padded walls of his cell—all the while cursing those who might dare to obstruct his plans.

God now calls Moses and Joshua to the tent. Moses is about to die, and Joshua is to succeed him as leader of the Israelites. So, some final words from

God and from Moses to the masses? Words of encouragement, such as a dying parent might address to his kids or the exhortation of a coach before the Big Game like, "You can do it! I believe in you."? Afraid not. Here's God's parting shot: "The LORD said to Moses, Soon you will be at rest with your ancestors, and then this people will prostitute themselves by following the foreign gods among whom they will live in the land they are about to enter. They will forsake me and break the covenant which I have made with them. At that time my anger will flare up against them; I will forsake them and hide my face from them; they will become a prey to be devoured, and much evil and distress will befall them."

And Moses' words of encouragement to the people? "For I know that after my death you are sure to act corruptly and to turn aside from the way along which I commanded you, so that evil will befall you in time to come because you have done what is evil in the LORD's sight and provoked him by your deeds." *With "parents" like God and Moses, how could the kids not screw up?*

God now tells Moses that he wants him to compose a great song, to be sung forever by the Israelites, enumerating God's great deeds. (I'm serious!) And Moses does it. He composes it and teaches it to the people until they've memorized it. And now, Moses is commanded to ascend Mount Nebo and give a good look into the Promised Land to which he is denied entry—as God reminds him for the final time. He is to die on a mountaintop, just as his brother Aaron did, for their joint crime: "Then you shall die on the mountain you are about to ascend, and shall be gathered to your people, just as your brother Aaron died on Mount Hor and there was gathered to his people, because both of you broke faith with me among the Israelites at the waters of Meribath-kadesh in the wilderness of Zin: you did not manifest my holiness among the Israelites. You may indeed see the land from a distance, but you shall not enter that land which I am giving to the Israelites."

And, finally, here's a description of Moses's death, ending with the statement that "To this day, nobody knows where he is buried." Wait! I thought he wrote these five books himself? In any case, it's a travesty of justice. All over the world there are shrines dedicated to "the tomb of the unknown warrior." In Moses's case, it's "the unknown tomb of the well-known warrior."

Perhaps the two most upsetting statements that are repeated throughout the book of Deuteronomy are "We left no survivors" and "Kill everything that breathes." These are boasts many tyrants have made throughout history as they slaughtered people in the name of territorial expansion. So, do you now want to recognize the biographies of these war criminals as the revealed Word of God and worthy of our admiration?

This is the kind of psychopath who puts serious hours into honing his murder skills. He has zero ability to empathize with the victims of His genocidal outbursts and the theft of property and the fruits of the labor of other humans.

Variety is the spice of life, so to change the mood, He punctuates mass murders with vendettas against individuals. He makes Aaron high priest and immediately kills two of his sons with a warning not to grieve for them. Then He arranges for Aaron's death, alone and naked on a mountaintop—never having even glimpsed the Promised Land. And, to round out the family feud, He arranges for Moses's death on another mountaintop and burial in an unmarked grave—but not before He has teased him with a look at the goodies that he will never enjoy. Imagine a parent that takes a normally model child into a candy store, shows him the sweets and then says, "but you're not gonna get any, 'cos you was a bad boy a couple of years back!"

As a chorus throughout the book, He alternates between a depressive paranoia about being jilted and a manic euphoria generated by self-praise.

The entire Torah is littered with evidence showing that, rather than being a historical, on-the-scene, blow-by-blow account of the 40-year safari from Egypt to Canaan, it is the poorly-edited foundation myth that may have been necessary, and certainly was successful, in both inspiring the remnant of the Israelites who found themselves in real exile in Babylon around 550 BCE, and in exculpating their real treatment of the other tribes among whom they had lived during the previous 600 years.

It will retroactively reflect not just the relationships between themselves and their "neighbors" but also the fragmentation and animosity among the twelve tribes themselves, with the winners—Judah—having the final editorial and redaction rights.

With that Dr. O'Sullivan concluded his presentation. The court sat is stunned silence.

Michael Newsome allowed a few minutes for the full impact of O'Sullivan's remarks to sink in. Then he rose to his feet, scratched reflectively under his chin and said, *"Dear jurors, I now want to summarize the charges of which Yahweh has been accused. I will organize them in three groups: first, murders He has committed; second, murders which He ordered the Israelites to commit; and finally, animal cruelty.*

God is a very resourceful killer whose range of options include the following methods: death by fire, stoning, swords, arrows, spears, drowning, plagues, snakebite, war and weather (brimstone, earthquakes and hailstones), and controlled demolition. Let's take a look at his lists of individual murders, mass murders, and genocides:

INDIVIDUAL MURDERS

a. He threatens to avenge the murder of the first murderer (Cain) by committing seven more murders.
b. He kills Lot's wife for looking back at the devasted Sodom and Gomorrah.
c. He kills Er and Onan (the sons of Judah) for their sins.
d. He tries to kill Moses for failing to circumcise his two sons (until his wife Zipporah intervenes).
e. He kills Nadab and Abihu (the sons of Aaron) for screwing up a liturgy the day after their ordination.
f. He leaves Aaron to die naked on a foreign mountain (Mount Hor) for a single act of impatience committed years before.
g. While teasing Moses with a look into the Promised Land to which he is forbidden entry (on account of a single act of impatience committed years before), He leaves Moses to die on top of another foreign mountain (Nebo).

h. His default option for a whole slew of sins is one of the following options:

1. the death penalty
2. to be "cut off from the people" which, in reality, means death or slavery for any nomad

i. Here's a partial list of his reasons for killing people:

1. They don't listen to the priest
2. They were witches
3. They were homosexuals
4. They were fortune tellers
5. Striking a parent
6. Cursing a parent
7. Fornication
8. Adultery
9. Followers of other religions
10. Nonbelievers
11. False prophets
12. The entire town if one member worships another God
13. Women who are not virgins on their wedding night
14. Blasphemers
15. Any non-priest who approaches the tabernacle
16. Working on the Sabbath

MASS MURDERS

Allow me to further divide this section into two parts: (a) Mass murder of His own people; and (b) Mass murder of other peoples.

Mass murder of His own people:

1. He killed 3,000 people for dancing naked around the golden calf that Aaron had fashioned.

2. He killed all of the military men who left Egypt (603,550 soldiers) because they upset him.

3. He put down a rebellion against Moses and Aaron by killing the rebels either with fire or earthquake. When the onlookers complained about this, He killed 14,700 more.

4. When the people complained about the manna menu, He killed an unspecified number by snakebite.

5. He threatened them that if they abandoned Him in favor of other gods, He would subject them to such violence and deprivation and siege by their enemies that even the most fastidious and refined among them would cannibalize their own offspring.

6. He killed 24,000 for "committing whoredom with the daughters of Moab."

MASS MURDER OF OTHER PEOPLES:

1. He killed the firstborn of all Egyptian families.

2. Then he wiped out the Egyptian army in the Red Sea.

3. In one battle with the Amorites, He boasted that He killed more of them with hailstones than Joshua's troops did with their weapons.

4. During another battle, as the day was winding down, He held the sun and the moon in place, so that Joshua could continue the slaughter.

5. He guaranteed to send His own angel before the invading Israelites to "bring you to the Amorites, Hittites, Perizzites, Canaanites, Hivites, and Jebusites; and I will wipe them out." (Exodus 23:23)

6. Then He killed 10,000 Moabites.

7. In one extraordinary engagement He killed 1,000,000 (yes, I mean one million) Ethiopians. (2 Chronicles c.14:7-12)

8. To help in a battle with the Assyrians, "That night the angel of the Lord went forth and struck down one hundred and eighty-five thousand men in the Assyrian camp. Early the next morning, there they were, all the corpses of the dead." (2 Kings 19:35)

9. Hugely insulted by the Arameans' claim that He, Yahweh, was merely a god of the hills and not a god of the valleys, He slaughtered 100,000 of them. When the survivors escaped to the city of Aphek, He made a wall collapse and kill another 27,000 of them. Imagine what He could have done with the Great Wall of China!

GENOCIDE

In the infamous "flood," He wiped out all of humanity except eight people. What kind of a God was it that mandated Noah to rescue snakes, skunks, and mosquitoes but abandon his grandpa, Methuselah—the most long-lived human in history?

Inciting others to commit murder and genocide:

To Yahweh's arsenal of execution technologies, the Israelites added: death by hanging, by the jawbone of a donkey, and by the tent-peg impaling of an asylum seeker.

INDIVIDUAL MURDERS:

For murdering an Israelite man (Zimri) and his Midianite wife (Cozbi) as they made love in their tent, He rewarded Phineas (grandson of Aaron) by guaranteeing that Phineas' progeny will always be priests.

Mass murders of their own people:

For worshipping another god, He had the Levites kill 3,000 of their own "brothers, friends and neighbors" (Exodus 32:26-29)

"THE BAN"

a. The City of Ai: "When the Israelite army finished killing all the men outside the city, they went back and finished off everyone inside. So the entire population of Ai was wiped out that day—twelve thousand in all. Joshua hung the king of Ai on a tree and left him there until evening" (Joshua 8:1-29)

b. City of Jericho: "When the people heard the sound of the horns, they shouted as loud as they could. Suddenly, the walls of Jericho collapsed, and the Israelites charged straight into the city from every side and captured it. They completely destroyed everything in it – men and women, young and old, cattle, sheep, donkeys – everything." (Joshua 6:20-21)

c. Any town that was just a waystation en route to the Promised Land was subjected to the "simple" ban, i.e., they killed only the men; and took the women, children and livestock as booty. But any town in which they intended to settle was subjected to the real deal, i.e., they killed "everything that breathed."

d. And Moses's final injunction—as God wished—was to wipe out the Midianites, who were descendants of Abraham by his second wife, Keturah, and the people who had given Moses himself sanctuary (and a wife) when he was wanted for murder in Egypt. Angry that in the first sortie his troops had spared the women and children, he sent them back to finish the job. An estimated 200,000 died.

In Moses's time, the dance is between (a) keeping women as part of the spoils of war and (b) risking that these foreign women might be Trojan horses smuggling other gods into Israel—no less a figure than Solomon fell for that one. Moses's decision? Better be safe than happy: "Kill 'em all."

And it wasn't just people whose lives were sacrificed to no end. Yahweh's insatiable thirst for blood caused unending suffering to the animal kingdom as well.

ANIMAL CRUELTY

The Permian Extinction of 252 million years ago wiped out 90% of all life on planet Earth, but God had a much better batting average than that. All animal life (except token "pairs") was annihilated in His vengeful flood. Then the "lucky ones" spent the next five months cramped in a three-story ark.

Not content with punishing the people of Egypt for the "sins" of Pharaoh with a series of plagues, He also lashed out at the animals by

- *turning all waters of Egypt to blood; subsequently, all fish and most waterfowl likely died*
- *sending a pestilence that killed all of the Egyptian livestock*
- *sending boils that affected humans and animals.*
- *sending hailstones to kill any livestock still in the fields*
- *killing the first born of all species*

He mandated non-stop ritual animal sacrifice of birds, goats, sheep, and cattle on the following occasions:

- *every morning*
- *every evening*
- *on the Sabbath*

- *at the New Moon festival*
- *at Passover*
- *at Pentecost*
- *on New Year's Day*
- *on the Day of Atonement*
- *and on the Feast of Booths.*

Their camp must have been a mobile cesspit of blood, urine, offal, guts, flies, and disease. As an integral part of the Ban, animals (when not taken as booty) were annihilated.

EVERY PERSON in the courtroom was aghast at these horrific descriptions. But one person was especially stunned by Michael Newsome's excruciating summation of Yahweh's crimes against humanity and creation as recorded in the Torah: Dermot O'Sullivan. This world-renowned Biblical scholar was quite familiar with the material covered in these five days of testimony, but never in his illustrious career had he seen and heard the horrific details of Yahweh's rap sheet listed by someone outside the halls of academia. If this hot-shot lawyer could gather such damning data on his own reconnaissance, it might just be possible for ordinary folks to begin to see the writing on the wall (to quote another Biblical image)!

"Well said, Michael!" O'Sullivan whispered (loudly) from his seat behind the prosecution.

The prosecutor gave a subtle nod, took a sip of water, and then introduced his next expert witness.

PSYCHOANALYZING GOD

Dr. Smith was a tall, gangly man, with a mop of white hair and the demeanor of someone who'd seen it all in his psychology practice. He had built a career on understanding the criminal mind. His mandate in this trial was to diagnose the behavior of the defendants.

After Smith was sworn in, Michael Newsome approached the

stand and asked, *What, Dr. Smith can you tell us about the chief suspect known as Yahweh?*

Well, Dr. O'Sullivan is a tough act to follow, but a quick run through volume one of God's journal (also known as the book of Genesis) quickly throws up the following data:

1. When God says, "Let us make humans in our own image and likeness," He is either suffering from what used to be known as multiple personality disorder or He is actually part of a collaborative group involved in the earliest phase of terrestrial human evolution.

2. He advocates that humans have dominion over nature—and we see how well that has worked out, with the human-orchestrated extinction of millions of species, and the possibility of ecological collapse.

3. He can't remember in which order, but over the course of six days, He created the world as we know it.

4. The constant anachronisms are red flags telling us that blatant mistakes have been made by the writers and redactors who assembled the Bible.

5. Sometimes God praises the search for wisdom and sometimes He punishes it.

6. His reactions are totally out of proportion to the situations that made him angry. His ethics are even pre Lex Talionis. (Or perhaps the flood episode was a fictionalized story of the Permian Extinction of 252 million years ago, which wiped out more than 96 percent of marine creatures and 70 percent of land species.)

7. Repeatedly, in this part of His journal, he oscillates wildly between (a) over-punishing the guilty and (b) punishing the innocent while rewarding and blessing the guilty. His reactions are utterly unpredictable. (I wonder if He has a drug-abuse problem.)

8. When He traces the family tree of His chosen ones, He frequently gets the names wrong.

9. In the story of the Nephilim, He really blows His cover: He is a physical being with physical sons who have physical sex with His physical creatures, and He is determined to exact a global revenge.

10. Just to keep His hand in, He personally kills both Er and Onan, the sons of Judah.

11. He is already en route to becoming the greatest serial killer and mass murderer in human history.

12. Once He starts making covenants, He constantly revises the conditions, and blames humans for changing His mind.

13. He curses the Earth, the serpent, the woman, and the man with all kinds of long-drawn-out punishments culminating in death.

14. He has all of the worst human characteristics— regret, anger, revenge, jealousy, and insecurity.

15. He is a misogynist.

16. I agree with Dr. O'Sullivan that he should have been reported to the Child Protective Services for kicking his prerational, premoral kids out of the house to wander vulnerably around the planet.

17. He may be suffering from early onset Alzheimer's, as he gets confused a lot. He can't remember what instructions he gave to Noah about the number of animals to put in the ark, nor how long exactly the rains lasted, nor how long it took for the first mountain peak to breach the surface of the receding flood waters.

18. He sets up slavery as a punishment, in perpetuity, for the unborn progeny of a giggling, embarrassed young man who had just survived a global disaster, and months aboard a fragile craft crammed with noisy and smelly animals.

19. He has no objections to the practice of slavery or the denial of basic human rights to women or "foreigners."

20. Probably the single most repeated chant in the Book of Genesis is His "promise" to take the land of Canaan from the natives and give it to the resident-aliens-become-invaders.

21. To "prove" His omniscience, He regularly indulges in what I call "retroactive prognostication"— a guarantee of 100% accuracy in prophecy.

22. He often behaves like a con-man or a used-car salesman, making promises that He doesn't or can't deliver on.

23. Confused about who the true holder of the covenant is, He eventually goes mute.

24. He is outsmarted by Abraham (whose ethics are also head and shoulders above Yahweh's) regarding the planned destruction of Sodom and Gomorrah.

25. And, in some circumstances, He seems to condone incest.

Michael Newsome stepped toward the bench and said, *Thank you for that succinct summation of Yahweh's behaviors. Will you please give us your clinical assessment of the defendant, Dr. Smith?*

Since I am not his personal psychiatrist, nor have I been granted an interview with the defendant, I can only reference the DSM with regard to this case, Smith explained.

That will be very helpful, Dr. Smith. But first, will you please tell the people of the jury exactly what the DSM is? Newsome asked.

Certainly, Mr. Newsome. The DSM is the Diagnostic and Statistical Manual of Mental Disorders. It's a compendium of the criteria, demographics, and etiologies for the full range (as presently understood) of mental states and pathologies. It examines the prevalence, course, familial patterns and differential diagnoses of each disorder, from those normally first diagnosed in infancy, childhood, or adolescence all the way to late stage dementias of various kinds.

In brief, from a psychological perspective, I'd make the following condensed mental status report on Yahweh. Of course, diagnosing God's mental status would best be done in a clinical face-to-face situation accompanied by a battery of paper-and-pencil and sophisticated medical tests, but until He presents Himself for such procedures, we can only go by written reports of His behavior. These, however, hold extra value given that His self-reports have been deemed inerrant.

I'm not going to bore you by comparing the 1,600 pages of a typical Bible translation with 1,000 pages of the DSM, but I will make a few observations based on my seventy years of reading the former and twenty-five years of applying the latter in my psychology practice. Here's a smattering of diagnoses and their codes that might fit Yahweh's profile:

1. Vascular Dementia with Depressed Mood – 290.43

2. Bipolar Disorder NOS – 296.80

3. Delusional Disorder, Grandiose Type (he thinks he's God) – 297.1

4. Generalized Anxiety Disorder – 300.02

5. Antisocial Personality Disorder – 301.7

6. Narcissistic Personality Disorder – 301.81
7. Borderline Personality Disorder – 301.83
8. Adjustment Disorder with Disturbance of Conduct – 309.3
9. Intermittent Explosive Disorder NOS – 312.34
10. Attention-Deficit/Hyperactivity Disorder – 314.01

If He were willing to undergo a more thorough scrutiny, I'm sure we could fine-tune these possible diagnoses and arrive at the bedrock issues that resulted in His alleged behavior. We could probably rule out childhood trauma and failure to bond with His mother.

There are lots of modern instances in which people have wanted to be associated romantically with jailed psychopaths or become followers of these sociopaths while they were still at large (like in the case of the Charles Manson gang). How is it different when fundamentalist monotheists—the latest incarnation of Yahweh's groupies—willingly get inducted into denominations that swear fealty to an off-world psychopath? Isn't it time we examined His credentials and track record and categorically reject Him?

Based on what we've read about Him, Yahweh's nature is seriously flawed. While proclaiming Himself both compassionate and just, His behavior suggests that He is neither. He expects humans to do better, but He occasionally rewards the devious while punishing their innocent victims. For example, He rewards Abraham and Sarah with slaves and herds for lying to Pharaoh, while punishing Pharaoh for being an unwitting stooge. He does precisely the same with Isaac and Rebekah when they take advantage of Abimelech. He rewards the barefaced lies of Jacob to his blind father while punishing his naïve brother Esau. When His divine sons have sex with human women, He ignores the sons' behavior but punishes the women and their families. He sets up slavery as a punishment, in perpetuity, for the unborn progeny of Noah's son, Ham.

He institutes a legal system that denies basic rights to women and foreigners. (Tell me again how children, whom He has created, can be "foreigners"?) His IQ level never quite reaches a hundred and so He is easily defeated in rational debate—once with Abraham over the fate of Sodom and Gomorrah, and twice with Moses, in the desert, where Moses shows Him the insanity of His plan to wipe out the Israelites where the Egyptians will discover the bodies and deduce that He ain't much of a God.

He would score really high on a sadist scale: He plays mind games with Pharaoh, continually hardening Pharaoh's heart, so He can have more opportunities to inflict damage on him and on his land. This game of taunting, promising, threatening, and punishing would get him a CEO position in Torquemada's Holy Inquisition.

He punishes all of Egypt for the sin of their king; and his vindictiveness is showcased when even Moses and Aaron are punished for an act of impatience. He's like a Mafia don who whacks even His own enforcers. He shows definite signs of dementia, regularly forgetting numbers, dates, and promises made.

His Impulse Control Disorder is only bested by his over-the-top road rage. He can't seem to appreciate the consequences of His outbursts, but rather is blinded by a very thin skin which is allergic to most any interaction with mere mortals. So, He curses the entire Earth—human and animal—for a single childish act of disobedience; and then makes good on His curses by wiping out all of life. Whatever happened to His "an eye for an eye" edict, let alone His boasting about being a God of compassion?

He is a dead-beat dad who ignored "His" people for four hundred and thirty years and then came back with a mighty show of power and lots of promises, took over and demanded total obedience from His cowering kids, and backed that up with physical and emotional abuse.

His inferiority complex is so extreme that He must compensate for it by constantly singing His own praises and commanding others to do likewise. He even insists that Moses, as one of his last acts, teach the Israelites a song with long, lugubrious lyrics extolling His many talents. All ritual, prayer and animal sacrifice are created to maintain focus on Him, because He is always afraid He will be abandoned in favor of other gods. With such abandonment issues you would think He must have had an evil stepmother like Cinderella's.

In brief, He assigns all human virtues—writ large—to Himself, while demonstrating all human vices—writ large—to His "children."

I'd love to have Him as a client in my therapy practice! We would have a lot of work to do.

Michael Newsome thanked Dr. Smith for his professional assessment of Yahweh's psychological profile and then looked to the judge for closure.

Court adjourned! Judge Grossler declared with a tap of his gavel. *Get some good rest tonight, everybody.*

HOLDING GOD ACCOUNTABLE TO HIS OWN COVENANTS

Day six of the trial began without any fanfare as the Prosecution began to wind up what appeared to be a clear case for conviction of Yahweh. As soon as the judge called court into session, Michael Newsome called his next expert witness, a contract attorney named Fidelma Murphy. In addition to her undergraduate degree in History from Trinity College in Dublin, Fidelma held a BA in Jurisprudence from Oxford University and an MBA from the Wharton School of the University of Pennsylvania. Her specialization in contracts and commercial law covers areas including the sale of goods, services and property; employment contracts; and franchises. Ms. Murphy's mastery of the Uniform Commercial Code, which governs contracts and commercial business transactions, makes her a frequent expert witness in cases involving breach of contract. Her background equipped her well to give a complete presentation of the devious, illegal, and self-excusing manner in which Yahweh repeatedly disregarded the many contracts he arranged with his clientele.

Thank you for making room in your busy schedule to testify today, Ms. Murphy, Michael Newsome began, but before he could pose a question, Fidelma Murphy, who certainly knew her way around a courtroom, launched into her well-prepared case against Yahweh.

It takes a particular kind of pathology to make an agreement, unilaterally change the terms, and then blame the other party for breach of contract, she began, as if she were about to interrogate the defendant herself. *And it takes a chronic form of this pathology to repeat that pattern with so many different parties. Yet, that is precisely Yahweh's track record.*

In an ecstatic burst of creativity, Yahweh fashioned Adam and Eve in His own image and likeness, lavished them with gifts, and placed them in Eden.

The plan is for them and their progeny to enjoy His protection and these blessings in perpetuity. But one childish mistake later, the contract is in pieces. Adam and Eve—and the rest of us—are locked out of the garden and a security firm is employed to keep us from sneaking back in as squatters.

Meanwhile, God's sons discover human women and take them as wives. This so infuriates Him that He determines to wipe out all of life on planet Earth, except for a floating zoo built and captained by Noah. Later on, He comes to His senses and makes a second covenant which, He insists several times in writing, is between Himself and "all living things." That agreement is soon restricted to Noah's progeny—humans only. But, of Noah's three sons, He condemns Ham's progeny to perpetual slavery, He pretty much ignores Japhet's offspring, and He limits the new version of the agreement to Shem's kids.

It seems, however, that Yahweh is confused by having to deal with large crowds so, out of Shem's lineage, He chooses "a wandering Aramean" called Abram, and makes him and his line the beneficiaries of the latest edition (version 5.0) of the covenant. Versions 6.0 and 7.0 follow quickly: He rejects Abraham's first born (Ishmael) and limits the covenant to Isaac's line. No, not to Isaac's entire lineage, but only to the descendants of Isaac's second son. Remember him? The deceiver, Jacob, who swore several times to his blind father that he was actually Esau, the first born of Isaac? That one!

Jacob is fertile and from his loins spring the twelve tribes. God, however, is unable to protect them and so, ten of the tribes (83%) are captured by the Assyrians and never heard of again. Now only the tribes of Judah and Benjamin are left to benefit from version 7.0. (This god has so many updates, He'd give Bill Gates and Microsoft a run for their money!) That is, until the arrival of Jesus; and then according to the claims of the New Testament, Yahweh creates His "final" covenant (version 8.0) in which He rejects the Jews and chooses the Christians. (Islam, of course, will claim that they are the "final, final" version (9.0)—with many more versions yet to come.)

So, what do we now have? Why, a situation in which, for the last 1,400 years, the "ignored" children of Japheth (the Europeans) and the "rejected" children of Ishmael (the Arabs) constantly persecute and hunt into exile the "chosen" children of Israel. I'm not so sure I'd want to be chosen by this God.

And with that, Fidelma Murphy paused, allowing Michael Newsome the opportunity to resume his role as prosecutor.

Thank you for that detailed listing of the many covenants Yahweh has made and, subsequently, broken, Ms. Murphy. I imagine this gave Yahweh a reputation as a bad business partner, the prosecutor prompted.

That would be an understatement, Michael, Fidelma Murphy snapped. *A quick sweep of the history of the "chosen people" reveals the full extent of God's incompetence. He is utterly unable to protect His people. While constantly beating His chest, tooting His horn and boasting of His own omnipotence—as demonstrated by His willingness to conduct regular genocide and mass murders even of His own followers—He is much more frequently on the other side, blaming them and their following of other gods for their much more regular defeats, exiles and losses. Here is a précis of that history:*

i. Around 1850 BCE, He promises Abraham and his descendants a land flowing with milk and honey, only to give them a land which is subject to regular famines so severe that even in his own lifetime, Abraham has to flee to Egypt twice, for extended periods, in order to eat.

ii. In the days of Jacob and Joseph, another famine in the "Promised Land" resulted in another journey to Egypt which turned into four hundred and thirty years of slavery.

iii. The "escaped slaves" then spend forty years wandering in the desert where they were regularly slaughtered by their God.

iv. On entering the Promised Land, they spend another two hundred years conducting genocides of their own.

v. In 1010 BCE, they capture Jerusalem and in 950 BCE, they build the first temple.

vi. Civil war breaks out in 933 BCE and the people are split into two kingdoms.

vii. In 722 BCE, the Assyrians wipe out the ten northern tribes.

viii. In 598 BCE, Babylon conquers Judah, destroys the temple, and sends the last two tribes into exile.

ix. In 538 BCE, the Persians set them free to return to Israel, where they rebuild the temple.

x. In 330 BCE, the Greeks conquer them.

xi. From 180-70 BCE, there is a brief period of freedom, courtesy of the Maccabean revolt. They manage to utilize this window of self-rule to conduct another vicious civil war, involving crucifixion as a tool of execution.

xii The Romans conquer them in 70 BCE

xiii. From 66 to 70 CE they revolt against Rome, but they end up getting crushed and the second temple is destroyed.

xiv. From 135 CE—the end of the Bar Kokhba revolt—to 1948 CE they live in exile, a people without a nation.

xv. So, from 1850 BCE down to 1948 CE, they are slaughtered, enslaved, ruled or exiled by the Egyptians, Assyrians, Babylonians, Persians, Greeks, Romans, Christians, Muslims and British.

xvi. The persecution runs the gamut from local Easter pogroms in European and Russian villages to genocidal holocausts.

xvii. In 1948, the state of Israel is set up and the very next day four Arab armies attack.

xviii. More wars follow in 1967 and 1973; and later, two Intifadas, terrorist attacks, and counter retaliation.

So, over a span of 3,798 years, there have only been tiny pockets of freedom, which the Israelites managed to use for civil wars and succession battles. When you do the numbers, counting peaceful self-rule as a hit, this God's batting average is about 0.083! This wouldn't get Him even into a tee-ball league for five-year-olds. And His response? He blames them, saying it was they who broke the covenant and followed other gods. As far as being a reliable business partner goes, I'd say Yahweh struck out.

Thank you, Ms. Murphy. Michael Newsome said as he straightened his tie and readied himself for his final statement. It wasn't going to be easy to capture the essence of everything these three expert witnesses had covered, but he was prepared to give it his best shot.

Ladies and gentlemen of the jury, we have heard a startling amount of evidence over the past five days, much of which is the stuff of horror movies. I'd like to thank you for your willingness to pay such close attention to all of the atrocities Yahweh and his sidekick Moses have committed in the name of God. Please bear with me just a little longer as I offer a closing summary that will surely show that there is no innocence in these acts of cruelty, greed, jealousy, and spite.

Michael Newsome walked slowly to the center of the courtroom—leaving his notes at the lectern—and spoke from memory the details of the case of his career:

Not counting those killed in the flood, or the death of the Egyptian firstborns, or the victims of other "spats" where He didn't take time out to count the corpses, God, according to His own admission, killed 2,821,364 humans. When you extrapolate from the other mentioned but uncounted slaughters, a conservative estimate of His total killing is around 25 million people–not to mention the slaughter of untold billions of livestock and wild animals.

And how many people, according to the Bible, did Satan kill? Ten! The seven sons and three daughters of Job; and this was the result of a bet between Yahweh and Satan to test Job's fidelity to God. Instead of using the phrase, "The Devil made me do it!" as an excuse for antisocial behavior, wouldn't it be far more accurate to say, "The Bible made me do it!"? In fact, wasn't that the pretext and the inspiration for the Crusades, the Inquisition, and the Conquistadores? Michael Newsome blurted, unable to contain his own commentary on the subject.

Now add to that slaughter His inciting of the "chosen people" to imitate His brutal behavior, then factor in His wholesale slaughter of animals, add in His pathological profile and His pathetic record on keeping contracts, and you have a cosmic psychopath masquerading as our compassionate, albeit partisan, creator.

How can we explain our craven obedience to this monster? It has all the hallmarks of the Stockholm Syndrome or the Patty Hearst subpersonality.

How often have we witnessed Hindu gurus, Buddhist Rinpoches, and Christian Televangelists abuse their devotees (sexually and financially) while purporting to offer them samadhi, nirvana, or heaven? The followers are forced to resolve the cognitive dissonance between what they observe of the teachers' behavior and what these "masters" claim, by subduing common sense, intelligence, and a moral code to the overriding demands of the ego's fascination with self-proclaimed wonder workers.

What excuses have Judeo-Christians offered for God's egregious behavior? The excuses are as follows. Firstly, "He is God; who are we to question

His judgments?" That was Yahweh's final putdown of Job's attempts to seek justice or even a sensible explanation for his own mistreatment. Secondly, devotees will proclaim, "other tribes and religions committed the same kinds of slaughter back then; in fact, it has happened throughout all of human history, right up to our own times in Hitler's Germany, Pol Pot's Cambodia, the Armenian genocide and the mass murder of the Tutsi people in Zaire."

All this is true, but these criminals did it on behalf of what Judeo-Christianity would claim are false gods (or for purely political reasons). The Bible, on the other hand, says that Yahweh's actions and Israel's imitation of them were done by and at the instructions of the One True God, for spiritual reasons. And He was still being worshipped by 2.2 billion people as of 2010.

So, dear readers/jurors, you don't have to be a Supreme Court justice or a rocket scientist to appreciate the indisputable guilt of this God. I wouldn't expect your deliberations to last for even an hour, in order for you to return a verdict of "guilty on all counts." Thank you, Judge and jury. I rest my case.

WELL, dear reader, while you might think we have an open and shut case against this monster known as Yahweh, I encourage you to stay tuned as the Defense offers another perspective.

SECTION II: THE DEFENSE

KAYLA GOLDSTEIN'S presence was highly collegial throughout the prosecution's detailed presentations, even when the expert witnesses attacked her client's very character without mercy. The Defense calmly absorbed every bit of the Prosecution's vitriol without even blinking. Her calm demeanor could almost be seen as lackadaisical. But we're about to see all of that change as Kayla Goldstein takes command of the courtroom in a brilliant defense of God.

HEAVEN COUNTERSUES: HUMANS CHARGED WITH TAKING GOD'S NAME IN VAIN

For the last six days, we have listened to the carefully culled, impressive evidence presented by the learned attorney for the prosecution. My esteemed colleague Michael Newsome has done a stellar job assembling the many damning pieces of evidence, recreating the many crimes and telling all of the lurid details. The monster he describes surely deserves to be held accountable for His deeds. Although I rarely advocate for capital punishment, our world would, indeed, be far better off without a brutal god such as this.

However, I intend to show you, beyond any doubt, that the crimes—the very real and stomach-churning crimes—the prosecution has presented are attributed to a totally-innocent defendant. I do not dispute that such horrendous deeds do, indeed, occur in this world, but I will prove to you that the person on trial today did not commit them—not one of them!

Imagine if you will, faithful jurors, that I had written a novel in which the chief protagonist dictates his autobiography to one of his henchmen who is at once his scribe, the chief witness to many of his crimes, and a willing enforcer of many other crimes committed at his command. Some years later, a diligent investigator comes upon this record. This investigator has had a long, successful career in solving and prosecuting similar crimes. So, he is resolved to bring the protagonist to justice. For some reason, he is unaware that this "autobiography" is a work of fiction, and he pursues the case all the way to a live trial. The problem is that both the protagonist and his scribe do not now nor ever have existed. So, here we sit today having been buffeted by the strobe lights and stage sounds of a made-up drama, proving Shakespeare right in his assessment that "All the world's a stage."

In defense of "Yahweh," I will show you that the scribe/witness/enforcer called "Moses" never, in fact, existed, and that the main saga of an escaped slave-race being led across the desert by a blood-thirsty wannabe god, is part of a human-created projection that was designed to answer the human questions of the day. The resultant historical novel, however, is neither historical nor novel. It is a well-crafted fable based on the oft-manifested archetype of the projected human shadow.

A dull rumble of commentary passed over the room as the Defense attorney returned to the podium with reading glasses balanced on the tip of her nose.

"So then, let's get into it." Kayla Goldstein called Isaac Baruch, Ph.D., a professor of Biblical history from the Hebrew University of Jerusalem. In distinctly precise English diction, he began his presentation to the court after the Defense introduced him as her first expert witness.

THE BIBLE TOLD ME SO

Professor Baruch strode into the center of the room and, looking around him, said *I am a Sabra. A native-born Israeli. And I have long been interested not just in the Hebrew scriptures but also in the Christian testaments and, particularly, in the great Jewish prophet, Yehosua bin Joseph—better known as Jesus of Nazareth*—for most of my thirty-year career.

I will now walk with you through certain books of the Bible with an eye to four things. Firstly, I will examine and comment upon individual statements. Secondly, I will call attention to underlying themes. Thirdly, I will seek to identify the character (and the caricatures) of the God who emerges. And fourthly, I will try to uncover the personalities of the writers and the nature of the times that produced such ideas and such a God.

Then, I will show how this caricature of God came to be such an ogre. Perhaps the crimes outlined by the prosecution were indeed committed, but if so, why did we never find the actual culprit? Why were there no eye witnesses? But the real question I'm chasing throughout this comedy of errors is this: how can we find the real God instead of this evil twin we seem to be stuck on convicting?

I can't help but find the whole thing rather humorous! Baruch laughed in a squeaky squeal you might expect from a person half his girth. *And, besides, any God at whom or with whom we cannot laugh is too small a god. There is a great passage in the gnostic Gospel of Philip where Jesus, as he comes up out of the Jordan, having been baptized by John, begins laughing. He is not mocking life, he is just hugely amused at the myriad of illusions under which we labor—including our illusions about the nature of God. If Jesus's sense of humor had made a bigger splash in the canonical Gospels, we might have less fanaticism and more forgiveness in modern Christianity.*

So, I must sprinkle my testimony with humor and some tongue-in-cheek comments because, firstly, I'm Jewish and we Jews love to laugh. Secondly, to relieve the weight of the case I am making. And thirdly, I think the pious platitudes and fear-based projections that often accompany our discussions of God must really crack Her up!

All eyes were on him as he calmly opened his dossier on this Moses character. *What do scholars have to say about Moses? Let's look first at his alleged authorship of Torah. Using three forms of biblical criticism, it quickly becomes apparent that Torah was not the work of a single author, nor was it written in a forty-year period. Rather, it is demonstrably the work of many scribes over a period of several hundred years, beginning much later than Moses's putative era. I will explain this later.*

Of the five books of the Torah—Genesis, Exodus, Leviticus, Numbers, and Deuteronomy—only parts of one of them—Deuteronomy—is written in the first person singular. In actual fact, Deuteronomy—which began as a collection of laws in the Northern kingdom and was completed many years later in the Southern kingdom and during the Babylonian exile, when the Southern kingdom fell—is retroactively put into the mouth of Moses as a series of exhortations. This device was common in ancient times—anonymous authors ascribing their work to a famous, or even a fictitiously-famous, person in order to give it gravitas and appeal. Even in modern times, politicians use speech writers and movie stars' and athletes' books are written by ghost writers, yet we hear and read those words as if they originated with the person to whom they are attributed.

Why don't we see through this façade? Could it be that we so desperately want to hear from the person in question that we voluntarily suspend our disbelief? In the case of Deuteronomy, it's pretty obvious. How else could it be that the other three books describing events occurring in the time of Moses appear only in the third person singular, e.g., 'God said to Moses...'? Why not, 'God said to me...'? Moreover, Deuteronomy records Moses's death and the fact that nobody knows where he is buried. Was this a post-mortem addendum that he managed to append to his magnum opus from the other side? And what kind of a humble man describes himself as "the humblest man who ever lived?"

The simple truth is that Moses didn't write the Torah because Moses never existed.

A low rumble rolled through the courtroom as someone in the gallery let out an angry hiss.

Dr. Baruch waited for silence to return and then stepped away from the podium and approached the gallery.

I understand how this testimony might be unsettling for some in this courtroom today, but I assure you, my intent in giving you the most accurate historical assessment of Judaism is not to weaken the Jewish faith, but to honor it.

Abandoning his notes, he continued extemporaneously.

In spite of the fact that Moses is a fictional character and that the Exodus from Egypt never happened, the Moses-Exodus myth is arguably the most inspirational story of all time. If any people ever needed the inspiration of such a hero and the example of such an escape, it is the Jewish people. In my reading of history, I know of no other tribe that comes even remotely close to having had to survive so many real exoduses—beginning with the return from Babylon in 538 BCE and continuing almost unabated into our own times—in which they've been forced into exile by decree, intolerable restrictions or outright persecution from both Muslim nations and Christian nations. In the 20th century alone, over one million Jews—who for some 2,600 years had lived continuously in the Arab countries of the Middle East and North Africa—had to re-enact the exodus in their flight from Libya, Egypt, Iraq, Yemen, Morocco, and Tunisia, as well as from Iran; even as six million of their kin perished in the Nazi Holocaust. Our stories have helped us to survive and even thrive in the face of overwhelming odds. Moreover, the story has been the inspiration for countless Christians and Muslims as well. Dismantling the historicity of the myth must in no way diminish our recognition of and admiration for the genius of its creators, and of its millennia-long inspirational effects. Judeans of all eras deserve our deepest respect.

Holding steady eye contact with the people in the back of the gallery for a moment, Dr. Baruch smiled briefly and returned to his notes.

Scholars have come to the conclusion that Moses is a fictional character and that the Exodus from Egypt by a few million Hebrew slaves, and subsequently their entry into the Promised Land, never occurred. The scholarly consensus is that Moses is a legendary character based on the archetype of Sargon the Great (2334 – 2279 BCE), which was a familiar motif in ancient Near Eastern mythology, whereby a person of humble origins rises to liberate and rule his people. The inventors of Moses use this 'rags to riches' or 'log cabin to White House' story of Sargon—by then more than 1,500 years old—in imitation of the great king who founded the Akkadian empire (the first multi-national empire ever) by overthrowing the former king and uniting the region of Mesopotamia under his own rule. Here is what Sargon says of himself: 'My mother, the high priestess, conceived; in secret she bore me. She set me in a basket of rushes, with bitumen she sealed my lid. She cast me into the river which rose over me.'[1] *Sound familiar?*

Modern scholars concur. Dr. Michael D. Coogan, lecturer in Old Testament in Harvard Divinity School, writes: 'There is no historical evidence outside of the Bible, no mention of Moses outside the Bible, and no independent confirmation that Moses ever existed.'[2]"

The first nonbiblical writings about Judaism with reference to Moses appear in 323 BCE in Greece. This is almost 1,000 years after his alleged lifetime. Moses was therefore blessed with terrific insight, which was really hindsight. One of the greatest ways to shore up one's authority is to make retroactive prognostications. Your prophesies will score a perfect bull's-eye every time with the benefit of time travel. And the Bible writers are masters at this technique. Let me give you a few examples.

The Testament of Adam *is a Christian pseudepigraphical work, probably dating to the second half of the fifth century CE. It purports to relate the final words of Adam to his son Seth in which he prophesies both the coming of the Messiah and the Great Flood.*[3] *Its ability to foretell the future with uncanny accuracy must have been a huge bastion of faith for early Christian communities. Its specificity is truly wondrous. Here is a section of it:*

Adam said to Seth his son: 'I have heard, my son, that God will come to the world after a long time. He will be conceived by a virgin and wear a body and be born like a human being and mature like a child. He will perform signs and wonders upon earth—walking upon the waves of the sea, rebuking the winds so that they abate, beckoning the waves that they cease (rolling), opening (the eyes) of the blind, cleansing lepers, causing the deaf to hear, giving speech to the mute, straightening those who are bent, strengthening the paralyzed, finding the lost, expelling devils, casting out demons…[then quoting God, the text continues] For your sake I shall be born from the virgin Miriam, and for your sake I shall experience Death and enter the realm of Death. For your sake I shall fashion new heavens, and I shall set your descendants in (positions of) authority among them. After three days in the grave, I shall resuscitate the body which I wore on your account…I (also) learned, my son Seth, that a Flood will come and purge the entire earth on account of the descendants of Cain your brother. Because of (his) jealousy for Lebuda your sister, he murdered your brother Abel. Similarly, due to your mother Eve, sins came into existence. And after the Flood, the years for the (continued) appearance of the world will be 6000 years. And then its end will come.' And I Seth wrote down this testament. My father died and was buried east of Paradise, opposite the first city to be built on earth, which was named Enoch. Adam was accompanied (to the grave) by angels and heavenly powers because he was created in the image of God. The sun and moon grew dark, and there was thick darkness for seven days. We sealed the testament and placed it in the Cave of Treasures with the offerings which Adam had brought out from Paradise—gold, myrrh, and incense. And the Magi, the sons of kings, came and removed them, and brought them to the Son of God in the cave at Bethlehem of Judaea.

Pretty damned impressive, huh? Dr. Baruch chuckled. *But long before this was written, a book actually wangled its way into the canon of the Hebrew Bible illegitimately by claiming to have been written at the time of the Babylonian captivity—around 550 BCE—when, in fact, it was penned during the time of the Maccabean revolt (around 180 BCE). It's the Book of Daniel. And, of course, it makes several post-factum 'prophecies' with the benefit of almost 400 years of hindsight. The book is divided into two parts. First, tales like 'Daniel in the lions' den,' etc., which are fictional fables; and, second, eschatological predictions.*

This is the very same ploy that is used by the invention of Moses and his predictions; again, with a fictional character allied to post-factum 'prophecies,' now with almost 700 years of hindsight. But, for a credulous audience, fact and fiction, real prophecy, and retroactive prognostication are equally effective.

And then there's the matter of Egyptian records or, in this case, the total absence of them. The ancient Egyptians were fastidious record keepers, yet somehow it escaped their notice that over two million slaves had escaped; that ten devastating plagues served as their get-out-of-jail-free card; that the firstborn of every single Egyptian family died on the same night; and that Pharaoh's forces were swept away in a mass drowning.

Taking a drink from his water glass, he shuffled his stack of notes and peered over his reading glasses just long enough to confirm that his audience was still transfixed.

Egypt existed for a long time under the rule of various kings, but it was only in the 'New Kingdom' (1570-1069 BCE) that it became an empire. Incidentally, it was only at this time that their leaders were called "pharaoh"—before that they were simply called, 'king/queen.' The New Kingdom is the most completely documented period in Egyptian history. Its territory stretched from Nubia and Kush in the south to Libya in the west and to the Sinai, Canaan, and Syria (as far as the borders of the Hittite empire, which is modern-day Turkey) to the north. It saw the full flowering of Egyptian art, culture, architecture, trade, and military might. In this period lived some of the pharaohs that many of us can name from our high school ancient history courses: Ahmose I, who conquered Syria; Hatshepsut (a female pharaoh); Thuthmoses III, the great empire builder; Amenhotep III; Akenaten (who instituted monotheism in Egypt—it proved to be very unpopular and the priests of Amun undid his great work); he ruled with his wife, Nefertiti; Tutankamun (who went back to the old gods, as his name shows); Seti I; Ramesses II (the Great), who defeated the Hittites in 1274; Ramesses III. In 1069, under the pharaohship of Smendes I (1077-1051 BCE), the empire collapsed, and Syria, Canaan, and Libya were 'lost.'

Do we seriously think that any of the pharaohs who ruled this empire would allow a bunch of two million slaves to escape and wander aimlessly in the Sinai—which was under Egyptian control—and to conquer a land (Canaan) which was a vassal of Egypt? With no mention of this anywhere in their otherwise detailed historical record?

Even though the Bible does not name the pharaoh of the Exodus, the timeline of the story—1250 to 1210 BCE—falls within the reign of Ramesses II who ruled from 1279 to 1213 BCE and was called Ramesses the Great. He is regarded as one of the most successful of them all. No other pharaoh documented his reign as he did, nor built more monuments, nor left more inscriptions behind him. But there is not a single mention of plagues, drownings, or escaped slaves. Bible literalists claim all of these events did happen but that the embarrassed Egyptians destroyed all the records. In other words, 'this is my belief; I don't need any evidence.'

Among less biased researchers, the consensus is that the tradition of

Moses as a lawgiver and cultural hero only goes back to about 600 BCE, from earlier stories, as a theocratic blueprint for the then-raging battle with Egypt for territory. Early American scholar-statesman Thomas Paine, in his work The Age of Reason, *calls Moses a 'detestable villain' who committed 'unexampled atrocities.' Paine cited Numbers 31:13-18 (the slaughter of the Midianite men, in round one, and of the non-virginal women, in round two) as a case in point.*

EXPLAINING HISTORICAL EVOLUTION

Having shown that Moses is not the author of Torah—that he never in fact existed—and that the Exodus is a fictional fable, the Defense team's next task was to figure out who wrote Torah, when, and under what circumstances.

Dr. Baruch continued: *Let's begin by looking at how the notion of gods and God evolved in human thinking. Once* Homo sapiens sapiens *had arrived on the scene, we quickly put our newly developed abilities of language and self-reflection to wrestling with the great existential questions: Who created all of this? What is our relationship to them? Why suffering? What happens after we die? Where were we before we were born?*

It didn't take long to 'create' the notion of gods, and to figure out that we needed to appease them through prayers and sacrifices. It is part of the development of innate, scientific development of observation, pattern-recognition, prediction and, hopefully, some measure of control.

Those whom we originally worshipped—the gods—are really the thinly-disguised personifications of the vices and virtues of individual humans writ large. We took the very best and the very worst in our own behavior, magnified it, and then ascribed it to the sky beings. Looking at their behavior, these gods were no less and no more moral than ourselves. They had dalliances on the Olympian heights that overlooked us Earthlings, who simultaneously feared them and attempted to emulate the lifestyle of these divine beings. This allowed us to glorify greed and violence, while admiring the theory (though not the practice) of love, justice, and compassion.

Then about two and a half thousand years ago, Judaism graduated to monotheism. No more gods, only a one, 'true' God—the omniscient, the omnipresent, the omnipotent, the just, the vindictive, the irascible, and the jealous. He is the thinly disguised personification, not just of individuals, but of the tribe itself. We took the very best and the very worst in the behavior of the entire nation, magnified it, and then ascribed it to Him. And He returns the compliment, even today. That same God blesses both our National Security paranoia and our denominational chauvinism, and He allows us the right to conquer other tribes, enslave them, plunder their resources, and then convert them.

In its most virulent form, this human-created belief system results in progeny conceived by an IVF procedure in which the sperm donated by the secularists (politicians, economists, and the military-industrial complex) fertilizes the ovum of fundamentalist religion. It is assayed in a solution of xenophobia, fear, prejudice, and self-righteousness. And it gives birth to a demon child, an anti-Christ who promises salvation but delivers carnage and global destruction.

This is the divinity of which 13th-century German theologian Meister Eckhart spoke when he said, 'I pray daily to God to rid me of God!'

He is a God with three sets of rules. The first set is one that governs His own behavior. He is entitled to break all of His own commandments with impunity, e.g., 'Thou shalt not kill,' but He can wipe out all of creation in a fit of pique. The second set of rules is for His chosen people—He always has one, and it is always 'us.' This is a code that governs their internal relationships, and by and large, it's a pretty sophisticated one (unless you're a woman or gay). Then the third set is for His chosen people in their dealings with outsiders (gentiles, pagans, infidels, etc.). Here, not only murder but even genocide is permitted and, occasionally, even mandated.

He is a God who has long since outlived His usefulness. I hope Nietzsche was referring to Him when he wrote, 'God is dead!' in his philosophical novel titled Thus Spoke Zarathustra. *Moreover, I hope Nietzsche was correct in his diagnosis. We can no longer afford such a God. He is very high maintenance and has done far too much damage to the human family. But we shouldn't really be surprised. He's been messing with our heads since, having detected our efforts at building the first skyscraper at Babel, He declared in Genesis chapter 11, 'Let us go down and confuse their language...'*

It's high time to retire that kind of an insecure God, give Him a pension, *and then set out in search of a better likeness of our true Source. Surely, we can do better than this Creator called Yahweh that we've fashioned in our image and likeness. To really simplify the human psyche, we could say that it has three layers: first, the mask (persona) I wear to project the image of myself I want others to believe in (e.g., I am kind, intelligent, romantic etc.); second, the ego, which lies behind the mask and which most of us believe is the real me; and, third, the soul—the bite-sized bit of God, which is who I really am. The gods are to this "God" as the persona is to the ego, and this "God" is to Source as the ego is to the soul. Early humans mistook the masks (how they understood the moods/character of the gods—*prosopon *in Greek and* persona *in Latin) for Source. Then, they gave God an ego by collapsing all of those masks into one being—though a very volatile one. But thankfully, the mystics of every tradition realize that there is only Source—ineffable but experience-able. We know we are approaching Source when we begin to see that all life forms, in all dimensions, all worlds, all galaxies, and all universes are equally beloved and deserving of respect. Then we know that there are no chosen people, nor even a chosen species. And that there is only one rule for all. It is to love thy neighbor with all thy heart and soul and mind and body. Because thy neighbor is thyself.*

But in the course of this evolving theology, all tribes have developed Origin Myths that speak not only of how all creation came into being, but, in particular, how our tribe came to be. These founding fables are peopled with heroes and heroines, with villains and victims; and the more elaborate ones—those that take several nights around a campfire to tell—become sagas and epics.

Let's look, then, at how and when and why the Yahweh myth was developed. We can start with 550 BCE and work in both directions as the remnant of Judah simultaneously creates a way forward out of a real historically verifiable exile by remembering a real historical past (for example King David, the Assyrian conquest...) and fabricating an imaginary, inspirational past (for example, Moses, Joshua and the Exodus.)

Under the influence of Zoroastrianism, the great religion of the Persians who, when they conquered the Babylonian empire, liberated the remnant of the Judeans and introduced them to very different ideas about the gods. Zoroastrianism had reduced the pantheon of warring divinities to a cosmology of merely two gods—Ahura Mazda, the god of light, and Ahriman, the god of darkness—and, ultimately to a monotheistic eschatology (an "end times" of a single divinity.) Judaism, in its post-exilic period from 538 BCE onwards, would work these ideas into their own powerful monotheistic creed, and from that center, they would work in both directions; forward into a second-temple religion; and backwards into fabricated, inspirational stories that gave the crestfallen remnant heroic figures and an imagined history (Moses, Exodus, a Promised Land) to encourage them to new greatness. And it worked wonderfully.

Yahweh, courtesy of the politics of the ancient Middle East, worked his way up from being a minor divinity to becoming the god of Israel to, finally, claiming to be the one and only God. In a most creative retrofitting of His image, the Hebrew scholars managed to explain away His "apparent" failures. Here's how they re-wrote their history.

When the ten northern tribes of Israel were exiled by the great Assyrian empire in 722 BCE and permanently erased from the narrative, the scholars now claimed that Yahweh was simply using the gods of Assyria as His enforcers to punish the failure of Israel to honor the covenant. Then He used the gods of Babylon to punish the gods of Assyria for wiping out Israel. But, at the same time, He also used the Babylonian gods to exile the last two tribes—Benjamin and Judah—in 587 BCE. Next, in 538 BCE, He used the gods of Persia to punish the gods of Babylon for exiling Benjamin and Judah. Later on, He would use the gods of Greece and Rome (and maybe Britain?) to continue teaching "His own people" a lesson. It's a little bit like Oswald murdering JFK, Jack Ruby murdering Oswald, and Ruby succumbing to an early death due to a virulent illness. But I digress. The reaction of "His own people" is like abused children trying to make sense of their angry alcoholic father's irrational and unpredictable moods; like victims of the Stockholm Syndrome, they imitate him. Except in this case, the abusive father and the conniving kidnapper are both fictitious characters. The bewildered people of Israel and their priests, theologians, and prophets created Him in an attempt to make sense of their history. Meaning is even more important than freedom. And the self-created interpretation of the suffering is no less real. Imaginary fears are every bit as debilitating as the "real" ones.

So, let's take all of these pieces of the puzzle and rearrange them in chronological fashion so as to represent the actual historical sequence.

Beginning somewhere in the 13th century BCE, a group of nomadic Canaanite tribes began to attack the settled urban communities—who were also Canaanites. At some stage these separate tribes of nomads realized that a loose confederation would be more effective. This confederation may have been joined by other Semitic nomads who had travelled in the Sinai and possibly even as far as Egypt. The alliance proved so effective that the nomads themselves eventually settled down in the conquered towns. In time, they were welded into a more permanent alliance under king David around 1000 BCE. They developed a religion to help hold them fast. This religion was centered on the king as "son of God." (This phrase was actually part of the coronation rite, "you are my son; today, I have begotten you.") The center of worship was the temple built around 950 BCE by David's son, Solomon, in Jerusalem. Then began the task of recording the "sacred history" of Judah. It would come to be known as "J." Alas, the alliance fractured in 933 BCE on the death of Solomon; and the ten northern tribes—henceforth known as Israel—seceded. They began to write their own "sacred history" around 750 BCE, which is known to scholars as "E." But since these kings were not descended from David, and since they had no temple, religion depended on the prophets—Amos, Hosea, etc. The north also began to compile sacred laws which would eventually morph into the Book of Deuteronomy— "D"—some 400 years later.

Israel fell to the Assyrian empire in 722 BCE and the ten northern tribes were never heard of again. A few scholars escaped and brought "E" and an embryonic "D" with them to the south. Then "J" and "E" were fused in a rather sloppy fashion with different versions of the same event/story juxtaposed, e.g., the two differing accounts of creation found in the Book of Genesis chapters 1 and 2.

In 587 BCE, the two southern tribes were deported to Babylon and the temple of Jerusalem was destroyed. During this exile, the priest-prophet, Ezekiel, fearful that they, too, would go the way of their brothers in the north, set about fusing them into a believing unit. Writings and stories, laws and myths, heroes and sagas were invented that would help them make sense of their history and current predicament, yet, convince them that they were

God's chosen people. Ezekiel created the holiness-by-separation code that instituted the Sabbath, divided treif from kosher, forbade table fellowship with gentiles, vetoed intermarriage and insisted on circumcision. And it worked. Wonderfully!

At this stage the myth of Moses and the saga of the Exodus were born. To shore things up further, a new document, called the Priestly Document—"P" —was written. Finally, these four streams were woven into one— "JEDP" —and became the Torah.

While exiled, however, they came under the influence of the great Persian religion Zoroastrianism. This would help them to include belief in life after death, angels, and spirits in their theology; and to ponder the great existential issues, resulting in works like the Book of Job. These would later get appended to Torah as "Ketuvim" (writings) along with the teachings of the prophets, known as Nevi'im.

When Cyrus the Great, the Persian emperor who conquered Babylon in 538 BCE, set the Jewish exiles free to go back to their homeland and even financed the building of the second temple in Jerusalem, it wasn't a completely altruistic act on his part; he wanted "friends"/allies on his western borders as a buffer against Egypt. In fact, in 525 BCE, his son Cambyses II defeated the Egyptian forces and took the title and dress of "pharaoh."

Back in the homeland, the Jewish scholars, scribes and priests set about the final redactions and edits of their sacred writings, culminating in the Hebrew Bible that would serve as the foundation of Judaism, Christianity, and Islam.

Thank you, Professor, I have no further questions, the defense attorney said.

There was a long pregnant pause after Professor Baruch left the stand. Kayla Goldstein held the silence as a sacred space, allowing the full effects of his presentation to sink in before she called her next witness, an esteemed archaeologist named Saul Lieberman. He, too, was a Sabra—born and raised in a kibbutz in Galilee. His lean, muscular body was deeply suntanned from time spent in the sun on numerous digs in several parts of the world, including Jerusalem and the Sinai Peninsula, as well as Africa and the Americas. He held an MS from the University of Haifa in Israel and a PhD from Cambridge

University in England. While Cambridge is regarded at the top archaeology program in the world, it was Lieberman's experience at the University of Haifa that exposed him to the cultural mosaic representative of the region—where Jews, Muslims, Christians, Baha'i, Druze, and Bedouin all study their ancestors as preserved in the archaeological record.

ARCHAEOLOGISTS DIG FOR ANSWERS

Unrolling a rustic map that was propped up on an easel, Saul Lieberman began his presentation:

Let's look at what my fellow archaeologists have to say about the Biblical Exodus as they cite logical inconsistencies, new archaeological evidence, and the related Origin Myths of the preexisting Canaanite culture. From the 19th century CE onwards, archaeologists were surprised by the lack of evidence for the Exodus event. By the 1970s they had given up using the Bible as a field guide. Even a rather conservative archaeologist —William Dever—called the historicity of the Exodus "dead." Modern Israeli scholars like Ze'ev Hertzog concur.

What archaeologists are finding is overwhelming evidence that both the northern kingdom (Israel) and the southern kingdom (Judah) had their origins not in Egypt, but in local Canaanite cultures. The excavations reveal that the culture of the earliest Israelite settlements is Canaanite; that their cult objects are of the Canaanite god El; that the pottery is in the local Canaanite tradition; and that the alphabet is early Canaanite. The sole marker distinguishing Israelite villages from Canaanite sites is the absence of pig bones.

Painstaking efforts to excavate the locations of the many towns mentioned in the Book of Numbers as places the Israelites camped or massacred the locals, show that many of these places did not even exist for several hundred years after the Israelites' alleged time of conquest. As an example, the story of the destruction of the kingdom of Edom falls on its face because the region was not even inhabited at the 'time of Moses'; the nation of Edom did not come into existence until about 800 BCE; only then, according to radiocarbon dating, was the town built. It takes a lot of shadow boxing to exterminate a nonexistent people.

Even the two 'treasure cities' of Egypt—Pithom and Raamses—allegedly built by the Hebrew slaves—did not exist at the same time as each other. Pithom was an obscure garrison town until the 26th dynasty, which began in 664 BCE, while Raamses had been abandoned at the end of the New Kingdom, in 1069 BCE.

No Egyptian sources mention Moses or the events of Exodus-Deuteronomy, nor has any archaeological evidence been discovered in Egypt or the Sinai wilderness—not even from extensive 'digs' on Mount Sinai—to support the story in which he is the central figure. According to two highly respected Jewish archaeologists, Finkelstein and Silberman, "Repeated archaeological surveys in all regions of the peninsula, including the mountainous area around the traditional site of Mount Sinai, near Saint Catherine's Monastery ... have yielded ... not even a single shard, no structure, not a single house, no trace of an ancient encampment."[4]

It's been argued that a wandering band might not leave any evidence that would survive 3,000 years, but modern archaeological techniques can successfully trace even the meagre remains of hunter-gatherers and, in fact, has unearthed such evidence in the Sinai peninsula from 1,000 years earlier than the Exodus. And, if the Biblical account is to be believed, this wandering band is estimated to have been in the ballpark of two million people.

But Jewish and Christian scholars alike have been desperately trying to find evidence of the Exodus for many decades. Between 1967, when Israel captured the Sinai Peninsula from Egypt, and 1982, when it was returned in the peace treaty, Israeli archaeologists made dozens of expeditions throughout the peninsula. Yet, not a single shred of evidence for an ancient Israelite presence was found. Finally, despite numerous digs on Mount Sinai, on the southern tip of Sinai Peninsula, no evidence has been found of any ancient Israelite presence there.

The archaeological record simply does not support a reality in which the Israelites spent forty years perambulating around the Sinai Peninsula. The Bible says that after some initial wandering and a disheartening spy mission into Canaan, the Hebrews encamped at Kadesh Barnea and spent thirty-eight years there before starting the 'final leg' of the journey into the 'promised land.' And the Bible tells us that of all the people who left Egypt, only two souls—Joshua and Caleb—made it into Canaan. This means that the vast bulk of the two million people—not to mention their flocks—died in that encampment. And yet not a single human skull, not a single cooking pot, not a single jawbone of a donkey (sorry Samson!) has been found there.

Moreover, a group of two million immigrants into Canaan, whose 'native population' was significantly smaller, would have left a huge archaeological imprint. In fact, of the thirty-one cities supposedly conquered and destroyed by Joshua, only one—Bethel—shows that kind of destruction. The 'famous' Jericho was "small and poor, almost insignificant, and unfortified" *and* "there was also no sign of a destruction," *according to Finkelstein and Silberman.*[5]

It's important to understand the genre to which these stories belong. Almost universally, scholars say the Exodus is best understood as a charter/foundation myth, a way of explaining a nation's origins, culture and institutions.

With that, Dr. Lieberman folded up his map and sprang back to his seat.

Kayla Goldstein flashed her nimble witness a grateful smile and then turned her eyes toward the jury box, silently making eye contact with each juror, giving them ample time to digest what the science of archaeology had laid bare in their hearts.

By now, the courtroom was humming with excitement, but Kayla Goldstein was determined to keep the atmosphere calm and serene, as she could feel the historic significance of what was unfolding before her eyes.

When the members of the gallery settled down, Kayla called her next witness.

The Defense would like to call Father Seán O'Brien, PhD, to the stand. Father Seán completed his undergraduate work in Mathematics at the National University of Ireland, was ordained in the Roman Catholic church after extensive seminary training and has also earned a PhD in transpersonal psychology. But I'm not calling him to testify due to these credentials, as significant as they are. I'm calling Father Seán to testify in his role as a mythologist. Raised bilingually, speaking Gaelic and English from childhood, he absorbed Irish mythology from his druid grandfather and spent time immersing himself in the archives of the Irish Folklore Commission, which has the greatest cache of mythology and stories anywhere. He was also a very accomplished linguist with a working knowledge of several European and African languages.

Shooting him a quick smile, the Defense asked, *"Father Seán, will you please share with the court your understanding of the sagas and epic tales that make up this library of books we call The Bible?"*

Certainly, m'darlin', the avuncular Irishman replied with a brogue that gave his earliest heritage away. *I was raised on a double stream of them. The first stream came from my great-grandmother—a Catholic mystic who told me tales about Jesus which I never heard in Church but which I later read in the Gnostic writings and in the apocrypha. Somehow these had been translated into Gaelic in the 5th and 6th centuries and had gone underground because of the censoring croziers of the hierarchy, and thus survived in the oral tradition.*

The second river of stories I got from my grandfather—a Celtic druid and storyteller (called a seanachaí in Ireland)—and in it swam the great maidens and warriors of the Tuatha Dé Danaan (Etáin, Aonghus Óg...); of the Red Branch (Deirdre of the sorrows, Cúchulainn...); and of the Fianna (Fionn, Oisín, Oscar and Niamh of the Golden Hair.) There was also a smattering of historical patriots (Brian Ború, Daniel O'Connell, Páraic Pearse, Michael Collins—to name a few.)

Every culture has developed their own version of these founding fables; and the objectives are twofold. First, to make sense of the past and the present; and, second, to unite them as a tribe and inspire them for the future. I have written extensively on the difference between truth and fact. Something can be factual but not true, or true but not factual. There are, of course, two other possibilities: something can be both true and factual, or something can be neither true nor factual. An example of the former would be Gandhi's famous Salt March which transformed a subcontinent under military dominion into a free country, without a single act of violence. Examples of the latter are the propaganda which have been promoted for the purpose of "inspiring" fear, xenophobia, and war.

All founding myths (the basis of a culture's identity) utilize all four of these combinations. Unfortunately, the fourth possibility (neither true nor factual) is far more heavily represented in all the world's "historical" stories, including the Bible. They glorify war, conquest, military heroes and heroines, and the slaughter of the enemy, who is dehumanized even by the nomenclature employed: infidels, barbarians, pagans, gentiles. In story form, this can be exciting, entertaining, and inspiring. In reality, it simply means human suffering on a gigantic, gory, terrifying scale.

It's time to abandon these "heroes" and "heroines" and these tales, in favor of a global—nay a cosmic—story based on compassion for all sentient beings, all of whom were birthed from the same smiling grandmother God.

In the case of Yahweh, a myth that was meant to inspire has locked its followers into subservience to a fictitious psychopath and robbed them of any possibility of mystical union with the True Source. Furthermore, it has cast them into a perennial battle with others who appeal to the same fictitious divinity to justify inter-religious genocide! Isn't it time to awaken from this nightmare?

When Homo sapiens sapiens *developed language around 70,000 years ago, I bet the very first use to which they put it was storytelling. And I imagine there was a sequence and a protocol to the process. Imagine with me: Arap Chito had just encountered a leopard in the bush of East Africa. Luckily, he escaped, but even as the adrenaline and cortisol began rushing through his system, he was rehearsing the encounter with his internal language skills —what de Saussure would call the* signified *(internal image) and the* referent *(the real live leopard), so as not to forget its significance. That night, around a campfire of his twenty-five-person tribe, he would share with them his encounter using* signifiers *(words.) He would thus accomplish four objectives: firstly, he would transfer this new knowledge to the other twenty-four minds; secondly, he would archive this knowledge in the tribal memory for future generations; thirdly, it would be a bonding exercise; and, fourthly, it would be entertaining. Indeed, stories are the archived wisdom of any culture, and pithy proverbs its distillation—the "cheat sheet" to be accessed when time is of the essence.*

In the summer of 1963, between my junior and senior years in high school, I spent three months in a Gaeltacht (places where the working language is still Gaelic) called Cúil Aodh collecting proverbs— seanfhocail ("ancient words") is what we call them in Irish. I systematically visited all of the elders asking, "Can you give me some proverbs and tell me the context in which each one would be used?" At the end of the summer I had collected 432 of them.

One old man said to me, "If Christianity had never come to Ireland, we could live according to the seanfhocail." He was probably correct, because I came to realize that there was a proverb for every situation.

I learned something else as well about proverbs: they frequently contradict each other, because for every situation "A" demanding proverb "X," there is an opposite situation "B," demanding proverb "Y."

In Irish: "Níl aon tinteán mar do thinteán féin" (there's no fireside like your own fireside) is contradicted by, "Bíonn blas ar chuid an chomhairsin" (there's a special taste to the neighbor's food.)

In English: "Look before you leap," but "He who hesitates is lost."

In Kiswahili: "Haraka, haraka haina baraka" (hurry, hurry has no blessing), but "Chelewa, chelewa mtoto si wako" (delay, delay and the baby will not be yours). Go on, figure that one out!

In Latin: "Festina lente" (hasten slowly) but "Carpe diem" (seize the day).

This exercise alerted me as a teenager to the realization that I should listen to all sides of a debate because, if an intelligent "decent" person holds a viewpoint contrary to my own, there must be some merit to it. I grow more by listening to that gem in the other person's ideas than by imposing my viewpoint or refusing to listen. Earlier and wiser minds than mine had already figured that out with the philosophical and logical teaching of "thesis—antithesis—synthesis."

And then there are plenty of examples from disparate cultures that actually support each other. All popular wisdom to the contrary, scientific studies in psychology show that multitasking is not an efficient use of time. Irish agrees: "I ndhiadh a chéile a thógtar na caisleáin" (one after the other are the castles built). Kiswahili concurs: "Upole ndiyo mwendo" (slowness is sureness). And the Greek story of the hare and the tortoise says it elegantly.

Or take the notion of family and elders. The Hebrew scriptures tell us: "Honor your father and your mother that you may live long in the land." Confucius claimed that the notion of the separate self was an illusion created by the sum of our social roles; hence his core teaching is about the "five constant relationships," i.e., that of husband and wife; that of parents and children; that of elder brother to younger siblings; that of teacher and student; and, finally, that of emperor to subjects. Mammals, who arose about 200 million years ago, introduced sustained parenting into the equation of evolution; the sciences of psychology, sociology, and anthropology managed to codify it—with a few notable blunders like behaviorist B. F. Skinner raising his daughter in a stimulus-response "Skinner Box," or the campaign to end breastfeeding in favor of a pharmaceutical formula[6]*. But ultimately, most healthy mammals adopt behaviors that support the species. Kalenjin has an interesting proverb, "Nda samis muryat, ko bo go nebo" (even though the rat is dirty he is part of the household.) It's their version of loving even the "black sheep" of the family. And what about the Howard Loomis story? Back in 1918, Howard was abandoned by his mother at Father Flanagan's Home for Boys. Howard had polio, wore leg braces, and found it very difficult to manage stairs. Older boys sometimes carried him up and down the steps. One day Father Flanagan asked one of these boys—Reuben Granger—if this was difficult. Reuben replied, "He ain't heavy, Father, he's my brother."*

Remember the famous detective Joe Friday from Dragnet, who regularly insisted, "Just give me the facts ma'am, just the facts." Joe had no time for stories. But when you nix storytelling, you demythologize life, thus reducing the person to merely a set of numbers, e.g., Social Security Number, bank codes, a ticket that allocates your place in line in the supermarket, car registration, phone number, postal address—even your jail identity.

Some cultures value the details of the story, while others sterilize their stories, thus losing the texture and nuance of life. For example, a Maasai herdsman knows all of his very many cattle by name, while your modern European Union farmer has a number stapled on to the ear of each of his nameless cows. Or, from my own family: for the last 20 years of his life my father lived in a house with a red door in a remote area of West Cork. His actual postal address was:

Teach Dearg
[The Red House]
Scairtínacillín
[near the little bush by the children's graveyard]

Béal an Dhá Chab
[at the mouth of the two river fords]
Contae Chorchaigh
[in the county of the marshy lands]

In comparison, where I live (in the forest where they don't deliver mail) my postal address is:

P.O. Box 427
Healdsburg, CA 95448

I suspect that they could actually drop the name of the state and it wouldn't make a difference to the USPS. So, dear reader, tell me this and tell me no more (to use an Irish idiom): which of these two addresses tells you more about where my father lived and where I live? It's like we have taken a vibrantly alive, high definition, color video and reduced it to a still photo draining it of all but gray tones.

When you drain life of stories, you drain it of meaning; and when you drain it of meaning you create a nightmare out of God's dream—stripping the cosmos of the miraculous.

MYTHOLOGY, MEME-MAKING, AND "NEWS" AS REVELATION

Self-described "modern" scientifically grounded people constantly confuse the idea of "myth" with "made up." They do not appreciate that the reason myth lives on in the wisdom traditions of the world is that the most entertaining, enduring, and inspiring way to archive and promulgate a deep truth is to embed it in a story. To the literally minded, this, then, is "just a piece of folklore." To the cognoscenti, it is a gem to which an individual can return at various stages of her life and harvest new insights. Myths, when properly understood, are evergreen and every generation can find hints which empower it to engage with the current era and issues of life on planet Earth.

I have a much-younger sister, Dearbhla, to whom I told many of the great Celtic and European myths when she was a young child. When she was a first-year college student majoring in psychology and sociology we revisited the old myths, extracting age-appropriate inspiration from them. For example, even a simple tale like Jack and the Beanstalk could now be interpreted as one of Joseph Campbell's "hero with a thousand faces" and provide the encouragement to face the demons and giants of life-after-high-school.

Mythology—in fact, storytelling in general—is a container for a seed called a "meme." The story protects, encapsulates, and allows the meme-seed to germinate in the consciousness—and even in the subconscious—of a community. To use a different analogy, a meme is to a culture as a gene is to an organism. Each organism is a story told by DNA; it is a structure whose building blocks are genes. Similarly, each culture is a story told by memes. The memes are the great organizing principles of any movement. They create the intersubjective reality spoken of earlier. Probably, if you meet an "-ism," you are meeting a fully developed meme, e.g. capitalism, Catholicism, communism, fascism, consumerism, etc.

On the historical, international stage, the following are examples of successful memes: the great religions, empires, multinational corporations, and what I call, "the migrating oligarchy"—the powerbrokers who, throughout history, have followed or maybe even created the seat of power as it moved from empire to empire. At a national level, political propagandists are the meme-makers. And at the local, village, or tribal level, the storytellers are the meme makers.

A meme attempts to create a culture in its own image and likeness, and it can either be a healing agent or a cancer in the body of the community. Each one of us is meant to be a meme maker. So, it is incumbent upon us all to awaken to the memes in which we are awash and learn to be discerning. There are three stages to the process. Stage one: your decision making is driven by unconscious, preprogrammed ancient propaganda. At this stage, you are under an illusion if you think you are exercising free will as you make your choices. Stage two is where you are beginning to wake up; your choices are semi-free, but you are still manipulated by current propaganda. You still get sucked into angry debates about politics as you defend your candidate or party, not realizing that it is basically a Punch and Judy Show to distract you while confederates of the hidden puppet master circulate among the partisan disputants picking their pockets. And stage three is where you operate from your superconscious Self. Now you are fully free, inured to all propaganda—ancient and current— and filled with compassion for a world mesmerized by the illusion known in Hinduism as maya. You are a change agent, not so much by what you do but by who you are. You realize that you, and everybody else, had volunteered to incarnate at this critical juncture of human history, to move the world from the edge of the cliff into the arms of Christ Consciousness. You have rolled back the amnesia about who you really are and why you've come, and with love, forgiveness and patience, you hold even the "enemy" in your heart.

"News" or the "Fourth Estate" was created after the invention of the printing press to educate and inform the public in the belief that "the truth will set you free." It quickly became the ordinary citizen's access to what is happening all over the world. It made us "neighbors" with the entire human family. It informed us of injustices at home and abroad, and investigated, on our behalf, corruption in high places. It kept the powerbrokers on their toes. Journalists were the early warning system of the community. Next to "it's the gospel truth!", the ultimate clincher in settling any disputed facts was the statement "I read it in the paper!" Journalists were the locust-eating, camel-hair-clad John and Jean the Baptists of the 18th, 19th, and 20th centuries—prophets who spoke truth to power, the Sherlock Holmes figures who put the memes and the meme-makers under the magnifying glass.

THE SHADOW SIDE

When we begin to take myth and meme as literal truth, we are in danger of tumbling headlong into what I will call "the intersubjective pitfall." And, thus, the unexamined meme becomes a time-bomb. It is often the first misstep of the slide into despotism. The meme-makers massage the message to create fear, anxiety, anger and xenophobia. These are always the result of force-fed, preprocessed, predigested pablum the oligarchs use to put us to sleep, until they need us outraged by a concocted crisis, whether it's killer bees approaching from Mexico, the zika virus from South America, the Russians hacking our elections, or Middle-Eastern terrorists.

Driven by the lust for power, the desire to own and control the world's resources, and a fascination with bloodletting in endless wars, the memes are planted in the "news" media in order to have us cry out for protection, to surrender our civil rights in exchange for security, and as a patriotic sacrifice. At the apex of this pinnacle of power sit the "megameme-makers," such as the Bank of International Settlements which presides over the IMF and the World Bank, and which controls the fictitious "fiat currencies" now fully digitalized. And, of course, the hidden policy-making moguls like the Bilderberg Group, the Trilateral Commission, and the Council on Foreign Relations. Of these three groupings, Jesus might have said, "render unto Caesar the things that are Caesar's and to God the things that are God's." My understanding of this statement of Jesus is not simply the segregation of secular and spiritual authority, but the much deeper realization that "Caesar" represents the illusions of maya. We may need to work with it during incarnation, but in no way does it define who we are or what our true purpose is during incarnation—which is nothing less than the activation of our Buddha nature and the bringing about of Christ Consciousness on our beloved planet.

Propaganda is as old as storytelling, and its modern costume is "fake news." The problem is that most of the fake news is coming from the mainstream accusing the prophets of being the ones propagating the fake news. This deception is as old as the book of Jeremiah of 600 BCE, where the "court prophets," who were aligned with the ruling class, accuse Jeremiah of promoting lies that could lead to the overthrow of the kingdom of Judah. As it turned out, of course, he was correct. Within a few short years the royal family, "court prophets," and the bulk of the populace were taken into exile in Babylon and the first temple (the one Solomon had built in 950 BCE) was destroyed.

In our times, the fourth estate (the current crop of court prophets) has become a willing partner to the oligarchy and is used by them to distract, misinform, and disinform us. And there are myriad pieces on their chessboard of divide and conquer: ethnicity, racism, sexism, ageism, denominational affiliation, political parties and class (lower, working, middle, upper, elite, aristocratic, and royal). These strident, finger-pointing "presstitutes" in the employ of the powerbrokers have abandoned their sacred mission as guardians of the truth and promoters of revelation. It is a well-known fact that if you want to succeed in a coup, you must first capture the mass media.

Jesus said, "By their fruits you shall know them." [Matthew 7:16].

Look at the fruits of Jesus's "good news"—which was both good (God is a loving Abba, not a punitive rage-aholic) and new (a far cry from the business-as-usual of famine, disease, and war). Now compare that with the fruits of the fake news of a divided nation which manages to savage itself even as it conducts foreign wars. Why would we continue to believe in a "news machine" that told us lies about weapons of mass destruction, quickly followed by the invasions of Afghanistan, Iraq, Libya, and Syria, causing the deaths of millions of real, innocent human beings and creating a tsunami of refugees? Fake news tells us that we are always the heroes and good guys, even as we steal, lie, invade, and murder people on the other side of the globe.

These are the same folks who told us that the Patriot Act was patriotic, and that the National Defense Authorization Act (NDAA) was actually defending us. In reality, these pieces of legislation are dissolving our constitution and causing the outside world to both fear and despise us. Fake news and bought airtime have sold us Citizens United to ensure that the US gets the best "representatives" corporate money can buy and convinced us to reject state propositions that would have halted the race to the top of GMO foods. Perhaps it's time to do a "news fast"—to put my TV and radio to bed and to save a tree by cancelling my subscription to my morning newspaper.

If you set out on a hike without a map, you may get lost; if you take an inaccurate map, you'll probably get lost; but if you take an intentionally drawn wrong map, you will certainly get lost. If you're a cook and decide to be creative by not following a recipe, the results may taste foul; if you follow a bad recipe, it will probably taste foul; but if you follow a bad and poisonous recipe, not only will it definitely taste foul, it will also kill you.

Whether you're hiking or cooking, examining your cosmology or pursuing a PhD in astrophysics, it is vital that you exercise critical thinking and not simply swallow what you are fed.

Those who sneer at mythology and boast about science are demonstrating ignorance of both. I have been lucky enough to have had extensive exposure to and training in both fields: a childhood with a storyteller grandfather followed by a Bachelor of Science degree. It was amusing to me that the church expected me to park my brain at the door and believe only in faith when I dipped my hand in the holy water font and made the sign of the cross;

and that the university expected me to park my soul at the front gates of the college and believe only in science.

Mythology is the cultural interpretation and articulation (in story form) of its collective experiences. It forms the basis of "reality" for subsequent generations. It then becomes very difficult to experience anything that the culture says does not exist. Science is simply a more modern form of myth. Using different criteria and a new methodology, it simply creates a new story that has formed the basis of "reality" for the last several generations. Once again, it then becomes very difficult to experience anything that the culture says does not exist. Science has made as many serious errors in its models of reality as has religion. And its current story of a big bang explaining the origin of the cosmos (which ironically was first proposed by a Belgian Catholic priest-scientist, Georges Lemaitre, in 1927) is as infantile as the religious story of an irascible God sending a flood to wipe out this little corner of it.

Ultimately, all we have are stories, whether they fall into the religious category or the scientific one. So, using Aquinas's insight ("Truth is found only in the judgment"), we have to choose very carefully which stories to believe.

Fundamentalist science gives us a cosmos without God, a cosmos without purpose and, as a bonus, weapons of mass destruction and ecological devastation. Fundamentalist religion gives us a God without love, a theology without compassion and, as a bonus, hell for all eternity for the nonbelievers. Based on all the evidence of which I am aware, I choose to not believe in a cosmos without God (fundamentalist science) or in a God without love (fundamentalist religion). Instead, Credo in Unum Deum—I believe in one (unconditionally loving) God.

The court broke out in a spontaneous smile as this Irish Catholic priest ended his impassioned discourse, joined his hands in front of his face and offered them all a hearty *Namasté*—the Hindu prayer meaning *"the divine in me recognizes and honors the divine in you!"*

As he returned to his seat, everybody in the courtroom was feeling a whole lot better about life and about God. After a short break, the judge called order and invited the Defense to resume its presentation.

ANALYZING YAHWEH

Once again Kayla Goldstein stood up and addressed the judge. *Your honor, I would now like to call my final expert witness—a Jungian Analyst, trained in Zurich, a noted author and lecturer and an international speaker. Her name is Silvia Moorehouse and she is here specifically to explain the notion of "projection."*

After being sworn in, Ms. Moorehouse began to explain the phenomenon of projection, illustrating her presentation with lots of allegories.

Imagine you're watching a movie screen and you think that John Wayne is actually riding across the stage from left to right when, in fact, the action is happening in the projection box. But it is very boring to go into the projectionist's box and scroll through the celluloid roll, watching the movie one frame at a time. By projecting it onto a screen, we get the illusion of change, of time, of speed and of size. It allows us to see very clearly what is happening on the celluloid frames. But if we think it is actually happening on the screen, we are deluding ourselves.

And that is what we've tended to do with "God"—we project our inner images onto the screen of the heavens and paint it with all of our own attributes—good and bad. So, let's look at this.

The oldest and most vexing issue is the problem of evil, called "theodicy" in theological circles like Father O'Brien's. I want to offer a way of understanding evil from the vantage point of psychology. One of the most impactful archetypes driving human behavior, according to Carl Jung, is the "shadow"—that unacknowledged part of us which we typically project unconsciously onto others. It's a pity that we don't recognize that the shadow is 80% gold—the unrealized potential, the gap between who we could become and who we presently are. But more problematic is the other 20%, the repressed material that makes it difficult for us to see the log in our own eye, thus enabling us to ascribe it to others.

When we do this as individuals, we simply project this material onto another person, typically onto someone with whom we have a significant relationship—good or bad. Then we wind up, literally, shadow boxing, often with disastrous results.

When we do it as a community, we form prejudices and dump the shadow of the entire group onto another group. I remember watching the movie Mississippi Burning *several years ago. The part of the movie that most upset me was an interview with a young White woman who was nursing her infant, all the while vilifying the Black community and claiming that if they weren't kept in their subservient role, the Blacks would be raping White women, killing White menfolk, and burning White homes and churches. This is precisely what the White community had actually been doing for years to the Black community! That is what happens when a group fails to acknowledge and work on its own shadow.*

The nation, also, has a shadow, and so it creates a major industry to convince the citizens that the "bad guys," the "axis of evil" is the other group. Billions of dollars are spent on propaganda and trillions of dollars are spent on war machinery in order to project the nation's shadow onto the "enemy" and then in attempting to conquer it. All wars throughout human history have been fought on the basis of this one-two punch.

All shadow-casting results in a double-sided illusion. Firstly, a failure to see ourselves as we are. And, secondly, a tendency to see others as they are not. This skewed reality creates a misalignment—a background/foreground disorientation—which leads to psychological and sociological crippling. It's rather like seasickness, which is produced by the contradictory sensations being delivered by vision (the eyes) and kinesthetics/proprioception (the stomach). So, for instance, if you're in your cabin in a ship that is being tossed about by a storm, relative to the interior of the cabin you are not moving or pitching or yawing, so the eyes are deceived, but the gyroscope of the stomach can detect the motion. It's this conflict between the eyes and the stomach that leads to seasickness. Hence, you'll feel less sick if you go up on deck where eyes and stomach are giving you the same message. Well, the unrecognized shadow operates something like that and, depending on the numbers involved (individual, community, nation etc.), the results can be anywhere from mild discomfort to a category five hurricane.

But it's not just nations that have shadows; the entire human species, qua species, has a shadow. This is projected onto nature and is so severe, in our times, that we run the risk of a murder-suicide pact, in which we destroy nature's ability to feed and support us, and, thus, we have become a cancer which, having killed its host, now finds itself in the clutches of death.

"God" may well be the aggregated shadow material of Homo sapiens sapiens*—a cancerous archetype of the unacknowledged but destructive energy of this dark part of the human psyche.*

Nestled between the east coast of Asia and the west coast of North America lies a huge gyre, a swirl of ocean currents that has trapped a massive amount of human garbage. It has been called variously "The Great Pacific Garbage Patch" and "The Pacific Trash Vortex." It consists of plastics and chemical sludge, 80% of which comes from land-based dumping and 20% from ship-based dumping. It is made up of a host of items—from abandoned fishing nets to micro-pellets used in abrasive cleaners. Typically, it takes the North American currents about six years to ferry their contributions to the dump, while the Asian currents can manage it in less than a year. Depending on how you measure the items in this dump—from microscopic plastic particles to soda bottles—this garbage pile is either the size of Texas or twice the size of the continental USA. As you can imagine, it results in the deaths of millions of sea creatures, and the poisons ingested by them, and hence by their predators, work their way up the food chain to be delivered to you on the shiny antiseptic shelves of your local fish market.

This vindictive, bloodthirsty, genocidal "God" of whom we read in the Scriptures may well be the psychospiritual equivalent of the "Great Pacific Garbage Patch"—the constellated island of the human community's unwillingness to face and heal its own darkness. He may well be the personification of the projected Great Garbage Patch of the unclaimed human shadow.

The court swished this idea of projection around in their minds as Silvia Moorehouse returned to her seat.

THE BEST DEFENSE

Once again Kayla Goldstein took the stage as if performing in a one-woman show on Broadway. She confidently strode to the center of the courtroom and, planting her feet, she began her soliloquy.

The prosecution has effectively created a lurid picture of Yahweh's pathology, appealing to clinical experience and its own "bible"—the DSM.

The reason, of course, that Yahweh has all of these pathologies is because He is a composite figure evidencing the combined traits of (a) the population of writers who created His profile, (b) the behavior of the peoples among whom they lived, and (c) the actions of their leaders.

Squaring her shoulders for her final arguments, Kayla continued. *"I'm sure it hasn't escaped your notice, dear juror, that the defendant Yahweh and his scribe Moses have been tried in absentia. This is not due to an oversight on the part of the prosecution nor a ploy on the part of the defense. They were tried in absentia for the very simple reason that they don't exist! Never have. The prosecution has accused a fictitious Santa Claus of breaking and entering. A set of purported autobiographical journals, which is largely a work of fiction based on observation of human nature and attributed to the imaginary culprits, is the only evidence the prosecution has presented. Their 'findings' may be of interest to students in a creative writing class, but they have no place in a court of law. And isn't it ironic that all of the prosecution's witnesses have been asked to swear upon the very book which is the subject of the entire trial? How can we not be biased when pledging to 'swear by the Bible that the Bible is the Word of God'?"*

Even the prosecution was stunned by this obvious flaw in the very foundations of the system.

If Yahweh's alleged behavior and the existence of his main enforcer—Moses—are fictitious, the case quickly falls apart. All cultures have created gods in their own image and likeness by taking human virtues and vices, magnifying them, and ascribing them to sky beings. A Hindu priest, a Tibetan Rinpoche, or a South American shaman would immediately recognize this deceptive divinity.

So, we have found the enemy and it is us! Humankind has acted violently in response to an idol made in its image and likeness. God—the real God—is innocent of all these crimes: those are not God's journals; God never said those things; neither did God ever commit nor decree such actions. I, thereby, move to dismiss this case on the grounds that we have tried the wrong "person."

Judge Grossler scanned the stunned faces of the jury, his own emotions well-hidden as he called an end to that session of the trial.

Kayla Goldstein had just dismantled the Prosecution's seemingly ironclad case, which had been painstakingly delivered over the course of six days of excruciating testimony, in a single day of counterargument. The jurors had paid close attention to every word from each expert witness, assessing each bit of testimony for accuracy and significance. But now, all of that was up for grabs if this was indeed a case of mistaken identity.

SECTION III: THE VERDICT

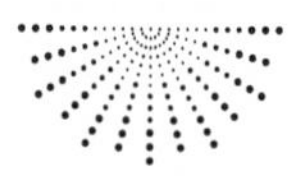

After a brief recess, Judge Jerome Grossler called the court to order, which was hardly necessary, as every person sat silently on the edge of their seat eager to hear the verdict. The judge wasted no time getting to it.

It's been obvious to me since the opening statements in this case that both the Prosecution and the Defense actually had the same objective. They brought this situation to our attention so that a very elegant and mutually satisfying solution could be found. In fact, they've conducted themselves in a manner suggestive of two loving parents attempting to deal with a much-maligned child. They both highlighted, in contrasting ways, the projection of the human shadow onto an ineffable, loving Source. The Prosecution sought to do so by highlighting the psychopathic nature of this global thought-form run amok—and he did a damn fine job of it! Judge Grossler said, shooting a proud smile to Michael Newsome. Turning to face Kayla Goldstein, the judge continued. *Then the Defense utterly dismantled this theology of taking God's name in vain by systematically, thoroughly, and quite brilliantly showing how such dark projections became dogma, even scripture, over time.*

Congratulations are in order to both of you. It will be my honor to present a verdict which will please you both; a verdict for which you painstakingly laid the groundwork; a verdict that sets Source free from the libelous thoughts of generations of 'believers' and, in setting God free, will liberate God's children to bathe in a love so deep and so irresistible that it inspires and compels us to treat others—indeed, all sentient life—with the same kind of compassion. By virtue of this trial's evidence being presented in a case of mistaken identity, I release the members of the jury from their duty to deliberate.

A shockwave rolled through the courtroom as members of the jury, gallery, the Prosecution, and the Defense wondered aloud where the judge was going with this. No jury deliberation? How could that be?

Pounding his gavel on the desk, calling for order in the court, Judge Grossler waited until he could hear a pin drop. *What we have here is a case of mistaken identity*, he whispered, and then victoriously bellowed— *Set God free!*

This verdictless verdict momentarily knocked the wind out of every gasping set of lungs in the room. Then the packed courthouse witnessed a very unusual event. With broad smiles and open arms, Michael Newsome and Kayla Goldstein walked across the courtroom and embraced each other in a warm, genuine, celebratory hug. And with that, every person present breathed a collective sigh of relief.

ON THE COURTHOUSE STEPS

Hordes of microphone-wielding reporters and their video crews surrounded the defense attorney as she emerged from the courthouse, making it impossible for her to leave the scene without providing a few juicy sound bites for the evening news. Both exhausted and exhilarated by the trial, this brilliant young attorney composed herself for a moment and then gently but firmly spoke these words directly into the sea of cameras before her:

Religion has shot itself in the foot. By concocting and accepting such a vile and vicious God, many of the founders and followers of the Abrahamic religions have caused global fallout with the repercussions of a nuclear holocaust.

First, and worst, is the way the all-loving true God has been reduced to a threatening, hateful monster. It's simply unthinkable that Love has been hijacked in this way.

Second, this fictional caricature has been used as a bludgeon to keep generations of believers cowering in fear of immediate torture and eternal damnation.

Third, millions of innocent people have been dragged before inquisitions, tortured, and murdered on behalf of this "God."

Fourth, 'God's' behavior became the justification for every manner of evil committed by humanity, including colonial conquest, genocidal wars, and the practice of slavery, to name a few.

And, finally, when it was safe to do so, millions of thinkers escaped into the twin deserts of agnosticism and atheism, fleeing not only this caricature of God, but the True God as well.

That's quite a rap sheet, wouldn't you say?!

But God is not responsible for any of these crimes; people are. In attempting to promote devotion to God—which can only ever flow from the natural, beautiful human mystical impulse that exists within us all—organized bureaucratic religious oligarchies have vilified God, thus driving many true seekers into the wilderness of despair.

My prayer today is that God and humanity—believers and nonbelievers alike—would be set free to love and be loved as the True Loving Source of all intended from the start."

IN THE JUDGE'S CHAMBERS

One week after the trial ended, both attorneys were surprised to get phone calls from the judge, inviting them to a private meeting in his chambers. They contacted each other but neither of them could figure out what the purpose of such a meeting might be. When they arrived, they found Judge Grossler dressed in street clothes, amiable and relaxed. He greeted them with a broad smile and bade them be seated. *Drinks, anybody?* he asked, as they settled themselves into the soft seats. Both opted for water as he decanted for himself a glass of Sauvignon Blanc from the Quivira Winery in the Dry Creek Valley of Healdsburg, California.

No doubt you're wondering why I requested this meeting, he said as he took his seat. Both attorneys nodded silently. *Well,* he continued, *I was so impressed with what you accomplished during the course of the trial, and I am so convinced of the importance of the topic, that I have a proposition.* He swirled the wine around in his glass, closed one eye, and watched the sunlight refracted by the liquid. Then he said, *I'm old enough to remember when the idea of mediation was first introduced into the justice system. I watched how this novel way of dealing with divorce cases and civil litigation eased the burden on us—judges and attorneys—and shortened the wait time for the public. Many of my older, retired colleagues utilized their experience to help couples and litigants deal more efficiently and amiably with what heretofore would have been stressful and divisive issues.* He paused reflectively, sipped his wine and continued. *I was so impressed with how you handled and presented the material of this trial, and of how vitally important this topic is, that I am convinced many others within the legal system could learn from what you did and how you did it. I really believe that many of our fellows—judges and attorneys alike—could benefit from being exposed to those same data which you covered so thoroughly in the course of the trial.*

He glanced at them. Both of them were smiling, accepting this great compliment from someone whom they greatly admired. They mumbled their thanks and self-consciously sipped from their own water glasses. Both of them, however, intuited that the meeting was not merely about congratulations. So, they tentatively awaited what the judge might say next. He didn't disappoint them, but he certainly surprised them.

He set his glass firmly on the table, leaned forward and looked intently at them. *I have a strong feeling that this material could be the stuff of a seminar that could impact the judicial process even more effectively than did mediation! I want to suggest that we put together a seminar for interested judges and attorneys, to expose them to the material. I've privately run it by a number of them who'd already heard of the case and were hugely impressed by it, and the response was interest—even enthusiastic interest. What do you think?*

The attorneys looked at each other—a glance that flashed appreciation for the compliment and a tentative excitement at the prospect. Kayla Goldstein spoke first. *What would it involve and where would it be held?* The judge had an immediate response. *I foresee a group of perhaps fifteen to twenty people getting together once a week for three hours. We could probably comfortably fit in these chambers. Each week, we'd have one of your expert witnesses present the material, field questions and moderate the subsequent discussion. I think we'd have enough material to run it over a nine-month period.*

Michael Newsome exhaled audibly as he took in these suggestions. His heart was pounding with excitement and a quick look at Kayla Goldstein confirmed that she, too, was thrilled by the possibilities. He blurted out, *I don't often find myself without words, but I do now.* This wasn't just a figure of speech, as he smiled wordlessly. All three held the silence gracefully—each visualizing what great good this collaboration might accomplish.

The judge leaned back in his chair, took a long, satisfying swig of his wine and surveyed his guests. Then, once more he leaned forward —even more intently—and looked earnestly at both of them. Lifting some papers, he donned his spectacles and said, *During the trial, I received three Amici Curiae—pleading letters from three parties who would be affected by the outcome. I was deeply moved by them, though I chose not to read them aloud during the actual trial. But, if you will indulge me, I will read them to you now.* He adjusted his spectacles, coughed politely to clear his throat, and began. *The first is from a group calling themselves the "Devastated Faithful" and it says: "The prosecution's case is attempting to dismantle our home. It may be a dysfunctional family, but it is the only one we know. God may at times appear to be an irascible, punitive father, but He is Our Father. We may live in a ramshackle, outdated house but it is a place that has long afforded us shelter. Please do not allow a wrecking ball to destroy it!"*

The second one is from a group calling themselves "Suddenly Interested Agnostics" and it reads: "At last somebody has had the courage to point out the glaring inadequacies of orthodox religion, the intelligence to put the mind on a par with faith, and the ability to show that science and spirituality might be God's two arms, not irreconcilable enemies."

And the third one is from a group calling themselves "Recovering Judeo-Christian-Muslims" and it reads: "We can now dare to admire the lotus growing out of the mud. The pearl in the jaws of the oyster. The buried treasure hidden in the field of dreams."

He laid down the paper and continued, *I want to use the allegory of the house contained in the first Amicus Brief. I, too, grew up in a faith tradition that was more like a hovel; it had no electricity, no indoor plumbing and its foundations had been seriously compromised by many earthquakes. Lots of family members left over the years, forced out by feelings of insecurity and by their distrust of raging 'parents' who used inquisition, crusades and excommunication to keep us in line. During this trial we learned instead that "in my father's house, there are many mansions." (John 14:2) There is space for everybody and security for all. No family member needs to feel unloved.*

He paused, and it was obvious to the attorneys that the best was yet to come. Once more he did not disappoint. Taking off his spectacles and twirling them in his hand, he said, *I realized over the last week that we've only just begun. We demolished the house of fear-based fundamentalism in which many people— the "Devastated Faithful"—lived in unsafe, unhealthy conditions where they continued to shelter because it was the only home they knew. But there are other houses that are equally unfit for human occupation—other homes which are also unsafe and unhealthy. We need to persuade those residents also to abandon their abodes. I am speaking of the hovels of fundamentalist scientism, which sacrifices meaning and dishonors Nature, and of a psychology which has lost its soul—even though psychology literally means "the study of the soul." We have, I contend, only half finished the job!*

We need to visualize and build a magnificent new home where the Devastated Faithful, Suddenly Interested Agnostics, and Recovering Judeo-Christian-Muslims—as well as True Scientists and Transpersonal Psychologists can live and thrive. It must be a new home designed by a master architect, checked by a first-rate structural engineer, built by a reputable contractor, decorated by a very talented interior designer, and whose grounds will be created by a wonderful landscape artist.

The seminar started one month later with twenty people packed into the judge's chambers. Word soon got out. The following week, the seminar had to be moved to a larger venue that groaned under the energy of some fifty people—all of whom were connected to the justice system. But God's desire for liberation was not yet quite satisfied. Within a month an auditorium had to be rented as five hundred people, including peace officers, local politicians, some scientists, and religious leaders of all stripes clamored to be included.

Fast forward twelve months. The original seminar worked with all of the material that had been used in the trial, with the lectures being given by most of the original expert witnesses who had taken part in the trial. At the end of seminar, there was an overwhelming desire to dig even deeper and to actively build "the new house" mentioned by Judge Jerome Grossler. So, it was decided to do a second yearlong seminar using the same format. The attendance at this second one was as impressive as that of the first.

As the final scene of our imaginary courtroom drama fades out and the credits roll, before the curtain falls, take a bow for the part you have played in this imaginal exploration, dear reader. To the extent that you are able to see yourself as a member of the jury, you really do play a part in the trial of the century. As we prepare to reenter the narrative we began in Part One, take a moment to imagine yourself signing up for Judge Grossler's seminar as, together, we engage in the dual objectives of setting spirituality free and setting science free.

PART III

SETTING SPIRITUALITY FREE

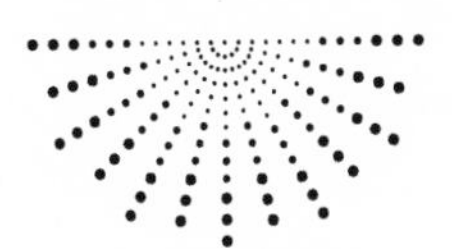

INTRODUCTION TO PART III

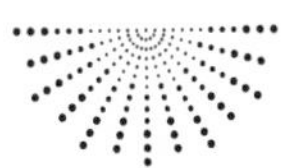

GREATER THAN PHYSICAL FREEDOM—THE ability to *go* where you will—is mental freedom—the ability to *think* what you will. But the greatest freedom of all is the ability to fall in love with God, the real God, and then *love* as you will.

Humanity has long hitched its soul to the projection of a dark, devious deity who led us through fear and intimidation into Hell-on-Earth and the threat of eternal damnation in the afterlife. But you've seen the phantom dissolve. Now, you are free to find the light—the healing compassion emanating from the heart of the One True God. And so, you may now dismantle a religion of legalism and, instead, mindfully fashion a spirituality of love. You've been held captive for too long. Now, set yourself free and begin the journey home.

SECTION I: THEOLOGY

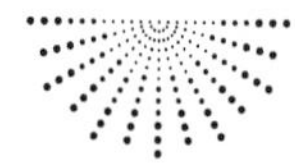

LET MY PEOPLE GO!

THE FOUNDATIONS of all cosmologies rest on the universal human dialectic between fear-based thinking and love-based thinking.

I believe that infants are born with only two emotions—love and fear. When love is inner-directed it becomes self-esteem; when it is outer-directed it becomes compassion. When fear is inner-directed it becomes depression; when it is outer-directed it becomes anger. And the deepest fear of all is the fear of being unloved. Every infant unconsciously wrestles with this because, being yet at the age-appropriate stage of narcissism, it believes that the absent mother (who may have gone to the store or to the bathroom) has abandoned it due to its innate unlovability. This deeply embedded oscillation between love and fear, then, is the genesis of all of the other virtues and vices. All relationships are buffeted by this struggle. Kids and adults alike compensate for this by creating a plethora of defense mechanisms to protect the fragile self-image or gain an advantage in the interpersonal wars inherent to human social life. It is a major cause of apparent superiority complexes, which are simply overcompensation for the horrible reality that I am inadequate.

Writ large, it is the reason why nations and religions need to claim chosen-ness or specialness. All wars are dramatizations of this inner conflict and all warring ceases when people realize who God really is, who they themselves really are, who their neighbor really is, and what the real mission of life is. But the road to that realization is a long, narrow, winding path punctuated with potholes.

YOUR INNER CHILD: WHEN WE LOVE TO HATE

You've witnessed it many times. Perhaps you've been the victim yourself or even been the perpetrator of the crime: a two-year-old throwing a temper tantrum in a supermarket after his mother has said, "No! You may not have another candy bar!" and the enraged reaction, "I hate you!!!" accompanied by stomping feet, bitter tears, and lashing out at her. So what, then, is your greatest strength, or your ultimate defense mechanism? Your ability to hate those who love you, or your ability to love those who hate you? Are you most frequently like the two-year-old in the supermarket or the Galilean carpenter who set a very true example of loving his enemies?

This is not just a question that individuals need to ask of themselves; it's an even more important question when asked by communities or by nations. Precious few "Christian countries" or "Christian political leaders," in their international policies, have acted according to the "love those who hate you" principle.

Spiritual development that leads to unconditional love has the power to change the world. I'm always on the lookout for such spiritual adaptogens. An adaptogen is any commodity that can configure its elements to address the needs of a situation. In medicine, the term is used to refer to a substance that can rearrange itself to identify, target, and treat a disease—Ginseng, for example. Anything that boosts the immune system—the body's own healing cornucopia—will *ipso facto* act as an adaptogen. In nature, water is perhaps the ultimate adaptogen. Not only will water find its way under, over, around or through any obstacle, but when it is "domesticated" and placed in a container, it will organize its shape to conform precisely to the inner contours, no matter how complex or irregular those contours may be.

In human relationships, the two greatest adaptogens are fear and love. They've never met a container to which they cannot conform nor a situation which they are not able to conquer. Which brings me back to my original question: What is your greatest strength, or your ultimate defense mechanism: your ability to hate those who love you or your ability to love those who hate you?

What happens, then, when love and fear *confront each other*? What happens when an irresistible force (love) meets an immoveable object (fear)? This battle of the Titans is the entire point, the *raison d'être,* the mission, the very purpose of incarnation! Mostly, it looks as if fear (also known as anger, greed, violence, war) is winning the contest hands down. But that is a misreading of the data, because fear—intrinsically—is simply a misplaced form of love. Fear involves two missteps. Firstly, it is a succumbing to the illusion of separate identity: believing we are separate from God, separate from each other, and separate from nature. And, secondly, then attempting to love (desperately, passionately, and protectively) this isolated, vulnerable, little self. Scaled up, xenophobic nationalism or fanatical fundamentalism is simply a group version of this lonely, fragile self.

Since, then, fear's primary energy is that of love—albeit a deformed version of love—ultimately Love is the victor. Eventually, all forms of Love return to their Source, erasing any and all deformations in the process. Absence makes the heart grow fonder. Hence Jesus's famous saying, "There is more joy in heaven over one sinner who repents than over ninety-nine who do not need repentance." A victory wrested from the jaws of death is the most satisfying win of all.

If bringing to superconscious awareness our heretofore subconscious personal cosmology is part of the task of incarnation, how can we choose among the very many popularly peddled philosophies clamoring for our attention? "Here is the kingdom!" "No! Over here is the kingdom." If, as each religion claims, we can only win heaven by adhering to its unique scriptural tradition; if we can only avoid eternal damnation by eschewing the "false" teachings of all the other "fake" scriptural traditions, are we then destined to stand immobilized or to drown in the cacophony of these competing "revelations?"

Gratefully, there are a few simple yet elegant orienting principles which can help us navigate these shark-infested ideological waters: any system that depends on fear to win and hold adherents is not true revelation; any system whose members are cemented together by prejudice or xenophobia is not true revelation. When you meet a system with pithy mantras such as "We are God's chosen people," "Outside the church there is no redemption," "You cannot be saved unless you accept our personal savior," or "Our prophet sealed the deal," you might want to smile compassionately and continue your search.

Conversely, when you find a grandmotherly God who is completely enamored of Her offspring—all of them, from bodhisattvas to banana slugs—tarry there, you're getting closer to home, weary traveler! Like Mirabai Starr's imagined conversation with Julian of Norwich illustrates, "The God you love is an unconditionally loving mother who squeezes your cheeks, looks into your eyes, and tells you that you are the most adorable creature she has ever created."[1]

If you find that you are waking up to a new way of seeing and being, know that it will be difficult. In the Gospel of Thomas, the canonical teaching "Ask and you shall receive, seek and you shall find, knock and the door shall be opened" is widened significantly to "Those who *seek* will find, and when they *find* they will be *disturbed*, and when they are disturbed they will *marvel*, and when they marvel they will *rule* and when they rule they will *rest*." Six stages, and the third one is "being disturbed." If your work on your cosmology doesn't disturb you, you are most probably not growing but, are rather settling for the security of old sectarian thinking. The temptation on first becoming disturbed is to go right back to sleep. Please don't. The world needs you to be awake and responsive to the Spirit.

So how do you know whether you are awake or asleep? You are asleep to the extent that you operate in fear, despair, anger, or unforgiveness. You are awake to the extent that you recognize the divine in yourself, in others, and in the "enemy." To the extent that you are willing to listen to the perspectives/beliefs/fears of the opposition, you are awake; to the extent that you can stretch beyond the confines of both positions to synthesis, you are awake. To the extent in which you realize that there are no longer good/bad guys but only God's guys trying to make sense of incarnation, you are well on your way to aligning with your Buddha nature. To the extent that you are ready to laugh at the illusion of reality fed you by society, you are ready to be an agent of Christ Consciousness, Buddha Nature, Shekinah, Nirvana, Great Spirit, or whatever name you give to That Which Is.

You may find yourself developing a new level of acceptance of previously unknown or taboo traditions, but you will also have to shed lots of prejudices, old beliefs, and judgments in the process.

In April of 2016, astrophysicist Neil deGrasse Tyson hosted a panel discussion to debate the theory—now gaining scientific traction—that we live within a simulated reality, a real live Matrix, if you will. The idea that we are simply characters in some Extraterrestrial kid's game is humbling, to say the least, and frightening, to say the most. Are we simply actors on stage, mouthing our lines and unconsciously following a preordained plot? Is that really very much different from Calvin's idea of predestination, except that, in Calvin's version, the ET kid is a sadistic god who drools at the mouth as he watches his own creatures suffer eternally? Not only has he got scant regard for those whom he created specifically to be damned, but in fact takes delight in their eternal suffering.

Neil deGrasse Tyson's scientific discussion is predicated on the following data: when you send a photo to a friend via email, the process involves two kinds of code. Firstly, a transmission code that sends the bits and bytes in discrete quanta (packets.) Sometimes a few of these packets get lost or corrupted in transit, so a second kind of code is also embedded, whose function is to auto-correct or infer and insert the missing or corrupted data. Thus, you manage to get a "perfect" photo at the other end. Now, when physicists wrestle with the mathematics of our universe, they find the same two kinds of code. Hence, the theory that our "reality" itself is the result of a transmission. We are characters in a novel whose author is so talented that he has made us believe we are real! That's the theory.

So, are we real? Is the universe real? *What is real?* I believe there is nothing that is not real, but that there are levels of reality. A greater perspective will immediately diminish or relativize the importance of any phenomenon which had been previously experienced from a lesser perspective—just like a bird's-eye view will re-perspective a flower or a stone that previously had been seen only from a worm's-eye perspective.

Hence, whatever can be sensed, remembered, dreamed, imagined, felt, thought up, or thought about, exists in some dimension—and is therefore real. Even what is experienced in a psychotic break is no less real than your daily breakfast. It is, hopefully, just a less frequent experience and, therefore, outside the narrow, culturally created bounds of consensus reality. But let's not conflate consensus reality with the real thing. The former is simply a subset of the latter. All experiences are grist for the mill of the awakening of the divine in the odyssey of incarnation. The important questions, then, are:

1. Do my personal experiences—in any dimension—move me into greater alignment with love?

2. Does the culturally sanctioned consensus reality move the group into greater alignment with love? But we still need to ask: do we live in a simulated universe? I believe we do. But the simulator-engineer-creator behind the enterprise is not a geek in a different dimension, and we are not the hapless, helpless, hopeless robots who naively believe that we are real. Rather the "mind" behind this reality is found in the soul of all sentient beings. It is a mind that designed an experiment to grow through the experience of separate self-awareness and the exercise of free will—from discrete chunks of Source (i.e., individual souls) into the realization that only God exists, and that we are

all God-probes into the adventure of Lila—the divine game of hide-and-go-seek. Our journey is from free will (the ability to do as we please) into freedom (the ability to do as pleases God); from narcissism into compassion; from service-to-self into service-to-others; and from sleepwalking into Self-realization.

What a pity that fundamentalist, close-minded, materialistic scientism collapses all of the above to the neuronal firings of a three-pound blob of wetware that humans carry between their ears. What a pity that self-appointed, orthodoxy-protecting devotees have created a jealous, violent God in their own image and likeness and attempted to bludgeon the rest of us into submitting to this idol, under threat of physical inquisition and eternal perdition. We are left with a caricature of God—created by the latter—battling a joyless, barren, depressing God-shaped hole—created by the former.

If we were to believe in that final scenario, then indeed we would be living in a simulated reality, but it would be a reality simulated by the human shadow, not one ordained by God. I prefer to believe that there is a great light—the light of unconditional love—from which fear hides, behind the obstacles created by our illusions. With enough lamps, there is no place left for the shadows to hide.

Do you have enough oil in your lamp? Do your beliefs sustain your life and lead you away from fear and toward love? Why do you believe what you believe? Do you even know what you believe?

It's up to each of us to craft and tend our own evolving cosmology. In crafting your own cosmology, what I'm really talking about is a return to the God that is Source—that from which you came. The first thing to realize as you begin to chart your course is the philosophical fallacy known as "the myth of the given." This belief—that our sensorium provides us with a radically accurate map of what exists—is actually a myth. The sensorium can't do that. All we can say is that we've got five senses with very narrow ranges. It's like we've got a tiny laptop. And when we apply our narrow group of senses to this little laptop we carry between our ears, we have a limited model of reality. If we had a bigger laptop and extended sensorium, we would have a totally different model of what's out there.

So, what do we need to do? We need to shift the frequencies constantly and move into different kinds of experiences. We need to begin thinking and experiencing outside the box so that we can make our maps of reality less inaccurate. They will never be perfectly accurate. But they can be less inaccurate.

So, imagine you're an explorer two hundred years ago on your way to Africa. You had heard of this continent called Africa, and you want to find out what kind of wildlife lives in the jungles there. So, you go with a hundred mousetraps. And you set them out in the forest. And then you come back a few days later and look and there's a mouse caught in each of them. And you write home to your expedition's sponsor: *"Africa's jungles contain only mice."* If you put out mouse traps, you're only going to trap mice. What did you expect? Is an elephant going to be caught in a mouse trap?

And that's what we're doing with our little models of reality. We're setting mouse traps in the cosmos and we're capturing just a little slice of reality. And we're claiming that's all that exists. How foolish! If you put out mouse traps in Africa, you're only going to catch mice. If you put out the all-too-common tiny mindset based upon the myth of the given, you're only going to catch material science. So, we need the courage to change the channels, to experiment constantly with altering our states of consciousness so we can capture more of what lies beyond the sensorium's reach. And when we do that, we'll have real-time experiences with different energies and entities. And then we can bring them back and cross-fertilize what we've learned with our current models and extend what we believe.

To that end, it will first be necessary to remove the last vestiges of fear and projected shadow material before we can truly gaze upon the face of the Beloved.

PURIFYING THE WATER

My home rests on a plot of land ten miles from "civilization" among the redwoods, madrona, manzanita, and scrub oaks of northern Sonoma County, California. And so, I have my own water system—a well that was dug two hundred and sixty feet into the hillside. The pristine source of these waters is the snowmelt from the Sierra Nevada Mountains, but the surrounding area is very geologically diffuse, layered with several strata of mineral-rich, rocky soil. So, by the time the water gets to my home, it has picked up traces of iron, copper, and several other "toxic" elements. Before I can drink it, I have to put my water through a three-stage filtration process to get it back to its pure state.

That's the kind of relationship religion has with spirituality. Spirituality is the pristine water of Source, or God, as we've been calling Her. Religion is, inevitably, contaminated by the dogma and fear that get picked up by people along the way. The wisdom of the avatars (such as the Buddha, Jesus of Nazareth, Gandhi, and Mother Teresa—among others) and their insights serve as the filtration systems by which we can glean pure spirituality from the religion we've been given. But these are not once-for-all-times interventions. Each era needs to purify the "water" it is drinking. So, let's first look at the contaminants we need to nullify in our times, in our sacred books, and in our religious beliefs.

Let's begin with a quick review of the origins and evolution of God in our theologies.

I've never found a satisfactory definition of religion, though I'm certain of its origin, which I take to be the impulse of Spirit. This is, in fact, a wonderful impulse. However, humans have a penchant for screwing up all great ideas. The least deadly screw-up, perhaps, is to allow the impulse to stagnate theologically—and the deadliest is to weaponize it.

Religion has many facets and serves many purposes, like creating community, formulating ethics, and devising rituals. All of these are vital to the life of the tribe, no matter the size of the tribe. Community should both support and challenge the theological thinking of its members. But frequently, community deteriorates into a mere institution that is inevitably taken over by an oligarchy. Soon, orthodoxy becomes the ultimate criterion of holiness, and heterodoxy (as defined by the oligarchy) is shunned. If heterodoxy, God forbid, should stray into heresy or, *horribile dictu*, into blasphemy (again as defined by the oligarchy), then shunning is upgraded to inquisition, torture, and execution—all to protect the thin-skinned sanctity of the bent-out-of-shape divinity. If the institution has enough clout—and if it has become a theocracy, it already has the necessary clout—then, having dealt with internal dissidents, it now turns its face and weapons to converting or exterminating the pagans/infidels/barbarians/gentiles who live outside its hallowed gates.

Eventually, some new prophet will arise from within its ranks to call the group back to its founder's intentions. And the time-honored template for dealing with the prophet is to first slander, then imprison, then execute and, finally, name a street after him (e.g., Martin Luther King Jr. Highway) or create a feast day in her honor (e.g., the feast of St. Joan of Arc). Under no circumstances, however, can their unexpurgated teachings be allowed to flourish. Rather, a sanitized, defanged version is packaged as sanctimonious pablum to anesthetize the masses to the prophet's real message.

And while the original religious community is becoming a vigilante group, the ethical primacy of love (*"Do not do to others what you would not want them to do to you"*) has given way to the canonization of law. (In Maggie Thatcher's strident words, "the law is the law is the law!") The enactment, imposition, and punishment-for-infractions of a legal code become the primary moral tools.

And rituals that initially were the practices intended to create altered states of consciousness so as to encourage encounters with extra-dimensional energies and entities (e.g., sound/music, dance/processions, art/stained glass windows, scent/incense, taste/communion, meditation, etc.), have now become dead rites that choke off mysticism and replace it with dogma.

By then, religion, instead of being a stage in the evolution of humanity, has disintegrated into the "revealed" concretized, unchangeable will of an irascible God. To make this stagnation stick, however, history must be either ignored or rewritten.

I see religion as the training wheels for spirituality—a form of support to be discarded once the practitioner has developed the skill to go it alone. This is not to say that community is no longer important. It is. But its function is no longer to herd and censor; it's to provide encouragement and challenge for the individual, mystical journeys of its members. The rigid schoolmarm approach must give way to the Socratic method and the mother must allow the kids to cut their social/religious umbilical cords.

When *Homo sapiens sapiens* first developed language around 70,000 years ago and learned to manipulate symbols intracranially, one of the firsts uses to which it put this newly emerged skill was to ponder the existential questions, e.g., Who "made" all this? What happens after death? Is there purpose or pattern to our world and our lives?

In an attempt to answer these questions, we created three kinds of gods: first, regional gods—divinities who settled in particular places. If you moved into their turf, you had to worship them. Rather like paying protection money to the local Mafia family who controlled the neighborhood. Then there were the tribal gods, nomads who wandered around with their chosen people. And finally, there were the portfolio gods—homeless and tribeless and available to anybody who was interested in their wares (e.g., art, war, agriculture, etc.)

And the journey, I believe, progressed through four main stages. First was the era of the theologians, where we began to talk about God (or the gods.) This is rather like moderns who are fascinated by the lives of movie stars whom they will never actually meet. Next came the era of the priests—experts who, having figured out what these gods are, set about contacting them. This is the era of talking to the gods. It gave birth to prayer, sacrifice, and rituals. Era three is the epoch of the prophets—those who claim to speak on behalf of the god. Their function is to establish covenants with their god of choice. This involves monolatry (the worship of a particular god) but not yet monotheism (the belief that there is only one God). Having established the covenant, the prophet's task is to continue to call the errant populace back into alignment with it. His function is not so much to predict the future as to prevent it; not to foretell it but to forestall it, because the future is almost always a dire, punitive situation created by the sinful ways of humans and the jealous, impatient ways of the god. The final era is that of the mystic, who speaks not about, not to, and not on behalf of, but rather, *as* God. It is the stage of the realization that only God exists, and we are holographic fractals spun off into incarnation, so that God may temporarily experience alienation from Self. Mystics are no longer interested in being discrete, permanent waves on the beach, but rather see themselves as temporary manifestations of the ocean.

In brief, we can wrestle with the notion of God at two levels. Ultimately, He is ineffable and so we can say nothing about Him, though we can experience Him—in His transcendence. But in Her manifested form She appears in all of Her creation—in Her immanence. This is not simply pantheism—the belief that God is just the sum total of all creation. Rather, it is pan*en*theism—the belief that God is the sum total of all creation and a lot more besides! It's the difference between Hamlet and Shakespeare: Hamlet is just one of Shakespeare's works, but Shakespeare is much more than even his collected works.

Similarly, there are several kinds of God-language. Theologians debate how many angels can dance on the head of a pin. They spent years in the great councils of the Church defining, in exquisite detail, the one nature but three persons of the Christian God. The Great Schism of 1054 and the resultant bilateral slaughter was triggered by a disagreement over a single Latin word: "Filioque" (rendered in English as "and from the son"). This dispute in a creedal formulation lasted almost 1,000 years! This kind of theological language employed to explain God is called cataphatic.

On the other hand, the language of the mystics, if they choose to speak at all, is apophatic language. Lao Tzu allegedly said: "Those who know, don't say, and those who say, don't know." Rather than claiming God is X or Y or Z—as do the theologians—mystics use the Sanskrit phrase "Neti! Neti!" which means "Not this! Not that!" Since God is utterly beyond human comprehension, and the experience of God is ineffable, we can only back ourselves into the realization by going transrational and cutting all anthropomorphic links. Hence, the enigma of the Zen koan, e.g., "What is the sound of one hand clapping?" Or of Meister Eckhart's "I pray daily to God to rid me of God," and of Buddhism's "If you meet the Buddha on the road, kill him."

Teachers, however, have a problem. In spite of Lao Tzu's statement, they are tasked with trying to inspire, if not explain. To avoid the cataphatic trap and to temporarily eschew taking refuge in the apophatic, they must resort to symbol—stories, parables, proverbs, aphorisms, metaphors, and analogies. The role of the listener is to engage the symbols at the level of the soul, not of the mind, and above all, to avoid the pitfall of literalism. But we have a very spotty record in this respect. When Jesus is spoken of as "the lamb of God" nobody thinks he's walking about on two legs of mutton, but when he's spoken of a judge or a king, we take these as literal descriptions. So, Christianity has managed, at times, to convert a compassionate avatar into a despotic psychopath.

Jesus chose to speak only in parables (rather than theological, philosophical, or scientific language) precisely because he did not want his message to be a one-size-fits-all-people-in-all-eras, but as Socratic seeds to be weeded and watered in the pristine garden of the human soul.

I have a dear friend, Arlen, whose mission in life is to rescue and protect abandoned animals. She once saved a sickly two-month-old stray kitten. He had been the recipient of her unconditional love, nursed back to health by her naturopathic genius and invited into self-confidence by her willingness to accept all of his idiosyncrasies. As he recovered, he began to deluge her with gifts. He started by chasing golden autumn leaves around her back garden. He would pounce on one, spear it with his sharp claws, clamp it firmly in his mouth, bring it inside the house and lay it triumphantly at her feet. She accepted without demur. He was finally old enough to understand, and grateful enough to begin repaying the debt he owed her for saving his life. Then one day he graduated from flora to fauna. His practice with leaves had proven invaluable and soon he caught a little mouse. He pushed his way through the animal flap in Arlen's back door and presented her with this new token of his appreciation. The greatest gift an animal can give us humans is to first draw us into its reality and then bestow membership of its species upon us.

"Isn't that cute?!" we say. And sometimes we reciprocate by anthropomorphizing them, ascribing all kinds of human characteristics to Fido or Kitty. Mostly, however, we reserve that kind of compliment for God. The greatest honor we can bestow on Him is to make Him "one of us." To make Him a "personal" God. To give Him a megahuman personality and to define Him by ascribing to Him human traits. God must love the leaves and mice we lay at His feet!

Theology is currently in a messy state—what with Atheism, Agnosticism, Nontheistic spiritualities, Deism, and Theism all competing for a spot in the human psyche. In particular I find the oscillation between Deism ("God doesn't give a damn about us!") and Theism ("God will damn you for saying that!") to be amusing. So, to complicate things even further, I'll throw in a distinction of my own: God is im-*personal,* but She is not impersonal. By im-*personal* I do not mean that She is distant, remote or uncaring but, rather, that She cannot be described as a *person*. That is far too limiting a descriptor because God is love unlimited. It's so difficult for us to imagine a love that is not confined to physical, emotional, or mental modalities. Specifically, we think that ultimate love is the feeling we have in special, intimate relationships. We think that if we regarded all equally, that would mean diluting our love. An all-embracing love seems impersonal and therefore generic and bland; it threatens our narcissistic egos that can only find self-worth by competing, by being told we are special, different, greater, more attractive or more appreciated than all other egos. We insist on a sun that neglects the gardens of others to focus its rays only on ours; we want a tide that doesn't lift all ships, but just our beloved boat.

God has already taken out membership in all Her created species but has a citizenship that transcends them all. So, if you offer Her a leaf or a mouse, incense or Eucharist, the Hajj or Puja, be prepared to laugh hilariously at these feeble attempts to detain Her within your trance.

By the same token, I do not believe that God is a creator who gets out of bed each morning, eats His breakfast and then spends a few hours in His workshop pulling rabbits and elephants, mountains and lakes, planets and stars out of His hat. Rather than this *creatio ex nihilo*, I believe, rather, in 'emanatio ab Deo'—as Plotinus put it. All that is, is "God stuff"—the unfolding of Her "isness." Just as a daffodil is not created by the bulb but is an emanation of it.

Nor do I believe that God is a lawyer—making, interpreting, enforcing and punishing laws, though the observable universe favors particular patterns like gravity or karma. Neither is He a micromanager who sticks His nose into everything and is upset when things don't turn out the way they should. And I certainly do not believe that She is partisan, favoring one solar system over another, one species over another, one tribe over another, or one religion over another. We often act like a besotted fan in a 5,000-person arena at a music event, convinced that the gyrating, guitar-wielding rock star on the stage a hundred yards away is singing only/especially to me. The lyrics were written for me, the passion is all about me, and for some odd reason the other 4,999 morons in the crowd don't realize this.

Theologies and cosmologies are maps; they are not the terrain. The best we can do is use metaphors and symbols when we need to speak about the ineffable. We need to constantly update our maps. Let's begin with the great archetype of Shiva, the Hindu master-God of reconfiguration and spiritual evolution.

SHIVA—THE THIRD PERSON OF THE HINDU TRINITY

"Taking God's name in vain" is not the prerogative of monotheists alone. Other gods, too, have been misunderstood and maligned. Take the Hindu trinity, for example. Brahma, basically, is the creator aspect of the divine, Vishnu is the preserver aspect, while Shiva is the destructive aspect. In iconography and imagery, Shiva is sometimes depicted as a fearful lay-waster dealing death and destruction—the master of mayhem. The truth, however, is quite different. Where Brahma is creator, Shiva is re-creator. Where Brahma is the expert at "*creatio ex nihilo,*" bringing into being that which previously did not exist, Shiva is the genius who disassembles old configurations and recombines the constituent elements into new, exciting manifestations.

Let's play around with a few analogies—some scientific, some artistic and some more prosaic.

Ilya Prigogine, a Belgian, Russian-born scientist, was awarded the Nobel Prize for Chemistry in 1977 for solving an old problem in science, namely: if the second law of thermodynamics is true—"all systems, left to their own devices, eventually run themselves down into chaos" (e.g., bikes left out in the rain will rust; a steaming cup of coffee left on the kitchen table soon becomes tepid) then how come more and more complex life forms evolve? Prigogine discovered that systems can reorganize their interior elements, dissipating chaos in the process, and leapfrogging into new and improved versions of themselves. He called this process "Dissipative Structures." I call it Shiva energy at work!

Next analogy: Imagine a little boy with his first box of Lego. Initially, he arranges all of the pieces in a one-dimensional "straight" line that starts in the sitting room and stretches all the way through the kitchen, the hallway and into his bedroom. He claps his hands in glee at his wonderful achievement! Some days later, he kicks his masterpiece into heaps, which his parent gathers and puts back in the box. The next week he tumbles them back onto the floor and now he is ready to try his hand at creating—from the very same pieces—a two-dimensional art piece. Perhaps he even manages to spell his name in Legos. That survives for a while and, once more, is taken apart. Very soon he will discover the third dimension and, from the original pieces, start creating exotic feats of engineering. Before you know it, he's on his way to winning a young inventor award! This ability to use preexisting, simple elements to solve significant issues is precisely what allowed the engineers of NASA and the crew of Apollo

13 to survive a near-fatal flaw during their 1970 mission. Shiva wins again!

Here's a scientific analogy: Bruce Lipton—a paradigm-busting cell biologist, and Steve Bhaerman—a witty political philosopher, combined their talents in a book called *Spontaneous Evolution*. Very succinctly, they tell the story of the caterpillar-into-butterfly odyssey, using it as an allegory for human survival and evolution in our times. When the caterpillar somehow realizes that he has gone as far as he can go as a caterpillar, he becomes a recluse, building a house about himself that disconnects him completely from the external environment—including food sources. So, he begins to devour his own body, reducing it to goo in the process. Somehow (through an embedded Higher Consciousness?) he releases or fashions "imaginal cells" which begin to promote a new program of transmutation. The old cells, however, fight desperately to keep the previous code intact. But this fight actually strengthens the imaginal warriors, who eventually win the day. The new program is fully installed and operational, and the result is "unimaginable": a delicate, angel-like, multicolored aeronaut. Nothing is added or taken away; the cells are simply reorganized by a different algorithm. Let's hear it for Shiva!

Here's an even more scientific analogy: About fifty years ago I saw a black-and-white portrait of a young woman. On closer inspection, I realized that it had not been done with pencil or charcoal or paint; it had been typed on an old-fashioned Imperial typewriter using the single letter "x." Simply clustering the "x's" at different densities created the perfect image. That's basically what your TV screen does, except the "x's" are pixels. If your screen were divided up into tiny boxes of six hundred rows by four hundred and twenty columns, you'd get over a quarter of a million spaces or pixels, each of which can either be on/live/occupied (a "1") or off/dead/unoccupied (a "0"). The almost infinite number of resulting combinations can be coded to represent letters, numbers, colors, sounds, symbols, etc. Thus, everything you read or hear or see on your screen is simply a sequence of filled or empty pixels. This is based on Boolean algebra—a system devised in the 1850's by the professor of mathematics—

George Boole—at my Alma Mater, University College Cork, part of the National University of Ireland. (Who knew Shiva was so good at math?!) You—or at least your bodily "spacesuit"—and, indeed, all life forms, are simply the hardcopy of an online program that, instead of "0's" and "1's," uses four nucleotides—Adenine, Cytosine, Thymine, and Guanine. Change the sequence and you get the blueprint for anything on the planet, from hermit crabs in the ocean to hermit mystics in the Himalayas. No need to add or subtract; simply rearrange.

How about an example from linguistics? When the Phoenicians invented the alphabet (around 1200 BCE) they managed to reduce the unwieldly (and very difficult to master) cuneiform of Sumer and the hieroglyphics of Egypt to twenty-two simple characters representing the basic phonemes of which most spoken human languages are formed. The Greeks, Romans and Hebrews quickly jumped aboard. The ancient Celts reduced it further, to twenty characters, in their written language called Ogham (pronounced Om), while English bumped it up to twenty-six characters. All Western and middle Eastern written texts, from Shakespeare to "How to assemble a sofa from IKEA" are just combinations of these twenty-plus symbols.

Shiva has been really busy in our times; the changes are coming fast and furious. Somebody once quipped, "*Things are getting better and better, and worse and worse, faster and faster.*" Shiva is committed to evolution. But here's the thing: if Shiva has favorites, it most certainly is not those immersed in greed, violence, and hoarding. Human hubris is exactly the opposite of what he rewards. His favorites are the life forms that are sensitive and responsive to the feedback loop of their own footprint on the belly of Pachamama. Those life forms that walk with humility and grace will ultimately thrive; those who grab and despoil will wind up in evolutionary cul-de-sacs.

All 7.8 billion humans on the planet are currently filling in our Boolean "0's" (fear) and "1's" (love) on the screen of our Reality TV. The question is: will there be enough love pixels to put us on the road less travelled? Will there be enough imaginal cells to release the angel-like aeronaut in us?

Shiva really doesn't mind which species wins—as long as Love is the ultimate victor.

DEALING WITH THE DARKNESS

Let's face the darkness head on. Imagine a spectrum joining narcissism and compassion, or service-to-self and service-to-other. Each of us will land somewhere along that line or, more likely, we will skip about at various stages of our lives and in different situations, occupying different spots on that spectrum. However, we tend to have a home base or center of gravity which defines our typical placement.

Similarly, each group or community—though it may also skip about—will tend to have a favored location. This is true all the way up to culture, nation, and species. As an example of service-to-self versus service-to-other, we in the USA are 4.4% of the world's population, but we consume 30% of the world's resources. And we have displayed a brutal willingness to defend that lifestyle with the most expensive military machine that world has ever seen.

In 1964, the Russian astrophysicist Nikolai Kardashev created a typology of cosmic civilizations in a hierarchy of technological advancement. He originally proposed three types. (More recently it has been expanded to five.) Type I is a civilization that has learned to sustainably harness all of its planetary resources. Were humans to reach that level—we are still a Type Zero, he said—we could use waves, wind, sun, volcanoes, and earthquakes, etc., to satisfy all of our energy needs. Type II's would manage to harvest the energies of their local star and entire solar system. Type III's could do that for their galaxy; Type IV's for the universe; and Type V's for all of the universes that exist.

Now imagine positioning those civilizations on the service-to-self/service-to-other spectrum. Any group on the negative side of that scale would prove to be powerful enemies if you got in their way or possessed what they wanted. Is this what St. Paul meant when he declared, "*Our struggle is not against flesh and blood, but against the rulers, against the authorities, against the cosmic powers of the dark world, and against the spiritual forces of evil in the heavenly realms*" in Ephesians 6:12?

In this cosmic struggle between compassion (seeing the God in everyone) and narcissism (thinking that only I am God), is Satan a leader of a dark Type IV or Type V civilization? A being equipped with freewill, who regularly chooses the selfish, violent, egoic alternative?

Counterintuitively, the Roman Catholic Church, in the process of investigating the life of a holy person before he/she is declared to be a saint, appoints a "prosecuting attorney" popularly known as "the Devil's Advocate." His purpose is to try to derail the process by ferreting out the dirt on the saint-in-the-making. This is the kind of guy you love to hate, but his purpose is to ensure that no unworthy person gets sainted only to have it subsequently surface that he had feet of clay and the church would wind up with egg all over its face. (Messy mixed metaphors for a messy situation!)

The first such account is found in the Book of Job, where God wants to canonize Job, and Satan appoints himself as the Devil's Advocate. In fact, "Satan" simply means "adversary." His function is to ensure that Job's mettle is well and truly tested.

I remember one occasion, around age four, when I caused consternation in my family during evening prayers. Every night, under the direction of my great-grandmother, the family would kneel for the rosary. The five decades took about fifteen minutes, but were followed by "the trimmings," in which each person got to pray for a particular cause (e.g., "I want to pray for Michael Murphy who just emigrated to England; please, God, protect him from the pagans who live in that country and make sure that he doesn't marry a Protestant!" or "Please, God, look after our chickens and don't let the fox kill any more of them.") One night—and I have no idea what prompted it—I exclaimed, "Please, God, forgive the devil and let him back into heaven." I don't know if I was being guided by a cosmic compassion or if I just figured we'd all be much safer if he was back at Source, where Jesus and Mary and St. Joseph could keep an eye on him. Anyway, there was a shocked silence and then my grandmother scolded, "In

God's name, child, what are ye sayin'?" To which her mother, my great-grandmother, snapped, "Leave the child alone, Frances, because God knows exactly what he means!"

So, maybe, after all, Satan is a very necessary ingredient in the plan of salvation. Let's examine that through the lens of "temptation."

TEMPTATION, THE ROYAL ROAD TO ENLIGHTENMENT

It would be hard to overestimate the importance of "Satan" in the story of human evolution—not that God/Source creates evil or even "approves" of it but, rather, allows it as a necessary element of the development of freewill (the ability to do as pleases me) and of freedom (the ability to do as pleases God.) Evil is a necessary ingredient in the move from service-to-self into service-to-others, in the move from narcissism to compassion.

Let me define what I mean by evil. It is the energy that is born and nurtured when beings who have free will continually make choices for selfishness. Over time this energy swells into a powerful, dark force which intersects with and influences the journeys of all other souls. To the extent that any soul marinates in that energy, violence (intrapsychic, interpersonal, intercommunity and even global) follows.

I believe that, as souls, we make what I will call "pre-conception contracts" that involve volunteering to incarnate in an environment in which we will meet and contend with the reality of "evil beings" and "evil energies." It's how the soul grows. This is not to justify or applaud evil, but to acknowledge that it is part of the equation that we voluntarily embrace in order to grow. As Rumi said, "*Out beyond ideas of wrongdoing and rightdoing, there is a field; I will meet you there.*" Rumi was willing to embrace the fullness of humanity, right or wrong, just as Shakespeare's Hamlet argued: "*There is nothing either good nor bad but thinking makes it so.*" Being human means being willing to span the full spectrum of right and wrong, good and bad.

Why would you volunteer to live in a universe that's subject to gravity, and in which you could fall or have a building collapse on you and kill you? Why agree to life on a planet that has earthquakes, tornadoes, and tsunamis? Why agree to a mortal spacesuit (your body) which is inevitably going to get sick, age, and die? We choose incarnation, not because gravity, earthquakes and illness are good or bad, but because they help us to learn how to love. Whoever or whatever Satan is, we are meant to work with that reality in order to grow spiritually.

Imagine a spectrum with utter foreboding darkness at one end, and brilliant compassionate light at the other. Satan, perhaps, is the archetype of one bookend and Christ the archetype of the other. Even a being of pure light has freewill and could, conceivably, begin to make selfish choices. Enough of these choices would cause that being to begin to slide towards the dark end of the spectrum. Then the ratio of light and dark, of narcissism and compassion, of service-to-self and service-to-other, begins to change. Is this the story of Lucifer's ("bearer of light") descent into Satan (creature of the dark)?

Each thought, word, and action moves us along that spectrum—towards the light or towards the dark. It affords us both the daily invitation to live consciously, and the instant feedback on what effect our living is having.

Choosing, with awareness, to do the loving thing is what perfection means. Perfection (*telos* in the Greek New Testament) does not mean a stainless-steel sinlessness but, rather, the radical commitment of the acorn to becoming that which is its core nature and final destiny—an oak tree. A "human oak tree" is a being fully and finally grounded in love.

Temptation, then, is not the awful invitation to evil but, rather, the life tool that allows one to hone the faculty of discernment—to learn how to choose love and light over greed and shadow. And each of the great avatars wrestled with temptation. Archetypically, it came to a head when they were about to begin their public ministries. The biblical accounts of Jesus's temptation in the wilderness, Hindu theology, and Buddhist theory, all illustrate the three categories of temptation that we must confront, if we are serious about the spiritual journey.

Hinduism says that for the young soul, the first temptation is to fixate on sensual delight. This results from identifying with the body and mistaking physical pleasure for happiness. It points out that sensuality, *per se*, is fine as long as it is accompanied by moral behavior. But eventually, Hinduism teaches, the soul yearns for a more satisfying purpose.

In the modern West, addiction to food, drink, drugs, and sex creates a multibillion-dollar industry that pampers our reptilian brain and leads to all kinds of medical, psychological, and social problems. Dealing with this addiction and healing from it is also a multibillion-dollar enterprise.

At the other end of the economy are countless millions of humans who die of starvation or children who suffer from marasmus or kwashiorkor. I saw this firsthand during my fourteen years living in East Africa.

So, while one group is tempted to overindulge, the avatars are expected to miraculously solve the world's food "shortage" with dramatic displays of power. The Buddha, when tempted by Mara, "*If you really are enlightened, turn the Himalayas, the king of all the mountains, into gold,*" replied, "*If all the mountains of the world were turned into gold, there would not be enough to satisfy one person's greed.*"

And that was the same temptation that Satan offered Christ, after he had fasted for forty days in the desert: "*If you are the Son of God, turn these stones into bread.*" He was not just inviting Christ to fill his own slack belly, but to mass-produce food for the world in order to show his cosmic compassion.

Jesus realized that if he were to do so, the "powers that be" would immediately get control over the supplies, hoard them, and use them as a reward and punishment tool.

This is precisely what happened with the Agricultural Revolution 5,000 years ago. The invention of the ox-drawn plow and of ceramic waterproof containers allowed humans to mass-produce and store great amounts of food. Then, for the first time, food was weaponized; it became a weapon of mass destruction. The enemy's food supplies could be stolen or destroyed, and his fields salted so that nothing could grow there for decades.

Monsanto and their ilk are a modern version of this. They have claimed patents on seeds that took 10,000 years (since the time of the "digging stick") to develop; they have poisoned the land, the air and the water with herbicides and insecticides; and they develop eunuch seeds incapable of producing second-generation crops. Farmers in India are being jailed for their temerity in attempting to farm as their ancestors had done. The European Union had "Butter Mountains" and "Milk Lakes"—rotting stores of food kept off the market to drive up consumer prices and fatten the coffers of the playmakers. The "first world" farmers are even paid to *not grow* their crops. The great American dustbowl was a stark testament to what happens when agri*culture* becomes agri*business*.

This is the temptation to which the Buddha, Jesus, and Hindu gods were all saying "No!" Feeding the hungry is not about a miracle, it's about the individual and community invitation and responsibility to love, to care, and to share. The temptation is an opportunity to discern what stinks in our economic models and reinvent new systems based on our shared incarnation. Dom Helder Camara, the archbishop of Recife, Brazil once said, "*When I feed the poor, they call me a saint; when I ask why it is that the poor do not have food, they call me a communist.*"

After many incarnations, with the assistance of karma (a feedback loop of cause-and-consequence), the soul, says Hinduism, begins to realize that simply pampering sensuality does not bring happiness. Modern psychology has come to the same conclusion: while our reptilian brain is excited by pleasure, the mammalian brain (limbic system) is designed to habituate to it. We need more and more to get less and less of a fix. In other words, pleasure must not be confused with happiness.

So, for the next series of incarnations, says Hinduism, the ego will fixate on achieving power, privilege, and prestige.

In the Christian temptation story, Jesus is taken to the top of a very high mountain and shown all the kingdoms of the Earth. Satan tells him, "*I will give you jurisdiction over all of these, for they belong to me, if falling down you will worship me.*" On the face of it this seems like a pretty pathetic proposal. He must have known that Jesus wasn't into personal power. But the temptation is actually a much subtler one, i.e., "You can have control over all the institutions, organizations, kingdoms, empires, militaries, economic systems and their resources; and bend them towards justice and compassion for all."

It is a temptation that has been gladly accepted over the last 5,000 years by the elites and oligarchies from Sumer to Wall Street.

As a naïve child growing up within the supposedly infallible Roman Catholic Church, I was convinced that, if only every nation were to install a Catholic bishop as president, there would be immediate and permanent peace on the planet. That was before I read Church history—from forced conversions instituted by Constantine in 313 CE, to the crusades, inquisitions, and Papal States.

Overhauling corrupt systems is a necessary but not sufficient element of transforming society. Unless these systems are staffed by persons who are themselves committed to individual holiness, then the water (people) flowing through the pipes (systems) will simply corrode the pipes. As Jesus would famously say, "New wine (transformed individuals), new wineskins (transformed systems)."

Even if we were lucky enough to have a truly enlightened leader in each country, somewhere down the line a corrupt service-to-self megalomaniacal minion would orchestrate a coup.

You can't legislate or force people into loving behavior. So, reluctantly, in response to Satan's second temptation, Jesus said, "Thanks, but no thanks!"

Again, according to Hinduism, during the third series of incarnations, we are subject to the temptation of "service." But this is still far short of Moksha (liberation), the realization that the sense of separate self (upon which service-to-other is predicated) is the final illusion on the road to enlightenment. There is no separate self; and both the Buddha's teaching (Anatma) and Confucius's contention that the self is an illusion created by the sum of our social roles, point in that direction. And this is the great temptation of religion: serving and saving others.

Satan takes Jesus to the pinnacle of the temple in Jerusalem, shows him the crowds milling below and suggests a third alternative: "Why don't you start a brand-new religion and kick it off with a really spectacular miracle? Why don't you bungee jump without a bungee cord, since it is written in Psalm 91, '*He has given his angels charge over you, lest you dash your foot against a stone*'? Alert the crowd below, then jump, land safely, start preaching and you're a surefire winner—the religion to end all religions!"

Wouldn't that change people's hearts? No, it would merely titillate their need for entertainment until Monday Night Football was invented. Although each of the great religions began with a deep mystical impulse on the part of the "original prophet," inevitably it goes through the following cycle:

Spiritual experience - charismatic prophet - community - death of prophet - organization - oligarchy - theology - dogma - crusades against outsiders - inquisitions against insiders - new prophet.

Personally, I don't believe that Jesus was a Christian, nor did he come to found a new religion. Rather, he came to fan into flames the mystical embers that lie at the heart of each one of us; a flame that frequently is smothered under the ashes of dogma and institution.

So, for the third time, Jesus's response was a resounding "No!"

How could you possibly develop free will, freedom or compassion without being tempted? How could you find Moksha unless your faculty of discernment were honed by trial and error? How can you hit the bull's eye unless you use the feedback of previous arrows to adjust your aim?

Without temptation we would be robots, preprogrammed to be "good." One who is unconsciously good is simply lucky; one who is unconsciously evil is simply "asleep"; one who is consciously evil is pathological; and one who is consciously good is enlightened.

Let me end with a wonderful story from the Talmud: Adam and Eve sneak back into the Garden of Eden one night to taste once more of the forbidden fruit. They hear a rustling in the leaves of the tree and discover an embarrassed God also feasting on the fruit.

Temptation may well be the royal road to enlightenment.

Are you ready to take another stab at understanding the theodicy issue?

THE PROBLEM OF EVIL – A NEW LOOK

We are all bite-sized pieces of God, small-scale fractals of Source. But like little children who insist, "I wanna do it myself!" we take the newly emergent pieces—self-awareness, free will and freedom—and attempt to develop our budding divinity.

Free will is the sticky part. It necessitates there being choices among which to decide. But the choice, originally, was not between good and a preexisting evil but, rather, where to land on the spectrum of service-to-self, at one end (let's call it A-street) and service-to-other at the other end (let's call it the B-street).

It's necessary, at the start of one's life, to make many choices at the A-end (food, air, warmth, attention...), otherwise the little infant would not survive childhood. But if we camp out there, survival morphs into selfishness, which morphs into greed, which morphs into fear, anger and, eventually, violence. Evil has arrived! We did not make a choice for a preexisting evil—and God certainly did not create it.

Evil, then, is an emergent phenomenon, an energy that comes into being, and coagulates into a solid state, from living at the A-end of the spectrum. Like all energies, it is contagious, and people are quickly lured into its embrace. Eventually even entire communities and future generations are affected. Babies are then born into a world in which evil is a major player. It spreads quickly and gathers both global and even cosmic harvests. That is the real meaning of "original sin."

And suddenly, creation, which was birthed only through love, has its elements rearranged into a configuration that breeds odiferous evil.

Are you up for a few more metaphors?

The Jigsaw Puzzle Postulate: Each soul is a fractal of God, a scaled down model with all of the same pieces and features of which Source Herself is composed. But each soul insists on being presented with the final image separated into all its constituent parts, so that "I can do it myself!" However, if I make poor decisions while I attempt to assemble the pieces, I will wind up with a buckled puzzle that has lots of gaps and many pieces left over. It won't look anything like the original. If I work the puzzle correctly, then I will reproduce exactly the image of God.

It's important to note that the buckled version with the gaps and extra pieces did not exist before my attempts. I wasn't choosing to do it like that because God had previously made that version available as a possible outcome.

Pure Water: Two animals drink from a lake in East Africa, one a cow and the other a snake. They drink the same water, but the cow turns it into milk to nurture its calf, while the snake turns it into venom to kill its adversary. Likewise, it's the way humans process their experience that will wind up nourishing others or killing them. But the experience itself (the water) is pure love. Evil was not a preexisting creation of God but, rather, a wrong reworking of the elements.

Playing the Violin: One of my grandfather's favorite poems was "The Touch of the Master's Hand," in which an old, discarded violin is being auctioned off for a pittance, until an old man approaches the auctioneer and asks if he may play a tune on it. The old man—the Master—plays it so beautifully that it brings tears to the eyes of the entire attendance. When the auctioneer restarts the bidding, he is now getting offers in the thousands of dollars.

Another person, without any musical talent, might have produced utter cacophony had he attempted a tune. The violin was made to midwife great music, but in the grip of the amateur, only discord emerges. Good music is what the violin was made to produce; cacophony did not exist until the amateur got involved.

The Artist: I'm sure that many of Fra Angelico's contemporaries had access to the self-same palette of colors that he had. But I'll warrant a guess that for every one of his masterpieces, other painters produced visually blah or even repugnant canvasses. It's the person holding the brush that determines what will emerge.

So, finally, a word about emergence. Emergence is what happens when the total is greater than the sum of the parts. It is never predictable from examining the separate pieces. For example, for the longest time, in cosmic evolution, both hydrogen and oxygen existed separately. However, when molecules of hydrogen and oxygen began to date, suddenly a brand-new substance that had never existed before emerged. We call it water! That's what happens when you get the jigsaw puzzle right.

When Timothy McVeigh orchestrated the Oklahoma City bombing on April 19, 1995, he simply combined two commercially available products—Ammonium Nitrate and Nitromethane fertilizer—to produce an emergent substance that killed one hundred and sixty-eight people. That's what happens when you get the jigsaw puzzle wrong!

Evil is not a piece created by God and tossed into the crucible of incarnation to separate the wheat from the chaff. It's a brand-new emergent phenomenon created by those who live permanently on A-street.

HUMAN SUFFERING

The Buddha, we are told, once said, *"Pain is inevitable, suffering is optional."* It's a great insight. Pain is the price of incarnation; it is inescapable. Suffering, however, is, I believe, mainly the result of the stories we tell and the interpretations we foist on that pain. As a psychologist, I have observed that perhaps 95% of human distress is caused not by pain, but by suffering. It's obviously a complex issue. So, here are some considerations on the causes of suffering.

Number one, as I've just stated, is the stories we tell about our pain.

Then come "acts of God"—natural disasters. We have volunteered to live on a planet that is subject to earthquakes, tornadoes, hurricanes, volcanoes, and even meteor impacts. That will keep us on high alert. Under the same umbrella—acts of God—if you are of the fundamentalist mindset, you can include direct punishment by God for our sins. (That'll larn ye!) Polytheists in the past would also have included collateral damage, as the gods duked it out amongst themselves in the heavens.

Cause number three, if we believe in the Gaia hypothesis, is that nature herself is giving blowback in response to environmental insult. When you disturb the carefully crafted balance of the natural world, it strives for homeostasis, and that sometimes involves violent mood swings to right the ship. It's a form of nature-karma.

Number four is caused by the very makeup of our bodily spacesuits—they're wired for aging, illness, and death. They were not meant to be immortal garments; rather, we all agreed to eventually *"shuffle off this mortal coil."* In the meantime, genetics, home environment, personal lifestyle, and personal belief systems will all contribute to the suffering.

Number five is interpersonal, intercommunal, and international conflict—violence, war, theft, lies... We have a lot of suffering-causing agents in our arsenal.

And finally, and perhaps most devastatingly of all, comes identification with the ego and its concomitant sense of separation from God, from others, and from nature.

Taken together, these are a surefire recipe for suffering. And the best solution? Firstly, differentiate between pain and suffering; and, secondly, disidentify with the ego, and realize that you and all others are spirits-in-spacesuits, each one on this planet for a limited time.

HEAVEN AND HELL AND PLACES IN BETWEEN

People have long created cartographies of the afterlife. Dante's version is famous. The Catholic Church had a four-tier model: heaven, hell, purgatory, and limbo. Limbo was the designated eternal home for babies who could never see the face of God because they hadn't been baptized, and were therefore forever soiled with Original Sin, but who didn't merit hell because they hadn't, personally, committed any sin. (Update: very quietly, some years back, with zero fanfare, limbo was shut down and, presumably, the babies were bussed to heaven.)

Whatever the map, such divisions are the ultimate in the Caste system—an eternal stratification from penthouse-dwelling saints to basement-dwelling sinners. It fits perfectly with a fear-based, fundamentalist mindset and has no place in the compassionate heart and awakened soul of a mystic.

Hell is a psychological reality (created by one's own fear) or a sociological reality (created by unjust systems) but not an ontological one. It is based on the ego's anxious concern for its own safety and survival, and on the willingness to gloat over the pain of the damned. And the notion of "final judgment" is the ultimate extrapolation of human small-mindedness and the complete anthropomorphizing of God. Wanting the enemy to suffer eternally and the ego to triumph eternally is a measure of our blindness and lack of love. Any response to the pain of others—even our enemies—that is not compassionate misaligns us. Any response to the success of others—even our enemies—that is not joyful, misaligns us. This mindset even coopts heaven into the schadenfreude, hoping we get plush balcony seats, from which lofty perspective we can witness the agonies of the damned in the pits of hell.

Heaven is not a reward for rule-keeping. It's the experience, even now, of a mindset utterly given over to love and compassion. Jesus said that the kingdom of heaven is *en mesoi* (meaning both 'within you' and 'among you'). We experience it within us by aligning with love and we create it among us by acting in love. It is not a selfish, personal reward for being good or confessing Jesus as your personal savior, but is the natural state of being in alignment with Source—which is our origin, our journey, and our destination.

At a Special Olympics some years back, a hundred-yard race consisting of a group of Down's Syndrome young adults came to a halt when one competitor fell halfway up the track. The whole group stopped running, came back to assist him and all of them linked arms and walked across the finish line together. That's what heaven is like; nobody gets there unless all of us get there.

The covenants of the Bible are simply the traces of the evolution of the notion of heaven. It started out, in Noah's time, as a promise made to "all living things"; then it deteriorated into a bargain with Abraham that guaranteed progeny as numerous as the stars in the heavens; Moses wanted real estate—the Promised Land; David wanted a dynasty to rule forever in Israel; and Jesus said heaven could be experienced before, during, and after incarnation.

Which version of the covenant do you choose?

THE BIRTH OF COMPASSION AND FEAR

When a soul volunteers for incarnation, it encounters many forms of limitation. Firstly, its cosmic spaciousness must now be cramped into a 3-D fetus-about-to-become-a-baby. Secondly, its cosmic intelligence is forced to operate in a tiny, three-pound piece of "wetware" that we carry between our ears. Thirdly, time has to be invented in order to break up the gestalt of Unity Consciousness that the tiny brain can no longer comprehend (this allows for the chronological apprehension of the pieces, in an effort to re-constitute the original whole). And fourthly, amnesia is created for who I *really* am and why I volunteered to come here.

Now the newly emerging ego begins to believe its own illusion, e.g., "I (ego) am ME," leading to "I need to *fight* to survive!" Then a very strange thing happens: upon meeting pure, unconditional love, the ego experiences fear. At a deep, primitive level, it realizes its days are numbered. Eventually, the ego will dissolve under the warmth of love. This subconscious realization creates panic—even terror.

To complicate things—and to shore up its own defenses—the ego quickly attracts all of the old fears generated, but not dissolved, in previous incarnations. Gratefully, these are modified by all of the love encountered and built up in those former lifetimes. Thus, the personality of the newborn is the mixture and balance of these previous experiences.

I used to believe that love and compassion were synonyms; now I realize that they are not. Rather, compassion only comes into being when love encounters fear. All-encompassing, unconditional love begets compassion as it encounters egos that are imprisoned in fear. Compassion is love's attempt to vicariously experience the pain of the fragile, suffering, separate self. At the other end of the meeting, upon encountering love, fear becomes terror, which then leads to anger, because it realizes its very existence is threatened. But no matter how long, how vigorously or how many lifetimes it resists, eventually it will succumb totally, and its own discrete, skin-encapsulated sense of isolated self will be drawn back into the seamless ocean of Source, on the ultimately irresistible waves of love.

The fear that held the ego in the prison of solitary confinement appears at very many different scales—like a fractal. It arises in all relationships, in illnesses, in competitions, and finally, when the time comes to die. At a mega level, groups also have an ego. When this national, religious or racial ego is threatened, it falls easy prey to the memes and propaganda of fundamentalism, in any of its many guises, and then even "ordinary" people can be led into the enthusiastic embrace of becoming agents of genocide.

Only love is real—everything you encounter is either an experience of love or a reaction to love. Love responds to all situations only with love. When the ego thinks angry thoughts, love responds only with loving thoughts; when the ego speaks angry words, love responds only with loving words; when the ego does angry deeds, love responds only with loving deeds. Love is infinitely patient and will wait out countless incarnations, and eons of Earth time, until Her children—individually and as a species—melt their egos and return to Source.

Congealed fear—at individual and species-wide levels—is the origin of all violence. Unconditional love is the antidote. Within the seventy trillion cells in the average human body (each cell containing about ten trillion atoms) are enough photons to light up a baseball stadium at one million watts for three hours. And there is enough love in one liberated human heart to light up planet Earth. Jesus did it, so did the Buddha and Mother Teresa, Martin Luther King, Jr. and Mahatma Gandhi. How 'bout you?

PRAYER

So, what happens then as we initiate conversation with God? Deep meditation is when we listen to Her—it's God's transcendence in dialog with His immanence. And prayer is when Her immanence (which includes us) is in dialog with His transcendence.

For my doctoral dissertation, I conducted what was then (in 1992) the largest double-blind, controlled, randomized experiment of the effects of prayer-at-a-distance on humans. I wanted to measure the effects prayer has on self-esteem, anxiety, and depression. Altogether, 507 people took part: 90 as agents ("archers" who did the praying for 15 minutes daily for 12 weeks) and 417 subjects (who were willing to be the "targets" of the prayer.)

In answer to the question, *"Does prayer work?"* I will synopsize a 393-page dissertation and reply, *"You betcha!"* And the biggest surprise? The agents (the archers) benefitted even more spectacularly than their targets.

Prayer does not work by bending God's arm to adjust Her will to our agenda but, rather, it creates a laser-focused intention of coherent human love-beams that can move mountains.

I suggest that there are six simple steps to effective prayer. First, we must do some housecleaning. It's counterproductive to offer water from a contaminated faucet to a thirsty traveler. So, as Jesus said, *"If you go to offer your gift at the altar, and there remember you have anger against your sister or brother, leave your gift at the altar, go and be reconciled with your sister or brother and then come back and offer your gift."* [Matthew 5:23] It's very important, before I begin to pray for any target, that I purge my mind of all gunk—anger, fear, anxiety and, especially, unforgiveness.

Stage two is to then fill myself with compassion, which is basically the realization that all beings are manifestations of the same Source; we are all sunbeams from the same star. There is no such thing as an "enemy" once we realize that. Compassion, then, is not so much one person feeling empathy for another, but rather, one finger feeling love for another finger on the same hand.

Stage three is to send out a laser beam of love at the target. This cannot merely be formulaic; it must have the cutting edge of the archer's focus on the target. It demands the energy of total awareness in a concentrated moment.

Stage four is to take whatever disciplined action is required in a situation a la the dictum *"Pray as if everything depended upon God; live as if everything depended upon yourself."* This may mean social justice work or simply smiling at everyone you meet. It should become a way of being—not a party piece to check off a box on the prayer protocol.

Stage five is a belief, a faith in some superpower (God? Combined Intention? Love?) to translate intention into outcome.

And stage six is detachment. This may seem counterintuitive, but it's not. Once we have done our part, we surrender to a much higher intelligence—that which designed an entire cosmos—to figure out the optimal route and the perfect timing for the intended outcome.

The mathematician in me can't resist putting these six stages in an "algebraic" formula:

$$\mathbf{AX_1 + BX_2 + CX_3 + DX_4 + EX_5 + FX_6 = \text{Effective Prayer}}$$

$\mathbf{X_1}$ is a clean heart.

$\mathbf{X_2}$ is compassion.

$\mathbf{X_3}$ is a laser-like intention.

$\mathbf{X_4}$ is a serious effort with quality, quantity (where two or more are gathered...) and frequency

$\mathbf{X_5}$ is alignment with the "natural order"

$\mathbf{X_6}$ is trust in the timing and methodology of the system

And **A, B, C, D, E** and **F** are the "weighting" of these six factors.

There are lots of different kinds of prayer. Most people only think of intercessory prayer, but that's just one kind. There's also prayer of praise, prayer of thanksgiving, prayer of adoration, liturgical prayer, and many others. But since most people think mainly about prayer of petition, let me focus on that for a moment.

Prayer of petition is where you want a specific outcome and you appeal to God to effect that outcome. And what might be the explanation for "successful" prayer of petition? Some people think it's merely chatting about the inevitable. Their argument goes like this: if God exists and is omniscient, then presumably he has factored all pieces into the equation. There is not going to be any change since God had factored in all the pieces and had come up with the final outcome. So, then, prayer of petition is just wasting your time or chatting about the inevitable, for God is going to do what God is going to do. I obviously don't believe in that model.

A second notion is that prayer of petition operates like a satellite dish. Suppose I want to pray for my brother Séamus who lives in Ireland, but because of the curvature of the Earth I can't pray for him directly, so I have to bounce my prayer off God like a satellite dish in the sky and God directs my prayer down to Séamus. God is some kind of intermediary bouncing my requests onto their targets. I don't believe that is true either, but a lot of people operate with that model.

A third explanation is what I call the Abrahamic model. It claims that you can argue with God. There's a great story of Abraham bargaining over the fate of Sodom and Gomorrah and saying to God, "If there are fifty good people in these cities are you still going to destroy them?" And God says, "Well, if there are fifty, I'll save them." "What if there are only forty-five?" "Okay." "Suppose there are only forty?" "You got a deal." "Suppose there are only thirty, or twenty?" And he goes right down to ten. So, is prayer about arguing with God, bending his arm to get what you want? I don't think that's how prayer works either.

A fourth notion is what I call the Mosaic model. There's a story of Moses in the desert where the Israelites are doing battle with the Amalekites. Moses goes up on a hilltop to pray. He's got his hands raised and he's appealing to God to help his side; as long as he can keep his hands in the air, the Israelites are winning. But his arms get tired and they begin to droop and then the Amalekites begin to win.

So two helpers come to his aid, one on the left side and one on the right side and they prop up Moses's hands—so the Israelites win. Thus, some people think there is a kind of trick to prayer. If you can figure out what the trick is, you get what you want; it may be a pilgrimage to Mecca or doing the Nine First Fridays or going to Lourdes or whatever. I don't believe there's a trick to it at all.

I think of prayer like a sprinkler system in a lawn; you have all these underground pipes connected to one faucet, which is the source: God. God's love for all of Her creation is the water that flows through the entire system and sprinkles the lawn that is life. But there are nexus points where the pipes join and when they get clogged up, an area of the lawn gets no water. The sprinkler in that area isn't going to work. What clogs it up are things like prejudice, unwillingness to forgive, and bad theology. The object of prayer, then, is to free up the blockages within the pipe system so that the water, which is within the system already, is free to reach the entire lawn.

I actually don't think God is involved in prayer at all. I don't think prayer is about asking God to make any change in the outcome. I think prayer is about human beings freeing the blockages in the water system so that others can benefit from our compassion. Prayer is about our consciousness and our mindfulness, which allow the blockages within the system to be dissolved so the water can flow freely to its targets; I call it laserized intentionality. We are not appealing for a transcendent entity to intervene in human affairs and change an outcome. But since we ourselves are bite-sized bits of God, we are, in a sense, praying to God as we're trying to access our own inner divinity. Except that, for most of us, it is really difficult to believe and so we create symbols outside of ourselves in order to try to focus what's actually within; we project this image outside in order to see it more clearly, but then we think that the action is really out there.

Prayer of petition involves a radical paradox because while it is true that this type of prayer has absolutely nothing to do with God, it is equally true that this type of prayer has everything to do with God. Hence Meister Eckhart, arguably one of the greatest Christian mystics of all time, said, "I pray daily to God to rid me of God." This God we need to get rid of is the partisan micromanager who created, interprets, enforces, and punishes "the law," and who doubles up as a cosmic bellhop, ever attentive to our egoic clamoring. He is ready to intervene at the drop of a hat—whether that hat be a yarmulke, a miter, or a turban.

THE EXPERIENCE OF GOD

The experience of God is, essentially, ineffable. In fact, while we may say that we had an experience of the ineffable, it is more precise to say that the experience *had us*. Once the experience has faded, and we are back again in this spacetime, 3-D reality, we are simply left with some residual symbol of the Spirit's passing. Inevitably, we try to make rational sense of it and clothe it in concepts. Eventually a bunch of these concepts are joined into a map, which we may call "theology." But theology is three stages removed from the actual experience, and each stage filters the experience through the multiple distortions of individual and group fears, hopes, and prejudices. A mystical experience can, then, be the basis for actions that span the entire spectrum from behaving like a Mother Teresa to becoming a suicide bomber. Meister Eckhart warned us about praying to or following this God.

The problem for us is our failure to make two kinds of differentiation: firstly, between the Transcendence of God (His mysterious ineffability) and the Immanence of God (how we experience Her through Her creative manifestation); and, secondly, in all forms of prayer.

Of God's transcendence, truly, we can say nothing. To ascribe any quality to this "God" (love, justice, jealousy—even the ontological category of "being"") is human hubris. If we must speak of it at all, it must be in the language of parable, proverb, poetry, story or art. If we choose to speak, we must use Zen Buddhist koans (that force the rational intellect to give up, e.g., "*what is the sound of one hand clapping?); or the Hindu "neti, neti" which means "not this, not this"; or Christian apophatic mysticism, e.g., "X? God is not X; Y? God is not Y." In these great insights, we are invited to go *trans*rational and *trans*personal.

We humans can experience the transcendent, but it cannot be reduced to philosophical, theological, or scientific data bytes. Immanence is how THE ALL THAT IS (the Transcendent) paradoxically experiences the "OTHER." In meditation, the transcendent initiates the connection with the immanent, while in prayer, it is the immanent that initiates the connection with the transcendent. Our job, as an expression of the immanence, is to give birth to God. Again, it was Meister Eckhart who said *"each one of us is meant to be the mother of God."*

This game of God, what Hinduism calls Lila, ends only when creation itself becomes both fully self-aware and filled with compassion. Then the immanent also becomes transcendent; as Buddhism says, then "samsara *is* nirvana." While this dance is in progress, however, and before the game is complete, it is important not to *reduce* the transcendent to the immanent. Just as the man Shakespeare is much more than his Collected Works, so too is the transcendent far greater than the totality of manifestation or creation (Her immanence.)

Am I guilty of anthropocentrism, then, when I say that prayer has nothing to do with God? Am I advocating a narcissistic infatuation with the ego? On the contrary, I am advocating not an anthropocentric focus but a cosmo-centric one. When we have, in the past, portrayed petitionary prayer as an appeal to an ineffable, transcendent Source, that was the *real* anthropocentrism, in which God was reduced to a ready-on-demand pizza delivery man to be summoned and controlled through a tool kit of tricks (e.g., Moses's raised hands to force God to grant victory over the Amalekites, or the Nine First Fridays winning eternal salvation for Catholics) or arm-twisting (Abraham haggling with God over the fate of Sodom and Gomorrah) or pilgrimages (Mecca, Lourdes, Rome, Jerusalem, Sedona, etc.)

Indeed, there are "thin places" on planet Earth which have been impregnated with the fervent longing-for-God of countless pilgrims and, hence, these shrines exude a transformative energy. But the Ineffable Transcendent One is just as much at home in a trailer park or homeless shelter as on a mountaintop to any soul whose GPS is tuned to Source.

If prayer of petition were really a successful technique to persuade the Transcendent Source to intervene in human affairs, then holocausts, genocides, and pedophilia would be evidence of either His culpable disinterest or His pathetic powerlessness. Of course, it is neither. The souls themselves make the pre-conception contracts with each other to evolve human society by activating the immanent divinity, while the transcendent honors a Prime Directive previously agreed to by all the parties. We have been given all of the resources to pass the exam, and the teacher is not going to retard our learning by feeding us the answers to the test items or doing parts of the exam on our behalf.

In talking about the dangers of anthropocentrism, it is important to distinguish between self-realization and Self-realization; the former is a tendency to inflate the ego, while the latter is the recognition and development of our true divine nature. We are, at core, bite-sized pieces of God—what Kabbalah calls Netzotzim (sparks of the divine light). "Realization" has two aspects: firstly, to intellectually appreciate and, secondly, to make it real by walking the talk.

So, when Hinduism speaks of Self-realization, it is not a New Age mantra to promote narcissism, but a deep, mystical understanding of our own core nature. Once I recognize the divine in myself, *ipso facto*, I recognize the divine in everybody and everything else, greeting them with "namasté."

Full self-awareness leads to the realization that ultimately only God exists, and that immanence is how transcendence experiences for Itself. Then the following procession is obvious: Life is a dream that the ego is having; the ego is a dream that the soul is having; the soul is a dream that Spirit is having; and Spirit is a dream that Source/God is having.

So, why should we commit to a life of prayer? I believe that the primary purpose of prayer is bringing to consciousness our relationship with the living God. I would add, however, that God is living *inside* every one of us, as well as being manifested in the totality of creation. This is not a relationship calculated to create beggars (us) and a benefactor (God) but, rather, to accelerate our dawning Self-realization and compassion: awareness of the divine in others.

It is important to realize that the transcendent is not a partisan, micro-managing lawyer who constantly intervenes in human affairs to decide the outcome of boxing matches or who does and does not survive cancer. Prayer of petition is, then, accessing our inner divinity, even if particular prayer techniques or sacraments *temporarily* encourage us to project our needs onto an "external" God; or place our trust in an "outside" divinity.

"You are my child; today I have begotten you" is all the soul needs to remember. The incarnation you volunteered for, and the life which is your mission, is like a jigsaw puzzle freshly spilled out of the box onto the table. The soul must trust that every piece that's there is necessary, and every piece that's necessary is there. The colors of the pieces and their contours, plus the image on the box cover, are all you need in order to reveal the face of God—which is the completed puzzle.

The greatest prayer of all, then, is Christ's *"the Father and I are one; to see me is to see the Father."* This was not a narcissistic, megalomaniacal, unique claim on Jesus's part. It was a declaration of what each soul is meant to achieve. Hence, in the same teaching—the Last Supper in John's Gospel—he also said, *"the same things I have done you will do, and even greater."* [John 14:12] Indeed, if we're paying attention, we have all witnessed these "greater things" happening all around us, but we need to know how to read the signs and interpret the messages.

In the 1950s Jomo Kenyatta was leading Kenya's independence struggle. The British authorities stationed police at each of his rallies to make sure he wasn't fomenting public unrest. He would constantly speak of "Wabeberu" (the Kiswahili word for "he-goats") and how they were grabbing food from the cattle and sheep and other domesticated ungulates because of goats' innate, belligerent nature. The cops reported to their superiors that Kenyatta was confining his remarks to agricultural advice. In truth, "Wabeberu" was a code word for the colonialists.

When I lived in Kenya from 1972 to1986, I worked with the

Kalenjin peoples where polygamy was still fairly common. Each wife had her own hut, as did the husband. When a woman got pregnant, intercourse would cease until the child was weaned—typically around age two and a half years. Then, one day the mother would send the child across the compound with a bowl of soup for his father. The little child would be so proud thinking, "What a big boy am I; I am bringing food to my daddy!" But what mammy and daddy knew was that this was an invitation to resume conjugal activity.

Literally-minded beware: things ain't always what they seem to be.

Inspired art and writings can also be interpreted in three different ways. Firstly, there's the literal level. But try using that on Jesus' statement: *"If your right eye causes you to sin, gouge it out and throw it away. It is better for you to lose one part of your body than for your whole body to be thrown into hell. And if your right hand causes you to sin, cut it off and throw it away. It is better for you to lose one part of your body than for your whole body to depart into hell."* [Matthew 5] Take this literally and you'd better be ready for a heaven peopled with blind amputees.

The next level is the symbolic one. Now you've gotta dig deeper to find the meaning. There are two sub-levels here—associative symbols which are best interpreted by the individual reader, and archetypal symbols which come from the Collective Unconscious and are found in all cultures, e.g., mountains as theatres for theophanies. Finally comes the mystical level.

Let's briefly unpack these three. When speaking of Jesus's teaching, the literal level is mostly predicated on fear, the symbolic level on pride, and the mystical level on pure, unconditional love. When Jesus speaks, the interpretation of his words is completely dependent upon the spiritual maturity level of the individual listener. Those raised on a diet in which God is a distant, demanding deity will cower in fear of eternal damnation and follow a mandate of blind obedience to law.

The people of the symbols, typically, will pridefully sequester themselves ("the believers") from the sinners, pagans, infidels, gentiles, barbarians (take your pick.) And if they have any compassion for these outsiders, it's to want to convert them so they can be saved from hell.

In early 1995, I was invited to give a series of seven lectures at the

Presbyterian Church in Palo Alto. I titled the series, "Will the real Jesus please stand up?" During the preparation period for the series, while I was meditating one day, I had a very powerful vision of Jesus. Before the meditation began, I had been reading the famous passage in John's Gospel where Jesus said, *"I am the way, the truth and the life. Nobody comes to the father except through me."* So, now that I had him 'in person,' I asked him, *"Did you really say that?"* He replied, *"Yes, I did. Because the only way is love; the deepest truth is love; and the whole point of life is love. Anybody who wants to find the father needs to walk only in love."* And then, without any prompting from me, he went on to say, *"And the Buddha is the way, the truth and the life. Nobody comes to the father except through the Buddha. Because the only way is compassion; the deepest truth is compassion; and the whole point of life is compassion. Anybody who wants to find the father needs to walk only in compassion."*

Another encounter with Jesus happens each time I ponder the eucharist. It was Last Supper time. Jesus, having lived for about 12,000 days, now had less than one day left—no time to fiddle about with literalists, in spite of the Apostles' best attempts to 'ground' his flights of fantasy. There's a hint of impatience as he attempts to elevate the thinking of both Thomas and Philip in the following exchanges. Thomas: *"Lord, we don't know where you are going, so how can we know the way!"* This prompted the rejoinder I've spoken about above: *"I am the way..."* Then literalist Philip asks, *"Lord, show us the father and that will be enough for us."* An exasperated Jesus replies, *"Philip, have I been with you all this time and you still don't know who I am? When you see me, you see the father."*

He's at his deepest, most profound and most mystical at this stage. Why oh why did his disciples, then and now, oafishly try to reduce these enlightened teachings to membership in the human clubs called churches?

Throughout his private life, beginning at age twelve when he debated the scholars while 'lost' in the temple, and especially during his public ministry, Jesus was answering the four great questions, namely: *"Who is God?"*, *"Who am I?"*, *"Who is my neighbor?"* and *"What is my mission?"* The enlightened answers to the first three questions can actually be given in the same, single word—LOVE. And the answer to question #4—what is my mission?—is, *"to come awake!"*

On the road to Caesarea Philippi, he asked his disciples, *"Who do people say that I am?"* And then *"Who do YOU say that I am?"* The Gospels don't record the third, even more important, question that I believe he also asked, *"Who do you [my disciple] think YOU are?"* Jesus knew who he was, who the father was, who his neighbor was and what his mission was. And his mission was to awaken, first his disciples, and then, through them, all humans to the same conclusions to which Jesus himself had come. Alas, we still have a long way to go; and the very leaders who should be opening themselves and their 'flocks' to the true answers, have retreated into fundamentalist fear and demonized the mystics who took Jesus at his word.

Let me revisit the notion that my mission is "to come awake." Real love is actually very difficult to attain unless one has first awakened. What passes for love, in a pre-awakened person, is either mawkish sentimentality or else just favoring one's family and friends.

When Gautama Siddhartha—who was not a priest and had no business in the preaching trade—was challenged by the "real priests" (the Brahmin caste) to say what gave him the right to speak on spiritual matters, he simply said, "I am Buddha." Literally, "I am awake." It became his nickname just as Jesus was given the nickname "Christ" after he rose from the dead. The Buddha's right to preach came precisely from the fact that he was awake; he had pierced the fog of maya. This immediately resulted in unconditional compassion, which is simply unconditional love-in-action.

Jesus himself would tell many parables about being awake, e.g., *"If the householder knew what time the thief would break in and steal, he wouldn't go to sleep."*

Another descriptor for "being awake" is the Hindu notion of Self-realization. The Christian equivalent is "salvation." But salvation is grossly misunderstood by church teachers, who see it as an action of redemption (literally "buying back") from the grip of Satan, occasioned by the mythical story of Adam and Eve disobeying Yahweh in the Garden of Eden. The solution? Get baptized, profess Jesus as your personal savior, and bingo!, you're saved.

Nothing could be further from the truth. Jesus did not come because an irascible divinity demanded innocent blood to satisfy his anger at being disobeyed. Jesus came as an avatar, accepting incarnation with all its limitations, temptations and vicissitudes, and yet never forgetting his divine nature. He was awake as he came in, awake as he lived in his human spacesuit, and awake as he committed his soul, on the cross, into the hugging embrace of his father. This is why he could say, "It is completed; mission accomplished; I never went to sleep; I never forgot who I am and why I came."

There is only one sin, and it has nothing to do with the ten commandments of Moses. Rather, it is to never attempt to awaken to one's true, divine nature. If I opt to stay asleep, then I have two choices. If I am a "religious" person, I will only believe in a transcendent, punitive deity and I will serve him in fear, so that I may dodge the fires of hell. If I am an atheist or an agnostic, then I don't really care about this Superman-in-the-sky, and I will live my life by the world's values. But if I awaken at any stage of incarnation, I will immediately recognize that only God exists. I will smile and offer Namasté to everything that I encounter, from a wave breaking on the beach, to an acorn full of the promise of growing up to be an oak tree, to the wrinkled old lady in the back seat of the church gripping her rosary beads. Everything that exists is simply God-in-drag.

That was the message Jesus urgently tried to deliver on the last night of his life to his motley crew of fishermen, housewives, and tax collectors. And some of them got it. Later, however, subsequent generations of church leaders would try to domesticate this outrageous heresy, rein Jesus in, and present us with a sensible theology of fear, obedience and the security of being "saved."

RELIGION AS REVELATION

Religions make a claim of revelation that none of the other sources (i.e., science and "news") make, because while the other sources depend upon observation, experimentation, and reasoning to form their positions and teachings, religions say up front that they got their teachings directly from God. So, while the others act as if they have unearthed revelation by their own efforts, religions say that God did all the heavy lifting for them.

Since "revelation" simply means to uncover that which was previously unknown, there are, I believe, two forms of this, as I've stated earlier: previously unknown but discoverable by human effort, e.g., the existence of Pluto before 1930; or what the top of Mount Everest looked like before Edmund Hillary and Tenzing Norgay summited it in 1953. The second kind is both unknown and undiscoverable unless God reveals it to us, e.g., why Adam and Eve got kicked out of the Garden of Eden—provided you accept that story as truth. So, while other sources claim to be revealing the "truth" and act as if they are infallible, while never actually saying so, religions claim infallible origins for their most closely held beliefs.

Therefore, now I want to focus on religions' revelation and its shadow side. All religions, I believe, originate with some kind of mystical impulse. However, the essence of "mystical" is "mystery" and "ineffability." As soon as you attempt to put it into words, you either lose some (or even all) of it or else corrupt it. The mystical "revelation" that the Aztec emperors received led to the annual ritual slaughter of thousands of specially chosen victims. The greatest was during the reconsecration of the Great Pyramid of Tenochtitlan in 1487. In a massive celebration to inaugurate their great temple, the Aztecs claimed that they sacrificed 84,000 people over a period of four days. During the reign of the Aztecs, an estimated 250,000 people were sacrificed across Mexico during an average year. They would have given the God of Exodus a run for his money!

The great insight of deep religion is to use altered states of consciousness (ASC's) to surf the many dimensions of reality in a way that is not only *not used* by science but is actively discouraged and even demonized by science. I define "imagination" as that human faculty which allows one to volitionally shift one's state of consciousness, visit other dimensions, interact there with other energies and entities, learn from them and bring back the lessons and insights to supplement and expand one's experiences in "normal" waking consciousness.

I have already introduced the analogy of the cylindrical skyscraper with many floors and eight rooms per floor to speak of the states (rooms) and stages (floors) of consciousness. Religion, at its finest, receives its revelations from the perspicacity developed when visiting these rooms and floors in a quest for truth. So, it is capable of taking the human experiment to much more lofty heights than is science—especially materialistic scientism.

The great avatar figures—Jesus, the Buddha, Mohammed, etc.—drew their inspiration from this ability. And the great, deep, true—true in my sense of transformation and alignment—teachings of love, compassion, and forgiveness are the harvests of such journeys. Alas, the disciples frequently are more fascinated by the power and status of the avatar than they are about marinating in the teachings themselves. Religion is frequently hijacked by a subsequent leadership that, consciously or unconsciously, seems dedicated to replacing love with law, compassion with judgment, and forgiveness with revenge.

In a marriage made in hell, religion is often happy to allow science to develop and provide it with more and more efficient ways of killing nonbelievers, while science is very happy to have customers who will try out their new weapons for them. In this cycle of mystical-impulse-on-the-road-to-crusades, "leaders" are not averse to infusing "new" revelations into the mix. Finally, the religion is headed in exactly the opposite direction intended by the founder. This is done gradually enough that no generation is shocked by a full 180 degrees "volte face." If the founder had said, "we need to set our course directly due West," the next incumbent of the leadership role is not likely to say, "what our beloved founder meant was, 'directly due East.'" Rather, bit by bit, the injunctions will be, "the founder actually meant 'directly West-South-West,'" then "South-West," then "South-South-West," then "South," then "South-South-East," then "South-East," then "East-South-East," and then finally, "East." Mission perverted! How else can one explain how Jesus's command to "love your enemies" got turned into religious wars? Or how "Allahu Akbar!" became the final "prayer" of a suicide bomber taking out a bus full of school children?

All of the claimants to revelation (including news media and science) are guilty of hypocrisy, but none sin as egregiously as religions who call God as witness to the "virtue" of their genocidal behavior. To them, a mystical experience in the mind of a young soul is deadlier than a nuclear device in the hands of a terrorist. And when the teachers/leaders themselves are young souls, then God help us!

SECTION II: JUSTICE

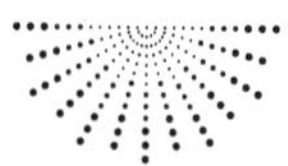

Homo sapiens, who developed about 200,000 years ago, could think, but could not think about thinking. That would come 130,000 years later with the arrival of *Homo sapiens sapiens*. Thinking about thinking involves language, which is the ability to manipulate symbols in the mind and then create external signifiers (e.g., words, gestures, writing). Soon *Homo sapiens sapiens* realized that they could experience altered states of consciousness by various practices, e.g., dancing, drumming, chanting, fasting, enduring extreme pain, or ingesting entheogens.

Among those altered states of consciousness, perhaps the most exciting were states of mysticism—the ability to experience and dialog with the gods. They quickly learned that this venture was fraught with danger; hence the caveat: *"It is a terrible thing to fall into the hands of the living god."* (Heb 10:31)

There were two main dangers—that of permanent madness (the inability to subsequently operate in the "ordinary" world) or inflation (a virulent form of narcissism.) So, very quickly, the elders set in place a bunch of restrictions to prevent the unprepared (uninitiated) from stumbling into such experiences.

We call these restrictions "taboos." The first notion of sin, then, was the willful disregarding of these taboos. Was this, perhaps, the "sin" of Adam and Eve?

In later eras, sin would change its meaning fairly radically. The second understanding of sin, I believe, was that it involved failure to honor a covenant between a tribe and a god. The tribe operated as a "corporate singularity." So, if one member sinned, the whole tribe was guilty and needed to be punished. For the "non-offenders" to protest their innocence would be the equivalent, today, of a murderer pleading that since it was only his index finger that pulled the trigger, only it needed to be punished and the rest of him should be set free.

This idea of punishing all for the sin of one has a long history. According to Genesis chapter 3, all of humanity was to be punished for the sin of our first parents. Even today, we kill millions of innocent civilians in order to punish the sins of political dictators (e.g., recent wars in Panama, Iraq, Syria.)

The third phase of sin was the notion that it was the breach of a commandment. Beginning with the Code of Ur-Nammu in Mesopotamia around 2100 BCE, the Law of Moses around 1250 BCE and the Brehon laws of the Irish, each culture created or received via "divine revelation" a law-code that legislated all aspects of private and public life. The infraction of any of these led to the punishment of the individual sinner (and, sometimes, his progeny.) This punishment was either meted out directly by the offended god or by his Earthly representative—the king or the priest.

This phase is still alive and well on planet Earth and is, currently, most violently represented by ISIS and fundamentalist Islam, which is outraged on behalf of Allah, and quite prepared to chop off limbs and heads to satisfy Allah's rage at his subjects' disregard for his laws.

Personally, however, I believe that the only sin is the selfish decision or utter laziness to stay asleep rather than do the work of aspiring to enlightenment. Infractions of precepts or breaches of covenants are simply epiphenomena that flow from this lethargy.

Let's survey, in rough chronological order, how various cultures and religions have treated "sin."

ORIGINS OF SIN

Middle Eastern language expert Zecharia Sitchin is one of a handful of scholars able to read the Sumerian cuneiform tablets. He proposes that civilization began with the Sumerians around 5,800 years ago. The Sumerians gave us science, astronomy, writing, mathematics, marriage, divorce, adoption, taxes, and religion. They claimed, however, that all of these were gifts brought from heaven by extraterrestrial beings called the "Anunnaki," who arrived on the planet about 445,000 years ago and genetically modified a hominid group, thus creating *Homo sapiens*. Later, they genetically upgraded *Homo sapiens* to *Homo sapiens sapiens*, giving him language skills. Then, although it was against their own law, they interbred with *Homo sapiens sapiens*, thus creating the demiurges or "sons of god."

So, strictly speaking, they didn't create us but merely modified us into their own "image and likeness," which is both good and bad news because not only did we pick up many of their skills, we also demonstrated an ability to be just as warlike as they.

According to Sumerian stories, having fashioned us to be a slave species (miners, gardeners, and house servants) they later pressed us into military service in their frequent internecine squabbles. And we learned that lesson really well.

When we failed to obey their rules, there followed immediate punishment. And finally, in exasperation at our inability to live lawful lives, they determined to wipe us all off the face of the Earth in a global flood. And they damn near succeeded.

You may recognize some Sumerian themes as they later appear in Judeo-Christian stories. Because of the nearly ubiquitous availability of the Bible, the Hebrews are probably the ancient civilization we know most about. It's important to look back to the earliest records to understand the various eras in the evolution of Judaism. First came a polytheistic phase—from Adam to Moses; secondly, a monolatry phase—from Moses (1250 BCE) to the Babylonian Exile (587 BCE), and thirdly, Judaism entered its monotheistic era after the return from Babylon (538 BCE) where they had come under the influence of Zoroastrianism.

The first era is characterized by a group of gods (the Elohim) who have a discussion about "making man in our own image and likeness." Once again, that image is a two-edged sword, since these gods demonstrate the same proclivity to anger, jealousy, and bloodshed that the Anunnaki did. These gods gave laws and punished the "first sin" by throwing Adam and Eve out of paradise and telling them that neither they nor their offspring were welcome back. However, the sons of these gods found the daughters of men to be very attractive and began to take them as wives, producing in the process a race of giants called the Nephilim or Anakim.

During the time of Moses, one of these gods, Yahweh, decided to make a covenant with the descendants of Jacob. An agreement of 613 laws was drawn up and Yahweh promised to give them a land flowing with milk and honey, if they would agree to worship only him. One of the 613 precepts said, "Thou shalt not kill," yet this god personally killed 371,186 humans and mandated that the Hebrews kill another 1,862,265 of their enemies. All in all, not a very exemplary divinity.

Post-Babylonian, monotheistic Judaism came to the following conclusions: God is one, God is just, there is no afterlife, and therefore behavior has to be rewarded or punished here and now. All suffering is the result of personal or parental sin. The Hebrews were influenced by the prophet Zoroaster, who had reduced the polytheistic pantheon to just two divinities: Ahriman, the god of darkness, and Ahura Mazda, the god of light. Suffering and sin are the result of their cosmic battles. The Book of Job in the Hebrew scriptures, and also the Essene movement within Judaism, were very heavily influenced by Zoroastrianism, as was John's Gospel in the New Testament.

But the cosmologies of the Greco-Roman World also gave us creator gods arranged in a strict hierarchy. Made in their image, we imitated their promiscuous behavior and warlike actions. They also had sexual intercourse with their human creatures, giving rise to a race of demigods. Like the Sumerians and Hebrews before them, these gods crafted, taught, imposed and applied laws, and punished any infractions with great anger. All human suffering was caused either as a direct punishment for our sins or merely as collateral damage during one of their own spats.

The introduction of Christianity was no different. Once again, intercourse between God and a human woman (Mary) results in a divine child—this time, not a demi-god but a fully divine and yet fully human figure called Jesus. This is the Christian mystery of three persons in one God, but two natures (divine and human) in one of these persons. St. Paul asserts that sin and evil are of three sources. Firstly, Law. He says that there was no sin before there was the Law. [Romans 5:13]. Secondly, the Flesh: *"The good that I would, I do not; it is the evil I do not want that I find myself doing."* [Romans 7:19]. Thirdly, Extradimensional Beings: *"For our struggle is not against human opponents, but against...cosmic powers...and evil spiritual forces in the heavenly realm."* [Ephesians 6:12].

It would be left to Augustine, who flourished around 400 CE, to invent "original sin"—not to be confused with the "first sin" of Adam and Eve. Rather, original sin was the indelible blemish imprinted on the newborn soul at the moment of conception by the ungodly act of orgasm. The results of this sin, said Augustine, were that our wills are weakened, our intellects are darkened, and our bodies are subject to sickness and death. And Christianity bought that preposterous proposition. The West, and fundamentalist religion in particular, has maintained this simultaneous fascination with and demonization of sex. For good measure—just to be sure to be sure—the Roman Catholic Church added a few more hell-meriting sins (e.g., missing mass on a Sunday or eating sausages on a Friday.) It's a minefield out there!

We don't often think of sin as being a primary tenet of the Eastern religions, but it is there as well. More interested in mysticism than dogma, the Eastern religions (especially Hinduism and Buddhism) added some very interesting dimensions. Sin is "Maya"—the illusion of believing and acting as if only the physical world is real. Karma—the law of cause and effect—serves as a feedback loop that leads to enlightenment. And reincarnation functions as the compassionate cycle of getting as many chances as are needed to reach full alignment with Source. Detachment is realizing the impermanence of pleasure and power. And Anatma (no-self) allows us to distinguish between pain (the price of incarnation) and suffering (the price of identifying with the ego.) The ultimate sin is choosing to remain unaware, and the chief virtue is Buddhahood—being fully awake. In the East also, divine beings, i.e., Devas (the good gods) and Asuras (the evil gods) manage to intervene and interfere and mate with humans.

An oft overlooked "religion," the United States' National Security State, is of course rife with sin and is often followed more blindly than a cult. In this Alice-through-the-looking-glass system, good and bad are turned on their heads in the service of the newest and most powerful of the gods. If you kill somebody in Texas, you get executed, but if they put you in uniform, give you a gun and send you to Afghanistan, where you kill lots of people, they give you a medal. If you tell lies in court, you get jailed for perjury; but if you tell lies on the campaign trail, you get elected to Congress. In fact, we spend billions of dollars each year on the 3-letter agencies (CIA, NSA, etc.) so they may invent spurious propaganda and assassinate democratically elected foreign leaders, topple governments, and destabilize entire regions of the world. If you cheat on your taxes or rob a 7-Eleven, you get years of jail time, but when the banksters collapsed the national economy in 2008, the crooks were too big to jail. So, Satan and Source have reversed their roles. Up is down and virtue is unpatriotic. Like Yahweh of old, the National Security State promises to be our loving protector, but then proceeds to turn all of its own precepts on their head.

So, the main sources of sin/evil appear to be of two kinds. Firstly, our relationships to the gods and, secondly, the battle between the soul and the ego. As far as the gods (and this includes the National Security State) are concerned, this includes the danger (taboo) of encountering them, agreeing to covenants with them, accepting their laws, interbreeding with them, realizing that we are built in their image, and being collateral damage in their interpersonal conflicts.

As for the ego-soul battle, it is the illusion (Maya) that keeps us asleep with its seductions of the flesh (pleasure and power seeking); and it is the cycle of karma that aims at restoring the balance.

It's easy to come to the conclusion that the gods represent a very mixed blessing. Could it be that we have actually created them in our image and likeness?

THE STAGES OF CULPABILITY

I've traced for myself, over the years, what I consider to be the development of the notion of culpability throughout the Judeo/Christian scriptures. I see it evolving in seven great stages. The first stage is what I call "passing the apple." It is Adam and Eve sinning and neither of them taking responsibility. Adam, when he's caught, blames his wife. His wife blames the serpent. The serpent blames God for creating him. So, nobody is taking responsibility. That's stage one in the evolution of a notion of culpability.

Stage two is that God then punishes everybody. The *Catechism of the Catholic Church* says (with St. Augustine's influence): *"By his sin Adam, as the first man, lost the original holiness and justice he had received from God, not only for himself but for all humans. Adam and Eve transmitted to their descendants human nature wounded by their own first sin and hence deprived of original holiness and justice; this deprivation is called "original sin." As a result of original sin, human nature is weakened in its powers, subject to ignorance, suffering and the domination of death, and inclined to sin (this inclination is called "concupiscence")."*[1] So, for this one sin, God is going to punish everybody.

Stage three is the notion of the scapegoat. When the people of Israel were in exile in the desert, once a year all of the people would come individually to Aaron, who was the high priest, and confess their individual sins. Then Aaron would take a goat from the herd and impose hands upon it while passing the sins of the entire group on to the goat. Then he would chase it off into the desert, hence the origin of the word 'scapegoat.'

Stage four was when God repented of the vastness and viciousness of His vengeance and decided to scale it back some. Henceforth, He was only going to punish the sins of the parents to the third and fourth generation. What a benign and compassionate God! He was only going to punish the great-grandchildren, not the great-great-grandchildren.

Stage five came about 600 years before Jesus with two great Hebrew prophets, Jeremiah and Ezekiel, who were practically contemporaries of each other. They quoted an old Hebrew proverb that said: "*The fathers have eaten sour grapes and the children's teeth are set on edge.*" Both prophets now declared: "*No longer will this proverb be true. No longer will the children's teeth be set on edge because the parents had eaten sour grapes. Henceforth, everybody is responsible for his own sin.*" [Ezekiel 18]. It may feel to you as if that was the culmination, and that it couldn't get any better. But there are two stages beyond that, and they are articulated by Jesus— the first one in his teaching and the second one in his life.

So, here is stage six: Jesus pointed out to the self-righteous religious leaders of his time, "*Woe to you scribes and Pharisees; you bind heavy loads and place them on people's shoulders, but you won't lift a single finger to help them!*" [Luke 11:46]. Therefore, authorities who make burdensome, unjust, or unnecessary laws are partially responsible for ordinary people's inability to keep them.

The final stage was not so much what Jesus had to *say* about things as what he *did* about things. Here was a man without personal sin, who lived his life in total alignment with God, but made a vow to dedicate himself to being responsible *to*—not responsible *for*—but being responsible to the sins of the world. He would take every situation he encountered and respond to it with love. That's as moral, as compassionate, and as courageous as it gets.

JUSTICE AND FORGIVENESS

Let's begin with a story.

A tribe in West Africa has an interesting protocol for a woman about to give birth. The elders sequester her, put her in a hypnotic trance, and then ask the baby-in-utero two questions. The baby, they believe, will use the mother's voice to respond. The two questions are, "*What is your name?*" and "*What is your mission?*" Then, during the labor, the women of the village dance around the mother-to-be, chanting the baby's name and reminding it of its mission.

Years later, if the child—now a young adult—engages in significant antisocial behavior, once more the villagers encircle him, chanting his name and reminding him of his mission. Inevitably the youth breaks down, throws himself to the ground in a fetal position and is rebirthed by the village in greater alignment with his name and his mission.

A tribe in North America has an interesting protocol for a woman about to give birth. The elders insist that she leave her home daily and go to work as usual and if she misses a day or is late, they ask her two questions: "*Why were you late this morning?*" and "*What the hell do you think you're doing?*" During the labor, masked strangers surround her, grab her newborn and whisk it off to be weighed, measured, and given an Apgar test.

Years later, if the child—now a young adult—engages in significant anti-social behavior, once more a group of strangers gathers round him chanting "lock him up" and incarceration separates him from free society. His former community is interested in neither his name nor his mission but merely in his sentence.

Before we go any further into this discussion of justice and forgiveness, I need to clarify a few things about the vocabulary we'll be using. Firstly, karma is not a punitive mechanism whereby one is punished in later stages of life (or in a subsequent incarnation) for sins committed in a previous stage (or life), but rather an opportunity to learn and grow from past experiences, both positive and negative. Karma means coming awake to the realization that the hand life dealt you is precisely the hand you *planned before you incarnated*. Fate is the hand itself and destiny is the result of how you *play* that hand. Neither fate nor destiny means a predetermined, unavoidable outcome. Both are utterly malleable.

Judgment is the ascribing of ontological value to a person or an event (e.g., "*he is a bad man*" or "*that was an unfortunate happening*"). As many avatars, including Shakespeare averred, *"there is nothing either good nor bad, but thinking makes it so."* Another of the avatars, Jesus, cautioned, *"Do not judge and you will not be judged."* Are we then to approach life with a blank, bland mind? No. Whereas judging is not helpful, *evaluating* is vital.

Evaluation is determining the appropriate response to a person or event. It is creative and life promoting, whereas judgment is stifling and shuts down the possibilities for growth.

Justice is not merely the application of logic to a human legal code, whether it be that of Hammurabi in 1776 BCE, the Brehon Laws of the Celts, or the Constitution of the USA. Justice is not about *judging* human behavior, but about *nudging* human behavior into alignment with love.

Yuval Noah Harari, in his brilliant book *Sapiens: A Brief History of Humankind*, talks about two kinds of order: Natural Order is how the universe behaves, no exceptions (e.g., gravity doesn't play favorites); but all civilizations are built on what he calls Imaginary Orders (e.g., money, religions, empires). Imaginary orders differ from culture to culture and from era to era but belief in them and allegiance to them is so strong that it can unite vast throngs of otherwise disparate peoples. I love his thesis, but I would prefer the phrase, "Creative Orders" to "Imaginary Orders" because we human beings are also an expression of nature, so whatever we invent is also a form of natural order. It is a very powerful order created by a branch of nature called humans.

These two kinds of order are the foundations on which the moral development of the planet can be gauged and built. Christ consciousness and Buddha nature weave these plaits together. These two, and other great teachers, were way ahead of their times. The trick is to embrace a long-term—even an eternal—timeline. The really important evolutionary trends and the truly significant shifts can only be perceived from that lofty perspective. And this shift in perspective is vitally important when we come to tackle the issue of justice and compassion.

Justice is one of those creative/imaginary orders, because it has varied widely and swung violently like a pendulum under the hand of a playful child. Here is a very brief look at some of the forms it has taken: crusades, inquisitions, torture, witch trials, executions—in a bewildering variety of really sick and grotesque forms—and honor killings in which the males of a family murdered their own daughters and sisters for shaming the family by being raped. Each "order" was formulated and administered by teachers who managed to convince the populace that the order was revealed by divine decree.

Within those larger, "revealed" orders, individuals and groups fashioned their own suborders to bless vigilante justice, revenge, and vendettas where they took the law into their own hands.

Wiser heads enacted the "innocent until proven guilty" principle and afforded the defendants the resources to prove their innocence. Of course, any system can be corrupted, so even this form can and has descended into "the best justice money can buy." If justice is meant to be blind, it appears to be a very selective blindness. According to the US Bureau of Justice Statistics, by the end of 2013, the USA had the highest incarceration rate in the world—716 per 100,000 of its citizens or 2.3 million people. We are only 4.4% of the world's population, but account for 22% of the world's prisoners. From the 1920s to 1980 the figure was less than half a million, but that number had doubled by 1990 and redoubled by 2000. Between prison, probation and parole there are now 7.5 million Americans under some kind of criminal justice control.

Three factors have led to this meteoric increase. The first was Nixon's "war on drugs" beginning in 1970. The second was Reagan's Anti-Drug Abuse Act of 1980 which led to mandated longer sentences. And the third salvo was the emergence of the prison-industrial complex. In 1980, private prisons did not exist in the USA. Now, as an example, Louisiana—which has the highest incarceration rates in the world—"houses" most of its prisoners in private, for-profit facilities. By 2007, incarceration was already a $74 billion industry—and I do mean industry. A 2013 Bloomberg Report states that in the previous decade the number of inmates in for-profit prisons had grown by 44%. These corporations, such as the Correction Corporation of America, negotiate deals whereby the states guarantee to fill at least 90% of the prison beds or else reimburse the companies for the short fall.

The final indignity is that these corporations then use their profits to lobby at both state and federal levels to introduce legislation such as "three strikes," longer sentences, and expanded definitions of "crime" to ensure a steady supply of client-inmates. For the lawbreaker, crime may not pay, but for the jail masters it pays handsomely.

If you believe that Laws are a revelation from a superhuman source, entrusted to a chosen elite, then justice is one kind of animal. When, however, you review the history and consequences of these competing and sometimes mutually exclusive systems, you realize that no taxonomy can explain their differences.

But what if true justice is not about assuaging the bruised ego of either a person or a tribe but rather the effort to align behavior with soul's purpose? What if it's about adding a piece of the jigsaw puzzle so as to unveil the deepest order of all: Unity Consciousness? What if its true destination is choreographing human interactions under the baton of "the better angels of our nature"? *Ipso facto,* justice can never be midwifed by anger; rather it is equal parts protection *of* society and compassion *by* society.

Both society as an entity and the person as an individual are entitled to protect themselves. But the balance between taking that into one's own hands versus depending on law enforcement officers is a tenuous one. Even the term "law enforcement officer" rather than "peace officer" alerts us to how easy it is to toggle between radically different emphases. Mostly, justice has been a system whereby powerful elites have controlled and exploited the masses by

1. Creating the laws—legislators
2. Interpreting the laws—judges
3. Enforcing the laws—police officers and military
4. Punishing infractions of the laws—"correctional" officers.

Inevitably these elites have appealed to some superhuman order as the origin and justification for their "laws." In the case of theocracies or even scripture-quoting regimes, superhuman means supernatural —some god through some prophet revealed the code. In the case of secular or atheistic regimes (e.g., Communism), superhuman means that the "natural order" itself is the origin. And they have their own prophets (e.g., Marx, Engels, Lenin and Mao Tse Tung in the case of Communism).

The revealed code is passed from the superhuman to the prophets, to the culture, to the teachers, to the parents, and finally to the children. Born, indoctrinated and cued continually into the "rightness" of this code, people can be trained to embrace even the most ludicrous of beliefs (e.g., the correctness of prejudices, wars, and even genocide).

The American philosopher Ken Wilber came up with a very neat way to analyze all sides of an issue. It's basically a 2x2 matrix (a four-paned window) whose vertical columns are the "interior" and "exterior" of a phenomenon; and whose horizontal rows are the "individual" and the "collective." The top left-hand quadrant is the inside of the individual, e.g., thoughts, emotions...; the top right-hand quadrant is the outside of the individual, e.g., biochemistry, neuronal firing, behavior...; the bottom left-hand quadrant is the inside or "interior" of the group, e.g., shared beliefs, culture...; and the bottom right-hand quadrant is the outside or "exterior" of the group, e.g., laws, infrastructure, school system, money, laws.[2]

4

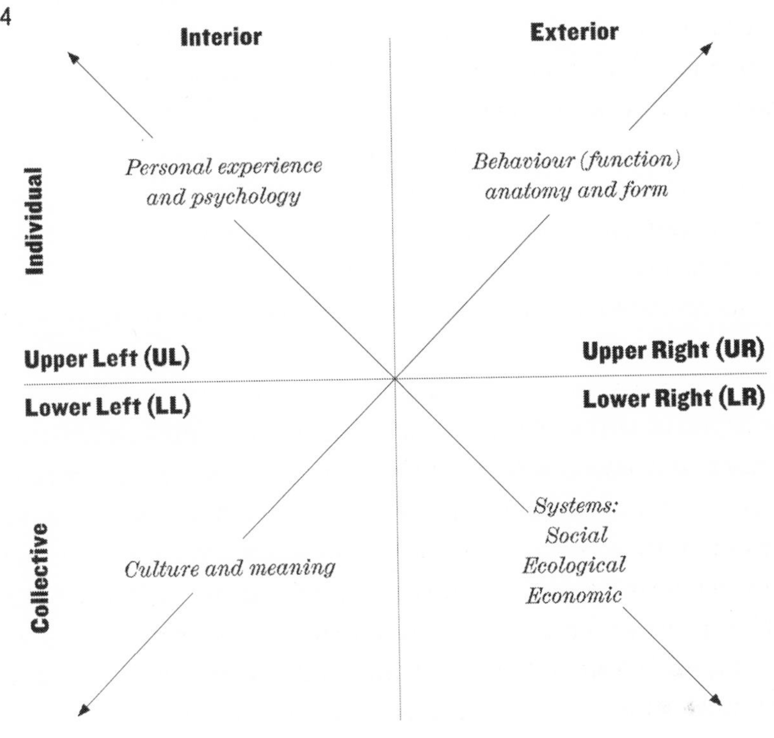

IN THIS MODEL, any attempt to understand the justice of a response must factor in all four quadrants. Typically, conservatives emphasize the top row, and so the lawbreaker is 100% responsible for his own actions; there are no extenuating circumstance such as low IQ, abuse as a child, growing up in an educationally and vocationally impoverished neighborhood. And liberals emphasize the bottom row so that criminals are always made by society and the individual lawbreaker is actually the real victim.

FORGIVENESS

I learned the *Pater Noster* originally in Gaelic and English, but I didn't really understand Christ's teaching on forgiveness. For that matter, I don't think the Christian churches themselves fully understood it either; and they definitely did not practice it, either in their dealings with insiders (inquisitions) or outsiders (crusades). When I learned it in Kiswahili and Kipsigis, I finally got it. The Kiswahili version says, "*Utusamehe makosa yetu kama vile tunavyowasamehe na wale wanaotukosea.*" The phrase, "*kama vile tunavyowasamehe*" means, "*in exactly the same fashion that we forgive.*" The little words "as" (in English—forgive us our sins *as* we forgive) and "mar" (in Gaelic—maith dhúinn ár bhfiacha *mar* a mhaithimidne) fail utterly to do justice to the concept of reciprocal and equal forgiveness. It's not that God is playing quid pro quo or advocating a tit-for-tat mentality, but rather that a heart holding hatred is commensurately incapable of letting love live. The grace of God, like sunlight, is ever present, but the moody clouds of our inner darkness and the outer umbrellas of our discordant behavior interfere with its effects.

In the marketplaces of Kenya, the traders use the "debe" as a measuring device. The debe is a second-hand tin container that once held petrol (gasoline). It measures about 12" x 12" x 18"; the traders used two different versions of it. The "whole debe" was the debe in pristine condition (sans petrol) and was used to measure grains (millet, wheat, maize kernels, etc.) It would be heaped up in a pyramid, so that if you were to add another single grain, you would start a landslide. It's interesting that Jesus used the same image when speaking of the reciprocal nature of giving, "*full measure, pressed down, heaped up and overflowing, will be poured into your lap*". [Luke 6:38] The other version of the debe was called a "crushed debe" and this one was beaten in on all four sides and at the bottom, thus radically reducing its carrying capacity. It was used to measure potatoes; and if a large spud got wedged in the waistline of the crushed debe, the entire bottom could be empty, while the debe appeared to be overflowing up top.

Many of these women merchants—and they were always women —were members of my parish, so when it came to explaining Christ's teaching on forgiveness, I would say to them, "When you approach God and ask Him for a whole-debe filled with compassion and forgiveness, He will do so; but if your sister approaches making the same request of you and, instead of a whole-debe, you only give her a crushed-debe of compassion and forgiveness, then don't expect God, to offer you a whole-debe the next time you ask Him for it." The image made complete sense to them. And I would emphasize to them, "It's not that God is ever unwilling to use whole-debes, but rather, when you insist on using crushed-debes for your sisters, you effectively crush your own debe."

There is actually no such thing as a half-hearted gesture. The heart cannot divide up its love output. Only the ego can measure out micro-doses of compassion or titrate forgiveness in milliliters.

Perhaps the greatest testament to our shared origin is attributable to modern resuscitative medicine; it's the phenomenon of the Near Death Experience (NDE). And of all the facets of the NDE, the one that most fascinates me is the Life Review. The NDE'r is temporarily outside of time and so every significant event of her life is reexperienced in full, 3-D, high definition, wrap-around Dolby sound. Moreover, as I reexperience an exchange that involved Mary and Denis and Larry, I get to experience it *as* Mary and *as* Denis and *as* Larry. And it's not just that I'm thinking, "I wonder how that exchange felt like to them?" Rather, for the purpose of the review, I *become* each one of them simultaneously, until I have understood the full, karmic, knock-on consequences of my every thought, word and deed. And that, of course, is merely the innermost circle of an *infinite* series of concentric circles that ripple out and affect the entire gene pool, present and to come. Love carries a truly cosmic responsibility; anger does truly cosmic damage.

As we've juggled the twin concepts of the utterly ineffable transcendence of God, and the palpable experience of Her all-present immanence, we've created schizophrenic theologies that oscillate between a Self-loving and a Self-loathing God; we fashioned a bipolar divinity in which compassion is God forgiving Himself and justice is God punishing Himself. Isn't it time for a new theology?

Somebody recently asked me: "Is there a faster way to learn forgiveness?" The following is my response. There are two quick tricks: firstly, changing your cosmology; and secondly, finding metaphors/analogies that make sense. Let me treat of them in sequence.

Check your cosmology. Really check it. If it tells you that you only live one life, then all insults have to be repaid in the here and now; otherwise, you're a loser in a zero-sum game. The winner, in that model, is not the guy who dies with the most toys, but the guy who gets in the most blows before the final bell. Life is a boxing match, and at the end only one fighter's hand is raised in victory by the referee.

If, however, your cosmology tells you that life is an *eternal stream* that occasionally goes subterranean (the bardo states) but always resurfaces (reincarnation), and if your cosmology further states that you make Pre-Conception Contracts with many other souls to incarnate together so as to create a life in which each one gets the ideal circumstances to develop the virtues that are especially meaningful, then the cut and thrust, the blow and parry are all part of the training. It doesn't make any sense to get mad at the sparring partner who just landed an uppercut, because your training is about how to ride with the punches.

Moreover, in this Pre-Conception Contract, you purposefully chose members from two different kinds of groups: your soul pod (people with whom you've had many previous *loving* incarnations) and a shadow pod (people with whom you've had many previous *difficult* incarnations.) And believe it or not, the latter group is the more important one for the purposes of your harvest. Forced to choose between fertilizing or weeding his crop, the experienced farmer will opt for the weeding, because fertilizer is blind and encourages the weeds and the crop with equal enthusiasm. The shadow pod agrees to be your weeders during an incarnation. You can say, "Ouch!" when they pluck, and then hang on to the pain and resentment, or you can say "Thank you!" when it comes to harvest time and you realize how they have helped you grow.

Nobody is in your life by accident or coincidence, but rather by design. It is a mutual agreement; that is the whole meaning of karma: the hand you were dealt at birth is exactly the hand you planned as you signed up for an Earth Experience. And all of the players—the good, the bad and the ugly—were interviewed and vetted for their contributions to your lessons in life. They get to play supporting roles in your life, in which you are on stage 24/7. And, of course, you are simply playing a supporting role in their lives, in which they are on stage 24/7.

Added to the mix is free will, so everybody is allowed to play their cards any way they want—well or badly—and then the drama takes on a life of its own. But the truth is that there is neither a designated plot nor a carefully written script for this life drama. It is always improv theatre. The only things you know for definite, as you enter stage left, are the previous performances of the characters—yours and theirs—and the lessons you hope to master by spending another life drama with the same cast of characters.

The second trick is to choose helpful metaphors and analogies. Here are two. First, imagine you are sailing by an archipelago of islands dotted along a 500-mile stretch of ocean. From your perspective, these are discrete, disconnected lumps of real estate; but if you were to trade your sail boat for a submarine, you would notice that as you go deeper, the islands reach out to each other until finally you realize that they are all simply eruptions from the one global crust.

Or second, take a mycelium, the underlying womb out of which mushrooms emerge. The biggest organism on planet Earth is a mycelium that undergirds four states of the USA. DNA sampling shows that the trillions of mushrooms are all siblings from the same mother.

Similarly, all human beings—in fact, all sentient beings on planet Earth or elsewhere—are just manifestations of the one, universal life Source. Once you understand this, you realize also that all forgiveness is simply letting go of my anger at myself. Why would I get angry at my feet for stumbling and hurting my wrist in a fall?

Just as all wars are civil wars and all violence is an autoimmune reaction, so too, all forgiveness is self-forgiveness. It means setting myself free—and, therefore, setting you free—from negative shackles and energies, which have benefitted neither of us, but rather have crippled both of us. Moreover, interpersonal conflict does collateral damage to the wider cultural environment.

The greatest toxins on the planet are not oil spills, chemtrails, fossil fuels, or garbage dumping—but anger, fear, anxiety, xenophobia, and revenge. While the former clog the physical arteries of the planet, the latter clog the etheric and astral arteries of Gaia. The most effective form of chelation is forgiveness!

SECTION III: MYSTICISM

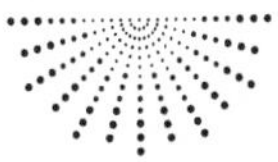

RECENTLY, I was making a pilgrimage near my home in the mountains of California where I have constructed the twenty-three stations of my "Eucharistic Prayer of the Cosmos."[1] At each station, I ring a bell and say the prayer for that station. As I walked, I had a realization: "I need to create a simple equation of enlightenment." Here's what I came up with:

$$\mathbf{E = AX_1 + BX_2 + CX_3 + DX_4}$$

If you add these four variables ($\mathbf{X_1\ X_2\ X_3\ X_4}$) and weight them appropriately (A, B, C, D), you have an Equation of Enlightenment.

"**E**" stands for Enlightenment.

$\mathbf{X_1}$ is Self-Awareness—to the extent that we identify with our physical bodies and the physical world—we cannot become enlightened. We have yet to realize that we are spirits in spacesuits, souls on safari on planet Earth, bite-sized pieces of God. Until we come to that self-awareness, there's no chance of becoming enlightened beings.

$\mathbf{X_2}$ is Intelligence—the ability to understand, manipulate and control our physical environment, our physical bodies and the communities in which we live—and maybe even our planet.

X_3 is Wisdom—the ability and faculty of understanding and aligning with the metaphysical universe —not the physical universe. It's the ability to understand and align fully with the kosmic principles.

X_4 is Compassion—the ability and practice of treating all sentient beings as my neighbor.

As I played with this equation, I began to wonder: "What if each variable were measured on a scale of zero to 100?" Zero being total absence of that attribute and 100 being perfection. What would it look like to score 95 on Self-Awareness? It would be to really understand that I have a body, but I'm not my body. I have emotions, but I'm not my emotions. I have an intellect, but I'm not my intellect. I have a personality, but I'm not my personality. I'm a bite-sized piece of God.

Intelligence would represent my ability to understand how the physical cosmos works. How people operate. What creates cultures. What makes me happy or sad. Wisdom would be my realization of how the metaphysical universe works. When I came to Compassion, I realized that all of the others go from zero to 100. But Compassion goes from minus 100 to plus 100. On the others, you can't score below zero. On Compassion, you can. Not only can you lack Compassion completely, but if you're a psychopath, you would take pleasure in either watching or inflicting torture on somebody else. So you can actually score way below zero on Compassion.

Next, I created a six-column matrix. In the first column, I put the names of famous people: Jesus, the Buddha, Muhammad, Mahatma Gandhi, Einstein, and Hitler. The second column was Self-Awareness. The third column was Intelligence. The fourth column was Wisdom. The fifth column was Compassion. And the sixth column was the total.

THE MODEL

Person	Self-awareness	Intelligence	Wisdom	Compassion	Total
Jesus					
Buddha					
Muhammed					
Gandhi					
Einstein					
Hitler					
Yourself					

Then I plugged in a whole bunch of numbers. Where did I think Jesus was with Self-Awareness? How intelligent did I think he was? How much Wisdom and Compassion did he have? I did the same with The Buddha, Muhammad, Mahatma Gandhi, Einstein, and Hitler.

I'm not going to tell you the results. But I invite you to create a simple matrix of those four pieces: Self-Awareness, Intelligence, Wisdom, and Compassion. And plug in any character you want and give them grades. Add them up. And find out. Also, place yourself into the equation to see where you fit in.

LIFE IS LIKE A JIGSAW PUZZLE

Let me return to the illustration I gave in the section on epistemology: Life is like a jigsaw puzzle. Last time, we pulled all of the pieces out and determined which ones were legit and which ones were actually torn-up pieces of the corn flakes box. Now, trusting that we have all of the pieces we need and no extras, we're going to try to put the thing together. If you were to scatter all the pieces of a jigsaw puzzle on a table, I'm guessing the first thing you would do is identify the four corner pieces and put those in place. Next you would identify the straight lines and put those in place. Then you have three clues for the rest of the pieces: contours, colors, and the picture on the box.

So, it's up to you to determine the four pillars of your understanding of life. What are the lines that hold you together and frame your life? And what are the colors and contours of the experiences you had as you put the pieces together? And most importantly, do you have any idea of what picture is on the box? If you don't have any idea of what the picture is, there's no way you can create the puzzle.

I'd like to propose that the picture on the box is you. *You*. Your divine face. And the greatest truth of all is that when you throw the contents of the box on the table, you have to realize immediately that everything that's there is necessary, and everything that's necessary to complete your life's mission is there. You're not going to wind up with 15 pieces left over or a gap that requires new pieces.

The greatest tragedy of all is to come to your elder years with big gaps in the jigsaw puzzle of your life—and a whole bunch of pieces that have never been used. You know that you're living life to the fullest if there are no holes in your jigsaw puzzle and there are no pieces left aside.

THE TUG-O-WAR

The journey home meanders from religion to spirituality and, finally, to mystical union with Source. Unfortunately, the process frequently goes backwards; instead of moving toward spirituality, religion may calcify as fundamentalism. When a religion is hijacked by the ego of a leader or an oligarchy, it veers off into fundamentalism and stagnates. Fear and craven obedience become the basis of its relationship with God; law and dogma the basis of its relationship with its own members; and prejudice and xenophobia the basis of its relationship with the "others."

Fundamentalism then becomes the antithesis of mysticism. In four quick steps, it first reduces complex ideas, like God or nationalism (the secular version) to a few bumper sticker one-liners that even the dumbest among us can comprehend. Secondly, it identifies or fabricates an "enemy" who is a threat to decent living, democracy, or "truth." Thirdly, the enemy is dehumanized so that exterminating them is actually pleasing to God. And the final step is to set about the slaughter.

Mysticism does exactly the opposite. Its first step is to move from cataphatic to apophatic language; to realize that God cannot be spoken of in human terms, and that to ascribe any characteristics to Him is human hubris writ large. Awe at the mystery, not reducing Him to an effigy, is the only response to the mystical experience. The second phase is to realize that all people are my neighbor, to recognize that all sentient beings are sister and brother to me. Thirdly, instead of dehumanizing the "other," we divinize them. We offer them greetings of "namasté," which means "the divine in me recognizes and honors the divine in you." And finally, we reach out not in war but in unconditional love.

The temptation of religion is to jam the gear stick of the mass transit vehicle into neutral, glide to a halt and huddle safely in the bus. The insight of mysticism is to get out and walk.

WHO HIJACKED PENTECOST?

A story doesn't have to be true in order to be inspirational. In fact, the greatest stories of all never even happened and yet have been the foundational myths of great nations and powerful religions. Take the Passover-Pentecost-Promised Land legend for instance. We've already been over the fact that there is not a serious Bible scholar alive today who believes that the Exodus ever happened or that Moses ever existed. And yet the story of Moses leading the Israelites out of Egypt after 430 years of slavery became the rallying mantra for the survival of the remnant of the Judeans who returned from the historically factual exile in Babylon in the 6th century BCE, some 700 years after Moses's fictitious Exodus.

Pentecost was Act Two in the Moses drama. He received a new constitution of 613 articles from Yahweh on Mount Sinai, fifty days after the great escape. Hence the name, Pentecost (50 days in Greek) from the Hebrew, Shavuot (a week of weeks). This constitution would lick a ragtag bunch of disparate tribes into a united people and give birth to a powerful new religion—Judaism. The third act in the story would be the conquest of the Promised Land.

And piggybacking on this three-part story, Christianity will rework the Passover, Pentecost, and Promised Land tale and spin it into Easter, the Descent of the Holy Spirit and the Kingdom of Heaven—the backbone of one of the most successful religious organizations in history.

Great ideas and great stories inspire great transformations, but they don't have to be "real" to effect these changes. That is why oligarchies create their own "real stories" (fake news) and eliminate the dissenting storytellers (the prophets).

And storytellers have a fascination with special numbers. The numbers 7 and 40 keep appearing in the Passover-Pentecost tale: seven times seven days after the great escape, Moses ascends Mount Sinai and communes with God for 40 days. Thereafter the Hebrews will wander in the desert for 40 years before they enter the Promised Land.

The fourth book of Torah (allegedly written by Moses) is called "Numbers" because it contains the first census, by tribe, of the warriors of Israel. And in the most esoteric book of the New Testament, the Book of Revelation, the numbers $3^{1/2}$, 7, 12, and 144 play a central role. In his version of the Good News, Luke places the Ascension of Jesus 40 days after his resurrection; Jesus had previously spent 40 days fasting in the desert before he began his public ministry; and Luke places Pentecost 50 days after the resurrection.

Whereas the original Pentecost resulted in a 613-item code, written on stone and called The Law, the Christian Pentecost would be a single-item system, written on the heart (just like the prophet Jeremiah had predicted 600 years before Jesus) and based on love-of-God-with-one's-whole-being. What a pity this version of Christianity was not practiced by the leadership of the post-Constantine church.

And whereas the third part of the original story—the possession of the promised land—started with the Hebrews' bloody conquest of

Jericho in 1210 BCE, and ended with the bloody capture of Jerusalem in 1010 BCE, the third part of the Jesus version—according to the parable of the Good Samaritan—started in Jerusalem when a Hebrew traveler got mugged, left for dead, and ignored by both Jewish priests and Jewish Levites, and ended up when he was rescued by an enemy who took him to Jericho and saved his life. A conquest by violence gives way to a conquest by love. In the long haul, the surest way to overcome an enemy is to respond with love. For 5,000 years we've tried to solve human problems by killing each other. Couldn't we try love for even one century?

MYSTICAL SELF-EMPOWERMENT OR CENTRALIZED CONTROL

The essence of John's account of Pentecost is, I believe, the injunction to self-empowerment based on forgiveness. Let me explain what I mean. According to John, Pentecost and Resurrection happened on the same day. The resurrected Jesus materializes inside a fear-packed locked room. He first offers forgiveness to the cowards who, when he had been arrested, had run and even denied they knew him. Then he breathed on them and said, *"Receive the Holy Spirit* [Pentecost]; *whose sins you shall forgive they are forgiven them and whose sins you shall retain they are retained."* [John 20:22]. The church latched onto this statement and made it a centerpiece of its own power-play, claiming that only the hierarchy, and its delegated representatives (priests) were empowered to pronounce the awesome phrase, *"Ego te absolvo a peccatis tuis"* (I forgive you from your sins.)

What Jesus was actually enjoining, on *all* his disciples, was the *responsibility* to forgive, not the privilege conferred on a few to be able to sacramentally bind or loose. The very first gift of the Holy Spirit was the loving insight that when we respond to the sins of others with compassion, understanding and forgiveness, everybody—victim and perpetrator alike—is set free spiritually, psychologically, and eventually, sociologically. On the other hand, when we respond to insult by hardening our hearts, everybody—victim and perpetrator alike—is chained, spiritually, psychologically, and sociologically by fear and anger.

What a travesty that this extraordinary insight was hijacked and turned into a weapon of control. Eventually, all the "great" institutions and organizations learn that centralization of authority, pyramidization of power, and control of the narrative are the keys to bureaucratic longevity. The Roman Empire learned this lesson well: again, and again, the wild, independent Celtic chieftains defeated Rome in individual battles, but Rome always won the war by organizing itself according to those three principles. Once Constantine shifted the seat of his empire to Constantinople and had set the very resilient Christian church to be the guardian of his western flank, the church quickly adopted these three principles—and still operates according to them 1,700 years later.

The real message of John's Pentecost, then, is the antithesis of centralization, pyramids and power plays. And Luke's account of Pentecost spells it out in even more detail. In his version, Peter—the erstwhile bumbling fisherman—charismatically delivers a tour-de-force homily in which he quotes the prophet Joel. He tells his multinational audience—gathered from the Jewish diaspora for their own Pentecost:

> *"In the last days, God says,*
> *I will pour out my Spirit on all people.*
> *Your sons and daughters will prophesy,*
> *your young men will see visions,*
> *your old men will dream dreams.*
> *Even on my servants, both men and women,*
> *I will pour out my Spirit in those days,*
> *and they will prophesy"* [Joel 2:28].

St. Paul, in his letter to the Galatians, expands on this democratization of Spirit: *"There is neither Jew nor Gentile, neither slave nor free, nor is there male and female, for you are all one in Christ Jesus."* [Galatians 3:28].

By those criteria, neither the Christian nations nor the Christian Churches are really "in Christ Jesus." If there is neither Jew nor Gentile, how do we account for almost 2,000 years of Christian persecution of Jews (Jesus's own people and the founders of the Jesus movement)? If there is neither slave nor free, how do we account for the situation that led to the US Civil War—a war which saw Christian Americans kill 660,000 Christian Americans. If there is neither male nor female, how do we account for the Catholic Church's refusal to ordain women as priests?

To truly be "in Christ" is to recognize that all apparent differences among us (socioeconomic status, gender, ethnicity, religious affiliation, nationality) are merely colors on God's palette as She creates the masterpiece called "Incarnation." It's a form of hide-and-go-seek designed to see if we can penetrate the illusion of separation and realize that God is playing all the parts? If not, we will continue to make war as we attempt to impale our own shadows with the weapons given us by the masters of deceit.

THE ASCENSION PROJECT

This project, I believe, consists of three tracks. Track number one is the journey of the individual in the course of a *single* lifetime. Number two is the journey of the individual soul over *many* lifetimes. And track number three is the journey of the entire human race, in fact, of all sentient beings, and of the cosmos itself, over the lifespan of the universe. Let me unpack each of those tracks.

Every culture has ritually honored the progression of the heavens through "yugas," each of which may last thousands or even millions of years. They also map the seasons of the year, the phases of the moon, and the perennial dance of day and night. Embedded in this wondrous mystery are the equally mysterious stages of the journey of the individual human. "Sacraments" or "rites of passage" are vitally important in synching nature and culture, the cosmic and the individual. The stages vary in number and in length, and several thinkers have tried to record this mapping—e.g., Shakespeare's seven ages of man, Erik Erikson's eight stages of psychosocial evolution, Confucius and his "five constant relationships," the Celts and their three orders of wisdom keepers (bards, ovates, and druids), Roman Catholicism's seven sacraments, and the Kalenjin peoples' three initiation rites (arrival into life, into warriorhood, and into elderhood).

The family and often the entire tribe celebrates these rites of passage. Traditionally, they weren't just excuses to party or shower the initiates with gifts, but rather ceremonies that marked significant shifts in how the initiate was subsequently regarded by the group. With initiation came not just privilege, but also responsibility. Often these ceremonies ritually—and sometimes very realistically and frighteningly—involved a "death phase."

If I were to define the word "sacrament," I would say it is the mindful ritualizing of the significant shifts of both status and obligations of the initiate in the wider community. In its more important reaches, this community is the cosmos itself. I believe that there are, perhaps, twenty-plus sacraments in the many-lifetimes' trajectory of the soul. Let me very briefly enumerate and comment upon them.

i. God Self-fractures into individual fractal-souls.

ii. The more adventurous souls, having been spun off from Source, volunteer for incarnation. If I were to paraphrase Jesus, I would say, *"There is more joy in heaven over one soul who incarnates than over ninety-nine souls who stay at home."*

iii. At the launching pad, souls destined to incarnate in a variety of dimensions and worlds jump from the open door of the spaceship.

iv. The soul docks with the developing embryo or fetus at some stage of its in-utero existence.

v. Birth and the first breath—Ruah Yahweh—announce its arrival to the community.

vi. Round about eight months, the ego—with its sense of separate self—develops, accompanied by the horrible realization that I and my mother are not a single entity (with me calling the shots), but a locomotive and its tender (and mother is the engine, while I am the boxcar.) This is when defense mechanisms—that cover the entire gamut from toothless smiling to lung-searing screaming—develop as the baby attempts to level the playing field.

vii. Around age one year, the child becomes homo erectus, reinventing our ancestors on the plains of East Africa some 1.9 million years ago.

viii. Next comes membership in *Homo sapiens sapiens* with its newfound ability to speak.

ix. After trying out the crowd pleasers like "dada" and "mama," it soon graduates to "no!" and "me" and "mine!" This can be either cute or annoying, but it is a very important stage for developing a sense of personal identity. And it represents the deepening dive into separation from Source which is key to the game of Lila.

x. Age seven brings the ability to think rationally, to learn the rules and the roles expected by the family, teachers and community.

xi. At around age twelve, the child is now sexually mature and can act as a conduit for other souls to enter incarnation. This ability will be tightly regulated by the culture—and it is, perhaps, the rite of passage that has 'birthed' (no pun intended) more prohibitions, constraints, laws, and indeed, hypocrisy than any other.

xii. Shortly thereafter comes the stage of self-reflection. Now the adolescent goes beyond mere rule-keeping and role-playing into questioning the culture's very values, and working with feedback from his/her own personal behavior. This, too, is very upsetting for society, for it challenges the tribal stories—historical, theological and cosmological. Here is where we move from ethnocentric to worldcentric thinking.

xiii. Then comes the first significant romantic friendship. The erstwhile disinterest in romance evolves into a heart-dictated search for complementarity and love.

xiv. But number xiii is a kind of "puppy love"—the heart's training for emotional commitment. With this next sacrament comes the first committed long-term relationship which may lead to a socially sanctioned union.

xv. Then comes the adoption of a profession; formal education is more or less complete. Now the initiate is attempting to offer a skill set to society, earn a living and settle down. The world-centric mindset, unfortunately, may sometimes now regress to the ethnocentric phase.

xvi. This stage begins with the birth of one's first child. Falling in love with the baby may cause a regression even further than ethnocentrism, because all attention is now focused on the infant. Hopefully, this will later change.

xvii. And this change is what happens with the birth of the first grandchild. The anxiety around protecting the newborn in the previous stage now blossoms into a commitment to protecting and nurturing all the children of the world.

xviii. Inevitably, if one is committed to growing, this burgeoning of love will lead to the embrace of the entire planet and all of her life forms.

xix. Then comes enlightenment, with its laughter at the illusion. Now you will offer namasté to all sentient beings anywhere in the cosmos.

xx. Then comes the sacrament of "death"—of shuffling off this mortal coil and identifying with your soul.

xxi. You've earned your place in "heaven" but even that does not exhaust your capacity for love, so now you take the bodhisattva vow: to not rest until all sentient beings can laugh at the illusion, become enlightened and join you in the bliss of nirvana.

xxii. So once more you parachute into incarnation with its risk of forgetting; and the cycle begins all over. But now the forgetting is merely cryptomnesia; it will dissolve very quickly. Even as a child, grace will shine through you, and you will accelerate through the stages. You are a powerful wave recapturing the stranded water droplets from the beach of samsara and leading them back into the ocean-heart of God.

xxiii. In this final sacrament, the game of Lila is done and all souls merge once more with Source.

I wonder what game She will dream up next?

THE JOURNEY OF THE COSMOS ITSELF

The individual is a fractal of the tribe which is a fractal of the planet which is a fractal of the cosmos which is a fractal of the kosmos which is a fractal of all manifestation which is a fractal of Source. As above, so below. Rather than bore you by attempting to trace the trajectories of all these scales, I will just focus on one more of them—the ascension of *Homo sapiens sapiens*.

You could say that human evolution began with the Big Bang 13.8 billion years ago or you could say it began, specifically, with the arrival of the hominids about six million years ago or, to be really picky, just with the advent of modern humans around 195,000 years ago. In any case, the real question to ask is why would this development *stop* with *Homo sapiens sapiens*? It would be the height of anthropocentric hubris to claim, as do many scientists, that the human brain is the most complex organism in the entire cosmos, that we are the apex of evolution and that the only way forward is Artificial Intelligence and cyborgs—human-machine hybrids.

On a more inspiring note, we've gone from ego- to ethno- to Gaia-centric. So why not Cosmo-centric?

And all of these "-centrics" need to be love-based, not just resource-based. We desperately need to not get suckered into the lowest, crudest level of the game. There have already been many detours in the journey. It would be sad if the only way out of theocracy is corporatocracy. So, let's look at two versions of the future that hopefully complement each other.

THE "SECULAR" FACE

Culture is the personality of the community and it contains incarnated or physical needs and yardsticks of evolution. An easy metric to trace historically is the assignment of personhood. It's not that long ago since the only beings recognized as "persons" were the male rulers. Later, personhood was conferred on non-ruling-class males. At some stage, *all males* were persons. It took time before women ceased to be seen as chattels and became persons in their own right. Children followed some time later. For many empires, "foreign" races and indigenous tribes were not persons, but merely impediments to conquest or resources to be subjugated and used as slaves.

What then of the future? Who will become a person who is not currently so? The debate on abortion involves that issue. When does an unborn human become a person? Will we evolve enough to confer personhood on animals? We've already done it with corporations. When do forests, rivers, and mountains warrant legal rights?

Caste, creed and class have all been easily identifiable categories of separation and prejudice. The Untouchables of India had to back away, on their hands and knees, from the upper castes. They dare not show their backsides. Colonialists are always the last to let go of the privileges of being better than the "natives" who, in the not so very distant past, were not even regarded as human. The last permit to "hunt" the San people (Bushmen) in Namibia was issued by the government of South Africa in 1936[2].

Harvard psychologist Steven Pinker has traced the evolution of humans with the concomitant reduction in all kinds of warfare, violence, famine, and disease and the corresponding upswing of rights and longevity. Critics have taken issue with his blind spots, but in general his analysis is meaningful. The human scorecard shows some mixed results, in my opinion, with the deficits—continuing violence and ecological degradation—largely due to corporate greed, fundamentalist religion, and scientism—while the credits are largely due to deep spirituality, the democratic impulse, and true science. In my heart of hearts, I know that eventually the "good guys" will win, but watching it unfold can be like watching a train wreck.

THE "SPIRITUAL" FACE

Three powerful visions I had over the course of about ten years gave me a feel for how Gaia is breeding spirituality. In the first one, I saw her stand in front of God and volunteer to animate the third rock from the sun in our solar system. Her self-appointed mandate was to breed life in ever more complex forms until she birthed a species capable of recognizing its own divinity and, *ipso facto*, the divinity of all other species. Hopefully, that is us.

The second one was the vision of the pregnant cosmos. It showed how Gaia-health and Cosmo-health are affected by the thoughts, words and deeds of humans and presumably other agents who possess free will.

In the third vision, I saw the globe with beings of light stationed at the intersection points of each line of latitude and longitude and at the two poles—a total of 64,442 "angels." These angels were midwifing the birth of a new era in human evolution. I believe that we are at a bifurcation point at this stage of evolution. The two lines that will develop I've called *Homo spiritualis*—people committed to love—and *Homo sociopathicus*—people committed to greed. The latter will continue to pursue a creed of, at best, the minimal adherence to law and justice and, at worst, the blatant disregard for both, in the pursuit of control of the resources. *Homo spiritualis*, on the other hand, will navigate this rocky terrain using more benevolent road maps.

Some genius once opined that the larger the sphere of our knowledge, the greater the contact of its surface with the infinity of our ignorance. To extrapolate, if a little knowledge is a dangerous thing, then a lot of knowledge would be a very dangerous thing! This is the hubris of scientism and of the fundamentalist mindset. If humility goes along with knowledge, then more knowledge is better than less knowledge; but if hubris goes along with knowledge, then less knowledge is better than more knowledge.

Jesus broke this down brilliantly in his teachings that have come to be known as the Beatitudes.

I consider the Beatitudes (Matt 5:1-12) to be a love song, a mantra in the style of Hebrew poetry utilizing Semitic parallelism. In them, Jesus reduces the 613 precepts of Torah to a single injunction—love God and your neighbor. All virtues are simply love in different circumstances. The Beatitudes replace laws with ideals, inviting humans to access their divine best and not just circumscribe their greed.

In these teachings, Jesus plays around with the concept of time, speaking of some results/rewards as happening at once and some when the fullness of the kingdom arrives. Of course, in the heart of the awakened disciple, everywhere is here and everytime is now. In the eyes of the world, all of the virtues he enjoins (poor in spirit, pure of heart, peacemaking, being persecuted for the kingdom, mourning, being meek, being merciful, and seeking justice) are the signs of a "loser" and the rewards (the kingdom, seeing God, being called children of God, being comforted, receiving mercy and being fulfilled) are merely the "honorable mentions" of the also rans. But one of the Beatitudes worried the rulers: *"Blessed are the meek for they shall inherit the Earth."* This one must have raised some eyebrows and alerted the security guards, like Herod's reaction when the magi told him they had come to find the newborn king of the Jews. He, too, was anxious to meet the infant king—so he could delete him.

The meek inheriting the Earth? That could be really problematic. Is this meekness a cloak concealing a power grab? Do we need to identify them and take them out of circulation? Such are the thoughts of *Homo sociopathicus* when confronted with the demeanor of *Homo spiritualis.*

Just as we can breed plants and animals in order to either extinguish or amplify particular traits, cultures are petri dishes in which vices and virtues can be bred in or bred out. When you carefully study history, you can see that particular families or cultures or nations or religions have been groomed to extinguish virtues that are seen as weaknesses (compassion, patience, forgiveness, etc.) and to accentuate vices that confer power (anger, revenge, fraud, etc.). This can be selectively instilled, e.g., love your country, hate your enemy; or support your caste, obstruct the outcast. And Jesus is developing his own breed of humans via the Beatitudes. The Gnostic gospels call these people by a strange but very insightful name: *"true human beings."*

The dance between the two kinds of humans continues in how they view the increase in complexity of evolution. For *Sociopathicus,* it offers economic, political, military, and religious mandates for domination of the species by select groups within the species and by individual oligarchs within the group. For *Spiritualis*, it is the baton of the conductor inspiring harmony, balance and symphony.

The theories and personal story of Darwin is an example of the struggle. As an aristocrat he was fully behind the colonialist agenda of survival of the fittest. The full title of his first book (1859) is *On the origin of Species by Means of Natural Selection: The Preservation of the Favored Races in the Struggle for Life*." That says it all. His half-cousin, Francis Galton, coined the term "eugenics" in 1883 and was an avid promoter of it. Darwin followed up with a second book in 1871, *The Descent of Man*, in which he cautioned against marrying socially and intellectually retarded races—like the Irish! (I kid you not). He claimed that such "mating" would lead to evolutionary regression. Interestingly, towards the end of his life, he began to toy with the idea of the evolutionary advantages of love and altruism. This was too much for his disciples and so they claimed he had gone senile. You simply can't build an empire and enslave others if you espouse love and altruism!

And so, physical strength, street smarts, and cunning seem to be the preferred path of evolution until you meet the avatars who tell us that the meek shall inherit the Earth, while the self-proclaimed "fittest" will continue to fight each other over the carcass of the 3-D Gaia-abandoned Earth-suit. A time will come when this Sermon on the Mount will actually reflect human behavior at intrapsychic, interpersonal, international, and interspecies levels. It will have created a morphogenetic field for the next quantum leap. And the great spiritual avatars are the prototypes.

The soothing mantra of the Beatitudes, when sung into the deafening cacophony of tribal violence, will in time, dissolve all dissonance and lead to a cosmic symphony of love sound. Then, truly, we will see that we live in a *Uni*verse. In the meantime, the Sermon on the Mount must be sung again and again, as a mother sings a soothing lullaby to her fever-ridden infant.

FROM MORALITY TO MYSTICISM

But Jesus did not stop at reframing the moral code. It gets even more extreme. Not only is Jesus "disregarding" the law, he is blundering into blasphemy. To a thoroughly incensed audience, he claims, "*Before Abraham came to be, I am.*" And he calls God his father. They take up stones to kill him. Jesus forsook worship of a distant demanding deity and spoke instead of an Abba "Daddy" figure. When the apostle Phillip pleaded, "*Show us the father and that will be enough for us,*" Jesus responded almost in exasperation, "*Phillip, don't you realize that when you see me, you see the father?!*" But this is not unique to Jesus himself, so he goes on to say, "*I am in my Father, and you are in me, and I am in you.*" [John 14:20]

Morality may be the *sine qua non* of religion, but it only takes us to the ground floor. Ultimately, religion is supposed to take us to the penthouse suite—mystical union with God, a union in which the myth of separate identity disappears, and in which even compassion disappears because there is nobody left for whom to feel compassion. There is only God, and we are the characters whom She portrays in Her dreams.

Hinduism gets it right when it speaks of the four phases of spiritual evolution—an evolution that takes many thousands of incarnations to achieve. First, a soul spends many lifetimes consumed by a focus on sensuality. Hinduism insists that there is nothing wrong with this. A fascination with food and cooking and drinking is quite normal, as is a fascination with sex. Not only is sex not bad, Hinduism even gave us the Kama Sutra.

But eventually, the soul realizes that there must be more to life than sensuality. So, for the next series of incarnations, the focus will be on power, privilege, and prestige. Again, there is nothing wrong with power as long as it is exercised with justice. They realized also that there is a big difference between "power" *per se* (e.g., as exercised by Gandhi) and "power over" (e.g., as exercised by Hitler). However, this is a very dangerous stage. People who overbalance at the sensuality stage only create problems for themselves, family, friends, and neighbors. But those who overbalance at the power stage can create even global crises because they often work themselves into positions of high leadership in churches, politics, economics, and the military.

Stage three comes when the focus on power gives way to a focus on service. This is where compassion becomes the major player in our thinking, speaking, and behaving. We see our talent as our gift to the world and our problems as our gift to ourselves—an invitation to stretch into our divinity.

But in the fourth stage even compassion disappears, because service is predicated on the notion of "other." With this realization comes "moksha"—total liberation from the idea of separate selves.

Let me get back to Jesus's contribution. Within 40 years of his death, the Zealot War of 66-70 CE would lead to the sacking of Jerusalem by the Romans, the utter destruction of the temple and the end of its animal sacrifices, and the disappearance of Sadducees and Pharisees. I believe, however, that the dying mother—Temple Judaism—would, in her death pangs, give birth to twins: Rabbinical Judaism with its emphasis on home rituals (e.g., Shabbat, in which the mother was the "priest") and Christianity, which would create its own priesthood and sacrifice (Eucharist) and its own Pharisee class of theologians. Unfortunately, these twins would soon become rivals and enemies just as previous siblings had (e.g., Cain and Abel, Isaac and Ishmael, Jacob and Esau). Do I detect evidence of the fractal nature of history?

It's taken well-nigh 2,000 years for ecumenism to rise from the ashes of acrimony. It's up to us to fan these embryonic embers into the flames of a new Pentecost. And setting God free from the manacles of our own projected prejudices is the first step in the process.

LAUGHTER

I believe that laughter is the first sign of awakening. But it's a special kind of laughter. It has its origins in the smile of the neonate. Wordsworth put it beautifully in his "*Ode on Intimations of Immortality from Recollections of Early Childhood*" in the passage,

"Our birth is but a sleep and a forgetting;
The Soul that rises with us, our life's Star,
Hath had elsewhere its setting
And cometh from afar;
Not in entire forgetfulness,
And not in utter nakedness,
But trailing clouds of glory do we come
From God, who is our home:
Heaven lies about us in our infancy!"

It morphs into the laughter of little children who continue to surf their imagination on the waves of the ocean of God's own laughter. Alas, "life" and school soon suppress this in favor of the inculcation of factoids.

There is an interesting passage in the Gnostic gospel of Philip: *"Jesus revealed himself at the Jordan. It was the fullness of the kingdom of heaven. He who was begotten before everything else, was begotten anew. He who was anointed, was anointed anew. He who was redeemed, in turn redeemed others. As soon as Jesus went down into the water, he came out laughing at everything of the world. Not because he considers it a trifle, but because he is full of contempt for it..."*

Christ's laughter is *not* at the people who are trapped in the illusion, but rather for the mechanism itself and its fabricators. Let me give an analogy. The very first moving pictures were created in 1895 by the Lumiere brothers in Paris. Initially, they were merely 50- to 60-seconds-long "epics" showing workers coming out of their dad's factory. The next film was created by placing a movie camera between the tracks in the path of an oncoming locomotive hurtling towards it at 15 mph. When they showed it to a packed audience in a theater there was immediate bedlam as people ran for the aisles and jammed the exits to avoid being run over by the train.

Imagine for a moment that you are a time-traveler from 2021 seated in the balcony watching this chaotic panic beneath you. Your first reaction would be laughter—not because you are enjoying their discomfort, but because you realize that they are caught in an illusion, though they are absolutely safe. That's what it must be like to be fully enlightened. It is not about enjoying the fears of others but realizing that they are trapped in maya, though they are continually held in God's loving embrace. And that is the sense of Jesus's laughter.

Laughter at its core comes from the deepest wisdom, the innermost conviction that only God exists and only love is real. Armed with that knowledge, you can strap yourself into the roller-coaster of life and enjoy the ride, even as your stomach does somersaults and your companions scream in delighted terror.

The first laugh of enlightenment, then, helps to liberate yourself; all subsequent laughter is to liberate others. It is the reason that the Spirit of evolution gives us imagination and intuition as well as rational thinking, and why the Spirit of creation continually sends us children, storytellers, artists, dreamers, and prophets. A hug is physicalized laughter—a life raft thrown to a swimmer floundering in the choppy waters of incarnation. Laughter, then, means dreaming lucidly, realizing that you are immortal, indestructible and, if you wish, can even fly.

There is, of course, both healthy, loving laughter and unhealthy, unloving, ego-based laughter. Healthy laughter is spotting the incongruities in a situation. It should be a clue that you've touched the boundaries of the matrix; therefore, it is an invitation to break out of it into true freedom. It is to laugh, not in mockery, not as a sadist, but in realization of the fact that all of your own fears and all the fears of others are based on a fictional reality. Since it is from fear that all human vices spring, and from awakening arises compassion and all other virtues, this laughter is true awakening to your core, divine nature. It's the soul-smile of a parent watching his two-year-old child gaze in wonder on Santa's lap. It has even been built into hierarchical systems to hold the egos of the leaders in check—like the court jester, who was the only one allowed to criticize the king. The jester's role was not merely to amuse or entertain but to check the inflated self-image of the ruler and invite him to pierce the veil of maya and recognize the divine equality of all God's children.

But like all human achievements, laughter too can be weaponized.

It can be deformed into mockery or schadenfreude. It is Judas betraying the master with a kiss or the soldiers dressing Jesus in royal purple, placing a crown of thorns on his head and bowing before him.

It is the tool by which all hidebound "authorities" control those who think outside the box: parents and teachers who use it to control children; scientists who mock the mavericks and their breakthrough ideas; religions' treatment of the prophets; and the status quo reaction to great social movements like women's suffrage and the abolition of slavery. It is swearing allegiance once more to the matrix, and the vilifying those who have the courage to swallow the red pill of Reality.

It seems to me that life evolves in three stages, each with its own kind of laughter. Stage one is where we are sunk deeply in illusion, and fear is the dominant reality. We oscillate between depression and rage; our laughter is filled with mockery, schadenfreude, and humiliating others. In stage two, fear is still the dominant reality, but now it oscillates between shame/guilt and eat/drink/be merry; between religiosity (as a fire escape) and addiction to sex/drugs/rock-n-roll (as a tranquilizer). Stage two laughter is either escapism/entertainment or self-humiliation. In stage three, love is the dominant reality: it brings serenity to oneself and compassion for others; it responds to all life forms with Namasté, respect for the Divine in all; its laughter is liberty and Truth.

I believe, then, that you can measure the level of your own enlightenment by the quantity and quality of your laughter. It is a measure of your compassion or cynicism; of your inner wisdom or your disenchantment. In brief, the very first sign of waking up, I believe, is laughter; quickly followed by compassion—a compassion that starts with forgiveness for myself and ripples out to embrace others, including my "enemies," and finally, all sentient beings. And laughter is the difference between fanaticism and commitment. Any God at whom or with whom I cannot laugh is far too small a God for me. And the laughter is birthed by piercing the illusion that I am separate from God, separate from others and separate from nature. It is the sense of playfulness created by the realization that I had been seduced by mere appearances.

Life unfolds in three stages: looking deeply beyond the veil; laughing loudly at the illusions; and then silently offering Namasté to all we encounter—from incarnated bodhisattvas to slowly-sliding banana slugs. Then we can begin to create less-and-less-inaccurate maps of reality and allow unconditional love to lead us home. We will notice that the ever-patient ocean of God's immanence has washed clean the pock-marked beach of yesterday's feverish foot traffic, so that we may imprint new hieroglyphics—cosmically-inspired sacred writings—on the newly-rearranged sands of an awakened lifetime.

DISPLAYING THE GEM

Let's activate our inner architect and design a house of God in which there are many mansions; a dwelling where unconditional love, unity consciousness and pure awareness are the three dimensions.

Then, with St. Paul, we can cry aloud: *"Eye has not seen, nor ear heard, nor has it entered into the human mind, what things God has prepared for those who love Him!"* [1Corinthians 2:9]

I'm not a big believer that God made covenants with humans. Ever! I find it infantile to think that the Source of All That Is—the manifester of universes—would hammer out contracts with individual groups of humans, get outraged and murderous when the contracts were broken, and insist on getting not just his "pound of flesh" but the entire carcass.

There *are* covenants governing incarnation, but I believe they are pre-conception contracts made by groups of souls who journey together over many incarnations. Rather like a drama group that puts on a new play each year; the same people simply change roles, adopt new characters and swap gender, ethnicity, socio-economic status and denominational affiliation, in order to savor life in all of its multiplicity of flavors.

As we came in, we understood the ethos of the era into which we were being parachuted. We also knew the track history of each member of the cohort. And we knew the purpose of the mission. But it's still improv theater—there is neither plot nor script. We create the drama as we respond to the moves of the other players.

Though each one of us intends to focus on one or two specific virtues, all of us are committed—before amnesia sets in—to waking up fully, helping each other to wake up and trying to awaken *Homo sapiens sapiens* to our Buddha nature, Krishna mind, or Christ consciousness.

This will involve moving from freewill (the ability to do as I please) to freedom (the ability to do as pleases God); to move from a preoccupation with service-to-self into a commitment to service-to-other; to move from narcissism to compassion; to go from an isolating sense-of-separate-self into unity consciousness; to go from crippling fear to unconditional love; and to move from mere knowledge to wisdom.

Knowledge is information gleaned by the senses and processed by the brain. It allows us to navigate in the physical cosmos—to predict some of its laws and control some of its behavior. It is focused on self-preservation and discrete, separate identity. Wisdom, on the other hand, is information culled by the soul and processed by the heart. It allows us to navigate in the *metaphysical* realms—to align ourselves with its purpose rather than attempt to control it. We can, however, predict all of its "laws" because they are the code that inspires our every thought, word, and deed. And its focus is always on compassion for all, and its destination is a unitive identity.

The soul-on-mission is the interface between knowledge and wisdom. And it invites each one of us to be an agent of change and a prophet for our times. The prophet only appears to be telling the future because she is the one who sees the present, the players, and the spin for who and what they really are. The prophet sees all seven timelines we met earlier. She is able to distinguish between and calculate the effects of the actual past and the fictionalized past, the effects of the actual present and the fictionalized present, and the myth of the "inevitable future." And she encourages us to forsake the probable future and to create the possible future.

There are two ways to change the future. First, you can persuade the players to act differently. Second, you can spin off a parallel universe that becomes the fertile womb birthing a desired, different outcome, i.e., "Be the change you wish to see," as Gandhi put it.

In order to effect a change in the future trajectory of the human journey, we must become significant meme-makers. And you can do this also in two ways. You can convert your own thoughts, words, and deeds into love and radiate these outwards by intentional prayer. And you can also try to intervene sociologically through hands-on social, national, and international projects.

MULTI-PERSPECTIVING

After laughter, your ability to walk in the shoes of another may well be the best gauge of how your spirituality is progressing. Since "creation"—the immanence of God—is how God's transcendence generates experiences, then each "creature"—whether it is a river, an elegant stag, a lily, or a human—affords God a unique perspective on life. Thus, God takes *all* perspectives. When, as humans, we learn to adopt/imagine the perspectives of endangered species or "enemy combatants" we become God-like. In your dreams, without realizing it, you are the director, producer, costume designer, and location planner; you also write the script and fashion the plot; and you play *all* of the parts—though, for purposes of enjoyment, you pretend to be playing only the part of the dream ego.

When you learn to dream lucidly, and then *live* lucidly, there comes an Aha! moment when you realize that all perspectives have value. It's a tiny step from there to deep compassion for all of the other actors whom you—God-fractal—are playing.

So, a practice of regular visualization is really helpful. Imagine and experience life as a planet, an oak tree, a sea anemone or, *horribile dictu*, a democrat/republican—and stretch outside the narrow confines of your current spacesuit and the even narrower strictures of your belief systems. If you're familiar with the season and purpose of Lent (40 days of preparation for Easter), don't just give up beer or chocolate, give up a prejudice. I guarantee you'll lose weight—the weight of carrying judgment and anger on your shoulders. The fools think that nobody can teach them anything; the wise ones know that everybody is their teacher.

I remember one very interesting seminar during my seminary training. Since we were being readied for missionary work in "foreign" countries with "foreign" cultures speaking "foreign" languages, it was important to have some kind of a game plan so as to not offend local custom. We needed to get a head start on learning, aligning with and loving the cultures and languages into which we would be parachuted.

For the first class, we were divided into two groups that met in separate rooms, and each "tribe" was given a made-up language and taught a made-up culture. Once each member of the tribe was conversant with the language and culture, it then had to send an ambassador/missionary/anthropologist to the other tribe. The results were hilarious. The two languages and cultures were devised in such a way as to be radically opposite from typical. No matter what the emissary tried—and each tribe got the opportunity to send several subsequent emissaries—it didn't work. They either provoked laughter, derision, anger, or even incarceration for trying things as innocuous as attempting a handshake, a smile or even just talking. It took a lot of time and a lot of jailed emissaries before we began to figure out the system.

Something similar pertains to being parachuted into incarnation. There are rules of engagement, and it may take many lifetimes to infer them. In the meantime, we can be at best, ineffective and insensitive, and at worst, belligerent and domineering. Gratefully, human evolution can benefit from trial and error, from science, from philosophy, from religion, but, particularly, from spirituality, in getting the game right.

An important part, then, of the science of spirituality, is figuring out some Kosmic laws. A brief note here: by *Cosmos* the Greeks meant the physical universe, while *Kosmos* meant its metaphysical origins and foundation.

Whether or not you have ever studied Newton's or Einstein's ideas on gravity, or even if you don't believe in gravity, if you fall off the roof of a ten-story building, you're gonna die. And whether or not you saw the 30-mph sign when you drove into a new part of town, you're gonna get busted by the cops if they find you doing 50 mph. It's the same with Kosmic laws. Ignorance of them is neither an excuse nor a bypass. But here, I'd add two caveats:

First is to beware of promoting human precepts as divine decrees, e.g., pre-Vatican II Catholics merited hell by intentionally eating meat on a Friday. Jesus inveighed against this kind of law when he said, *"Man was not made for the Sabbath; the Sabbath was made for man; therefore, the son of man is lord even of the Sabbath."*

And the second caveat is to beware of thinking that science has discovered or even can discover all of the laws that guide our existence or control our destiny.

KOSMIC LAWS

The Law of Love: Given that, in my opinion, the universe is a manifestation of a loving Source, then laws that create fear or that privilege our species, are "bad" laws—they're simply not accurate. God does not give with the hand of religion and take with the hand of science, or vice versa. The right and left "hands of God" are directed by the same divine heart. The entire purpose of incarnation is to remember the Kosmic rules while we are still away from home.

The Law of Unity: There is only one Source; nothing exists except God; all that is, is a manifestation of that One. Discrete, separate selfhood is an illusion of incarnation and to identify with it is to bind the blindfold even tighter. Your true identity is your God-self; and the true identity of all whom you meet is that One; you acknowledge that with a namasté. I am THAT, you are THAT, all is THAT. Whatever you meet is a Word-of-God-made-flesh. That was Jesus's teaching, not his claim to uniqueness. Therefore, all war is civil war, and all violence is like an autoimmune disease whereby the incarnated-body-of-God is made to attack itself.

The Law of Manifestation: In the game of Lila, Source, in order to experience the paradox of separation-from-Self, fractured into souls, bite-sized pieces, fractals containing the All-in-miniature. The Buddha put it beautifully: "form is emptiness and emptiness is form." Vietnamese mystic Thich Nhat Hanh explicated one wing of that when he said that a flower consists completely of non-flower elements: remove the rain, the sun, the wind, insects, earth minerals—and there is no flower. Celtic spirituality explicated the other wing of it, in the realization that darkness—the fecund soil of the womb—is the conceiver, carrier and birther of light. For the Celts, light and darkness, form and emptiness, nature and culture, goddesses and gods are lovers who dance and mate, not enemies who go to war.

The Law of Impermanence: Everything that is born will die. And it is important to also realize that everything that dies will resurrect. Impermanence is not a curse on life, it is the blessing of variety, of shifting states of consciousness and forms of incarnation. It is the Dissipative Structures of Ilya Prigogine which bring increased complexity out of the apparent death of entropy. It is Shiva dismantling the old in order to recombine its elements into something even more exciting. It is the painful exit from mother's womb into the light of another life-filled incarnation. It is Shakespeare rearranging the 26 symbols of the English alphabet into his Complete Works. It is the four nucleotides—A, G, C, and T—recombining into all the forms that have ever flown, run, crawled, or swum on Gaia. The permanence of impermanence is the guarantee of evolution—physiological, psychological, and spiritual.

The Law of Entanglement: Not only are all the particles of the cosmos 'talking' to each other, but *communities of particles* also engage in mega-conversations. It is a Kosmic brain in which every single neuron is in dialog with every other one. Some of these 'brain cells' are on the other side of the veil. We may call them 'our dearly departed,' 'angels,' 'avatars' or 'saints'—it matters not. We are the way God talks to Herself and guides Herself through incarnation. Moreover, even 'individual souls' have two aspects—Atma, who never leaves the presence of God, and Jiva, who dips regularly into a spacesuit; which leads me to the next law.

The Law of Interdimensional Communication: All of the neurons are in dialog, but we are, perhaps, most aware of the Atma-Jiva conversation. They are like two birds sitting atop a very tall tree; Atma never leaves the perch but Jiva often swoops to the forest floor examining the underbrush, feeding on worms and singing to other multicolored Jivas engaged in similar pursuits. Atma watches from afar. When Jiva returns, they compare perspectives in order to create a total picture.

They are very creative in their communication technology. Here is a partial list of devices they use: Intuition, inspiration, déjà vu, synchronicities, moments of awe, memorable dreams, visions, meditation, time spent in nature, "psychic" moments, brushes with death, and significant illnesses.

The Law of Attraction: Since, as Einstein's famous formula showed, everything ultimately reduces to energy, then energies of various frequencies interact differently with each other. If you overlay two sine waves, you get a whole spectrum of effects by moving them closer or further from alignment with each other. Trough on crest (or crest on trough) will annihilate the amplitude of both waves and cause them to 'flatline'; crest on crest (or trough on trough) will double the amplitude. There is an art to pushing a child on a swing set, as she screams, "Higher, I wanna go higher!" The art is to match the frequency of your push with the frequency of the swing.

Similar frequencies attract and amplify each other; dissimilar frequencies repel and negate each other. Fear, anger, and despair attract further reasons for fear, anger, and despair. Misery loves company. Nothing satisfies the victim mentality like another negative incident. They are the hardest people of all to work with in therapy because they resist all efforts at healing or solutions to their problems. It's as if you were trying to take their livelihood away from them. Maybe they regard such efforts as the oldest form of identity theft.

In the same way, love, peace and compassion attract and amplify love, peace, and compassion. There is a long history of prayer, ritual, and "magic" that builds upon that realization. Jesus called it the faith that can move mountains. In the prayer research I conducted for my doctoral dissertation, the single most intriguing result was that the improvement in psychological, physical, and mental health of the agents (the people who were praying for others) was even more spectacular than that of the subjects (the people being prayed for.)

The Law of Deliberate Intention: Whether we realize it or not, the future hinges largely on our own choices—even when they are done unconsciously. Gravity is equally effective whether a person jumps off a building or "falls off it" because of an unconscious death wish. Fate lies in our own decision-making. We are creators of our own destiny. When decisions are made consciously, we are *masters* of our destiny; when decisions are made mindlessly, we are its *victims*. When Gautama Siddhartha spoke of being "buddha" (awake), and advocated mindful living, he was talking not just about accelerated enlightenment, but about doing an end run around suffering. Attention and intention coupled with Self-belief and belief in a benevolent universe are the key elements of conflating nirvana and samsara; of realizing that the kingdom of heaven is "*en mesoi* (within you and among you.)"

The Law of Allowing: If you really believe in creating your own destiny and in the unity of all life, then, *ipso facto*, you must accord others the right to make their own choices. "Restrictions may apply" as advertisements warn us in the fine print, tucked away from the headline promotion of the item they want you to buy. Obviously, in some cases, "authorities"—parents, teachers, police etc.—may be mandated to intervene when decisions that negatively affect the life or wellbeing of self, other, or property are involved. Barring these situations, however, we do not have the right to control the lives or decisions of others. This is a lesson, unfortunately, that has been frequently ignored in personal relationships and as oligarchies of various kinds manage the lives of the masses. But, like charity, the law of allowing begins at home.

The Law of Karma: As I have been at pains to point out, karma is not a system whereby I am punished in this or future situations for mistakes I made in past or present situations. Karma, within a single lifetime, is a law that pertains both in the cosmos and in the kosmos. In fact, it is probably the single most important law of science: cause and effect. Between lifetimes, as I've said, karma is the planning of the next lifetime's hand, based on the lessons the soul wants to learn there. Essentially, it is very simple: you do A and B happens. Did you like B? If yes, keep doing A; if not, stop doing A. It's so simple a rule that it is mostly ignored; and we spend years repeating the same choices that got us the results we keep complaining about. To put it in Einstein's words, *"You can't solve a problem from the same mindset that created it."*

The Law of Deferred Outcome: Children are fascinated by speed. "Go faster, daddy!" a typical eight-year-old strapped into the back seat will encourage his father at the wheel of the car. Fast forward ten years and the same kid, on his own 800 cc motorbike, will open up the throttle and take off down the road, once released from an intersection's red light, often with his front wheel feet above the ground.

Chuck Yaeger broke the sound barrier (750 miles per hour) in 1947. Einstein told us we can never break the speed of light (186,000 miles per second), but in actual fact, we do it all the time. The speed of thought is almost instantaneous. If I say to you, "Think of Neptune," which is 2.7 billion miles from Earth, you'll get there in nanoseconds.

Only one thing is faster: the speed of love, because it doesn't depend on the electro-chemical firing of neurons, synapses, and dendrites. Love is the God-stuff always present everywhere and everywhen in all creatures. For fully-enlightened beings—angels and avatars—every thought has immediate manifestation. But for the rest of us, we need a time buffer. Otherwise, the freeways would be littered with the corpses of those inconsiderate drivers who cut us off and drew *"Die, Asshole!"* reactions from us.

Eventually, every thought, word and deed does have manifestation, but the time buffer gives us a reprieve so that we may reconsider or cool down before it indulges our wishes. Even thoughts create energy-forms which, if they are subsequently reinforced, will acquire physicality—almost like a tulpa. "Count to ten before you respond!" is sage advice. The Kosmos may count even to a thousand before it obeys our commands. In the meantime, we get ample opportunity to cancel the delegated highway assassin.

This is part of the importance of our dream life, where we *do* have the magical ability to instantly incarnate a thought. It's the training wheels for the real thing. There may be three stages to the process. First, learning to dream lucidly; second, learning to dream not just lucidly but lovingly—to be moral and compassionate even in the dream state; and third, *living* lucidly—with unconditional love for all sentient beings.

Results: All of these laws interact; they provide the ground rules of the Kosmic game: the laws of Lila. And, as I said before, they apply whether or not we are conscious of them. Being awake, then, means knowing these laws and getting into alignment with them.

THE JOURNEY INTO GOD'S HEART

The journey from gods, to God, to Source is a long, arduous one. It starts with the amnesia of incarnation, and wanders through the labyrinthine illusions of ego, until it finally finds itself on the pathless mystery of the soul, on the verge of merging. We desperately need to clean the slate and start afresh with a myth of mysticism in place of the stories of a partisan, human-writ-large bully. Let's identify once more the spiritual impulse in the soul of humanity, the glowing ember which the mystics of all traditions have secretly tended, and blow upon it so it grows into the purifying flames of unconditional love for all sentient beings.

The entire safari of incarnation is archetypally represented by the birth, life, death, resurrection, and ascension of Jesus. Of course, many other great avatars provide the same template for the faith-filled in many other wisdom traditions. The feminine face of this journey is represented very beautifully in Luke's account of the virgin-mother, Mary. Let me briefly recount what Catholicism calls "the five joyful mysteries of the rosary." Number one, the angel Gabriel appears to a young Jewish woman and tells her that she has been chosen to be "theotokos" (God-bearer). This is true of all of us. Each person, upon volunteering for incarnation, is tasked with the mission of conceiving the Word of God—which essentially consists in remembering our true nature. Mystery number two I call, "the Christian namasté"—Mary visits her pregnant cousin, Elizabeth, and the two babes-in-utero recognize the divine in each other. Stage three is the birth of Jesus, i.e., when the fulness of the conception arrives, each one of us, as Meister Eckhardt said, "is meant to be the mother of God." At this stage, we must have the courage to walk the talk of Christ consciousness. Number four—called, "the presentation in the temple"—is when the parents of the eight-day-old babe induct him into his Jewish religious heritage. All of us, initially, need the training wheels of a wisdom tradition to get us started on the spiritual path. The fifth and final joyful mystery is called, "the finding in the temple." It is the story of the twelve-year-old Jesus in deep dialog with the teachers. It is the beginning of the move from identification with a single religious and cultural tradition to seeking out the wisdom of other traditions also.

And Jesus's story complements that of his mother by extending it beyond death into resurrection and ascension.

PART IV
SETTING SCIENCE FREE

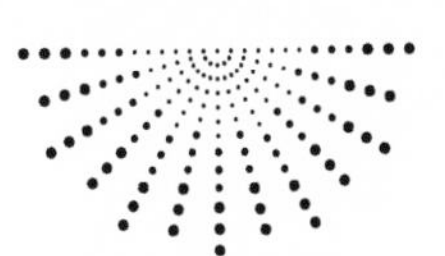

SETTING SCIENCE FREE

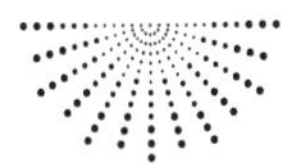

SCIENCE IS the youngest child in the family. It has a genius IQ. Unfortunately, it can suffer from huge hubris, even denying it ever had parents who were wise and loving even as they were fallible people of their times. But science's genius and creativity must be wedded to wisdom—which is data generated by the soul and processed by the heart. Science must not simply worship knowledge—which is data generated by the senses and processed by the brain.

For true science is the progeny of deep mystical wondering. Like a bright child who, when she reaches puberty, thinks her parents' IQ drops precipitously, time and life will allow her to realize that parents have a deeper knowing that only becomes apparent as the teenager becomes an adult and an elder herself. The ideal combination is the enthusiasm and inspiration of the child wedded to the wisdom and experience of the parent.

The spotty performance of science, side-by-side with its wonderful achievements, shows that real science is best situated somewhere in between its ability to positively influence spirituality and its need to be informed by mysticism. The merging of science and spirituality gives birth to a new level of intelligence, (heretofore only made visible in the insights of outliers like Teilhard de Chardin and

Jane Goodall) which is now becoming more and more visible in our time. I call these harbingers of this new level of wisdom "the mysticists." Here's what their birth announcement might look like:

"Mr. and Mrs. Enlightenment
(Samuel the Scientist and Mary the Mystic)
wish to announce the birth of their first child—
a beautiful, bouncing baby
called Marcia the Mysticist."

Here's the story of that infant's maturation.

PURE MATHEMATICS

Those who mock mythology and sanctify science understand neither, because both systems are just stories predicated on unproven and unprovable postulates. Yes, my friend, all of science is based on faith! This is true in pure mathematics and physics, in philosophy, in geometry, and in every branch of science—just as it is in religion.

Often called "the queen of the sciences," Pure Mathematics is abstract reasoning at its most elegant and unencumbered. And yet, it is based on faith. In 1889, Giuseppe Peano, an Italian mathematician, created the five axioms of natural numbers. Thereafter, they have been known as "the Peano postulates" and are meant to be a rigorous basis for the natural numbers (0, 1, 2, 3…) used in arithmetic, number theory, and set theory. I'm not going to bore you by enumerating and explaining them; suffice it to say that *none* of them can be proven. But if taken on faith, they can build very powerful and very useful theories.

By the early 20th century, scientists in general and mathematicians in particular were becoming convinced that they were on the verge of a system that could be built from the ground up without any need for faith or postulates. Alas for human hubris, along came a brilliant young Austrian mathematician called Kurt Gödel, who in 1931 proved that no axiomatic system of natural numbers could be both complete and consistent. It can be one or the other but not both. It was the equivalent of the Heisenberg Uncertainty Principle in quantum mechanics. And it's not just that mathematicians aren't yet clever enough to manage it; Gödel proved that it *can't* be done, ever, by anybody. Faith in at least one unproven postulate will always be necessary. Whether this makes you say "Amen!" or "Phooey!" doesn't really matter. Just as the numbers are useful in spite of themselves, so is this awareness of their limitations.

THE THREE COMPONENTS OF LANGUAGE

Ferdinand de Saussure (1857–1913) was arguably the greatest linguist of his time. He identified a model of human language that suggests language consists of three parts—referent, signified, and signifiers. Let me explain via metaphor. You are walking in the bush in East Africa and you come upon an animal that is 18 feet tall, has long legs, and a long neck. You automatically internalize an image of it that is part visual (what it looked like), part auditory (what it sounded like), and part olfactory (what it smelled like.) Then you go back to your village and you tell others about it. The actual animal is the "referent," the internalized image is the "signified," and the words you use to describe it (e.g., "twiga," if you are speaking Kiswahili or "giraffe" if you are speaking English) are the "signifiers." It's important to note that you are making an act of faith at each of these levels. As we saw earlier in our exploration of the myth of the given, we have no idea whether the referent is real or merely a fabrication of our consciousness.

Secondly, the signified (the internalized image) may also be a construction of personal perception. Attend any court case or ball-game and you will immediately realize that there are wild differences in the perception of the referents. The plaintiff and the defendant in court and the partisan fans in the ballpark manage to create very different signifieds and will swear that these internalized images are truly reflective of the referents.

And, thirdly, you cannot be certain that the signifiers (words) you use are understood by others to mean precisely what they mean to you. To try to remedy this latter situation, we've invented dictionaries in order to standardize the meanings of words. The problem is we have to use *other* words to nail down the meaning of the words we are trying to define! So, it leads to an infinite regression, a circular argument: X means Y because Y means Z; but Z has previously been defined using X. We are like dogs chasing our tails.

All things considered, it's a major miracle that we manage any level of communication. And this major miracle is based on faith: faith that the other person understands the meaning of the signifiers *in precisely the same way as you do*. So, language depends on three acts of faith: in the referents, in the signifieds, and in the signifiers. And since philosophy is totally dependent on all three, philosophy sits squarely and fully on faith.

Moreover, we can extrapolate from Kurt Gödel's work that *any* axiomatic system (not just of numbers but of any set of propositions) cannot simultaneously be consistent and complete. So, any logical set of axioms (and these are the building blocks of philosophy) must have at least one postulate which cannot be proven. Without faith, no philosophy is possible.

GEOMETRY

Some 2,200 years before Giuseppe Peano's time, Euclid ran into the same issue with his "Elements"—his set of geometry propositions. These are based on five unproven and unprovable postulates. The frustrating thing is that these postulates appear to be self-evident, e.g., "the shortest distance between any two points is a straight line." Obvious? Yes! Provable? No!—not even by the finest mathematical minds over the last twenty-three centuries. Faith, once again, is necessary.

SCIENCE AND THE SCIENTIFIC METHOD

Basically, all of the sciences operate by observation of the natural world/cosmos and/or by experimentation. Science gathers data, looks for patterns, creates hypotheses to explain these putative patterns, conducts experiments to "prove" or negate the hypotheses, replicates the experiments in other scientists' laboratories to ensure that the first "successful" results were not simply by random chance, establishes "laws"/principles, creates models of reality, tweaks these models if new anomalous data arise, and finally, discards old models that are so leaky they can't be tweaked enough, and creates newer models that can accommodate both the old and the new data.

In theory, this is a very elegant, humble, and open methodology. It has conferred lots of very useful benefits in everything from transportation to communications, medicine, agriculture, etc. However, like anything invented by humans, it has a shadow side and some glaring inadequacies.

Since even its instrumentation is basically an extension of the human sensorium, it is subject to all of the sensorium's limitations and illusions. For instance, if the entire electromagnetic spectrum were represented by a 3,000-mile-long line joining Los Angeles to New York, the visible portion of that spectrum would be the diameter of a dime! Add to this the fact that dark matter and dark energy (about which science is absolutely ignorant) account for 95% of all the "stuff" in the universe. Throw into the mix science's refusal to admit data from any state of consciousness except the so-called "waking state" (denying the input of altered states of consciousness, e.g., dreams, visions, transpersonal experiences, and meditation), and factor in the reality that the experimental method itself is based on probability theory. This means that it can only *infer* a causal connection between events but can never actually *prove* it. Add all of these limitations up and it's obvious that science has very fragile feet of clay.

SCIENCE AS A RELIGION

In the good ol' days, all important questions were laid at the feet of the priests, and religion was the arbiter of truth. Nowadays, science fulfills that function, and as a result it has become a new religious denomination. Its saints are the Nobel laureates. Its scriptures are the peer-reviewed journals. Its vestments are lab coats. Its rituals appear in the form of experiments. Its churches are laboratories. They even practice a form of excommunication—the refusal to grant tenure to outside-the-box thinkers who are often hounded out of their academic positions. And it has its own version of infallibility. When pushed, science will concede that its findings, *per se*, may not be infallible, but rather that they act as if the scientific method itself is infallible, since it is a self-correcting system. This claim, however, is flawed.

Firstly, there are many areas of life—very important areas (like, "what is the meaning of life?", "what is love?")—where science has nothing to contribute to the dialogue or enquiry. When it occasionally and foolishly attempts to give its opinion, it is hopelessly inadequate. So, mainly, it says these domains don't exist (e.g., the mind and consciousness) or are so unimportant as to not warrant spending time or resources on them (e.g., parapsychology and spirituality). So in effect, what they don't understand they choose to ignore. Secondly, we have the problem of the well-known "experimenter effect" which appears to be able to penetrate even the holy of holies: that of the double-blind, controlled, randomized, prospective experiment. A friend of mine, who was an internationally known researcher in parapsychology, once invited a group of skeptics to participate in a joint study in two laboratories (one of their choosing, and the other her own lab). They both followed the exact same protocols—from design to statistical analysis—and had observers in each other's labs during the course of the study. At the end, my friend had significant results and the skeptics didn't! It seems that the mindset of the researcher can influence— without any unprofessional behavior—the outcome. But why would we be surprised? Quantum theory has been telling us for almost 100 years that "observation" influences outcome.

Thirdly is the "file drawer effect" (particularly egregious in pharmaceutical research) where failed experiments are hidden away so as to skew the stats and bolster the dominant claims. And of course there's the ubiquitous "placebo"—the innate ability of any organism to readjust itself and find homeostasis. Science regards this reality as a nuisance to be discarded rather than being treasured, studied, and pressed into service.

So basically, science is another form of storytelling which, like all stories, is only consistent within its own rules. Once you accept the postulates, parameters, and methodology of any storytelling culture, then its "findings/truths" are consistent, elegant, and utterly satisfying.

THE INTRANSIGENCE OF SCIENTISM

Science continues to cling tenaciously to "laws" that are initially merely offered as possibilities, but harden over time into immutable principles. Scientists are often either unaware or unwilling to incorporate even their own most recent findings into the canon of their scientific scriptures. And so they rely upon their own creation: a *de facto* fundamentalist religion based entirely on materialistic science known as "scientism."

For example, the most recent DNA/genetics research does not support Darwinian Theory when it comes to human origins.[1] Biological research shows that some other factors/energies/entities intervened in project *Homo sapiens sapiens*. But you're not going to find that in any of the textbooks, even at the college level. Neither will you find a refutation of Darwin's 1859 claim that evolution proceeds by random mutation and by survival of the fittest. Nature is not merely "red in tooth and claw," but mostly operates through symbiosis and cooperation. However, the older belief suited the greed and hubris of colonialism, corporatocracy, international economic policy, and politics. It will have to be dragged kicking and screaming into examining, with an open mind, "alternative research." Thankfully, intelligent and curious people can read books like Bruce Lipton's *The Biology of Belief* to get beyond the limited views offered by scientism.

Another quick example: the claim that civilization began only 6,000 years ago, in Sumeria, is palpably false. Excavations in Gobekli Tepe in Turkey show that earlier civilizations emerged at least 12,000 years ago and may very well be cyclic, as many indigenous cultures have long claimed. We've been here many times before.

And one other datum: the notion that the brain creates consciousness is still entrenched in the scientific corpus of medical literature, when it is more likely that consciousness creates matter. The ancient mystical systems pointed that way. Erwin Schrödinger, who won the Nobel Prize for Physics in 1933, said "Consciousness cannot be accounted for in any physical terms. For consciousness is absolutely fundamental. It cannot be accounted for in terms of anything else."[2]

And then we have the big bang theory, which in spite of its name, many scientists accept as *fact*. Perhaps the single most important tenet of science is the law of cause-and-effect, which says that: (1) every cause results in an effect, and (2) every effect has a previous cause. And yet science asks us to believe that the entire universe (the effect) came "*ex nihilo*" (without any previous cause or agent). We are being asked to make a cosmos-sized act of faith that the very universe itself is the one and only exception to the law! In comparison to this article of blind faith, any religious belief is far less demanding of such naïve credulity.

Scientism's materialistic claims that "God is dead," "religion is irrelevant," and "freewill is an illusion" are interpretations of a series of experiments based on postulates that are falsely represented as "facts."

But not every scientist has bought into this house built of straw. The father of quantum mechanics and winner of the 1918 Nobel Prize for Physics, Max Planck, speaking of science's intransigence to new ideas, once quipped "Science advances one funeral at a time." In the meanwhile, keep your eyes peeled for the radical school of mystical scientists who will eventually break free from scientism's grasp. Original thinkers always seem to arrive in the nick of time!

RELIGION

All human enquiry into "reality" and "truth" is predicated on faith. That is the case with religion also. Whereas philosophy set out to establish reality and truth by logical induction and deduction, and science attempted to do it by observation and experimentation, we have seen that both science and philosophy, ultimately albeit reluctantly, are forced to admit that their lofty edifices are built on faith.

Religion, on the other hand, admits that up front. It *begins* with faith that a particular book (the Tanakh or Hebrew Bible, the Gospels and Epistles, the Upanishads, the Koran, etc.) is the revealed, inerrant Word of God. Its adherents then believe that all subsequent enquiry, reality-building, and truth must be in alignment with the scripture. Christian theology says "*credo ut intelligam*" (I believe in order that I may understand), whereas philosophy and science might say "*intelligo ut credam*" (I understand in order that I may believe).

Of course, Truth (with a capital "T") must be consistent, so *real science* and *mystical religion* will be found to be complementary lenses. The future is in the hands of what Carl Jung called "gnostic intermediaries"—people who are so thoroughly steeped in two cultures that they can be a bridge between them, cross-fertilizing both. In the case of mysticism and true science, I call these people "mysticists." And the prototypes have already walked among us—Pierre Teilhard de Chardin, Albert Einstein, Jane Goodall, Erwin Schrödinger, Temple Grandin, Buckminster Fuller, Jill Bolte Taylor—to name just a few.

When it comes to religion, however, I need to fine tune what I mean by "faith." Faith is frequently confused with giving intellectual assent to a mere human, institutionally affiliated dogma. But it is not that at all. Faith, in fact, is not so much an affair of the head as it is of the heart. It is much more "cordo" (I give my heart to) rather than "credo" (I give my head to). A better word might be "trust." The infant nestling securely in his mother's arms and sucking contentedly at her breast is not giving intellectual assent to a proposition that says, "you have to *believe* that your mother loves you and then she will." Rather, he is archetypally imprinted with a deep, soul-level trust in her existence and love. That is the level of "faith" that true spirituality depends upon and fosters. The old prayer that said, "*credo in unum Deum*" (I believe in one God) is far better rendered, "I trust in one unconditionally-loving parent known as Source."

IMAGINATION—THE APEX OF HUMAN FACULTIES

Imagination is the single most important faculty of mystics and scientists alike. The ability to imagine is the difference between a creative genius and a plodding technician, between invention and merely manufacturing the imagined device. It was the only equipment in Albert Einstein's laboratory. It is both palette and canvas for a true artist. It's the hallmark of childhood curiosity and the most telling identifier of somebody who lives and breathes "outside the box." It is, as "imaginal cells," what turns a caterpillar into a butterfly and the tadpole into a frog.

Often confused with fantasy, which is merely the ability to make up stuff that's not real, imagination, on the other hand, is the ability to volitionally shift one's state of consciousness, enter other dimensions, interact with other energies and entities who reside there, learn from them, and bring the harvests of those sorties back into this dimension of "ordinary consciousness." Imagination can create *ex nihilo*—thinking what nobody else has ever thought, dreaming what nobody else has ever dreamt, and birthing new possibilities into the psyche of the world.

It can also make contact with the ultimate stratum of reality, which is the divine Source, of whom we—and all manifestation—are holographic fractals, patterns that repeat at an infinite number of scales. For instance, electrons orbit about a nucleus just as moons orbit around a planet, just as planets orbit around a sun, just as suns orbit around a galaxy. And we are all fractals of God—bite-sized bits of divinity dressed in the clothing of humanity—or, as I like to put it —God in drag. Similarly, the human body is holographic. A hologram contains the whole of the original in all of its fractured parts. There is no system in the total organism which is not also contained in every one of its 70 trillion cells—our immune system, endocrine system, elimination system, and respiratory system all reflect the whole of our being.

So, if the fully awakened soul is indeed God in drag, imagination is a powerful tool for experiencing this reality. Once it has been experienced, imagination's favorite ploy is to bypass the left-brain intellect and express itself in some right-brain format: dance, art, music, proverb, or story. Zen Buddhist koans are a way of coaxing the seeker-after-truth to go beyond the mind by proposing conundrums which have no rational solution—like "what is your original face before you were born?"

And Jesus was a master at it. In Matthew's gospel in chapter 13, on two separate occasions, he is queried about his use of parables. "Why not speak plainly in philosophical, theological, or scientific language?" The first time he answered, "I speak in parables so that seeing you may see and not understand, hearing you may hear and not comprehend." And the second time he responded, "I speak in parables so that I may reveal things which have been hidden since the foundation of the world." He seems to be teaching that the deepest truths can only be met by going beyond intellectual jousting—into the soul, the heart, and the imagination. Having accessed wisdom by going transrational, imagination can effortlessly surf the transpersonal (no longer identify with the ego), the transtemporal (move backwards and forwards and even out of time) and the transspatial (no longer confined to physical matter.) Imagination is what gives wings to this flight into Spirit.

SCIENCE AS REVELATION

Science has become the new religion, its discoveries the most trusted form of revelation. The scientific method has, indeed, given us many great benefits—with some serious side effects. But, like all revelation, science is far from infallible and needs to be constantly evaluated using Aquinas's criterion (truth is found only in the judgment) and, I humbly suggest, using my own definition of "truth" (something is true if it transforms me and aligns me with God/Love.)

The scientific method itself, though it does indeed deliver significant practical benefits, is based on *probabilities*, typically at "p-values" at less than 5%—which means there's only a 5% chance that the results happened randomly. Thus, "probable" is conflated with "proven." So in fact, science can never prove anything but merely establish probabilities based on an acceptance of its postulates and methodology. And it's a very recent and young story. Other stories have been just as satisfying to the populace and lasted much longer. Since it's another kind of storytelling, then like all stories and storytelling cultures, it is only consistent within its own parameters and methodology. Once you accept the postulates and parameters and methodology of any storytelling culture, then its "findings/truths" are consistent.

WHEN THEORIES BECOME LAWS

The brilliant biologist Rupert Sheldrake has written a book called *Science Set Free: 10 Paths to New Discovery* in which he points out how ten major "tenets" of science are, in fact, just theories that have been iterated so often that they have morphed into "laws."[3] He has been censured by some in the scientific community and accused of blasphemy. His 2013 TED talk, *The Science Delusion*, was taken down until popular protest got it reinstated. Here is a quick synopsis of these theories-become-laws:

1. Nature is simply a machine and all its parts are machine parts—the cosmos itself, plants, human—so brains are merely programmed computers.
2. Nature had no consciousness until it "emerged" in some animal/human brain.
3. The laws of nature were fixed at the moment of the Big Bang and can never change.
4. The total amount of both matter and energy in the cosmos has been unchanged since the Big Bang.
5. Nature is purposeless; there is no teleology to it. Evolution is blindly going nowhere.
6. Biological inheritance is purely material via DNA.
7. Memories are stored materially in the brain.
8. Mind is nothing but the activity of the brain.
9. Psychic phenomena are an illusion; a mind confined inside the head can't possibly have effects at a distance.

10. Mechanistic medicine (i.e., surgery, radiation, and chemotherapy) is the only kind that works.

Taken together, Sheldrake's criticisms assemble powerful evidence for the way in which our notions of reality are often constructed upon *hypotheses* rather than upon proven facts. And the scientific community's response to Sheldrake, and many other brave scientific souls before him, shows us that power corrupts, and that questioning authority is frequently seen as antisocial, unscientific, or irreligious. No prophets are accepted in their own households.

FUNDAMENTALISM IN SCIENCE

For all its braggadocio, militant atheism has a much more difficult time trying to prove that God does not exist than timorous, doubt-filled theists/believers have in proving She does exist. This is true, firstly, since absence of evidence is not evidence of absence; and, secondly, even a single black swan, however long it takes us to discover it, immediately negates the proclamation that "all swans are white." Moreover, when you get down to the individual arguments, the application of Occam's Razor heavily favors the existence of some kind of mastermind behind project cosmos. Parsimony and elegance favor God's existence.

Of course, it is very healthy to exercise discernment in dealing with the issue. I find that the spectrum of reactions to any proposition can be divided into five basic stances. First, come the *Innocent* who have no boundaries to their credulity. They are totally open and simply swallow any thesis without objection. In group two are the *Naïve*. These, while not being quite as gullible as the Innocent, have very permeable boundaries and after a few tentative objections or questions succumb completely to the arguments of the proponent. In group number three are the *Critical Thinkers* who examine all of the evidence with an open but very discerning mind, and are prepared to abandon even fervently held prior positions in the light of powerful new evidence. This, I believe, is the optimal stance when dealing with any topic, including religion, revelation, and science.

In group number four are the *Skeptics*, who are partially closed, and who only open up to "extraordinary" evidence. I find myself here in opposition to Carl Sagan's statement that extraordinary claims demand extraordinary evidence. I have great regard for Sagan, but this is one of those statements that sounds very profound but is actually pretty dumb. Why would *any* claim need to be subjected to test criteria or protocols that we would also not apply to the "hard sciences"? For example, the standards which mainstream science demands of parapsychological research are way in excess of what it demands of its own research. And even when top class research in parapsychology uses these "ultraprotocols," the skeptics (and especially the debunkers) are still not convinced.

Finally, comes the *Debunker* group. These are people who are totally closed and whose modus operandi is to arrogantly act as if they already have the full truth, and any claim that might make a dent in that infallible edifice must *ipso facto* be false. Without ever examining the evidence, they "know" that the new claim cannot be true. All that remains to be done is to find the best way to discredit the research, or failing that, the good ol' "argumentum ad hominem" is frequently summoned to the fray. This group cleaves to its positions with a religious fervor that would put even the most fanatical God-fearers to shame.

I've never heard anybody ever describe himself as "a close-minded scientist." Each of us thinks we are in the correct place, all others are (too far) to the right or left of us in their opinions. Self-perception is a very fallible science. Latin warns us: *"nemo iudex in causa sua"* (nobody can be the judge in their own case.) As an example of that, 90% of Americans consider themselves "above average drivers"!

In the search for truth, in any discipline, we must allow the data to construct the theory, not the preconceived theory, to decide which data are admissible. I want to emphasize that this must be true in all forms of revelation—science, religion, "news," or scriptures.

MAJOR FAUX PAS BY PROMINENT SCIENTISTS

In 1807, Thomas Jefferson, who was then president of the American Philosophical Society (the equivalent of today's American Association for the Advancement of Science) reacted to a report of a discovery of a meteorite by two Connecticut astronomers with the statement, "I could more easily believe that two Yankee professors would lie than stones fall from heaven."

In the nineteenth century, much of what is now twentieth-century science was laughed at. The renowned physicist and former president of the British Royal Society, Lord Kelvin, stated in 1900, "X-rays are a hoax!" Kelvin had a reputation for hubris and a sense of his own infallibility. Here are some more of his decrees: in 1895, he opined to the Australian Institute of Physics, "heavier-than-air flying machines are impossible." And in an address to an assemblage of physicists at the British Association for the Advancement of Science in 1900 he stated, "There is nothing new to be discovered in physics now. All that remains is more and more precise measurement."

"The theory of germs is a ridiculous fiction," said Pierre Pochet, professor of physiology in Toulouse, France, when he learned of the germ theory of disease developed by Louis Pasteur, who was a crystallographer, not a doctor. Others even refused to look at his data.

"The abdomen, the chest, and the brain will be forever shut from the intrusion of the wise and humane surgeon," said Sir John Eric Erichsen in 1837; he was later to become Surgeon-Extraordinary to Queen Victoria.

Perhaps the most famous "expert statement" of all came from Charles H. Cuell, commissioner of the U.S. Office of Patents, who urged President William McKinley to abolish the Patent Office in 1899 with the assertion, "Everything that can be invented has been invented."

Even Albert Einstein, the face of science for the 20th century, spent the latter half of his life trying to disprove the findings of Quantum Mechanics.

Even when these grievous errors have been acknowledged, a smug scientific attitude will then say that, though individual scientific claims have been subsequently discredited, the scientific method *per se* is infallible, since it always, eventually, corrects its own errors. This is a very handy blank check that absolves it from all previous sins and promises that even present hidden sins, once they are discovered, will be remedied. Nice piece of self-exculpation! So, we are expected to still trust science since its present truths will be abandoned once contradictory truths have been established. Thus, not only does it forgive itself for past sins, it prophylactically forgives itself for its current crop of errors because someday they, too, will simply be past mistakes. How can you lose with that kind of deft footwork?

Of course, there are two kinds of ignorance: first, stuff we don't know but we know that we don't know (e.g., how to define "consciousness"); second, stuff we don't know, and we don't know that we don't know it (e.g., an undiagnosed and therefore untreated cancerous tumor).

Like all of the storytelling cultures that preceded it, science is very fond of patting itself on the back. But it too will prove to be a temporary story and will give way to a much greater future story. I believe that that future story will be some form of deeper mysticism whose adherents I've called "mysticists"—people for whom the mind, heart, and soul are a trinity of antennae, receiving, deciphering, and acting upon unconditional love, pure awareness, and unity consciousness.

THE SPIRITUALITY OF SCIENCE

Humans have been doing science since the first people began to observe their world, ask the great existential questions, and recognize patterns in the weather. At that stage "science" was a much more homogeneous affair. Over time, it would fragment into hundreds of subspecialties. Even the exalted profession of surgery, now involving years of specialized training for every possible bodily function, was originally just a sideline of the local barber!

Many of the great scientists of history were polymaths, and they were often deeply religious. Even in modern times, the truly great scientists tend to have mystical leanings. Humanity has benefitted tremendously from the ongoing work of these hybrid geniuses who inherently understand the unbreakable link between science and mysticism. That's why I call them "the mysticists." Filled with awe for mysteries of all kinds, they approach the task of real science—its core spirituality—as a never-ending attempt to explain the immanence of God (aka the natural cosmos) while bathing in its ineffable transcendence.

Properly undertaken, then, there is a spirituality of science, and its rigorous methodology is a template that can be of huge value to spiritual seekers. An empirical approach is necessary for true spirituality. I'll say it again: *an empirical approach is necessary for true spirituality*. But to say such a thing would be hypocritical—empty words—lest I show you evidence from which you might empirically observe this to be true. So, rather than tell you, let me show you some examples of this truth in action.

From 1973 to 1979, I lived in a mission called Kipchimchim in the middle of the tea-growing district of western Kenya. The nearest town was Kericho and it sported a grand hotel called, appropriately enough, the Tea Hotel. It was a holdover from colonialist times and had a nice swimming pool and a first-rate restaurant, one wall of which was floor to ceiling glass. The glass was a one-way system; those on the inside could see outside but those on the outside could only see their own reflections.

I was sitting at a window seat having lunch with a friend one day when up from the pool came a woman in a yellow bikini. She was obviously a stranger and did not understand the glass situation, for she came right up to the window less than a foot away from where I was seated and began to preen herself—pursing her lips, adjusting her bra, examining her makeup, and finally picking her nose. Everybody in the dining room could see this performance, but she was blissfully unaware and quite pleased with what she could see.

This memorable moment became a metaphor for me of materialistic scientists—those who can only see the outside: the physical universe and their important place in it. They cannot be persuaded that an "inside" exists. New-Age practitioners who use, but misunderstand, the Hindu notion of maya, do the opposite. In their case, the mirror is on the inside of the window and they claim that the outside does not exist. People who are waking up realize that both inside and outside are real, and they can dance between them as appropriate.

During a lecture in Palo Alto, California, I once heard a mysticist named Bernard Haisch make the following statement: *"By limiting infinite possibilities, we create finite reality."* I found it very insightful. He called this idea "creation by subtraction." Here's what I took away from this brilliant theory: Imagine you are in an old-fashioned movie theater watching a black-and-white film. What you see on the screen is the result of a bright focused light in the projectionist's box shining through a rotating spool of celluloid still photos. But what you probably don't realize is that you are watching not what's actually there—the light—but what is *not there*—the places where the light is being obstructed. The moving images are, in fact, different sections in which parts of the celluloid frames are blocking out the light. Your brain is reversing foreground and background. So, the infinite possibilities resident in white light are reduced to the moving shadows we call "reality." The trick of awakening is to *unlimit* finite reality by reentertaining infinite possibilities. This is paradigm-busting at its most glorious. It is the spirituality of science.

I'm sure you've played the game Twenty Questions, where one player imagines a person, place, or thing and another player gets twenty opportunities to ask yes-or-no questions in an attempt to zero in on what it is. It is a predetermined, one-right-answer-only, e.g., Mount Blanc. But John Wheeler, the famous American physicist, created another version of the game. It's a little more complicated than the first version. Let's call the "thinker-upper" of the target Mary and the questioner Tom. In this case, Mary decides *not to think of anything in particular*. Tom, however, doesn't know that. In response to each of Tom's questions, Mary has to give consistent, truthful answers. If Tom is really good, he can actually force Mary into a situation in which there is, ultimately, only one possible answer. As Polonius said, *"by indirection, find direction out."* Through an intelligent series of questions, Tom can back Mary into choosing an object she did not, initially, have in mind, e.g., cabbage or the Milky Way or polar bears or the Book of Kells.

And that is how science finds "God." By asking the right questions and giving consistent, truthful answers, it forces the cosmos to cough up a right answer from the fertile womb of divinity.

About 20 years ago I received one of the most useful gifts I've ever been given. It was a car-plug-in GPS. The donor, a friend of mine, knew that I have a penchant for getting lost. I have no sense of direction in a city. When I lived in Africa, in places where there were no roads, I had no problem. I could easily follow directions, e.g., "*drive across the river and then turn right on the far bank; when you get to the mountain, turn left and drive around the base of the mountain until you meet a grove of Acacia trees, and you'll see the village straight ahead of you.*" But in a city, all of the streets and all of the buildings look the same to me. And when somebody says, "*Just drive east for 3.7 miles and then turn north onto Highway 101*" they may as well be speaking Greek. When I'm in a car, I have no idea where north is.

So, the GPS was my savior. I like lots of things about it. Firstly, it always knows where I am, even when I have no idea where I am. Secondly, no matter how many times I misunderstand the directions the GPS gives me, and I take wrong turns anyway, it still presumes that I want to go to the destination I originally entered, so it keeps altering its instructions accordingly. And, maybe most importantly, it never yells at me for making mistakes. With the GPS, I always get there. Eventually!

That is how science finds truth, and therefore, how it finds "God." Science is a patient, self-correcting system with its eyes always focused on the same destination—the hope of understanding the cosmos (which is the immanence of God). True scientists have a combination of virtues: commitment to the search; humility in admitting errors; and realizing that, sometimes, by asking the "wrong" questions and conducting the "wrong" experiments, they learn what the right questions and right experiments might be. Also, the true scientists are willing to trust their imagination and are willing to share their data with and challenge colleagues. The science of spirituality needs the same virtues.

There's a second way that the GPS has proved very useful to me—and it's a little like John Wheeler's version of Twenty Questions. Occasionally, I don't have a specific destination in mind, e.g., I'm hungry and I just want to find the nearest Mexican restaurant, or I am low on gas and I need to find a petrol station (as we say in Ireland) as quickly as possible. Then, I simply ask it the appropriate question and before you know it, I have a full tank of gas in my car and a belly full of burrito. There again is the spirituality of science—its ability to let the universe guide it to where the nuggets of Truth may lie.

In Ireland, we've used stories as a form of GPS for millennia. Storytelling is not only the oldest form of entertainment, it's an ancient way to archive the wisdom of the group and create social cohesion. And there are many forms it can take. Mostly, we're used to one seanachaí (storyteller) spinning the yarn while the rest of us listen and learn. But there's another form that children sometimes use in which one person makes up the first line of a brand-new story, and then the story grows line by line as the "baton" is passed around the group. Sometimes, it will flow like a river in spate; sometimes it will meander; and sometimes, a single statement, from a rambunctious member, can send it off in an orthogonal direction.

Here, once more, we see the spirituality of science in action as each scientist builds upon, adds to, or seriously diverts the flow from the work of previous scientists (e.g., Relativity Theory and Quantum Mechanics). The churches of the world would be well advised to follow this pattern by listening to the promptings of "the little people in the pews" who sit where the rubber of the organization meets the road of real life. There would be far less dogma and far more mysticism if it were an organic family-wide journey rather than a hierarchically controlled institution using inquisition, crusades, legislation, and censure instead of listening to the Spirit wherever and whenever She whispered Her inspirations. Participatory storytelling is much more likely to lead to spiritual evolution than a crozier-wielding oligarchy imposing the "one, true, catholic and apostolic truth" on the unwashed masses. The meme-making of the future must be the outcome of all of the voices adding to the storyline.

Real scientists know that we do not live in a clockwork cosmos, a billiard game in which the Big Bang set all the balls in motion, and whose initial trajectories have predetermined their final configuration. The great scientists have pointed to the overarching importance of intelligence—and not just human intelligence, as in the double-slit experiment—but a cosmic intelligence, a universal consciousness. Here are a few statements to that effect from some famous Nobel laureates in physics:

> *"As a man who has devoted his whole life to the most clear-headed science, to the study of matter, I can tell you as a result of my research about atoms this much: There is no matter as such. All matter originates and exists only by virtue of a force which brings the particle of an atom to vibration and holds this most minute solar system of the atom together. We must assume behind this force the existence of a conscious and intelligent mind. This mind is the matrix of all matter."* —Das Wesen der Materie[4]
>
> *"It was not possible to formulate the laws (of quantum theory) in a fully consistent way without reference to consciousness."* —Eugene Wigner[5]
>
> *"Consciousness cannot be accounted for in physical terms. For consciousness is absolutely fundamental. It cannot be accounted for in terms of anything else."* —Erwin Schrödinger[6]

When Jesus said, "*Unless you become as little children, you will not enter the kingdom of heaven,*" three of the qualities of children he may have had in mind were awe, curiosity, and their constant questions. Great scientists have all three. And as such, they are close to God.

THE SCIENCE OF SPIRITUALITY

"*Science is not only compatible with spirituality; it is a profound source of spirituality.*" —Carl Sagan[7]

While spirituality is an esoteric experience, involving both the transcendence and the immanence of God, it is mediated through our senses, perceptions, emotions, and relationships—to self, others, and the very cosmos—and, therefore, the discipline and insights of science are important bulwarks when constructing the "cathedral" of spirituality.

The scientific method of observation, pattern-recognition, hypothesizing, experimentation, comparing notes with other scientists before principles are established or models of reality erected is also vital to the spiritual journey. When you study the mystical traditions of all the great spiritualities—as distinct from merely the exoteric shells that regularly censor them—you find the same steps at play. Mysticism, also, is solidly grounded in observation, pattern-recognition, hypothesizing, experimentation, comparing notes with other mystics before principles are established or models of reality erected. In lieu of physical instruments, e.g., telescopes, linear accelerators, and petri dishes, the mystics use introspection, nature, meditation, and other deliberate practices to experience altered states of consciousness, and thus become cartographers of Ultimate Reality by assembling its building blocks from all levels of experience. In the mystical models, physical reality is maya/illusion, not in the sense that it doesn't exist, but in the sense that it is only a particular level of reality; it is a subset of Reality. Unlike a child who learns to count to a 100 and thereby thinks she has exhausted all numbers, the mystic knows that even the positive integers are an inexhaustibly infinite set. Materialistic science stops counting at 100, whereas real scientists and all mystics know that awe at the mystery is even more important than trapping a few of its laws.

So here is the paradox: as bite-sized bits of God, we are infinite and "perfect," but as incarnated souls, we learn that discipline, rigor, and practice are vital to our spiritual evolution. One of the greatest tools of science is the falsifiability principle which measures every claim against its performance and results. Christ articulated that very succinctly when he said, "*By their fruits you shall know them.*" The application of that principle has knocked many monotheistic dogmas off their hypocritical pedestals.

Let's look then at some of these instruments and practices which esoteric systems have discovered.

FALLING TREES

If a tree falls in the forest and there is no human present, does it still make noise? And the correct answer is, "No! It doesn't make noise." What does happen is that the falling tree sets up shock waves that cause air vibrations which, if they reach the human ear in a particular, narrow band of frequencies, will be translated/interpreted/represented by the ear as sound. Air vibrations outside of that very narrow band will *not* be experienced as sound. Even if other animals still hear them, two things are true; firstly, the air vibrations must be within the specific range of each animal, otherwise it won't be "heard"; secondly, the "sound" is still an interpretation/translation/representation.

The same thing is true of all of the other senses; they are valves that reduce a deeper reality into a secondary "image." According to science, this deeper reality is some form of wave, e.g. acoustical or electro-magnetic, that can be fully expressed in Boolean zeros and ones. But what if these too are merely other reducing valves of a still more pristine level of reality? What if there are an infinite number of such reducers between us and ultimate reality?

CHAKRAS AND DREAMS

The chakra system with its concomitant seven levels of body—gross, etheric, astral, mental, causal, atman and brahma—may be an effort to wrestle with this issue. Each higher level reveals a more pristine and powerful order of reality and the chakras act as transducers between levels. The chakra system as developed by Hinduism teaches that we have seven levels of body. First is the physical body, which can be apprehended since it vibrates in the 400 to 700 nanometer range (between infrared and ultraviolet.) Next comes the etheric body (the aura) vibrating at a higher level. Each subsequent level vibrates at higher and higher levels, i.e., the mental body, causal body, soul, and cosmic consciousness. And the chakras act as transformers allowing energy at one level to be modified in order to express itself at other levels. Each chakra is like a household electrical component that allows you to shift between 120 volts (the number needed to light up a lamp) and 240 volts (the energy needed to drive the clothes dryer in your laundry room.)

And what of Jesus's famous saying from John 14:2, "In my father's house, there are many mansions"? Maybe this does not refer merely to separate heavenly living quarters to segregate Hindus from Buddhists, and Catholics from Protestants, but perhaps refers to different abilities in exploring the levels of reality. I suspect that the core, ultimate level is pure unconditional love, which is so overpowering that it dissolves not just all fears, violence, anxieties and prejudices but all sense of personal identity and separation from Source.

"Eye has not seen, nor ear heard, nor has it entered into the human heart, what things God has prepared for those who love him," said Paul of Tarsus. What if this actually means that "heaven" is beyond the reducers of the sensorium and even of the heart? What if heaven offers Unity Consciousness, where there is no separation between observers, nor even between the observer and the observed? What if there is merely pure observing and full awareness?

Pure awareness and unconditional love may well be the pre-reduction state, the original and only reality before the game of Lila began; a game in which God plays hide-and-go-seek with Herself, creating all forms of illusions, distractions and detours to make it an exciting adventure. Lucky us that we get to be the characters in this dream of God's. Like children at a campfire fearfully encouraging each other to tell ghost stories, this dream occasionally feels like a nightmare. But the trick is to become lucid—to first *dream* lucidly and then *live* lucidly. When we do that, the nightmares dissolve and laughter begins. Then we creep up on God, grab Him from behind and yell "Gotcha!"—only to realize that we've grabbed our own shoulders.

Then, again, what if the senses are not really reducers, but enhancers? What if the senses are the most basic form of imagination, with the extraordinary ability to transform the dull series of science's

0's and 1's into the image of a daffodil or the sound of children laughing? What if the myth of the given is a PlayStation devised by God to turn boring electromagnetic data into sensual symphonies of sound and awe-inspiring visions of a sunset?

If only we could keep the lenses of perception clear and not corrupt imagination by inventing greed and wars, would we then experience heaven on Earth? Would we then know what Jesus meant when he said that the kingdom of heaven is "*en mesoi*" (within you and among you)?

What if the entire process is actually a circle that begins and ends with God, who is both the origin and the destination of the journey? And what if the "scientific interval" is actually the lowest point of all, the result of the greatest, most limiting reducer of the lot; one that mangles the original mystery and spits it out as waves and bits, formulae and bytes? The living, tranquil, cud-chewing cow reduced to mincemeat.

What if the "imagination of the sensorium" is the first stage of restoration, reconstructing the miracles of music and the wonder of a waterfall, from the dull, gray, repetitive sequence of mere numbers? And what if pure love, in all its many manifestations—compassion, courage, forgiveness, patience—is the final transformer, resurrecting the separated souls into the bliss of full awareness and unity consciousness?

FINALE: BRING ON THE MYSTICISTS

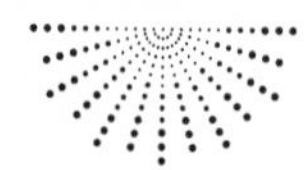

EVERYONE IS POTENTIALLY A MYSTICIST. But one must be willing to embark on the adventure of a lifetime to discover what that means first-hand. Though community is very important and "belonging" is vital, it must be predicated on individual gnosis (personal knowledge of spiritual mysteries.) In other words, it's more important to paddle one's own canoe in the river of Spirit than be an obedient, unthinking rower in "the barque of Peter" (or Mohammed, Moses, etc.) Mysticists live where real science meets true spirituality.

The mystical impulse is the umbilical cord connecting us to Source. It's the deepest instinct of the soul that lies behind all real evolution of the individual and the group. Problems start when the CEO of waking consciousness (aka the ego) thinks it's the center of the psyche and then the mystical impulse hardens into religions and conventions. Human history is littered with diversions and distractions that have hijacked this energy in the service of fear and greed and violence perpetrated on other individuals, other communities, and even on Gaia herself. We owe God a species-wide apology; not because God needs or even wants it, but in order to clean the slate and start afresh with a myth of mysticism in place of the stories of a partisan, human-writ-large bully.

Spirit cannot, ultimately, be suppressed. Like water or the Tao, it will gently, patiently and inevitably find its way over, under, around or through any and all obstacles and will eventually awaken even those in the deepest sleep. Lest we lose heart, it is vitally important to remember that we *volunteered* for incarnation in these very times. We are not here by mistake. We weren't unlucky and it's not random. It's by design. By the willingness of the soul to be an agent of transformation for the self ("the kingdom is within you") and of ascension for the species ("the kingdom is among you") we become paratroopers for Pachamama.

To that end, we must make partners, not enemies, of science and spirituality. The ancient Celts, when they spoke of goddesses and gods, meant that the goddesses were the archetypes of nature and the gods were the archetypes of culture. These were not in competition with each other, nor was one merely a resource to be exploited by the other—as we find, unfortunately, in the Book of Genesis and in Western thinking—but, rather, they were lovers and partners in the dance. And that is how real science and true spirituality must be. The offspring of that union are the people I call mysticists. Their mission will be to once more identify the mystical impulse in the soul of humanity, the glowing embers which the mystics of all traditions have secretly tended, and blow upon them so that they burst into the purifying flames of unconditional love for all sentient beings.

And the way of the mysticists gives us the final TOE (Theory of Everything). It is the weaving of the physical and the metaphysical, the merging of the immanent and the transcendent. It bespeaks a huge evolutionary shift for our species: the transformation of fear-generated vices into love-generated virtues. In this case, it is phylogeny recapitulating ontogeny—the tribe following the Ascension process first forged by the fully Self-realized Christ. It is the challenge and the possibility of the times in which we live. It is why you volunteered for incarnation at this stage of human history. Can you remember?

So, let me take the most famous scientific formula of all time, created by a proto-mysticist, Albert Einstein. It's $E = MC^2$ where 'E' is energy; 'M' is mass; and C^2 the speed of light multiplied by itself. A modern mysticist might rework it as follows: It's $E = MC^2$ where 'E' is enlightenment; 'M' is the mass of humanity; and C^2 the speed of God's-love-for-us multiplied by the speed of the-love-of-the-awakened-heart-for-others.

In the game of Lila, in which God plays hide-and-go-seek with Herself, She first self-fractures into perfect fractals, each of which contains the All in miniature. These we call "souls." In a downward spiral of devolution, souls then limit themselves to just their psychic powers—and this stage we call "the causal body." The third phase of obfuscation is called "the mental body" where we identify with the mind. Next comes the "astral body" where we believe we are our emotions. Then, "the etheric body" where we think we are the energy or vital force. And finally comes "the physical body" where we are radically convinced we are separate from God, from each other and from nature.

This is the low point of devolution, a phase in which existential angst, fear, greed, and anger are the primary responses to meeting "others." But this is precisely when evolution begins as we claw our way back out of the pit of isolation, reversing the previous stages of descent, back into the heart of God in our ascension project. We are like the individual waves pounding mercilessly on the coastlines of separate islands, who finally realize that we are simply movements of the one global ocean massaging the body of a single global land mass. We are both the yin and the yang.

And then comes the laughter of Lila, dissolving the illusion of separation from Source, and the rapturous homecoming of rushing into the arms of God, which prompted Jesus's final words on his cross of incarnation, *"Father, into your hands, I commend my spirit."*

AFTERWORD

As I finish writing this book, our world is in lockdown because of COVID-19. The United States is in crisis as bedlam and chaos, arson, robbery, and murder have hijacked protests against institutionalized inequalities. So, I need to append a prayer of hope and a final example of how victory can be snatched from the jaws of seemingly inevitable defeat.

I've only seen one NFL match in my life—I've never owned a TV—but I found it fascinating. I was invited by a friend to watch it in his house. Before the match began, he was singing the praises of a local boy named Tom Brady who was the quarterback for the New England Patriots in the 2017 Super Bowl against the Atlanta Falcons. It was a very one-sided affair and at halftime the Falcons were leading 21-3. Brady hadn't done diddly squat. The announcers reminded us that, in the history of the Super Bowl, no team had overcome a deficit of more than ten points. The second half got off to a disastrous start—the Falcons got another touchdown. Now the score was 28-3. At this stage, my friend got up and left me alone in his house! I was determined, however, to see the game to its bitter end. And I was not disappointed. Brady rose from the dead and by the end of normal time, the teams were deadlocked at 28-28. It went into overtime—a first in Super Bowl history—and ended in a 34-28 victory for the Patriots.

It became a vivid inspiration for me. No matter how dire the game of Lila appears right now, each of us has the ability to play like Tom Brady.

I began this book by taking the Celtic triple knot—which St. Patrick adopted by plucking a shamrock—and expanding it into a four-leafed clover—a mandala consisting of science, psychology, spirituality, and an adequate understanding of God. Hopefully, all four pieces have now been liberated.

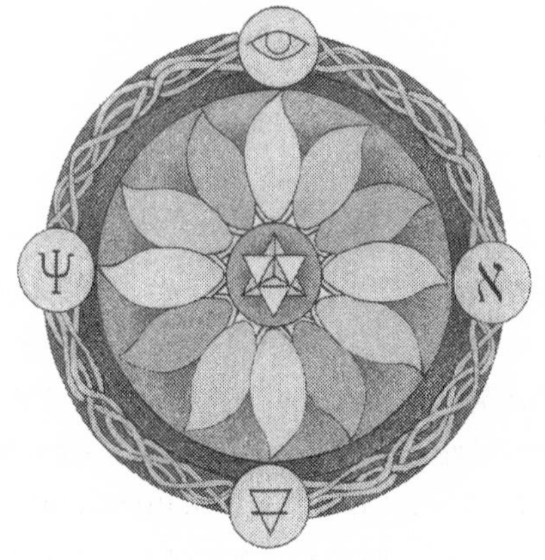

ACKNOWLEDGMENTS

It takes a whole village to raise a baby, especially when the baby is a book! First came the parents—a father (the mind) who conceived of the basic idea, and a mother (a fertile womb) who grew that seed into a thesis. Then came the readers who reviewed various drafts of the manuscript: Bishop Rosamonde Miller of the Gnostic Sanctuary, Gerry Murphy—a fellow Irishman and a grounded mystic, and Karen Rubin, who went through two versions of the embryonic book with a keen eye and a fine-tooth comb. Karen is also the artist who captured the essence of this book in the beautiful mandala on the back cover.

There are times during childbirth when the mother thinks, "Get me outta here! I want the pain to stop. Can't I just go home and pretend I'm not even pregnant?" I was getting to that point while writing this book, and then along came a doula whose presence and words made it possible, once more, to cooperate with the contractions, give one final push, and birth a brand-new bundle of joy into the world. Such a doula is John Mabry of the Apocryphile Press. Just when it was beginning to look like I was going to be pregnant with this book for the rest of my life, this wonderful man arrived in the labor ward. Along with him he brought Janeen Jones, a copy editor with an encyclopedic knowledge of all the pertinent literature, coupled with an eagle eye and a great sense of humor.

I've read a lot of books in my life and, inevitably, in their acknowledgement sections, the authors claim that their particular editor is the world's greatest. Don't believe them; I have no doubt that the gold medal here goes to Kate Sheehan Roach. At no stage of this book's delivery did she lose hope or show signs of fatigue. When three other maternity units turned us down, she found a fourth, far better choice and guided me there. This healthy, glowing baby you now hold in your hands is breathing and smiling because of her.

So then, extended-village-of-mine, I hope this book-baby can inspire you to set God free in the sacred scriptures of your own life story. And may God continue to hold you tenderly in the hollow of Her hand.

Seán ÓLaoire
(Tír na nÓg – Bealtaine 2021)

NOTES

SECTION I: EPISTEMOLOGY

1. Interview in "The Observer" (25 January 1931), p.17, column 3. https://www.newspapers.com/clip/25590070/max-planck-observer-12531/
2. mind-altering plants used in sacramental contexts
3. Lynne Twist's original statement can be found on the *"Everybody Matters Podcast: Lynne Twist and the Soul of Money"*:
   https://www.trulyhumanleadership.com/?p=3468
4. a concept attributed to many—including the Talmud, Anaïs Nin, and Steven Covey.

SECTION II: COSMOLOGY

1. Lynne McTaggart, *The Power of Eight: Harnessing the Miraculous Energies of a Small Group to Heal Others, Your Life, and the World* (New York: Simon & Schuster, Inc., 2017).
2. Matthew 7:16
3. *In epistulam Ioannis ad Parthos* (*Tractatus* VII, 8).

SECTION I: THE PROSECUTION

1. *The Jewish Chronicle* (July 9, 2010).

SECTION II: THE DEFENSE

1. Joan Goodnick Westenholz, *Legends of the Kings of Akkade: The Texts* (Winona Lake, Eisenbrauns, 1997), 33-49.
2. Michael D. Coogan, *The Old Testament: A Historical and Literary Introduction to the Hebrew Scriptures* (New York: Oxford University Press, 2010).
3. https://pseudepigrapha.org/docs/text/TAdam
4. Israel Finkelstein and Neil Asher Silberman, *The Bible Unearthed: Archaeology's New Vision of Ancient Israel and the Origin of Its Sacred Texts* (New York:Touchstone, 2001)
5. Ibid.
6. In the Baringo desert, I once encountered a young Tugen mother with a very sick two-year-old child. She had sold a dozen eggs from her own chickens in order to buy and feed her baby a bottle of Coke because of a tin poster nailed to a duka (little shop) proclaimed, "Coca-Cola huleta nguvu na afya!" (Coca-Cola always brings energy and health!)

SECTION I: THEOLOGY

1. Mirabai Starr, *The Showings of Julian of Norwich* (Charlottesville: Hampton Roads Publishing, 2013), xiii.

SECTION II: JUSTICE

1. *"Catechism of the Catholic Church - IntraText". Vatican.va. (Retrieved 24 January 2017).*
2. https://integrallife.com/four-quadrants/

SECTION III: MYSTICISM

1. You can find the Eucharistic Prayer of the Cosmos at http://www.spiritsinspacesuits.com/liturgy/_02_eucharisticPrayerCosmos.pdf
2. (http://www.mar.umd.edu/chronology.asp?groupId=56502)

SETTING SCIENCE FREE

1. See the work of Bruce Lipton and Greg Braden.
2. *The Observer* (11 January 1931); also in *Psychic Research* (1931), Vol. 25, p. 9.
3. Rupert Sheldrake, *Science Set Free: 10 Paths to New Discovery* (New York, Random House, 2013).
4. "The Nature of Matter," speech at Florence, Italy (1944) (from Archiv zur Geschichte der Max-Planck-Gesellschaft, Abt. Va, Rep. 11 Planck, Nr. 1797).
5. Eugene Wigner (1902 -1995) from his collection of essays "Symmetries and Reflections—Scientific Essays"
6. Erwin Schrödinger, 1984. "General Scientific and Popular Papers," in Collected Papers, Vol. 4. Vienna: Austrian Academy of Sciences. Friedr. Vieweg & Sohn, Braunschweig/Wiesbaden. p. 334.
7. Carl Sagan, *The Demon-Haunted World: Science as a Candle in the Dark* (New York, Ballantine Books, 1996).

Made in the USA
Middletown, DE
25 September 2022

11201891R00236